T0358718

Students Learning in Communities

Education, Culture, and Society

VOLUME 4

The titles published in this series are listed at *brill.com/ecas*

Students Learning in Communities

Ideas and Practices from the U.S.A., India, Russia, and China

By

Eija Kimonen and Raimo Nevalainen

BRILL

LEIDEN | BOSTON

Cover illustration: Photographs by Raimo Nevalainen

All chapters in this book have undergone peer review.

The Library of Congress Cataloging-in-Publication Data is available online at https://catalog.loc.gov

Typeface for the Latin, Greek, and Cyrillic scripts: "Brill". See and download: brill.com/brill-typeface.

ISSN 2590-0005
ISBN 978-90-04-51776-9 (paperback)
ISBN 978-90-04-51777-6 (hardback)
ISBN 978-90-04-51779-0 (e-book)

Contents

Preface

The main principles of educational reforms being implemented in the countries under study in this volume support a school culture that stresses interactiveness, both in the school and between the school and the surrounding community. In the future, schools in the United States, India, Russia, and China will naturally change and develop in diverse directions. This book aims to provide schools, their teachers, and other stakeholders with qualitative and contextual information on the foundations and practical applications of community-based learning. The purpose of this volume is to study the philosophical views, educational aims, values, and practices of schools in these four countries.

The experiences of working educators and other participants as implementers of the new curriculum that stresses community-based learning should also be utilized in the preservice and in-service training of educators and others, such as administrative and social personnel. One important area of training is to develop forms of education offering the people involved an opportunity to construct internal models of action. They can connect different theories of learning and instruction to these models of action, to utilize later in their work. During the continuous formation of these models, experiences gained in practical work play an essential role along with critical deliberation on these experiences. The goal is to learn strategies that change school practices by means of transformative and experiential learning. Alice Y. Kolb and David A. Kolb (2017) wrote that "the journey to become an experiential educator can be challenging, surprising, frustrating, and, ultimately, rewarding. ... We become educators by learning from our experience and it is this hard-won wisdom that is the foundation for our work" (pp. XIX, XXI).

Overview

Community-based learning is seen here as constructed through the manifestations of the direct interaction between school education and reality outside the school. The concept thus designates the relationship between the pedagogy inside and outside the school. The most central function of this process is to articulate, internalize, and change the essence of reality, during which time intentional activity directs itself toward certain physical, mental, and cultural subcomponents of reality. In the early industrial United States, nature study and school gardening were particularly oriented toward the physical elements of reality. The learning context was a constituent of reality that consisted of physical objects and states as well as nature and the material outputs of human intellect. The Naturalistic Dimension was the primary socialization environment. School camping prioritized the constituent of reality that was made up of human mental states, the subcomponents of which were subjective experiences. Experiences originate in the personal context of learning based on each individual's emotional, affective, and cognitive structure.

In neo-traditional India, craft-related education and social service marked the sociocultural context of learning. The intention of activities had as its object the constituent of reality that included the physical products of human cultural activity. Characteristic of craft-related education was its special concentration on the Productive Dimension of the socialization environment.

In the early Soviet Union, under the Narkompros, socially productive work was particularly oriented toward the physical elements of reality. The learning context was a constituent of reality that consisted of physical objects and states as well as nature and the material outputs of human intellect. In the early People's Republic of China, productive work was similarly oriented toward the physical elements of reality. The learning context consisted of nature and the physical elements and physical outputs of reality. Each individual had experiences that originated in the personal context of learning based on an affective, emotional, and cognitive structure. In the early Soviet Union, the Sociocultural Dimension was the primary socialization environment, while the early People's Republic of China prioritized the Productive and Martial Dimensions of the socialization environment.

Community-based learning in these four countries being studied has traditionally focused on the cultural subcomponents constituting reality. In the United States, the Republic of India, the Russian Federation, and the People's Republic of China, emphasis was also placed on the sociocultural context of learning, even though the Scientific-Technical Dimension was primarily stressed within socialization environments. The central pedagogical approaches to community-based learning favored not only the Scientific-Technical Dimension but other dimensions of the socialization environment. In the United States, outdoor education prioritized the Sociocultural Dimension, while environmental education highlighted the Ecological Dimension. In India, work-experience education emphasized the Sociocultural Dimension, whereas socially useful productive work focused on the Sociocultural and the Productive Dimensions. In the Russian Federation, nature protection accentuated the Ecological Dimension, while conservation projects prioritized the Sociocultural Dimension. In the People' Republic of China, characteristic of agricultural protection was its special concentration on the Practical-Agricultural Dimension of the socialization environment.

Acknowledgments

We would like to express our thanks to all who, in one way or another, contributed to the realization of this book. We are grateful to the Emil Aaltonen Foundation, the Finnish Cultural Foundation, and the Alfred Kordelin Foundation for their financial support. The writing process for this volume was carried out in the RICEI Project at the University of Jyväskylä, Finland. We would like to take this opportunity to extend our sincerest thanks in particular to the following colleagues from the University of Jyväskylä for their support and encouragement in this project: Päivi Seppä, Director of Finance and Service; Hanna Sahinen, Financial Planning Coordinator; and Tuija Koponen, Head of the International Office.

We express our warmest thanks to the following colleagues for their invaluable support and advice over the years: Professor Emeritus Robert R. Arnove from Indiana University; Professor Emerita Shakuntla Nagpal from the National Council of Educational Research and Training in New Delhi; Professor Dhruv Raina from Jawaharlal Nehru University; Dr. Gennady Bordovsky, Vice-Chancellor from the Herzen State Pedagogical University of Russia; Professor Congman Rao from Northeast Normal University; and Professor Weiping Shi from East China Normal University. We are thankful to the reviewers who kindly commented on this volume and provided constructive feedback. We are indebted to Lea Galanter for her invaluable contributions in performing the language and copy editing of the entire text. We express our sincerest appreciation to Arjan van Dijk, Publishing Director, Evelien van der Veer, Acquisitions Editor, Alessandra Giliberto, Associate Editor, and Jolanda Karada, Production Editor, for making publication of this book possible.

Reference

Kolb, A. Y., & Kolb, D. A. (2017). *The experiential educator: Principles and practices of experiential learning.* Kaunakakai, HI: EBLS Press.

CHAPTER 1

Introduction

Abstract

This chapter describes pedagogical approaches to community-based learning that are commonly applied for the purposes of building strong school–community relationships and creating profound learning experiences. This chapter examines the traditions of educational aims and their value dimensions and the tense and dynamic relationship between continuity and fundamental change in education. The chapter emphasizes that in addition to the historical dimension, the various educational philosophies, theories, and practices are linked to the prevailing sociocultural, political, economic, and ideological circumstances. These create social and structural conditions for education that either preserve and maintain educational theories, policies, and practices, or reform and change them. The chapter describes dimensions of school culture and key features of the learning environments. It offers several definitions for the concept of education, since the idea of what constitutes education has varied in different periods and in different societies. This study is based on definitions of education that represent the central social approaches to it, even though those descriptions aim to promote divergent views on the role of education in society as well as on the nature of the interrelationship between education and society. This study is part of a broader research project, the aim of which is to examine the interplay between education and society throughout the course of the 20th century. It applies the historical-hermeneutic approach to comparative education. The overall aim is to demonstrate the existence of fundamental educational patterns, policies, and practices in a social context.

Keywords

philosophy – aims – values – community-based learning – continuity – fundamental change – educational reforms – school culture – learning environments – society and education – historical-hermeneutic comparative education

• • •

This study addresses philosophical views and educational aims, with their associated values, as well as pedagogical activities for community-based learning in the context of social change. The examination focuses on the philosophical background of community-based learning, the changing quality of the value-oriented aims of community-based learning, and the pedagogical activities of this form of education, specifically in the United States, Russia, India, and China. Finally, the main philosophical background views and the aims of education and their value dimensions are compared from the perspective of social change. Similarly, the properties of pedagogical activities are compared in light of the approaches to community-based learning and their links to the dimensions of the learning environments at different times in the context of social change. The nature of pedagogical activities in these countries is examined through case studies and program descriptions, a further object of interest being the means, content, and settings of action.

This inquiry analyzes the processes of educational policy borrowing and lending. Previous studies have indicated that the ideas underlying an international school of thought can be adapted or assimilated to a national philosophical tradition as they cross national borders (see, e.g., Steiner-Khamsi, 2016). Phillips (2004) concluded that this kind of assimilation is possible if the new current of ideas is experienced as philosophically or ideologically interesting and the national context is also receptive for political, economic, or social reasons. The specific national conditions in one country thus create the need to experimentally utilize the experiences others offer (pp. 56, 58). The philosophical background of community-based learning in the countries studied here can be considered to rely both on national philosophical traditions and on the reformist ideas represented by international schools of thought. This study also shows that over the course of time strong opposition to the influence of certain international pedagogical ideas has surfaced in these countries.

This study is part of a broader research project, the aim of which is to examine the interplay between education and society throughout the course of the 20th century. It applies the historical-hermeneutic approach to comparative education (for methodological decisions, see Kimonen, 2015). The overall aim is to demonstrate the existence of fundamental educational patterns, policies, and practices in a social context.

1   Pedagogical Approaches to Community-Based Learning

Pedagogical approaches to community-based learning are commonly applied in various parts of the world for the purposes of building strong school—community relationships and creating profound learning experiences. Prast and Viegut (2015) viewed "community-based learning" as an educational strategy that educators can use to increase student engagement, make the curriculum more relevant and experiential, and strengthen school–community connections (p. 2). The present study regards community-based learning as a broad framework that includes a wide variety of instructional methods educators use while making connections between experiences obtained in the community and the different subjects in the curriculum. These methods offer various out-of-school and work-related approaches.

We can distinguish universal, reformist, and radical trends in the development of community-based learning. Different roles have been attached to the educator in these three versions of community-based learning. The universal life-centered form of such education, the reformist movement that highlights processes, and the awareness-raising radical version all differ with respect to the emphasis of the educator's role.

The American universal version of community-based learning can be seen as resting upon the educational theory and sociocultural practice of John Dewey (1859–1952). This approach regarded the educator's role as based on the ideas of both the progressive education movement and the life-centered community school movement. The Deweyan progressive school was to be part of the larger whole of a functional social life in such a way that teaching was based on the social activities of the surrounding community. Through various kinds of work-related activities and projects, schoolwork could become part of the child's immediate experiences (Kimonen, 2015, p. 197). In the early 20th century, these progressive ideas in education also inspired many other educationists to conduct experiments in education. Among them was Elsie R. Clapp (1879–1965), Dewey's distinguished adherent. She worked as the director of school and community affairs in the village of Arthurdale in West Virginia and documented her experiences in the book *Community Schools in Action* (1939). Her successful work in Arthurdale reveals Clapp as a major contributor to the development of life-centered community-based learning. This approach extended the educator's role further toward the community, with the focus on improving living conditions.

The reconstructionist educational ideas that underlie reformist community-based learning proposed that education must alter the prevailing social and financial structures in order to make the world a better place to live in. The theory of reconstructionism requires the educator to promote processes that enhance social transformation. The following brief list details that these types of processes sought to:
– recognize societal problems by critically analyzing the prevailing conditions;
– promote human growth and development by trying to analyze and solve social problems; and
– be actively involved in initiating social changes and reforms (Gutek, 2009, pp. 371, 375, 384–387).

Process-centered, reformist community-based learning requires that the educator have a broad understanding of the concepts of education and familiarity with the educational system. The educator is in charge of accelerating, facilitating, and coordinating the school–community process by identifying the problems, needs, and resources in the community.

Radical community-based learning has been influenced by Ivan Illich's (1970) ideas related to learning networks and grassroots communities of local people. Furthermore, Paolo Freire's (1970) pedagogy of the oppressed and the closely related process of awareness-raising have also impacted the approach. The educator who uses the ideas of radical community-based learning in practice assumes the role of an animator who enhances awareness among community residents regarding local problems and assists them in developing the knowledge and skills that can help solve these problems (see Brookfield, 1983, pp. 177–178). This approach sees that schools and their educational methods are intimately related to the communities in which they are embedded (Gutek, 2011, pp. 459–460).

Teachers have to make their own professional decisions about which pedagogical approaches they will use in their community-based instruction. Hlebowitsh (2007, p. 94) stated that a philosophy of teaching has to be receptive to three factors in decision-making: learner, society, and subject matter:

> Any philosophy of teaching resonates at the center of three sources for professional decision-making. Articulating a given philosophy involves answers to questions like these: What is the conception of the learner supported by a particular philosophical point of view? What is the ideal of an educated citizen? What knowledge (subject matter) is the most worth knowing, and how should it be organized and taught? Each of these points of departure leaves room for the expression of a different philosophical position and the formation of different school purposes and practices. (pp. 94–95)

2   Traditions of Educational Aims

An understanding of educational aims, purposes, and values, and their philosophical and historical bases, is one of the central elements in the teaching profession (see Shulman, 2004, p. 227). Aims and values, which give reform-minded educators direction in terms of what they hope to accomplish, are influenced by changing economic, political, and social forces as well as by educational philosophies and theories. This could be interpreted as meaning that the process of teaching in community settings is linked with the broader development of educational policy within a particular social context.

2.1 Functionalist and Pragmatistic Approaches

The nature of educational aims can be examined in relation to certain distinctive traditions of thought. This study interprets the aims of community-based learning from the perspective provided by the functionalist and pragmatistic traditions, as well as through a global approach, based on the framework presented by Rizvi (2007, pp. 65–67, 88).

Durkheim (1922/1956) approached the aims of education from the standpoint of the functionalist tradition, attaching a central role to a systematic socialization process through which young people are socialized to a particular society (p. 71). The instrumental aims of education reflect the processes that provide a foundation for society, as the educational system is a historical output constructed by society. A society attempts to reproduce commonly accepted beliefs, norms, and traditions through the school system. Even though school is intended to be developed in compliance with the requirements of the day, an educational system is always influenced by the society's earlier developmental stages (pp. 72, 89, 94–95). According to Durkheim, one of the key pillars of any national educational reform is analyzing and understanding the historical characteristics of a society, and only then reflecting on how to develop the society by restructuring the educational system (pp. 152–153). Following this approach, the aims of education express the social needs of a particular era and location. Society constructs the educational system by promoting and reproducing social ideals (Durkheim, 1938/1977, pp. 11, 14).

In turn, if the aims are viewed from the perspective of a pragmatistic tradition, it is understood that education refers to continuing growth, which is a goal in itself. The value of school education can be determined based on how well it can generate the willingness to continually grow and provide the means to realize these efforts (Dewey, 1916, p. 62). Dewey (1916) suggested that the aim of education is to provide individuals with opportunities to continue their own education. Education is thus both the end and the means. Nonetheless, Dewey admitted that although certain aims also apply to teachers' practical work, they must be linked to the educational activities in a natural manner so that they are flexible and arise from the circumstances. Moreover, they must be based on activities and needs that are typical of the individual being educated. Ultimately, the teacher bears the responsibility for translating the aim into a method that suits the learning situation (pp. 117, 121–124, 126).

The functionalist and pragmatistic traditions, however, can also be analyzed critically. It has been argued that the pragmatistic tradition presents the aims at an overly general level, and that the functionalist interpretation of goals leaves little room for social critique or radical change (Rizvi, 2007, pp. 66–67). Conflict theoreticians have found that functionalism does not recognize the ideological supremacy of the dominating class, which is why society regards its values as natural.

2.2   *A Global Approach*

Education has become a global issue, and this imposes new pressures on educational systems and their functioning. Rizvi (2007) argued that traditional approaches to the aims of education are no longer sufficient, as they are not fully engaged with the new global, transnational economic, political, and cultural interdependencies. Traditional approaches cannot be used to develop broader educational outlooks that aim to prepare students to be critical and committed to meeting the new challenges, threats, and opportunities of globalization. The global economy requires a new kind of employee who is multiskilled, service-oriented, adaptable to changes in the nature and conditions of work, and able to function in global, multicultural environments. Such an employee must also possess the ability to utilize new information and communication technology (pp. 64–65, 88).

3   Aims and Their Value Dimensions

This study explores the aims and values of community-based learning in the United States, India, Russia, and China within the context of social change. The aims and value dimensions of this form of education are compared in light of the main currents of educational philosophies and ideologies as well as related pedagogical approaches that prevailed at different times. The aims of education and the value dimensions intertwined in them are analyzed in these four countries from the standpoint of society- and school-centered community-based learning. Such an analytical process makes use of a classification framework based on the value theories used in this study (see, e.g., Spranger, 1914/1928; Allport et al., 1960; Schwartz, 1992).

4   Continuity and Fundamental Change in Education

The historical tradition of education shapes the tense and dynamic relationship between continuity and change. In addition to the historical dimension, the various educational philosophies, theories, and practices are linked to the prevailing sociocultural, political, economic, and ideological circumstances. These create social and structural conditions for education that either preserve and maintain educational theories, policies, and practices, or reform and change them.

Societal change can be seen as variations in behavioral patterns, culture, norms and values, and societal structure. Change is inevitable and ubiquitous. It can be rapid, or gradual and evolutionary (Ballantine & Roberts, 2009, p. 546). Changes from the post-World War II years to the 1970s have been seen as "an ever-present process that constantly forces schools and other organizations to adjust to new demands" (Ballantine & Hammack, 2009, p. 2). Perceiving change as a radical process rather than as incremental growth and rational adaptation became, however, an important aspect of organizational change in the 1980s. According to this view, real change is a period of discontinuity and disruption that can be called *transformation* or *revolution* (Demers, 2007, pp. 9, 43). At the same time, researchers gave special importance to the theory of organizations as cultures, since it provided a new perspective on the inner reality of organizations. Every organization has its own deep spiritual structure, which guides people's thinking, choices, and activities. Culture describes the organization's prevailing ways of thinking and acting, which have been shaped and strengthened through shared experiences (Harisalo, 2008, pp. 40, 265, 266). Schein (1985) suggested that the birth of an organizational culture is a dynamic process of collective learning that evolves with new experiences. Culture can be changed if people understand the dynamic of the learning process (Schein, 1985, pp. 7–8).

In the 1990s, open systems models based on systems theory were introduced as a basis for research on organizational change. Systems theory provided an opportunity for organizations to analyze themselves as part of broader systems. According to this theory, it is essential to understand the dependencies and interactions between different components and the effects of organizations' operating environments on their processes (Harisalo, 2008, pp. 38–39). *The Fifth Discipline* (1990), by Peter Senge, presents a dynamic and natural form of systems thinking that targets ever-changing systems and their components. Senge stated that to realize its potential, systems thinking integrates with other four disciplines: personal mastery, mental models, shared visions, and team learning (Senge, 1990, p. 12). The following summary of Senge (1990), defines these five disciplines:

– Systems thinking is the conceptual cornerstone of a functional system that supports other principles of the learning school. Systems thinking, aimed at perceiving the whole, is needed in order to understand and control the complex world.

- Personal mastery is learning by which persons expand their abilities to achieve the results they want. It is the mental foundation of a learning organization that clarifies and deepens a person's vision as well as develops patience. Personal mastery includes objectives and visions, the creative tension between the current state and objectives, a commitment to the truth, and the conscious utilization of the subconscious.
- Mental models that guide action are deep-rooted assumptions, generalizations, or perceptions that affect an individual's behaviors and understanding of the world. Mental models are active in nature, as they are shaped by how an individual functions.
- The shared vision reflects the view of the future that team members develop together. It is the compelling force in people that fosters the courage to act and promotes real commitment and alliance.
- Team learning is a prerequisite for organizational learning. It begins with a dialogue that allows the group to find insights that individuals alone would not have achieved (pp. 5–12).

When it comes to organizational change, the complexity approach has gained increased popularity since the 1990s. Demers (2007) wrote that the complexity approach "views organizations as nonlinear dynamic systems whose behavior can be unpredictable and far from equilibrium, yet adaptive" (p. 154). In the following, Demers (2007) concludes:

> The complexity approach is a very abstract framework that can be applied at every level of analysis and to any type of dynamic nonlinear system. It contributes a vision of organizational dynamics as the emergent product of a series of nested self-organizing systems. This perspective allows us to see inside the organization as it continuously evolves, by transforming it into an "idealized" system whose agents adapt by following simple rules. (p. 170)

Educational change can be understood as a paradigmatic shift in the philosophical starting points, goals, and practices of education, that is, a revision in the generally accepted doctrinal structures, ways of thinking, and tendencies behind them. New ideas and needs in society related to political, social, and economic factors can give impetus to a paradigm shift in education. The aim of the change is to adapt the value base, goals, and forms of education to new ideas and to meet emerging needs. The literature examining the theories of change in education comes mainly from North America and Europe.

Changes in school organization can be categorized as first-order or second-order. First-order, or incremental, changes are deliberate efforts to enhance the existing system by overcoming deficiencies in policies and practices. The aim is to improve the efficiency and effectiveness of current systems without disturbing the basic organizational features. Such alterations are aimed essentially at improving the core features of the organization. Second-order, or fundamental, changes seek to alter an organization's essential composition and involve identifying new goals, structures, and roles (Cuban, 1992, pp. 218–219; Fullan, 1991, p. 29). Changes in schools have hitherto been first-order. Second-order changes have, in most cases, failed. The challenge of the 21st century is to find second-order changes that will have a fundamental effect on school culture and structures.

Many factors and forces may promote or slow down educational change. The scale and complexity of change; the potential for different change options; motivation or philosophical commitment to change; the stability of society and organizations; the availability and adequacy of human, material, and financial resources; and the effectiveness of organizational structures and technological solutions can create or prevent change (Bray, 2004, pp. 253–254).

Johnson (2006) noted that schools can also develop a defensive culture of resistance to change. As it is often difficult to modify a school's operating culture, teachers may maintain their educational principles and practices for decades. Change can be slowed or prevented by the implementation of school routines, various traditional ties, and the institutional role of the school in society, as well as the practical nature of the teacher's work and phenomena related to the social behavior of the teaching staff (p. 98). Teacher beliefs can also conflict with new ideas, leading to resistance to change. Educational reforms do not necessarily alter the way a teacher teaches, as a profound and fundamental shift in education requires reframing beliefs, values, expectations, habits, roles, and power structures (Sahlberg, 1997, pp. 180–181, 184).

5 Educational Reforms in a Changing Social Context

Reforms involving an entire society usually lead to major changes in the nation's social, economic, and political structure. Social reforms can also bring about gradual or abrupt changes in educational principles and their implications. Fullan (1993) stated that school reform is a continuous process of change that can be characterized by dynamic, complex, contradistinctive, and unpredictable features (p. 20). This chapter observes that the term *reform* is closely related to the concept of *educational change*.

The change processes at different schools can vary significantly. The foundations of formal education services may remain relatively unchanged if the teaching methods, curriculum, and learning environments are considered. The school system may gradually adapt itself to the prevailing demands of society. Such a process of change can be regarded as an incremental adaptation (see, e.g., Hawkins, 2007, p. 143). Cuban (1992) argued that changes in schools have often been merely gradual attempts to develop the current system in order to eliminate insufficiencies manifested in operating principles and practices. The aim has been to make the operations of the organization more effective and to develop its special characteristics without actually addressing operational principles. Educational reforms that focus on changing the central structures and processes of school organizations have generally been unsuccessful. A challenge for the future school is to develop change efforts that fundamentally affect school culture through such means as identifying new objectives, structures, and roles (Cuban, 1992, pp. 218–219).

A straightforward, rational, and systematic change process reflects an approach in which the reforms school administrators propose are meticulously and thoroughly followed. The change process can also be characterized as eclectic when the teacher implements only part of the reform, guided by individual practical ethics, but does not change the basics of practical theory. Alternatively, the school reform may cause profound and radical changes in teachers' thinking and action models if the changes represent a view in which the teachers accept the principles, educational philosophies, and beliefs behind the reform (Snyder et al., 1992, p. 402). Waks (2007) observed that such fundamental educational change is "primarily about change in educational ideas, norms, organizational arrangements, and frameworks that constitute education as a social institution" (p. 294).

A reform based on particular educational thinking can be used in an effort to adapt education to new social requirements. For schools, such policy could mean that teachers should familiarize students with the reality of what a society needs. This study notes that during major social changes, the education system can be required to accelerate large national reforms. Under these circumstances, attempts can be made to have schools increase economic productivity through such measures as promoting the developmental trajectory of scientific and technological modernization. Characteristic of this type of change is a deterministic belief that school reform could be the key to effectively achieving social goals (for more details, see Kimonen, 2015, pp. 174–177).

Hopkins (2013) concluded that although we understand a great deal about school reform, we do not systematically realize its potential. This lack of understanding has not had any positive impact on students' learning and achievement. The ultimate mission would be to formulate relevant information for the purposes of creating theories of action within a comprehensive plan for school reform (p. 317).

This dilemma Hopkins presented could be approached by leaning on the ideas of Botkin et al. (1979), which state that an answer to the prevailing problem must be sought through a new type of learning that diverges from everything previously used (p. 10). This educational reform is characterized by something innovative and societal.

6   Dimensions of School Culture

The school organization can be examined as a collaborative system that gathers and integrates different resources in order to implement desired objectives. The theory of organizations viewed as cultures provides a new perspective on the internal reality of organizations. Every organization has its own deep mental structure that guides people's thinking, choices, and actions. Culture represents an organization's prevailing ways of thinking and acting, which have been created and strengthened through shared experiences (Harisalo, 2008, pp. 31, 40, 265–266). Arends (2009) defined *school culture* as the philosophies that members of the school community use to justify their actions. It reflects their beliefs, values, and history (p. 488).

A school culture is a multidimensional entity. Schoen (2013) noted that the following four dimensions must be examined when changing a school culture: the staff's professional orientation, the organization's structure, the student-centered focus, and the quality of the learning environments. Developing the professional orientation and the quality of the learning environment are integral dimensions of the teacher's work. All staff members must participate in development work in order to achieve real changes in the school's internal reality as well as to develop the school organization and learning environments and make its activities increasingly student centered (pp. 13, 29–31).

In addition to the dimensions above, the nature of school culture is connected to the prevailing curricular thinking in a society. Previous studies have identified that curricular thinking in many countries, for example, in Finland, has moved away from a centralized and subject-centered model toward a decentralized and school-centered curriculum model emphasizing locality (see Nevalainen et al., 2017, pp. 209–210, 214–217). Marsh (1997, pp. 141, 149) brings together some advantages and disadvantages of curricula in centralized and decentralized school systems:

A centralized curriculum development refers to head office administrators or senior project officers in an educational system making decisions about what is to be taught, how it is to be taught, and how it is to be assessed. Some advantages of centralized curriculum development are that it provides a uniform delivery system, saves time, ensures continuity, concentrates expertise, provides tighter coupling between the school and the system, and provides high-quality materials. However, there are many disadvantages of centralized curriculum development. For example, it assumes that there is general consensus on value orientations and approaches and that specific curriculum materials will be acceptable to a wide range of educators (Marsh, 1997, pp. 137, 140–141).

School-based curriculum development and site-based management are specific examples of decentralization. The term *school-based* suggests that all pedagogical decisions are made at the school level. Some reasons for moving toward school-based curriculum development are that it allows schools to have increased autonomy, that is, it provides schools the freedom, opportunity, responsibility, and resources to determine and direct their own affairs, and it enables teachers to develop their professional work. There are a number of problems that educators experience in undertaking activities pertaining to school-based curriculum development. Generally recognized obstacles to independent curricular work include lack of time, insufficient expertise and resources, and challenges related to school culture (Marsh, 1997, pp. 146–147, 149). More profound problems than these are, however, seen in obstacles to teachers' professional development, such as resistance to change both in teachers and in environments.

7   Key Features of the Learning Environments

A school's culture has a significant impact on education and instruction at the school and thus on learning environments. The concept of a *learning environment* has a wide diversity of definitions, depending on the learning approach:
- Wilson (1996) defined a *constructivist learning environment* as "a place where learners may work together and support each other as they use a variety of tools and information sources in their guided pursuit of learning goals and problem-solving activities" (p. 5).
- Stein (1998) believed that *situated learning environments* place students in authentic learning situations, where they are actively immersed in an activity while using problem-solving skills. These opportunities should involve a social community that replicates real-world situations (para. 3).
- Based on the contextual learning approach, Kauppi (1996) suggested that the *contextual learning environment* moves learning out of the classroom into authentic environments or environments that imitate reality (p. 95).

Land et al. (2012) wrote that student-centered learning environments "provide interactive, complimentary activities that enable individuals to address unique learning interest and needs, study multiple levels of complexity, and deepen understanding" (p. 3). Land and Hannafin (2000) explained further that these learning environments are based on the following five core foundations:

- Psychological foundations that emphasize theories and research related to thinking and learning;
- Pedagogical foundations that include the qualities that exist and can be developed in the environment;
- Technological foundations that influence how information technology supports, constrains, or enhances the learning environment;
- Cultural foundations that reflect the prevailing values in a learning community; and
- Pragmatic foundations that emphasize the reconciling of available resources and restrictions when teachers are designing a learning environment (pp. 3–4).

The concept of a learning environment can be understood comprehensively as a socialization environment. The family has traditionally been regarded as the most important environment for primary socialization, however, the family's role as a child's primary socializer has decreased over time (Gauvain & Parke, 2010, pp. 239–240). The main environment for secondary socialization is linked to the contexts of pedagogical processes inside the school as well as to the physical, personal, and/or sociocultural contexts outside the school that are connected with these processes (for the learning contexts, see Braund & Reiss, 2004, p. 7). The world of work after the years spent at school can be seen as a tertiary environment for socialization (Jarvis, 2009, p. 45).

The study at hand demonstrates that the Naturalistic, Sociocultural, Productive, Economic, Martial, Ecological, Horticultural, Practical-Agricultural, Scientific-Agricultural, and/or Scientific-Technical Dimensions are emphasized in accordance with social trends in environments that are geared toward secondary socialization.

8 Society and Education

Parsons (1966) defined *society* as a social system that attains its highest level of self-sufficiency in relation to its environments (p. 9). It is an element in the concrete whole of human social life and consists of the total complex of human relationships. A society is also affected by its cultural elements, which play an important part in its concrete manifestations (Parsons, 1934, pp. 225, 231). Parsons (1971) asserted that all social systems have four primary functions

that are essential for maintaining those systems: pattern-maintenance, integration, goal-attainment, and adaptation. Primacy of pattern-maintenance is
attributed to the cultural systems in society. These include institutions that
aim at transferring values to new generations, such as the family and the
school (Parsons, 1971, pp. 4–5, 7, 98–101). The purpose of integration, in turn, is
to maintain societal norms and ensure that they are followed. The integration
of society is secured by such constructs as different kinds of associational organizations. Goal-attainment is related to functions in administrative and political systems, for example, in which collectivity in particular is emphasized.
Efficient management of resources, in turn, has objectives such as contextual
adaptation when purchasing equipment to achieve the intended goals. The
economic and technological fields bear responsibility for this task (Parsons,
1971, pp. 7, 11–12, 15–18, 24–26; Parsons, 1967, pp. 203, 348).

Furthermore, Berger and Luckmann emphasized the idea that individuals
and their social worlds are in constant dialectical interaction. According to
Berger's (1969) interpretation, the individuals encounter society as an external reality that is subjectively opaque to them (p. 11). Individual go through
a series of events in life during which they acquire the requisite faculties for
participating in social interactions. Society assumes form within the framework of a continuing dialectical process of internalization, externalization,
and objectivation. The starting point of these phases is internalization: the
objectivated social world becomes rooted in consciousness as socialization
proceeds (Berger & Luckmann, 1967, pp. 61, 129). In relation to this, Berger and
Luckmann (1967) described socialization as the comprehensive and consistent
induction of an individual into the objective world of a society or its different
sectors, such as the physical environment and nonmaterial culture (Berger &
Luckmann, 1967, pp. 130, 138; see also Berger, 1969, p. 6). Primary socialization,
people's first socialization, takes place during childhood, and makes them a
member of society. Secondary socialization is understood to encompass all
the consecutive events that take place afterward that guide individuals into
new sectors of the objective world of their own society. It involves the internalization of institutional or institution-based subworlds. The scope and nature
of secondary socialization thus depends on the complexity of the division of
labor and the social distribution of knowledge.

A variety of theoretical premises may be used to examine the processes
of social change. Within society we can distinguish between processes that
maintain the status quo and those that bring about change. According to the
consensus approach, society is, in the first instance, an action system aiming
at stability, a system where social change occurs gradually, with the system
adapting to it (Parsons, 1967, pp. 203, 216–217). The conflict approach, in turn,
emphasizes a society under continuous change that is based on the struggle for

power between the various social groups. Contradictions are a prerequisite for bringing about social change (Dahrendorf, 1959, p. 162). The syntheses of these two interpretations explicitly show, in a quite parallel manner, how social conflicts should be addressed, why they are important for the development of the society, and what conditions exist for managing them. The consensus-oriented approach emphasizes in its synthesis that, even though different kinds of conflicts intersect in society, conflicts must be tolerated and utilized, as they have an equilibrating and stabilizing impact on societal structures (Coser, 1956, pp. 153–154). Conflict theorists, in their synthesis, approach social changes from the perspective of evolution. A social conflict can be changed into an institutionalized pattern of social life by means of regulation (conciliation, mediation, and arbitration). As a consequence of effective regulation, social change can occur through gradual development (Dahrendorf, 1959, p. 230).

Development theory approaches have attempted to describe and explain the factors that promote or hinder social change. According to the views of modernization theory, economic development relies directly on a modern society. This has a causal connection with the attitude and value changes that define the individual's modernity, and correspondingly, these fundamental changes are followed by behavioral changes. The transformations in the individual give meaning to and support for the changes in the political and financial institutions that lead to the modernization of society (Inkeles & Smith, 1974, p. 312). On the other hand, the dependency theory approach, founded on the thoughts of Marx, observes social underdevelopment in the context of the external factors related to society. According to this approach, the economic development of the core group of industrialized countries is based on the exploitation of peripheral, nonindustrialized countries. This exploitation is also manifested in the relationship between the elite and poor population groups (Frank, 1969, pp. 8–12, 135–137). Willis (2005), however, wrote that sociological theories of development have been criticized for their lack of engagement with cultural diversity. They have been accused of adopting a specific social organizational form as their starting point or their goal, without taking into account the thousands of different religious, ethnic, and social groups in the world (p. 120).

Education is a social phenomenon and a part of social reality. Society and its specific features determine what is to be achieved through educational practice. Growth depends on the environment, and it takes place in social interaction with that environment. Education thus has an intentional, social, and, to some extent, an instrumental nature (Durkheim, 1922/1956, pp. 67, 70–71, 80–81, 114). Durkheim concluded that:

> Education is the influence exercised by adult generations on those that are not yet ready for social life. Its object is to arouse and to develop in the

child a certain number of physical, intellectual and moral states which
are demanded of him by both the political society as a whole and the
special milieu for which he is specifically destined. (p. 71)

Several definitions exist for the concept of education. The idea of what
constitutes education has varied at different periods and in different societies.
Different scientific disciplines have also defined it from their own perspective.
This study is based on definitions of education that represent the central social
approaches to it, even though those descriptions aim to promote divergent
views on the role of education in society as well as on the nature of the interrelationship between education and society (see, e.g., Sadovnik, 2011, pp. 3–9).

In the classical conception of an ideal capitalist society in the United States,
the means of production are predominantly in private ownership in accordance with the principle of classic economic liberalism. The purpose of such a
market economy system is the production and sale of commodities for profit.
In this type of early industrial society, Dewey's progressive ideas concerning
education were based on the epistemological tradition of pragmatism and the
naturalistic view of the human being held by functionalism. Dewey (1916) considered education to be primarily a constant reorganizing or reconstructing of
experience (p. 89). Education is a social process, the aim of which is familiarizing those entrusted to it with the physical realities of life and providing them
with practice for becoming members of society (Dewey, 1899/1943, pp. 9, 27–
28). The educational event is regulated primarily by psychological and social
factors (Dewey, 1897/1940, p. 6).

In India, Gandhian neo-traditionalism within national educational thought
was the central method during the nonviolent struggle for independence, as its
philosophical background of education relied on the national legacy of Indian
traditional society. Gandhi (1947) viewed that social freedom in the form of self-
government is achieved by acquiring the ability to resist authority when it uses
its position wrongly (Gandhi, 1947, p. 7). This ability to resist authority involves
internal strength that is achieved through character-building. The central function of education is thus to strengthen the spiritual essence at the heart of
human nature. It is essential to learn what the soul is and what hidden powers
it contains and to internalize that in the struggle of life, hate may be conquered
by love, lies by truth, and violence by one's own suffering (Gandhi, 1948d, p. 254;
Gandhi, 1954, p. 140). Such a process of spiritual awakening should be part of
the development of the body, mind, and soul, when the mind proceeds with the
education of the physical and spiritual faculties of the student (Gandhi, 1962, p.
58). Gandhi (1948d) held that this type of education provides practice in being
responsible for doing one's own share and will usher in a silent revolution. This

will do away with the contradictions between social classes, thus laying the foundation for a just social order in traditional Indian society (pp. 259–260).

In Marxist ideology, the means of production are primarily publicly owned. This idea entails a planned economy utilizing a centralized system of economic control to direct national economic activity toward goals specified in plans lasting for a span of years. In the Soviet Union, for instance, the First Five-Year Plan lasted from 1928 to 1932. This type of socialist society understood that Marxist dialectical and historical materialism maintains that a continuous process of change and development based on economic contradictions determines the development of society. In the same manner, all other human activity is subject to the general law of the development of economic relations (Marx, 1932/1978, p. 250). For Marx (1867/1974), the function of education is to produce individuals with all-around skills and knowledge for whom the various social duties are but different modes of activity in the new society (Marx, 1867/1974, pp. 436, 439). In a process of this type, the interpretation of phenomena is guided in accordance with the social laws prevailing in economic relations (Engels, 1852/1926, p. 22; Marx, 1932/1978, p. 250).

The successful Bolshevik Revolution and its implications strengthened Marxist-Leninist thinking in China. After the ideological conflict between these two countries arose, China returned to its own social processes. Mao understood that instead of the proletariat, the peasantry would the leading group of the preindustrial societies. From the 1950s, Maoism was the political and military ideology of the Communist Party of China (C.P.C.), until the late 1970s, when Maoism developed and transformed into Marxism–Leninism–Maoism. This type of socialist country was convinced that education could be best organized by guiding students to work in material production. This was due to a firm belief that the willingness for revolutionary practice will also be created through human work and, consequently, the information gained will contain the structure of social organization. Mao (1937/1966b) was convinced that the active function of knowledge not only manifests itself in the active leap from perceptual to rational knowledge, but, and this is crucial, in the leap from rational knowledge to revolutionary practice. The knowledge that enables us to grasp the laws of the world must be redirected to the practice of changing the world, that is, it must be applied in the practices of production, revolutionary class struggle, and scientific experiment. This is the process of testing and developing theory and, therefore, it is the continuation of the whole process of cognition (p. 14).

In addition to these four macro-level approaches, the relationship between education and the surrounding society is defined from the perspective of individual interaction (see Mead, 1934, pp. 189, 191). Berger and Luckmann (1967)

stated that individuals and their social worlds are in constant dialectical interaction. This view concludes that socialization is a process by which the individual is inducted comprehensively and consistently into the world of society and
its different sectors. Individuals thus undergo a series of events in life during
which they acquire the faculties required to participate in social interactions
(pp. 61, 129–130, 138).

Education maintains, but also changes and reforms, the structures and functioning of society. Social conditions, in turn, affect education. This dialectical
process takes place differently in different societies. Education in every society
is also a part of the dialectical process, with social, economic, and political
dimensions. The education system affects each dimension of society, which
in turn affect each other and the education system. This dialectical process
produces changes from gradual to revolutionary (Fägerlind & Saha, 1989, pp.
226–227). Different views of the developmental trends in society are associated with the different underlying value objectives and views of the people
who hold them. A view of the human being, that is to say, a system of concepts
pertaining to the people, in turn, reflects the values and ideals prevailing in
society. The concept is related to the overall concepts of worldview and outlook on life. In this study, outlook on life is defined as a person's comprehensive concept of the knowledge and values relating to the world. The body of
knowledge is also controlled by epistemological views concerning the manner
in which knowledge is acquired and justified. A worldview is part of an outlook
on life. It originates in beliefs concerning the world.

This study regards education as a socially organized, intentional activity
in which knowledge, skills, and attitudes are transferred and acquired for the
purpose of preserving or changing individual and social activities. Education
is regarded as being connected with other cultural and human activity and
thus intimately linked to society and its economic and political power structure. Education is a superordinate concept that also contains the concepts of
instruction and schooling. Instruction is seen as intentional interaction having learning as its objective. Schooling, in turn, aims particularly at imparting
knowledge and skills. A significant part of education is given within the school
and educational system.

This study considers that education is closely related to the totality of culture and human activity. The dialectical process between education and society is realized in a different manner in accordance with the different value
objectives that constitute the background for different societies. A society is
defined as a social system forming a cultural totality in a specific geographical
area. A society is also a unified structure for human life that is based on the
mutual relationships between the inhabitants of a specific geographical area.

This study classifies societies on the basis of political and economic criteria, with the subjects studied being the following societies: the United States of America, the Republic of India, the Russian Empire, the Soviet Union, the Russian Federation, and the People's Republic of China. The present work views the interrelationship between education and society from the perspective of community-based learning.

9   Historical-Hermeneutic Comparative Education

9.1   *Comparative Education*

Comparative education is a cross-disciplinary research method that has as its point of departure the investigation and comparison of foreign cultures. Comparative education studies the structure and functioning of ideologies and institutions. The comparison aims to identify the similarities and differences between educational systems. It examines education over national boundaries so that each country expresses one variant of the collective educational experience of humankind (Bereday, 1964, pp. 4–5).

Comparative education has been defined and implemented in many ways. Ideas about comparison have varied at different times, and different disciplines have approached it from their own standpoints. Comparing educational systems in their social context has been examined by scholars such as Sir Michael Sadler (1861–1943), the founder of scientific comparative education, and Isaac L. Kandel (1881–1965), the pioneer in consolidating the new trend.

According to Sadler's views of comparative education, the functioning of educational systems is to be interpreted against the background provided by more comprehensive social phenomena. Sadler (1900/1964) believed that when studying the educational systems of foreign countries, the things outside the school must not be forgotten since they can mean even more than the phenomena inside the school. They govern and interpret the phenomena found inside the school. Consequently, an educational system is a living totality that is the outcome of early national struggles and difficulties (p. 310).

Kandel's educational comparison is based on an interpretation of the social ideals that are manifested in the school. Kandel (1936) considered the purpose of comparative education to be the investigation of the differences in the forces and causes behind various educational systems (p. 406). In this manner, comparison is based on an analysis of the social and political ideals reflected by the school (Kandel, 1933, p. XIX).

Comparative education has no specific research method or body of data. King (1968) emphasized that the research method should follow the purposes and problems set by the researcher (King, 1968, p. 56). This expression of an interdisciplinary orientation has, on the one hand, been accepted throughout the 20th century. On the other hand, one can also speak of different method-ological orientations that can even be understood in the Kuhnian sense of par-adigm conflict between positivist and hermeneutic concepts of science (see, e.g., Holmes, 1981, pp. 41–49; Holmes, 1985, pp. 334–336; Holmes, 1986, pp. 179–199; Kelly et al., 1982, pp. 509–526). The paradigms do, however, complement each other and are used for different functions in comparative education, since research problems have to be approached pragmatically from the perspective of the appropriate theoretical orientations.

Benefiting thus from different approaches, comparative education tries to answer many types of questions linked with education. According to Kelly and Altbach (1989), comparative research has included the following different points of departure:
- understanding national identity or national character;
- quantitative analysis of the teaching methods used and the educational out-comes achieved;
- application of structural functionalism;
- examination of the structure and internal functioning of educational sys-tems; and
- analysis based on the issues and problems of education (pp. 138–142).

Since the 1990s, studies of comparative education have, even more than before, analyzed the phenomena of education detached from its structures. At the same time, methodological studies have focused on conceptual issues rather than, for example, data collection or data-analysis strategies (see, e.g., Rust et al., 1999, p. 107).

In the new millennium, comparative research has more commonly approached education in the context of the broader cultural framework (Kazamias, 2009, p. 139; for a contextual comparative analysis, see, e.g., Alexander, 2000). This compels the researcher to consider how the extensive research material can be ordered and the extent to which the comparison of different cultures is possible at all. King (1979) regarded acquiring contextual information about the subject of research and continually being true to it as the prerequisites for comparing cultures (p. 52). An essential aim of such research is to conceptualize the subject matter. This allows the area of research to be delimited and made more precise, and the concepts to be defined. The concepts used in the study should also be institutionalized. Their appearance should be examined in genuine systems. A central feature here is the operationalization of the inquiries, that is to say, the study of the functioning of the systems (King, 1969, pp. 5, 7, 11; King, 1979, p. 57).

According to the rationale for this study, education is intimately connected with all other aspects of culture and human activity. Analysis of national identity or national character is thus a prerequisite for understanding the structure and functioning of educational systems; it is the methodological basis and point of departure. According to Sadler (1900/1964), comparative education is based on the concept of national character (p. 310). National character can be seen as the mental constitution of a people and nation that gives rise to common goals and creates common efforts to attain them (Mallinson, 1957, p. 4). Every nation tries to protect and preserve its traditions and aspirations through education. In this way, the properties that are characteristic of the nation will also be reflected in educational ideals and goals as well as in the measures the educational system takes to achieve them (Mallinson, 1957, p. 8; Hans, 1950, p. 10).

National identity molds the educational system, while the educational system, correspondingly, changes the essence of national identity. Mallinson (1975) concluded that national identity consists of the social, economic, and political factors in a society, with the groups of factors vacillating in the mutual patterns of emphasis and influence. This combination gives rise to cultural values and educational forms. These regulate, in contrast, the features of national identity (p. 272). Nevertheless culture and education do have similarly oriented goals. The prevailing cultural patterns determine educational systems. Education, for its part, supports general judgments concerning morals and values while preparing individuals to think critically. This gradually leads to constructive changes in the emphasis accorded different cultural values (Mallinson, 1981, p. 55).

The factors influencing the development of nations and national identities form, according to Hans (1950), a background for comparative research against which the phases in the development of an educational system can be followed. At the same time, the different value objectives with respect to education reveal themselves, which, in turn, justifies the comparison (pp. 7–8). Such a comparative study also includes examining the structure and functioning of an educational system within a historical perspective.

9.2   *The Historical-Hermeneutic Approach*

Every scientific approach is based on certain basic assumptions that reveal themselves in the concepts and principles used by different schools of thought. According to von Wright (1971), two main traditions can be distinguished in the history of ideas. They differ from one another with respect to the conditions that scientific laws and explanations have to fulfill in order to be scientifically acceptable. The opposition between these two traditions of explanation is characterized by the terms *causal* and *teleologic*. In the development of science, these explanations have run parallel. Proponents of positivism have generally explained phenomena causally, the basic underlying idea being methodological monism. Representatives of a hermeneutic philosophy of science have favored understanding over explanation, this being realized as different meaning structures in the consciousness of the interpreter. The point of departure for the hermeneutic way of thinking is the concept of the intentionality of human activity (pp. 2–6, 29–30).

This study applies a historical-hermeneutic approach to comparative education. The historical approach in comparative education aims at a holistic interpretation of culture for the purpose of clarifying the cultural factors that typify different nations. This yields understanding of the specific features of educational systems within their social context (Kandel, 1955, p. 13). Today's pedagogical reality can be understood by examining the national issues of the past (Schneider, 1961, p. 126). The historical approach often examines the diachronic development of the educational system and society, focusing on a specific case. Combining the vertical and horizontal approaches, Ulich (1961) observed that an increased insight could possibly be gained into the links between the life of people and societies (p. 303). This is also how the relationship between education and society is compared synchronically in different societies at given periods. Nevertheless, Harré (1978) argued that neither mode of examination leads directly to general principles and regularities, because different types of social-psychological mechanisms may involve the processes of change that have taken place in different societies at different times (pp. 46–47). For this reason, according to Hans (1950), the historical approach in comparative education attempts to delve into the different value objectives that constitute the background for education while simultaneously leading to as justified a comparison as possible (p. 8).

Combining an examination of educational systems with a societal and historical framework facilitates identification of the factors serving to differentiate national educational systems. Points of departure for investigation include cultural patterns and traditions, such as political theories and ideals (Kandel, 1955, p. 13). Hans (1950) suggested that, when studying in the historical context, attention is first focused separately on each national educational system, following the development of national character and culture. Before the comparison, yet more data is collected concerning the structure, administration, and achievements of the educational systems of the countries in question (p. 7). Concerning this, Kandel (1955) proposed that the comparison should focus more closely on the similarities and differences between educational systems. At the same time the common problems come to the fore, as do the manners in which different nations have responded to them in their specific types of conditions. The study of educational systems is thus actually an examination of the political, social, and economic reflections of a society (Kandel, 1955, p. 13).

The holistic interpretation and subsequent comparison of comprehensive and complex phenomena is indeed challenging from the scientific standpoint. The suggestion has been made that a new approach, better suited to the needs of comparative education research, should be developed for the historical approach. Kazamias (2001) wrote that historical analysis should adopt and implement theories and concepts in order to "select, organise and interpret the historical material" (p. 446). The present study aims to interpret and compare the past processes through concepts and theories. It examines the developmental trends of educational policy within the context of social change and trends so that the phenomena are studied utilizing the frameworks provided by the hierarchies of concepts and through lenses suggested by sociological theories. In this analysis, the hermeneutic approach is also used to facilitate the process.

The term *hermeneutics* refers to a scientific approach that attempts to identify the significance of phenomena. Sometimes the term *method of understanding* is used, a term that includes intentionality. Essential to hermeneutics is interpreting the contents of the meanings within the entire context of social reality (see, e.g., von Wright, 1971, pp. 6, 29–30).

The historico-hermeneutical sciences acquire, according to Habermas (1970), their knowledge by understanding meaning. In hermeneutic research, the interpretation of texts corresponds to the systematic verification of the hypotheses put forth by positivist research (p. 157). Hermeneutic thought is a holistic process of interpretation that constantly moves in a spiral hermeneutic circle formed by pre-understanding and understanding (Gadamer, 1965, p. 275). Its purpose is to clarify or make comprehensible the subject of study (Taylor, 1971, p. 3). In this manner, research approaches reality guided by the interest of preserving and extending the intersubjectivity that is required to understand through the interpretive activity. This means that the process between the interpreter and the text is dialectic by nature. The interpreters attempt to place themselves into the perspective of the world or language from which the text mediating the tradition acquires its meaningfulness. The semantic world of the text reveals itself to the interpreters to such an extent that their own world also becomes clearer. The interpreters form a communicative contact between these two worlds. They attain the content of the tradition by applying it to themselves and their situations. Hermeneutic research thus has a practical interest in knowledge as one of its components (Habermas, 1970, pp. 157–158). The knowledge thus acquired may be termed *intentional knowledge*, the basic property of which is the internal intention to preserve and expand it. Knowledge is always verified again as new interpreters' meaning structures in their world of experiences.

The interpretive process in hermeneutic thinking moves within a framework of re-understanding and understanding, where understanding always functions as the pre-understanding for the next level of understanding. This spiral-like relationship between parts and whole can be mastered by the use of abductive, deductive, and inductive reasoning. Peirce (1966) concluded that abduction is the first step in scientific discovery. It is a process involving the creation of an explanatory hypothesis (p. 136). The first premises, perceptual judgments, are extremely flexible. The abductive suggestion itself originates as a sudden flash of insight within the framework of which the idea of combining the unknown with that previously known produces a new suggestion to be investigated. On the basis of these guiding principles of inference, as they are termed, facts are examined that suggest the hypothesis. For deductive thought, a hypothesis takes the form of an ideal state of affairs appearing as an analog of experience. Deduction involves proceeding from an already existing hypothetical viewpoint while attempting to trace the necessary and probable consequences of the hypothesis. Certain recognized facts, according to deduction, cannot exist without either an inferred fact or its inferred objective probability. The functionality of the ideal prediction developed in deduction is, for its part, tested in induction. The justification for a conclusion made in induction is to be found in the fact that it has been reached using a method which, if adhered to unwaveringly, will, in time, lead to valid knowledge (Peirce, 1935f, pp. 99, 106; Peirce, 1966, pp. 122, 124–125, 137; Peirce, 1868/1935e, p. 113; Peirce, 1877/1935a, pp. 227–228).

Abduction and induction may be perceived as being intertwined, but Peirce (1966) saw them as forming opposing poles in the process of scientific reasoning. Abduction begins with the facts without a specific theory, even though it recognizes that this is necessary in order to explain unexpected facts. Examination of the facts suggests a hypothesis. The mode of the suggestion is the similarity of the facts with respect to the consequences of the hypothesis. Induction, in contrast, proceeds from a hypothesis, which is not linked to facts, even if these are necessary to support theories. Investigating a hypothesis suggests experiments that reveal the facts to which the hypothesis had pointed. The mode is the recognized knowledge that the conditions of the hypothesis can be realized by means of specific experiments. The rejection of incorrect hypotheses is always followed by an experiment with a new hypothesis, but the basis of all abduction is the conviction that the human mind will hit upon an acceptable hypothesis in a finite number of conjectures (Peirce, 1966, pp. 137–139). This study is a comparative investigation that uses the historical-hermeneutic method and proceeds by means of abductive, deductive, and inductive reasoning.

The following briefly examines the phases of the hermeneutic process of interpretation by analyzing the principles of textual interpretation. Danner (1979) thought that hermeneutic educational research generally involves the understanding, explanation, and interpretation of texts (p. 88). The interpretive process used in this comparative historico-hermeneutical investigation utilizes the canons of textual interpretation set down by Betti (1962, pp. 14–16, 19–20, 53–54), and the rules and phases of textual interpretation proposed by Danner (1979, pp. 89–91). Actually, this type of systematic methodological procedure has been considered unreliable, since not even rules and principles are sufficient to ensure that correct interpretations are reached (see, e.g., Hirsch, 1967, p. 170). Application of the interpretive guidelines is nevertheless justified, because interpretation always involves using some method, either consciously or unconsciously.

Over the years, an extensive body of interpretive rules to follow when forming an interpretation has been developed in order to attain trustworthiness in hermeneutic research (see, e.g., Hirsch, 1967, pp. 198–199). Betti (1962) viewed that the canons of textual interpretation primarily apply to the subject of the interpretation and the interpreter:

- The rule of textual autonomy views that the text is to be interpreted solely on the basis of the author's intentions at the time.
- The rule of textual totality understands that the parts of the text and the text as a whole are to be investigated in relationship to each other. Each text is also to be related to a larger whole, for example, the life, language, and culture of the authors and their other works dealing with the same subject.
- The rule of topicality considers that the interpreters are to create the meaning conveyed by the text personally step by step, beginning with the final text and ending with its initial stages.
- The rule of correspondence regards that the interpreters are to overcome their preconceptions and thus open-mindedly project themselves into the authors' positions (Betti, 1962, pp. 14–16, 19–20, 53–54; Betti, 1967, pp. 218, 220–222, 226, 228, 230).

The rules for textual interpretation also include guidelines applicable particularly to pedagogical texts (see, e.g., Danner, 1979, pp. 88–91; Groothoff, 1975, p. 165). According to Danner (1979), the process of interpreting a text consists of a preparatory interpretation, an internal interpretation of the text, and a coordinating interpretation. The preparatory interpretive stage involves creating the overall meaning of the text. The text's authenticity is checked by relating critically to the text and its sources. The interpreters must also be aware of both their pre-understanding and the questions they are posing to serve as a framework for approaching the text. The internal interpretation includes detailed semantic and syntactic examination of the text. The totality of the text is compared with its parts, with the parts, in turn, being compared with the whole, according to the hermeneutic circle. Logical rules are used to supplement the rules of grammar so that the meaning of the text would open as a whole. The finished interpretation should be as consistent as possible. In the coordinating phase of interpretation, the text is compared to other works by the same author in order to determine its locus and position with respect to those other works. At the same time, the authors examine conscious and unconscious points of departure. The meaning of the text is also topicalized, that is, translated to the world of the interpreter. Additionally, it is acknowledged that the connections of meaning and influence that have been understood are hypothetical. Something that has once been understood may change as a result of a new interpretation (Danner, 1979, pp. 89–90).

The following guidelines presented by Danner (1979) can also be followed in the process of interpreting a text. These guidelines pertain to interpreting the interaction between the whole of the text and its constituent parts:

1. Reading the entire text
2. Studying the details of the text and clarifying its contradictions
3. Reading the entire text again
4. Familiarizing oneself with secondary literature and other texts of the same type produced by the author
5. Culling specific thoughts from the text
6. Breaking the text down into components
7. Noting the content of the textual components
8. Reading the entire text again (p. 91).

The internal phase of textual interpretation in the present study primarily utilizes the first five phases listed above. A text is thus reinterpreted several times. A complete overall interpretation should be as consistent as possible.

Danner (1979) did not, however, see the rules for interpretation as offering a precise plan with a specific order. Neither is the content of the rules strictly technical. What is most significant is the attainment of a certain type of scientific attitude. A researcher has to adopt a positive readiness containing such elements as patience, modesty, tolerance, self-criticism, and openness (p. 91). Such an attitude is the prerequisite for understanding a pedagogical text.

This study follows the hermeneutic trend in epistemology. It is a multidisciplinary study that examines the diachronic development between education and society in the societies under investigation. The development occurring at different times in the societies in question is also compared synchronically. The point of departure for the study is arriving at an understanding of national identity, that is to say, of national character. The structure and functioning of educational systems is examined in light of the factors expressing national identity. In this study, national identity comprises social, economic, and political factors in a society. An educational system is thus seen as the means for implementing the national cultural values springing from the combination of these factors.

This historical-hermeneutic comparative study is also a holistic process of interpretation that proceeds within the hermeneutic circle through abductive, deductive, and inductive reasoning. The source material has been interpreted using the hermeneutic-dialectic method. The study utilizes the rules and phases of hermeneutic textual interpretation to attain trustworthiness.

CHAPTER 2

Ideals for Learning in Communities in the United States of America

Abstract

The aim of this chapter is to analyze the foundations of community-based learning with a focus on the philosophical views, educational aims, and associated value dimensions in the United States. It also aims to examine the changing nature of the pedagogical activities of community-based learning and their authentic learning environments. This analysis concentrates particularly on the activities of community-based learning and their central pedagogical approaches in a context of social change. This chapter shows that the American philosophical tradition of community-based learning is founded on the ideas of progressive education and is based on the tradition of pragmatism and the naturalistic view of the human being held by functionalism. Consequently, the primary focus is on experiential education. This chapter demonstrates that community-based learning can take place in a variety of learning environments prioritizing the Naturalistic, Sociocultural, Horticultural, Practical-Agricultural, Productive, Ecological, or Scientific-Technical Dimensions, in accordance with the general direction of political, economic, and social development. The chapter shows that, starting in the early 20th century, the United States focused efforts on expanding learning environments from schools to the real world outside of schools. During the past seven decades, pedagogical approaches and their learning environments have increasingly given special importance to the use of technology-based applications. The study concludes that approaches to community-based learning could provide a way for teachers and communities to prepare students to participate and become engaged in solving local problems.

Keywords

philosophy – aims – values – practices – community-based learning – pedagogical progressivism – essentialism – pedagogical activities – pedagogical approaches – learning environments – experiential education – United States

1   Pragmatism and Pedagogical Progressivism

The present analysis sees the educational philosophy of community-based learning in the United States as related to the principles of pragmatism, which is traditionally considered to be the earliest independent American philosophical trend. The basic ideas of pragmatism developed in a philosophical discussion group that met at Harvard University during the 1870s. The members of the group included natural scientists, lawyers, and philosophers interested in current problems in the field of science and philosophy (see Peirce, 1906/1935b, pp. 7–9). In particular, they were concerned with the principles of epistemology, ontology, and ethics. The best-known members were philosopher Charles S. Peirce (1839–1914), the founder of pragmatism, and psychologist William James (1842–1910), the founder of the functionalist approach to psychology, which was based on pragmatism.

Peirce initially presented the epistemological ideas of pragmatism regarding the relation between meaning and action in his 1878 article "How to Make Our Ideas Clear." Peirce (1868/1935e) concluded that thinking is based on signs or conceptions that are produced through experience (pp. 151–152). The meanings of the conceptions can be ascertained by studying their practical consequences, and human consciousness and beliefs thus develop in close association with action (Peirce, 1877/1935a, 1878/1935c). The beliefs in reality, however, are not, in Peirce's pragmatistic view, based on personal experience, but rather develop in connection with such objective action that is related to an infinitely continuing process. Therefore, action is the prerequisite, aim, and guarantor of knowledge.

Peirce also presented a three-category classification of consciousness—firstness, secondness, and thirdness—and considered that these levels are in a triadic relation to each other. The following from Peirce (1931/1960) describes these kinds of relations in detail:

> A *Sign*, or *Representamen*, is a First which stands in such a genuine triadic relation to a Second, called its *Object*, as to be capable of determining a Third, called its *Interpretant*, to assume the same triadic relation to its Object in which it stands itself to the same Object. (p. 156)

When analyzing Peirce's classification of consciousness formation from the perspective of community-based learning, it could be interpreted that the first category of human consciousness (firstness) consists of feelings related to an authentic experience and its properties, while participating in activities within different learning environments. The second category (secondness), in connection with the first category, consists mainly of conscious observation as the individual participates in activities in and outside the school. The third category (thirdness) is a thought, the function of which is to govern the second category. It determines the idea and its form and, therefore, interprets action with the conscious observations obtained in different learning environments, thus gaining a conceptual meaning (Peirce, 1931/1960, pp. 152–153, 284).

James interpreted Peirce's pragmatistic principles specifically from the perspective of an individual's experiences, expectations, and feelings. James (1890) stated that the source and origin of reality is subjective, and therefore knowledge also expands on the basis of an individual's practical and esthetic interests (pp. 295–297, 344–345). An idea's significance is determined by its value and usefulness in the individual's experience. Practice reveals truth, which is manifested as something good (James, 1907, pp. 75–76, 222). Practical activity consists of valuable experiences to which new incentives are linked through action. Images in a stream of consciousness are also linked together in a similar fashion (James, 1899, pp. 66–67, 79–81). Consequently, according to the pragmatism-based functionalist approach to psychology, humans are primarily practical, thinking, and active creatures. It has also been stated that such creatures are capable of adapting to social transformation in a democratic culture (Garrison & Neiman, 2003).

Many American educationists were also interested in the ideas of European philosophers and pedagogies such as Herbert Spencer (1820–1903). Spencer's work *Education* (1861) talked about a school that prepares children for life (p. 8). His book emphasized educational ideas pertaining to freedom, independence, creativity, and activity propounded by Jean-Jacques Rousseau (1712–1778), Johann H. Pestalozzi (1746–1827), and Friedrich Fröbel (1782–1852).

Spencer (1861) proposed that school should, above all, teach the knowledge and skills required to cope with life and, in this process, provide guidelines for educating future generations, help in developing social conditions, and introduce means for acquiring educative interests (pp. 8–10, 37). Teaching, which follows the child's developmental level, proceeds from the particular to the general and is based on immediate experiences that the child obtains while solving problems independently in their own fields of interest (pp. 73–80).

Romantic naturalism, best represented in Rousseau's writings, grew into a well-known modern philosophical approach to education in the early 20th century. Examining the conceptual features of romantic naturalism using Hlebowitsh's (2007) classification, from the perspective of American community-based learning, can be interpreted to mean that the ideal student has an innate proclivity for self-education. This proclivity can be subjected to minimal adult guidance only by giving students an opportunity to engage in free activities within the context of open learning environments. The ideal educational program must also be content neutral, with an emphasis on free activity. The student is oriented toward a fragmented, ideal society where various kinds of individual efforts occur in the communities of an early industrial country.

The epistemology of pragmatism, the concept of truth in functionalism, and Spencer's educational ideas as well as Charles Darwin's (1809–1882) naturalistic theory of evolution inspired an interest in the possibility of individual growth. This, in turn, also aroused criticism of the U.S. educational system (Cremin, 1961, pp. 100, 116–117). Many people thought that the textbook- and teacher-centered teaching methods were not adequate in preparing children for the challenges of industrialized society. Supporters of a new type of schooling demanded a closer relationship between teaching and practice, immediate experiences, and real life in society. The ensuing lively discussion resulted in the progressive education movement (from the early 1890s to the late 1950s), which also influenced school reform in Europe and Asia (see, e.g., Dewey, 1929a, pp. 100–102; Kerschensteiner, 1913, p. 36). The central figure of this new movement was philosopher, psychologist, and educational reformer John Dewey.

1.1   *John Dewey and the Progressive Education Movement*

Pedagogical progressivism, when it emerged in the United States at the turn of the 20th century, became the new philosophical mainstream of education. This powerful branch of pragmatism was connected to the American philosophical tradition, particularly with regard to experimentalism and, consequently, also constituted a national philosophical foundation for community-based learning. The progressive education movement was principally related to school experiments by its major figure, Dewey, as well as to his publications on reforming teaching methods (see Dewey, 1897/1940, 1899/1943, 1902, 1916; Dewey & Dewey, 1915).

Dewey's thinking in the philosophy of education developed within the context of the philosophical trend of pragmatism and the social and economic changes taking place in the increasingly industrialized United States. After studying philosophy at Johns Hopkins in Baltimore (from 1882 to 1884) with George S. Morris (1840–1889), Dewey moved to the University of Michigan in 1884 to teach philosophy (Dewey, 1939/1951, pp. 14, 16, 19). By this time, he had been strongly influenced by the ideas of his colleague George H. Mead (1863–1931) and German philosopher Georg W. F. Hegel (1770–1831) (see Dewey, 1930/1960, pp. 3–11). After familiarizing himself with the psychological ideas of James in particular, however, Dewey gradually adopted the epistemological tradition of pragmatism (Dewey, 1930/1960, pp. 12–16), an American system of thought that he applied to his studies, as he also developed an interest in educational sciences and the societal significance of educational procedures.

Dewey's thoughts in the philosophical field of education could be interpreted as a combination of Hegel's view on dialectical change in society and the naturalistic evolution theory represented by Darwin, to the extent that Hegelian social development is seen to take place gradually. Here, the absolute idealism Hegel developed is replaced by the constant reconstruction of situations implemented by individuals and groups (for the influence of Hegelianism on Dewey's thought, see, e.g., Hickman, 1996). In this analysis, Dewey was convinced that the individuals are unique living beings who, through education, can not only realize their latent abilities but also contribute to society while actively adapting to the demands of the environment in a new industrialized and urbanized America (for more on neo-Darwinism, see Garrison & Neiman, 2003). In essence, Dewey's pragmatism could be described as a material counterpart to Hegel's absolute idealism. The following summary illustrates the significant role of Dewey's school experiments on the construction of his philosophical thinking in the field of education:

> John Dewey was one of the most influential educational philosophers and progressive educators in the United States. After becoming interested in education and the social significance of educational principles, Dewey accepted an offer from the University of Chicago in 1894 to head the combined departments of philosophy, psychology, and pedagogy (Dewey, 1939/1951, p. 27). Inspired by the atmosphere of pedagogical reform in Chicago (see Parker, 1894, pp. III–VI), he founded a laboratory school for his own teaching activities that served as a workshop for his students' personal observations, experiments, and research. It eventually became an experimental school for progressive educational ideas (see, e.g., Mayhew & Edwards, 1936/1966, pp. 42–52). During this period, Dewey wrote his first significant works on education, which were based on combining teaching with activity and school with life (see Dewey, 1897/1940, 1899/1943, 1902). While a professor of philosophy and education at Columbia University in New York City from 1905 to 1930, Dewey published, in addition to innumerable philosophical essays, his main pedagogical work, *Democracy and Education* (1916). He visited the early Soviet Union and was invited to lecture in China and other countries (for more detailed information on Dewey's impressions abroad, see Dewey, 1929a; for biographical details, see Cremin, 1988, pp. 165–173; Gutek, 2011, pp. 351–358).

Dewey's progressive pedagogic ideas are based on the epistemological tradition of pragmatism and the naturalistic conceptions of the human expressed by functionalism. Dewey claimed that reality is evolutionary, as it is constructed through interaction between humans and the environment. Knowledge is not related to absolute truth but evolves from experience generated by active effort (see Dewey, 1916, 1933, 1938). It is constantly being tested by new theories more in accordance with experience. Theory is thus an instrument for organizing experience and evaluating activity. The reconstruction of experiences proceeds by means of problem-solving based on reflective thinking. This involves recognizing and defining the problem and testing the hypotheses developed for solving it (Dewey, 1916, pp. 89–90, 188–189, 192). An essential characteristic of reflective thought is the suggestion of possible solutions, the intellectualization of experienced difficulties, the proposing of hypotheses, the mental elaboration of ideas, and the verification of hypotheses by action (Dewey, 1933, pp. 107–115). Thinking is consequently a means of mastering experience that furthermore promotes adaptation to the surrounding world (Dewey, 1916, pp. 192, 401). Such an interpretation, that of instrumentalist and experimentalist pragmatism, sees learning as occurring best in connection with doing and the associated immediate experiences. For this reason, school teaching should also be combined with practical work.

The progressive trend in education developed within the sphere of influence of international reform-pedagogical ideals. The representatives of progressive pedagogics, such as Dewey, Clapp, William H. Kilpatrick (1871–1965), Helen Parkhurst (1887–1973), and Carleton W. Washburne (1889–1968), were influenced by the national scientific tradition. Kilpatrick and Parkhurst made significant efforts to relate learning activities to the needs of the student. Kilpatrick emphasized the comprehensiveness of teaching. His project teaching method was ideally based on cooperative community activities chosen by students. These were projects in which students were required to participate in the planning, investigation, and assessment related to many school subjects in order to solve the problem in question (Kilpatrick, 1918, pp. 16–17; Kilpatrick, 1940, p. 38). Parkhurst developed an educational program that gave importance to students' independent activities in special subject classrooms. Her Dalton Plan, as it was termed, was based on a range of curricula, for a day, a week, a month, or a semester, according to students' abilities. The curricula were implemented alone or in groups, the teacher's function being that of a counselor, supervisor, and facilitator (Parkhurst, 1922, pp. 34–44, 85–90).

1.2   Aims and Values

The ideal progressive school offered the opportunity to articulate reality in such a way that connects teaching and education with situations of social reality, in which learning can be connected to the student's life and experiences. Dewey (1899/1943) stated that an individual's uniqueness and initiative are expressed as a desire to interact socially as well as to create and construct. These instincts also form the foundation for the need to investigate and invent as well as to express oneself artistically. The essential function of school is to provide students with the opportunity to develop their specific functional traits, but in close contact with the reality prevailing in society (pp. 42–45). In this manner, progressive pedagogy intended to combine motor, sociomoral, and intellectual education, an essential component of which is mental and moral consciousness (pp. 131–132).

The aim constituting the background for this type of work-related pedagogy was to teach children personal responsibility and to provide them with practice for the physical realities of life. To some degree, practical work would contribute to the school itself becoming a genuine manifestation of active community life (Dewey, 1899/1943, pp. 9–11). The ultimate socioethically value-oriented goal for child-centered progressive education was to teach students to understand the social meaning of work and, therefore, to help them cope with the demands of a capitalist, early industrial state.

During the 1920s and 1930s, the society-centered pattern of community-based learning in the United States can be seen as emphasizing motor and sociomoral aims. These aims had been designed to educate a real American, a citizen who has internalized "the American dream" for an early industrial, classical liberal society. The goal of the progressive school, rooted in pragmatism, was to educate individuals in a way that took their interests and needs into account while socializing them to the requirements and values of the society at that time. Progressive educators believed in fulfilling the values embedded in the founding of the United States, as established in the U.S. Constitution in 1788. The U.S. Constitution created the United States as a federal republic, with the president having the highest executive power and with a considerable degree of autonomy granted to the states. The national legislature, or Congress, consists of the Senate and the House of Representatives. With the Senate's consent, the president also appoints an advisory group, or a cabinet, consisting of secretaries who are politically responsible only to him or her. The highest judicial power is held by the Supreme Court.

In light of an approach to progressive education based on experientialism, it can be observed that community-based learning emphasized active involvement in the learning experience. Pedagogical progressivism was, by nature, a universal pedagogical approach that, in a down-to-earth manner, strove to narrow the gap between education and society. Dewey (1899/1943) suggested that by performing different work-related activities, students could familiarize themselves with the skills, current procedures, and principles needed in society (p. 11). The central idea in this process was that resolving problem situations through active efforts in cooperation with others would prepare

students for life outside the school. As Dewey (1899/1943) indicates, this form of community-based learning aimed to:
- integrate the curricula of the various subjects and grade levels;
- teach manual skills so that students can utilize the experiences of their daily life in school, where they acquire experiences that they can, in turn, apply outside school;
- teach students the ideology of classical liberal democracy, that is, to act as members of the embryonic society of the school and in the real life of society; and
- unite school directly with life, work, and activities in the community (pp. 11, 27, 72–76, 80).

The strengthening of the progressive education movement in the United States also revived the camping education movement. Both organized and public school camping emphasized motor and sociomoral aims and their value dimensions. As a reform-pedagogical implication of progressivism, the school camping movement was based on closeness to nature. This approach had only infrequent connections to school curricula. In the early days, the purpose of organized and public school camping was to offer students outdoor life experiences under camp conditions. An attempt was made to develop camping skills in order to promote virtues related to nature as well as to promote the students' character, health, work, love for their fellow people, and citizenship.

Organized camping intended to offer city children experiences with open spaces and sunshine. Sharp (1941) wrote that camping represented "a way of life" that was to be based on the past struggles of the people and on the role of nature in life as a whole. It was to relate to the way people used to live and still do in the open, close to nature. The aim was the development of the whole child involving, in addition to character-building, the advancement of aspects associated with physical fitness, spiritual balance, and health (pp. 4–6). Organized camping aimed to:
- teach the knowledge, skills, and attitudes that are necessary for a simple and healthy life;
- develop camping skills and leisure activities;
- teach respect for work, that is, to adopt a conscientious attitude toward work and to appreciate work as a joy in life;
- develop character through music, books, play, and worship;
- promote love of nature and fellow human beings;
- raise the national spirit; and
- offer experiences in the great outdoors (Gibson, 1939, pp. 2, 5–6).

The relatively few public school camps that existed in the 1930s and 1940s intended to offer students real-life situations under such conditions. In addition to offering regular outdoor activities, these camps also provided opportunities to observe nature in order to learn about it and understand it better. These were just the preliminary intentions for integrating school camping with school education. Emphasizing the universal values associated with nature and life also represented an aspiration for socioethical values related to the individual's inner self, fellow people, and national spirit.

By 1950, there had been no significant increase in public school camping, particularly regarding school camps functioning during regular school hours. The early public school camps were, to a great extent, based on progressive ideas of education. Vinal (1936) observed that school camps provided a learning environment of realism where human and natural values were more important than academic ones. "The materials of camp" were to be "the materials of life." Working "in the laboratory of life" led to the socialization of the individual (p. 424). This method of education aimed to:
- integrate camping with school teaching;
- teach camping skills and knowledge of nature;
- enhance initiative and independence;
- develop social skills;
- promote national spirit; and
- provide real-life situations under camp conditions (Sharp, 1935, pp. 26–29; Sharp & Osborne, 1940, pp. 236–237).

No doubt exists that Dewey's ideas represented an understanding of education and its practices that differed completely from the prevailing traditional and mentalistic education of the time. The traditional school was based on formalism, verbalism, and authoritarianism, whereas pedagogical progressivism can be seen as resting upon the ideology of an American early industrial society. The ultimate goal of education was to promote the students' sense of responsibility, thus leading them to membership in a free, democratic society. A progressive school of this type aimed at familiarizing the students with skills and courses of action needed in society. The integration of school education with activities and real life in the community was consequently a prerequisite for progressive, experiential education.

From the philosophical perspective, the progressive thoughts on experiential learning remained ever-present in many of the functions of the reformed school. American teachers and their students continued participating in community-based workshops, field trips, and resident outdoor schools, even though these had assumed new goals and forms. In Ravitch's (1983) point of view:

Neither the Russians nor the critics killed progressive education. It died because it was, ironically, no longer relevant to the times; it did not meet the pragmatic test of "working" in public schools except as curricular innovations for below-average students, which was far from its stated intentions. ... When at last it disappeared in the mid-1950s, there was scarcely a trace of what it originally meant to be, though surely the influence of its pioneers was present wherever projects, activities, and pupil experiences had been intelligently integrated into subject matter teaching, wherever concern for health and vocation had gained a permanent place in the school program, and wherever awareness of individual differences among children had replaced lockstep instruction and rote memorization. (pp. 79–80)

1.3   *Summing Up*

The conceptual features of experimentalism can be analyzed from the perspective of community-based learning by applying the three-level classification represented by Hlebowitsh (2007, p. 107). There the ideal relationship between education and society is outlined from the standpoint of the student, the educational program, and society. Experimentalism sees the ideal student as a problem-solver who is socially conscious, democratically inspired, and capable of thinking while actively participating in experiential activities based on collaboration in different learning environments. Similarly, the ideal educational program must contain problem-centered and goal-directed activities, this being consistent with authentic personal and communal experience. The student is oriented toward an ideal democratic society, the strength of which is based on public social discourse and mutual consensus, and the citizens of which work in early industrial production and, increasingly, in the service sector.

The progressive school reform continued its path to success in the United States during the period between the two world wars. Surprisingly, however, the popularity of progressive education diminished rapidly soon after the end of the Second World War (1939–1945). Cremin (1961) concluded that the collapse of the progressive trend in education was primarily the result of the professionalization of the movement, the rise of a new political trend, and far-reaching changes in American society. Being connected with these contextual factors, progressivism in education encountered the following process-related obstacles:
– The progressive education movement could not be revitalized, but rather it became professionalized and drifted into internal contradictions. The previously popular movement became vulnerable to criticism leveled at its

policies and practices. Some of progressivism's ideas were adapted in schools with no commitment to its overall pedagogical thinking (see also Dewey, 1952, p. x), nor could the supporters of progressivism revamp their program.

– The conservative political and social thinking of the postwar period accelerated criticism of the school revision movement. Many educationists imagined that they could preserve the progressive school as it had been, without change, although nobody could predict with certainty what kind of institution would ultimately arise to replace it (see also Dewey, 1891/1929b, p. 3).

– The progressive education movement did not keep up with the continuing transformation of society. The major technological innovations of modern society revealed the school's ultimate responsibility for organizing and transmitting knowledge. The ideas that the progressive school in education offered, which were devoted to traditional activity-oriented learning, seemed outdated (Cremin, 1961, pp. 348–351).

2   Essentialism and American Educational Reform

2.1   *Philosophical Views*

In the United States, a philosophical turn in education occurred in the late 1950s that was comparable to the later Indian neocolonial approach in the mid-1960s. The catalyst for this change was the threatening atmosphere that pervaded the country in the late 1940s during the start of the Cold War. The educational system was necessary to strengthen the power of national defense, particularly against the potential supremacy of the Soviet Union. The social goal was now to train experts for an ideal American society following capitalist ideology. In accord with these changes, emphasis was placed on the idea that the philosophical background of community-based learning evidently relied on the principles of essentialist education, these being primarily consistent with the philosophical tradition of realism.

The basis of this educational trend, essentialism, lies deep in the history of the American school. The concept was introduced to the wider public in the late 1930s and early 1940s by William Bagley (1874–1946), a professor at Columbia University who challenged the freedom, individualism, and engagement in activities promoted in progressive education (Gutek, 2000, p. 66). Essentialism is an educational theory rooted in traditional philosophies, particularly realism, and its ontological, epistemological, and axiological postulates are largely in harmony with the tradition of realism. From the perspective of realism, reality is objective, independent of the observer's experience, because reality consists of the physical world. Consequently, knowledge is built through the rational observation and interpretation of natural laws, which means that values are also seen as absolutes based on natural laws (for realism as a systematic philosophy, see, e.g., Gutek, 1997, pp. 36–40).

The essentialist theory of education became the dominant philosophical approach during the 1950s, a period in which the United States experienced widespread fear of communism. As the critical educational debate was churning, it became clear that the leading politicians and authorities responsible for educational policies were ready to favor an essentialist educational philosophy, particularly after the Soviet Union launched a small satellite, *Sputnik*, into orbit around the earth in 1957. The momentous National Defense Education Act of 1958 (1958) had the goal of training experts in science and technology for a society dominated by capitalist ideology (Section 101). Teaching was expected to emphasize academic expertise instead of Rousseauian child-centered education and its reform-pedagogical ideals.

The demand to increase the number of experts in the natural sciences also resulted in the development of pedagogical approaches of community-based learning represented by various programs of outdoor and environmental education. These had originated in such reform-pedagogical movements as the camping education movement and the conservation movement. The course of development was promoted by the environmental awakening of the 1960s, which involved a new public awareness of environmental issues. It can be claimed that the supporters of essentialism now offered an opportunity to operate in a familiar philosophical context of education, even though the ontological and epistemological starting points of their approach differed completely from those of their predecessor, pedagogical progressivism. Unlike the representatives of progressive pedagogics, essentialists emphasized examining the natural laws of the physical world as well as the mastery of essential knowledge, rather than concentrating on the mode of learning (Armstrong et al., 2009, pp. 268–269).

2.2   *Aims and Values*

Conservative social thinking strengthened in the United States in the late 1940s after the Second World War. This being the case, the popularity of the progressive reform-pedagogical movement also precipitously collapsed. Critical discussion of education took an unexpected turn during the Cold War period (1947–1989), a time when suddenly, in 1957, the Soviets successfully sent the first device into space. The event was interpreted in the United States as a major threat to national defense, and in order to raise the national defense level, it was necessary to raise the quality of scientific and technical knowledge among the citizenry. This required school reform, the goal of which was to produce competent experts for the new society following capitalist ideology and a full-fledged market economy. Many thought that experts who have special knowledge, skills, and training would be able to develop industries administered by the new technologically sophisticated society.

This major social change accelerated the development of the school-centered pattern of community-based learning so that the primary emphasis was on intellectual aims. The American essentialist school, influenced by realism, stressed the shared goal of these intellectual aims and the integration of motor, sociomoral, and intellectual education in accordance with the National Defense Education Act of 1958. Through these aims, the purpose was to train science and technology experts for the most developed capitalist society in the world. Education was harnessed to the international power struggle in an attempt to increase the country's political security and supremacy by accentuating intellectual aims, while, in fact, the intention was to promote theoretical values associated with truth, knowledge, and science.

The research studies from the period show that the society-centered pattern of community-based learning gradually started to become school-centered in the early 1950s, with more emphasis placed on intellectual aims. St. Clair (1958) found through her national survey that fewer than a fifth (approx. 18%) of the resident camp programs (N = 92) were started between 1937 and 1950. These camps were intended for third- to eighth-grade children and functioned during normal school hours (pp. 31–32). Weil (1950) stated that in 1950 the development of public school camping was a central focus of activity in nine states (p. 284), and Pike (1951) reported that in the 1949–1950 academic year 23 public school camp programs operated either for the entire school year or for a portion of it (p. 24). It appears that many educators discovered that the new concept of *outdoor education* offered a valuable method for their outdoor instruction.

Outdoor education can be seen as the earliest approach of the school-centered pattern in this era. The purpose of outdoor education was to provide an approach to learning in which teachers were urged to utilize pedagogical resources in various outdoor settings. School camps and field trips also began to employ, in addition to outdoor life experiences, relevant content areas of the school curriculum. Sharp (1947) emphasized that outdoor education was to advance from school to society in continuously widening circles, the activity reaching its peak in the school camp. The subject matter that could best be learned outside the classroom should indeed be learned outside of it (pp. 34–35). This form of outdoor education aimed to:
– integrate the contents of curricula;
– promote acquisition of knowledge, that is, to learn it faster, retain it longer, and understand it more deeply;
– arouse interest in learning;
– teach democratic ideology, that is, to respect one's fellow human beings and master cooperation skills; and

– offer immediate learning experiences in the community and its nature (Sharp, 1952, pp. 19–22).

The early 1950s and the mid-1960s were characterized by the standardization of outdoor education, which also included the uniformity of pedagogical aims (for a closer examination of the period, see Hammerman et al., 2001, pp. 239–242). The tendency in this process was the holistic integration of outdoor education into the school curriculum by concretely extending the classroom to form an outdoor laboratory in the natural or cultural environment. The purpose of such an approach to outdoor education was to enrich the curriculum, reinforce teaching, and stimulate learning, thus widening its dimensionality. The theoretical values of education were also prioritized in the spirit of realism so that the accent was on developing problem-solving skills and utilizing all the senses through research-based learning. Instead, less stress was placed on the aims related to universal values, such as enhancing the ability of students to appreciate and understand the natural environment. However, the idealistic goal of education was to develop students' ability to act as constructive members of a democratic society.

The Elementary and Secondary Education Act of 1965 (1965) had American teachers emphasize programs with out-of-school activities for the purpose of supplementing and enriching their instruction (Sections 301, 303). Fitzpatrick (1968) explicated that outdoor education was to utilize resources beyond the classroom to enhance and enrich teaching and learning (p. 78). Concerning this, Hug and Wilson (1965) explained that outdoor education was to be based on exploratory and discovery learning, which was to proceed by means of problem-solving while utilizing all of the senses in observation and perception (pp. 5–6, 8–10). Based on Fitzpatrick (1968), outdoor education aimed to:
– enrich the curriculum;
– develop the individual's intellectual, physical, and mental abilities;
– stimulate learning;
– develop the knowledge, skills, and attitudes needed for the wise use of leisure time;
– promote awareness of nature and its relationship to humankind, that is, to appreciate and understand the natural environment as well as the relationship between humankind and nature;
– enhance the individual's abilities to play a more constructive role in society, that is, to develop civic-mindedness and promote democratic human relations and procedures; and
– offer direct learning experiences beyond the classroom (p. 49).

In the United States in the 1950s and 1960s, the demand for increasing the number of experts in the natural sciences intensified the development of community-based learning to an unforeseen degree when the U.S. Congress also expressed the desire to direct public school academic studies to out-of-school environments. This trend spread when the environmental movement was accompanied by a revived awareness of the decline in environmental equilibrium. This affected decision-making within educational policy to prioritize intellectual aims consistent with the prevailing ideas in society. The purpose of the Environmental Education Act (1970) was to develop curriculum that promoted an understanding of the principles of the natural and cultural environment. Thus, attempts were made to support activities designed to improve the environment and maintain an ecological balance during the society's rapidly changing science and technology (Sections 2–3). In the same year, a Department of Health, Education, and Welfare publication suggested that the aims of environmental education were to guide students in making sound ecological decisions and to anticipate their consequences, prepare value judgments, and act accordingly (Office of Education, 1970, pp. 10–11).

In the academic year 1969–1970, about half (approx. 55%) of the environmental education programs in public schools (N = 702) of 1,000 students or more were termed *outdoor education*, the majority (approx. 65%) of all programs having some type of on-site resident experience. The program curricula most often focused on the natural and applied sciences (National Education Association, 1970, pp. 5–6, 9, 13, 49).

This kind of environmental policy appears to be focused on aims related to universal values. The intention was to enhance the will and ability of students and help them to understand values connected with the natural environment, ecological sustainability, and environmental protection. Stressing the universal values associated with nature also represented an aspiration for environmental ethics and values related to students' own ecological decisions and value judgments, and an awareness of their personal contributions. Values related to environmental literacy and decision-making were emphasized during active-learning projects that helped students build their ethical and mental abilities. These goal-directed activities were also used as a means to achieve the theoretical values of education that were prioritized so that the accent was on research processes concerning environmental issues and alternative solutions.

Many outdoor education programs were intended to be environmental education programs. The purpose of such programs was to study in various sites close to nature, these being forests, woodlands, ponds, lakes, recreation areas, or wild land natural areas. Stapp (1969) proposed that the aim of environmental education was to produce a citizenry that is knowledgeable about the biophysical environment and its associated problems, aware of how to help solve these problems, and motivated to work toward their solution (p. 31). Hungerford et al. (1980) stated that the goal of environmental education was to aid students in

becoming environmentally knowledgeable and skilled as well as dedicated citizens willing to work both individually and collectively toward achieving and/or maintaining a dynamic equilibrium between the quality of life and the environment (p. 43). This form of environmental education aimed to:
- provide knowledge of ecological foundations;
- develop the knowledge and skills needed to investigate environmental issues and evaluate alternative solutions for remediating these issues;
- promote skills required in positive environmental action;
- guide the development of a conceptual awareness connected with environmental issues and values; and
- provide environmental education programs in school and in the environment outside the school (Childress, 1978, pp. 5–6; Hungerford et al., 1980, pp. 43–44).

2.2.1   Summing Up

If the conceptual features of essentialism are analyzed by applying Hlebowitsh's (2007) classification from the perspective of community-based learning, we can conclude that the ideal student has a rational mind and concentrates on the basics of school subjects while examining natural and environmental phenomena using scientific methods. The ideal curriculum embodies programs of both outdoor education and environmental education, the experiential activity-based units of study of which are academic and subject-centered, with the contents being studied in a structured manner in and outside the school. The student is oriented toward an ideal democratic society that depends on the essential academic knowledge defined by experts in different fields, while operating in high-tech industrial production and service-based sectors.

Proponents of essentialism intended to emphasize teachers' central role in education. The whole learning process was to be centered on the teacher (see, e.g., Gutek, 2011, pp. 369–385). As a result, students were to take a passive role and, doing so, to be less involved in their learning. Essentialist education gained new strength in the late 1970s. Those years saw the neo-essentialist movement require that schools return to teaching essential academic content, such as mathematics, natural sciences, and social studies (see Webb, 2006).

3   Revival of Conservatism in American Education

3.1   *Philosophical Views*

The course of development in the United States was comparable to that in many European and Asian countries with regard to academic-oriented learning. This development is to be interpreted against the background provided by more comprehensive social phenomena. The Americans had earlier experienced a rapid remodernization of society by implementing education reform based on conservative functionalism. To achieve this goal, the teaching at a realism-oriented essentialist school would emphasize scientific investigation of the physical world as governed by natural laws. A teacher-directed teaching and learning process based on a subject-centered curriculum emphasized academic expertise, especially in the study of science and mathematics. The essentialist school developed into a center of structured learning connected with society in only a limited manner.

The supporters of neo-essentialism intended to improve on traditional essentialism. This new educational policy developed consistent with a neo-liberal social doctrine and its global economic, political, and ecological issues, which included unemployment, inequality, exclusion, conflicts, and environmental problems. The United States started to develop community-based learning in conformity with a realism-inclined, neo-essentialist educational theory. This also indicated vigorous efforts to standardize the experiential activity-based units of study within the ideal educational program as they were developed more toward the natural sciences, technology, and relevant applications. The new trend represented conservative neoliberal thinking in which the school's success, and thus the growth of human capital, was tightly linked with national economic productivity and growth.

Conservatism has seen a significant revival in the United States since 1980. Neo-essentialism is closely aligned with neoconservative ideology, as Gutek (2009) advocated:

> Neo-Conservatives and Neo-Essentialists agree that schools should be academic institutions with a well-defined curriculum of basic skills and subjects and that they should cultivate traditional values of patriotism, hard work, effort, punctuality, respect for authority, and civility. They argue that schools and colleges should stress the required core based on Western civilization and traditional American values. ... In addition to the congruence of Neo-Essentialism and Neo-Conservatism on traditional educational principles, they also concur that schools have an important economic role in enhancing U.S. economic productivity in a highly competitive global economy. (p. 329)

The approach to essentialist or neo-essentialist education, consistent with realism, became the undeniable mainstream of community-based learning in the United States. Since the 1960s, the development had been nurtured by the era of environmental awakening, which engendered public awareness of the environment's ecological balance and its degeneration. At about the same time, concern increased about the withdrawal of American youth from the social and political life of their communities. Consequently, an Ecological Dimension was more strongly included in the intellectual aims of community-based learning from the 1970s onward, represented by environmental education and, respectively, a social dimension since the 1990s, manifested as service-learning.

The aims of both approaches had been linked to the promotion of theoretical values, particularly through improving students' rational problem-solving skills. The aims of community-based learning shifted in an increasingly academic direction through the values sustained by the neo-essentialist school, which relied on the philosophical tradition of realism. This policy emphasized national standardized objectives for learning as well as assessment criteria that made it possible to test the achievement of these objectives. A conservative consensus advocated this alternative, which provided the background for the need to enhance school accountability in order to increase economic productivity in a neoliberal society. The intention was to support individual achievement in society, with such values of self-assertion as success, capability, and ambition considered important. Here, economic values were also given priority, as education was intentionally used as a tool to build a society with a competitive edge.

3.2   Aims and Values

Environmental education is a multidimensionally directed approach. It geared teaching toward an entirely new radical dimension, as the perspective of environmental awareness was integrated into community-based pedagogy. The aim was to promote student awareness of the environmental problems caused by economic growth and to hone skills in resolving these complex problems. This meant an overall effort to encourage attitudes of environmental responsibility in students by familiarizing them with the basics of ecology.

Community-based learning remained school-centered during the last decade of the 20th century, when intellectual aims were still being emphasized in accord with the doctrines of a classical liberal society. The goal was thus to train experts for a science- and technology-dominated society. The acts of 1990 and 2000 on environmental education stated that environmental engineering could make possible the development of an advanced scientific and technical education, with the aim of creating effective capabilities in problem-solving in the area of complex environmental issues (see National Environmental Education Act, 1990, Sections 5501–5504; John H. Chafee Environmental Education Act of 1999, 2000, Sections 2–5). Based on these documents, this form of education primarily aimed to:

– develop the skills needed to solve environmental problems;
– promote awareness of environmental problems and their origins, that is, to acquire an understanding of natural and cultural environments as well as the ability to comprehend the threats environmental problems pose on them; and
– provide environmental education programs in the classroom and in the environment outside the classroom.

School-based service-learning can be seen as one of the most recent approaches of the school-centered pattern in the United States. This teaching and learning approach intended to integrate community service with academic study for the purpose of enriching learning, teaching civic responsibility, and strengthening communities (National Commission on Service-Learning, 2002, p. 15). The service-learning approach appears to be flexible in relation to other American approaches, as it could be connected to environmental or adventure education programs. These would include attempting to implement such processes as identifying the needs of community members surrounding the school and resolving their problems. Readiness to achieve change and self-direction were new value dimensions, and attaining them was to be a matter of developing students' metacognitive faculties, thus enhancing the resolution of community problems.

School-based service-learning emphasized intellectual aims that paralleled sociopolitical connections in contemporary American society. The federal authorities published several documents giving special importance to the academic studies of this type of education. Of these, the National and Community Service Act of 1990, amended in 2009, pointed out that service-learning aimed at meeting the needs of the community surrounding the school. A learning process based on active participation was to be integrated into the academic curriculum of the school (Section 101). The report of the National Commission on Service-Learning (2002) concluded that school-based service-learning was to contain community service combined with curriculum-based learning, including the appropriate academic content and standards. The learning process was to proceed through problem-solving, utilizing critical and reflective thinking in each phase of the process (pp. 15, 17). Moreover, the Serve America Act (2009) endeavored to support high-quality service-learning projects that engage students in meeting community needs with demonstrable results, while enhancing students' academic and civic learning. It also aimed to renew the ethic of civic responsibility and the spirit of community (Sections 111, 1101). This form of school-based service-learning aimed to:
– develop the knowledge, skills, and attitudes necessary to define community needs and to meet and solve community problems;

- enrich learning;
- enhance metacognitive abilities, that is, develop skills pertaining to problem-solving, thinking, and cooperating;
- strengthen students and their community, that is, teach students civic responsibility and thus guide them to assist their community as needed; and
- provide service-learning programs in the school and in the community outside the school (National Commission on Service-Learning, 2002, pp. 15–17).

Some educators have also started their own "back-to-basics" revolution. Verhagen (2009) developed the Earth Community School (E.C.S.) model for secondary schools. This back-to-basics model is based on "a need to shift from an anthropocentric to a biocentric mode of instruction and learning, and from traditional subject area curricula to an integrated curriculum that has sustainability as its organizing principle" (p. 213). This type of community-based learning aims to:

- contribute to the societal ends of fostering sustainable, just, and participatory communities and societies;
- help make the sustainability challenge the guiding principle of the curriculum;
- guide young people to develop earth literacy, a perspective or set of values with which to respond to the major social and ecological challenges of the present and the future (p. 213).

3.2.1   Summing Up

The conceptual features of neo-essentialism can be examined from the perspective of community-based learning by applying Hlebowitsh's (2007) classification. Neo-essentialism interprets the ideal student as having a rational mind that concentrates on the basics of school subjects while examining natural and environmental phenomena through scientific methods. The ideal subject matter curriculum embodies programs of both environmental education and school-based service-learning, the experiential and standardized activity-based units of study of which are academic and subject-centered, and their contents are studied in a structured manner in and outside of school. This also directs students toward scientific and technological practices in conjunction with national and international evaluations. The school is expected to play an important role in enhancing economic productivity in a highly competitive global economy. The student is oriented toward an ideal democratic society that depends on essential academic knowledge defined by experts in different fields in the midst of social, economic, political, and environmental instability.

Educational policies based on a businesslike operational culture have also faced opposition. Many academics argued that the No Child Left Behind Act of 2001 (2002) had American teachers emphasizing national standardized school achievement tests to determine performance levels (see Section 1001). Darling-Hammond (2007) crystalizes this criticism in more detail:

> Critics claim that the law's focus on complicated tallies of multiple-choice-test scores has dumbed down the curriculum, fostered a "drill and kill" approach to teaching, mistakenly labeled successful schools as failing, driven teachers and middle-class students out of public schools and harmed special education students and English-language learners through inappropriate assessments and efforts to push out low-scoring students in order to boost scores. ... At base, the law has misdefined the problem. It assumes that what schools need is more carrots and sticks rather than fundamental changes. (para. 6)

The following section deals with the essence of community-based learning in the United States in a more concrete manner. The nature of activities is studied from the perspective offered by central pedagogical approaches and their dimensions of the learning environment. The primary focus is on experiential education.

4   Community-Based Pedagogical Ideas in the United States

4.1   *The Progressive School*

The post-World War I decades from 1920 to 1940 were the most vigorous time for progressive education in the United States. The pedagogical activities of the progressive school resembled those that had been implemented in the Indian neo-traditional school from the 1940s until the mid-1960s. The central challenge of pedagogical progressivism was to use education to adjust the citizenry to the new industrialized society. The Americans adopted a pioneering approach to meet this obligation: they combined teaching with practice, direct experience, and the actual life of the community in a methodological manner. During those times, various reform-pedagogical teaching methods and curriculum-focused approaches became known on quite a large scale in American schools. Characteristics of experience-based curricula included concentrating on the student, real-life content, and comprehensive themes as well as on actual problem-solving activities. The primary pedagogical activities in the school context were working in shops and gardens in addition to activity-based classes. Typical forms of teaching and learning in the out-of-school context were collaborative and individual study projects, visits, field trips, and school camps.

Dewey (1897/1940) declared that the basis of the school's function should be the social life of the child, and therefore teaching is to be based on the social activities of the community, such as weaving, sewing, cooking, and making wood and metal items (pp. 9–10). Through these fundamental types of social activities, termed *expressive* or *constructive activities*, teaching can emphasize ways in which the subject can become a part of the child's experience, settings in which its growth can be properly directed, and work-related activities that reflect the life of the larger society and are permeated throughout with the spirit of art, history, and science. According to Dewey's concept of *integration*, the true center correlating the school subjects lies in the child's own social activities. The processes that these activities offer provide an introduction into the more formal subjects of the curriculum. For example, science should not be regarded as a completely new subject but rather as a medium demonstrating factors related to previous experience and proving an effective means for the interpretation and direction of this experience (Dewey, 1897/1940, pp. 9–11; Dewey, 1899/1943, p. 27; Dewey, 1902, p. 30). Obviously, the activities of this kind of society-centered, community-based learning varied considerably from region to region and from school to school. The following three paragraphs describe instruction and its arrangements in the Laboratory School of the University of Chicago (Mayhew & Edwards, 1936/1966, pp. 225, 229, 383–384, 392):

> The Laboratory School of the University of Chicago served as the experimental school for progressive education from 1896 until 1903, during Dewey's time there as a professor of philosophy and education (Dewey, 1938, pp. 27–28). The functioning of the school was centrally based on the principles and methods of education that Dewey had presented (for the teachers' work at the Dewey school, see Mayhew & Edwards, 1936/1966, pp. 42–52). The daily program of the Laboratory School was to conform with the students' developmental level. For this reason, the school's comprehensive educational program was developed so that it proceeded in three phases, with separate curricula for the 5-to-7, 7-to-8, and 9-to-12 age groups. The program was constructed by balancing the amount of time used for active work and intellectual work in different ways, or, alternatively, the time used for constructive handwork such as shop, cooking, and sewing, and expressive activities such as modeling and painting. A specific amount of time for the students to spend in their overt activities was allotted for each different age group.
>
> The point of departure for the program was the 6-to-7-year-old students. These students spent 9 to 10 hours weekly in overt activities in addition to about 6 hours in expressive activities of an intellectual kind.

In the program for the older students (the 8-to-9-year-olds), the balance
between active work and intellectual work was changed so that about 3
and a half hours per week were spent on each, with the amount of time
spent on gym, shop, music, and excursions remaining the same as it had
been for the previous age group. The 10-year-olds used 4 hours for active
work and from 7 to 8 hours for formal intellectual work weekly. The program defined the division between these two activities with increasing
strictness in proportion to the students' age. This general proportion was
maintained throughout the entire 7 years of schooling.

The experiments with the students at the Laboratory School of the
University of Chicago plausibly widened to the natural and cultural sites
offered by the surrounding community. The students worked under a
teacher's supervision studying the contents of learning projects outside the school in as extensive and diverse a manner as possible from
the beginning of their school attendance. The excursions went to places
such as parks, waterfronts, greenhouses, museums, factories, university
laboratories and libraries, or other municipal institutions. The activities
that took place in conjunction with the excursions and visits were closely
linked with relevant study courses at the school. The course in local
physiography and geography, for instance, consisted almost completely
of field trips that were followed by write-ups of notes and class discussions. Then, the students also drew maps to illustrate the formation of
the Great Lakes and the St. Lawrence Valley by the retreating glaciers as
part of their studies.

Characteristic of an experience-based curriculum was a focus on problem-
solving in the active functioning of the school workshops. There, students
became familiar with raw materials, methods, and equipment through different activities, such as weaving, sewing, cooking, and crafting wooden items.
Simultaneously, all school subjects were integrated. Dewey (1899/1943) viewed
the ideal activities in the school workshops as being closely connected with
the economy, sciences, arts, and communication in the surrounding community. Working in the school kitchen and garden were to be associated with the
countryside, its processes and its products. Then the students could work on
projects to study topics such as factors related to growth, the role of agriculture in human history, and life in contemporary society. Activities on field trips
and study visits were linked to the topics being treated at school (pp. 66–67).
The students familiarized themselves with a variety of materials, tools, processes, and operations (Dewey, 1916, p. 230). They become acquainted with the
prevailing occupations in society and, simultaneously, all parts of the school
system were integrated to life. The students of the Dewey school applied the

Scientific-Technical Dimension when they studied the electric bell and motor in the Armour Institute and, later, constructed a dynamo motor. The following summary based on the work of Mayhew and Edwards (1936/1966) describes the pedagogical applications carried out at the Dewey school in Chicago:

> The students of Group 8 at the University of Chicago Laboratory School visited the Armour Institute, where they studied the electric bell and motor. The purpose of the course was to re-create Faraday's classic electromagnetic experiment with an iron core and a coil. The students planned the visit to the Armour Institute in order to familiarize themselves with a motor, a dynamo, a battery, and a telegraph, as well as a galvanometer for measuring weak electric currents. To conclude their course, the students constructed a dynamo motor.
>
> The next year, the same students visited the Armour Institute again during their course dealing with electric machines. During the visit, they familiarized themselves with a galvanometer, an ammeter, a voltmeter, and an electric magnet, as well as an electric-powered plane and jigsaw. Additionally, they had the opportunity to see direct and alternating dynamos as well as electric motors equipped with two kinds of armatures. In practice, the students thus learned that a dynamo is a machine that can be used to generate mechanical energy or, conversely, can be used to convert energy into electric energy. After the visit, the students decided to construct a galvanometer in the shop as well as considered constructing both a motor and dynamo as well if they could find the necessary components (Mayhew & Edwards, 1936/1966, pp. 208–209).

The guidelines Dewey introduced covering the selecting of activities to be organized in the school were also from the days of the Laboratory School of the University of Chicago. In his 1910 book *How We Think*, Dewey presented three briefly worded criteria for discovering and arranging the forms of activity. Dewey (1910) viewed that the activities organized in schools are to (a) accord with the student's stage of development, (b) help to form habits of acute observation and consecutive inference, and (c) prepare students for the social responsibilities of adult life (p. 44). In his primary pedagogical work, *Democracy and Education*, published in 1916, Dewey examined the essence of the organizing activities at school, particularly from scientific and social perspectives. Preparation for social responsibilities is not connected, as Dewey (1916) wrote, with the pursuit of economic advantage or vocational training, but the scientific content and social value of education should be revealed in the various school activities, such as cooking, gardening, and making articles from wood. For example, students can carry out intellectual investigations in the garden as they age when they consider factors related to growth, such as the nutrient requirements of plants, the chemistry of the soil, and the role of light. In the same manner, the garden affords an avenue of approach to knowledge of the place that farming and horticulture occupy in human history and in the contemporary social order (Dewey, 1916, pp. 234–235).

By the time Dewey published a revised edition of *How We Think* in 1933, the projects had already found their way into American schools. Dewey then presented his classical thoughts concerning the conditions that educative projects had to fulfill. Dewey (1933) argued that constructive activities or projects must be interesting and valuable from the standpoint of life. During the course of their development, they should present problems that awaken new curiosity and create a demand for acquiring information. An activity is educative if it leads the mind out into new fields. This is possible if the mind is led to ask questions that it had not thought of before. The questions are to create motivation for additional information to be obtained by observing, reading, and consulting experts. In order for whatever is being done to succeed, it must be continuous. Dewey held that these work-related activities are not a succession of unrelated acts but rather constitute a consecutively ordered activity in which every phase prepares the way to accomplish the next phase. The phase that follows increases the amount of information acquired in the previous phases and drives the activity forward in a cumulative way. The project's plan and objective have to be capable of development so that one thing leads naturally to another. The responsibility of the adult is to determine whether a specific level of achievement is guiding the students to seek new knowledge and new challenges (Dewey, 1933, pp. 217–219).

During that time, various types of teaching methods based on activity pedagogy were widely used at American schools. The progressive school was a workshop for the students' independent observations, experiments, and research. The entire school was equipped for active learning, and an effort was made to ensure that the integrated activities included in its instruction became more difficult in a rational manner in accordance with the students' abilities. In progressive schools, the students worked mostly in groups and under the teacher's guidance in the school's workshops, laboratories, library, office, kitchen, and garden. The students worked on arts and crafts, and wove and sewed. They prepared food, mended shoes, made items from wood and metal, practiced bookkeeping, and learned how to use a printing press. The school garden and field offered the students a place where they could learn about four primary environmental factors that affect plant growth: light, water, temperature, and nutrients. In this way, they carried out intellectual studies while performing various work processes (for the learning activities in selected schools, see, e.g., Andrus, 1935, pp. 337–338; Hanna, 1940, p. 66; Hentschke, 1935, pp. 556–559).

While activities such as organized camping certainly emphasized the Naturalistic Dimension of the learning environment, closeness to nature was also favored in other activity-pedagogical undertakings at that time. In nature study, the students explored plants and observed animals in fields, forests, and on shores. The school garden also provided them with a place for learning from spring until fall. The students prioritized the Horticultural Dimension in their learning environment when they plowed and prepared the soil, sowed seeds, planted and took care of plants, and reaped the harvest (for the activities in one school, see, e.g., Lauderdale, 1981, pp. 47–48). The following illustrates these activity-pedagogical processes at a high school in North Carolina:

> The students of Ellerbe High School grew trees and bushes in the school's nursery. They sowed seeds in beds to germinate and grow into seedlings, rooted cuttings, and planted them to continue growing in a nursery garden, as well as transplanted seedlings that were growing too densely to more open ground before planting them in their final location. As the work gradually progressed, the students became acquainted with the growth factors connected with such things as germination, the promotion of rooting, and transplanting. They also sold plants, planned gardens, and did planting jobs (Merritt, 1938, pp. 122–125).

An effort was made to adjust Americans to an unprecedented social situation that included a rapid change from a traditional agrarian society to one that was modern, urbanized, and industrialized. Various activities within the school curriculum also explored social change, with attempts at raising the quality of society. Curricula based on integrating different subjects were actively being developed in different parts of the country (for curriculum development in selected schools, see, e.g., Boutelle, 1937, p. 216; Loop, 1936, pp. 208–210; Odell, 1940, pp. 115–118; Pierce, 1941, pp. 70–73). A national survey by Hand and French (1937) indicated that curriculum development programs were underway in over 70 percent of the cities with populations exceeding 25,000, almost half of the communities with 5,000 to 25,000 inhabitants, and a third of the schools in communities with populations less than 5,000. By the mid-1930s, at least 32 states had statewide programs of curriculum development in progress (Hand & French, 1937, pp. 1–3).

The curriculum revision movement may well have included more than a quarter of the nation's teachers (Bruner, 1937, pp. 107–108). Hand and French (1937) found that teachers were noticeably in agreement about beliefs converging around progressive principles in the cities undergoing curriculum development programs (pp. 4–17). Spears (1940) observed that during this period, numerous approaches that intended to break with subject-centered curricula were actually applied to curriculum development. Schools' instruction was based on correlated, fused, core, comprehensive, and experience-based curricula (Spears, 1940, p. 53). At the same time, a national effort was made to renew teaching materials and premises as well as to arrange in-service training for teachers (Cremin, 1988, p. 231; Ravitch, 1983, p. 53).

The Lincoln Laboratory School, which continuously attempted to develop a reformist curriculum, functioned in conjunction with the Teachers College of Columbia University in New York City from 1917 until 1948. The progressive teaching and educational work done at the Lincoln School is thought to have greatly affected the course of the history of education in the United States (Cremin, 1961, p. 280). The school's operations were naturally influenced by Columbia University professors Dewey and Kilpatrick (de Lima, 1939, pp. 5, 41). Particularly from the early 1930s, curriculum development work at the Lincoln School was aimed at creating an integrated program, the core of which was subject matter related to social studies and an experience-centered approach to teaching (Buttenwieser, 1969, pp. 133–136; for the curriculum development work at the Lincoln School, see, e.g., de Lima, 1941, pp. 76, 78–80; Rugg, 1936, p. 257). A decade later, the school's program was based on a large structural pattern that included manifold variations in content and methods.

The Lincoln School's general courses were connected with the surrounding community where students lived. Hammond (1942) reported that these courses combined the various subjects into broad units of study. A general course intended for the school's seventh graders, called *Man and His Environment*, dealt with factors related to the study of the environment, such as climate, natural resources, land forms, soils, minerals, drainage, plant life, and water features. Three daily lessons were devoted to mathematics, science, social studies, and English. Applied, industrial, and household arts, as well as music, were also included in the program. The general course intended for ninth graders, *Living in a Power Age*, related all activities directly to present-day activities that the students carried out at home, school, and in the community. The course was structured around the needs of young people and concentrated on the individual, family, and community, the latter being examined in relation to other communities (Hammond, 1942, pp. 86–88).

The progressive schools made an effort to offer their students opportunities for active involvement in the surrounding community and natural environment. The environment was a laboratory for the students' precise observations and conclusions in which consistently organized activity elaborated on information that had been acquired in an earlier phase. During the course of their field trips and study projects, the students observed the functions of the nearby environment and nature. They became acquainted with work in the post office, mill, bakery, shops, workshops, and plants. They studied life in the fields, forests, shores, and farms. The students made notes, drawings, and illustrated studies; surveyed life styles, living conditions, and public services; collected plants, insects, soil, and stone samples; and observed the movements of animals and changes in the weather and seasons. They carried out projects that were connected with local sources of livelihood, modes of construction, and traditions of camp crafts; participated in health campaigns; and studied the consequences of serious social problems (for the learning activities in selected schools, see, e.g., Dewey & Dewey, 1915, pp. 44–47, 52, 91, 199–201; de Lima, 1942, pp. 59, 61, 161).

The progressive schools that applied activity-pedagogical approaches had a tendency to emphasize the Sociocultural Dimension of the learning environment in their community-based learning. This was evidenced in such activities as study visits to factories, laboratories, and other places in the community as well as projects devoted to local housing conditions, means of livelihood, or serious social problems (for the pedagogical activities in selected schools, see, e.g., de Lima, 1942, pp. 246–248; Wegner & Langworthy, 1936, p. 86). The following shows how teachers and students at one Kansas high school prioritized the Sociocultural Dimension in their learning environment:

> The ninth graders of Holton High School in Holton, Kansas, carried out a study of city planning and the prevailing housing conditions. They also surveyed the utilities in and the modern conveniences of houses on the basis of a questionnaire they had created. Drawing on this data, they made tables and graphs, as well as a map, in which the houses of the city were classified according to their convenience level. Finally, the students wrote an analysis describing the execution of the study and providing the study's findings and conclusions (Green, 1936, pp. 192–194).

Dewey (1916) argued that the objective of activity-pedagogical work at a school shop has neither economic nor vocational benefit (pp. 234–235). For example, the students at Holtville School, near Montgomery, Alabama, worked on the school premises in such places as the printing shop, the hatchery, the farm maintenance shop, the barber shop, or the beauty parlor. They also offered a variety of meat processing and soil transportation services or engaged in activities such as canning fruit and vegetables for sale and doing electrical wiring on contract (Lauderdale, 1981, pp. 47–49). This can be interpreted to mean that the Productive Dimension was justified by the neo-evolutionary theories that were holistically integrated with Deweyan activity-pedagogical methods and processes and their associated meanings. By virtue of these strategies, the progressive school oriented itself in a deliberate manner toward a transaction process with the early industrial society in accordance with the classical liberal trend of thought. An effort was made to adjust Americans to an unprecedented social situation that included a rapid change from a traditional agrarian society to one that was modern, urbanized, and industrialized.

The students of the progressive school participated frequently in various activities for the benefit of the school and the community (for the activities in some schools, see, e.g., Bowes, 1935, pp. 500–501; Gordner et al., 1938, pp. 632–633; Kendall, 1939, pp. 109–110; Merritt, 1938, p. 123; Spears, 1940, pp. 82–84). The students in Indiana and Kansas emphasized most strongly the Sociocultural Dimension of their learning environment when they renovated and furnished the old buildings of the school, instructed community members in gardening, and drew up a housing program with the city housing committee. When these students tended the school farm, they applied the Practical-Agricultural Dimension in their learning environment. The following exemplifies how teachers and students at selected schools in Indiana and Kansas organized various activities during the peak of pedagogical progressivism:

> The students of Public School 26 in Indianapolis, Indiana, renovated and furnished old buildings for use by the school and instructed community inhabitants in gardening. The students of Interlaken School, near La Porte, Indiana, planned and constructed buildings for the school, tended the school farm, and edited a local newspaper (Dewey & Dewey, 1915, pp. 87–89, 214–216, 220). In Kansas, the students of Holton High School took part in drawing up a housing program with the city housing committee. In this work, they made use of an earlier study done by students on housing conditions. This was a survey analysis on the utilities in and the modern conveniences of houses on the basis of a questionnaire they had created (Green, 1936, pp. 194–195).

About the same time as the progressive education movement was at its strongest, many related currents of reform-pedagogical approaches were being developed. In this manner, the camping education movement also began, which set the tone within the context of the progressive trend in education and the broad sociocultural change set in motion in the United States of the 1930s (Hammerman, 1961, pp. 169–172). During this time, there were still relatively few public school camps that usually lasted from a few days to over a week (Gibson, 1936, p. 28; Sharp & Osborne, 1940, p. 237).

In the 1930s and 1940s, American public school camps were principally summer camps with programs that followed traditional camp programs. The

Naturalistic Dimension was emphasized in this learning environment most strongly when students were practicing their camping skills out in the open or engaging in recreational activities at the camp center (for more details, see Hammerman, 1961, p. 134). The following describes the school activities and the community camp program at one school district in Washington State in the late 1930s:

> The school and community camp program for 1939 in the Highline School District in King County offered genuine camping close to nature at a campsite on Lake Wilderness. The summer camps for fifth and seventh graders of Highline Public Schools lasted for 6 days, in which students lived in tents, practiced camping skills, and hiked in the great outdoors. They learned such camp crafts as outdoor cooking, using knives and axes, and tying knots. They swam, played, made handicrafts, and spent nights around the campfire. They could also row and try horseback riding (Jensen & Burgess, 1952, pp. 7–8, 129–130, 133, 153, 161).

Only a decade later, the opportunities for studying outside the school in the great outdoors offered by camping education had already encouraged many reformist school teachers to conduct experiments in education, in addition to stimulating pedagogues, specialists in education, and administrative officials to engage in school development work (see, e.g., de Lima, 1942, p. 164; Spears, 1940, pp. 152–157; Uger, 1947, pp. 239–244). In a 1942 article, "The Role of Camping in Education Today," Kilpatrick presented his idea of combining camping and school education. Kilpatrick (1942) explained that learning is more successful at a camp than in a formal school setting because the children can experience more fully the things that they study in real situations. Camping education can be implemented naturally through living in a group. This offers an opportunity to live together in conditions that promote the development of emotional security and maturity. Participation in a group discussion and decision-making also provides the best environment for learning the principles of democracy. Kilpatrick considered that many activities that stimulate the child's mind, such as bird-watching, roaming in forests, and cooking over an open fire, permanently enrich an increasingly urban lifestyle, even though most of what is learned at camp cannot be transferred directly to an urban environment (Kilpatrick, 1942, pp. 15–16).

The quality of the Naturalistic Dimension of the learning environment changed by the 1950s. This decade saw the establishment of numerous resident outdoor schools whose programs were gradually supplemented, in addition to outdoor life experiences, with curriculum content: the study of nature, the environment, and conservation (Hammerman, 1961, pp. 148–151, 161–162; for two resident outdoor programs, see, e.g., Holland, 1955, pp. 16–18; Holland & Lewis, 1950, pp. 539–540). St. Clair's national survey (1958) revealed that 92 resident camp programs functioning during regular school hours were initiated between 1937 and 1958. They lasted for 4 to 7 days and were intended for third- to eighth-grade children. Most of these school camp programs (approx. 80%) were started between 1950 and 1958. Such programs were arranged in 23 states, but two-thirds (65%) of the programs were in only five states: California (21), Michigan (14), Wisconsin (9), New York (8), and Ohio (8) (St. Clair, 1958, pp. 31–32). The following description of a California camp based on conservation studies for San Diego teachers and their sixth graders serves as an example of a late 1940s resident outdoor education program:

> Camp Cuyamaca, whose program for the academic year 1947–1948 focused on conservation studies in particular, was set up in a California state park. The school camps for sixth graders from San Diego public schools usually lasted for 5 days, in which students studied in groups at a campsite and in neighboring fields, forests, and mountains. The students worked in the arts and crafts shops, visited the natural history museum, and spent time in the library. They planted seedling trees, took long hikes, and observed how nature functioned (Clarke, 1951, pp. 8–10, 27–28, 30, 51–105).

In the same manner, the teachers applied the content areas of nature and conservation to the school day camp programs arranged in places such as city and state parks, national parks and forests, or on privately owned property in rural regions, such as wooded areas and creek banks. School day camping was supported by the scouting movement, Christian associations, churches, schools, and many other organizations and institutions (Freeberg & Taylor, 1963, pp. 248, 250–251). Freeberg and Taylor (1963) estimated that at the end of the 1950s more than a million children and young people were participating in school day camping (p. 248).

This type of change in the nature of the Naturalistic Dimension was also seen in other community-based teaching, which was increasing in many out-of-school sites, such as the schoolyard, garden, forest, and farm (Smith, 1955, 1970). Freeberg and Taylor (1963) reported that by the 1960s more than half of the states in the country were actively running public school forestry programs. Many schools had their own school forest, for example, in Arkansas, the County of Nevada offered every school its own forest. At the same time, in various states many high schools either owned or rented a farm, particularly for teaching practical agriculture. For example, in California, agriculture was taught at almost 200 high schools, of which almost 50 also owned their own farm. The size of the tract varied from a few acres next to the school to as large as 120 acres (Freeberg & Taylor, 1963, pp. 170–171, 202). The following exemplifies pedagogical applications of the Naturalistic Dimension when students hiked their school's forest in Missouri; applications of the Practical-Agricultural Dimension when students visited the school farm in Texas and followed the farmer in his daily work; and applications of the Horticultural Dimension when students took care of garden plants in Michigan in the late 1950s:

> In Steelville, Missouri, the students of Steelville School District hiked in the school's 250-acre forest. They familiarized themselves with forestry methods and conservation practices, planted trees, and studied natural organisms. The public school students in Tyler, Texas, visited the school farm, where they observed the farmer in his daily work. They became acquainted with growing legumes, repairing fences, feeding penned animals, and other farm activities. The school farm of Battle Creek Public Schools, near Battle Creek, Michigan, also had a garden in which fifth and sixth graders took care of their plants from spring to fall (Freeberg & Taylor, 1963, pp. 171–173, 209).

4.1.1   Challenges

After the Second World War, American society experienced sweeping changes. The conservative political and social thinking typical of the period exacerbated criticism of reform-pedagogical movements, particularly from the late 1940s (Cremin, 1961, pp. 348–351). This also meant a downfall in the popularity of progressive schools. The final setback occurred in 1957, when the treatment of themes connected with national defense was suddenly linked to international competition in the fields of science and technology (see National Defense Education Act of 1958, 1958, Section 101). Moreover, progressive teaching was a challenge for many teachers. The following from Gutek (1997) describes the challenging role of progressive teaching:

> Because the Progressive classroom was oriented to purposeful activity, the Progressive teacher needed to know how to motivate the students so that they initiated, planned, and carried out their projects. As learning was centered in the participating group, the Progressive teacher needed to know how to use collaborative processes.
>
> Perhaps the most difficult challenge for the teacher was to act as a guide rather than the center of learning. The skilled teacher, in the Progressive

context, did not dominate the classroom as its focal point. Rather, he or she made the interests of the learner central. The teacher was properly a guide to discussing, planning, and executing learning. (p. 301)

No wonder that the school reform failed to change the fundamentals of the pedagogical work of teachers. Progressive teaching procedures in the United States were only combined with traditional teacher-centered instruction externally. The teachers tended to implement procedures unevenly and only for certain parts of the school day. The large groups of students were heterogeneous and often weakly motivated to study. Additionally, American schools of reform pedagogics suffered as a consequence of poor economic, mental, and physical resources. This relates to three facts: (a) sufficient economic resources were simply not allocated for the school reforms, (b) insufficient teacher education, in particular, was reflected in the low quality of the instruction the schools provided, and (c) school furnishings were old-fashioned, with inadequate teaching premises and equipment (Cuban, 1993, pp. 142–144). At the same time, the population explosion after the Second World War required rapid changes in the American school system (Ravitch, 1983, p. 70).

4.2   The Essentialist School

In 1957, an unforeseen foreign policy event initiated a school reform movement in the United States that continues today. When the Soviet Union successfully launched the first satellite into space, the U.S. Congress maintained that the country needed to rapidly raise the degree of science and technology through education in order to revamp national defense. For this reason, the schools were expected to enhance remodernization in the country by providing experts capable of functioning effectively in a technologically sophisticated industrial society. There was a widely held view that essentialist education provided the best alternatives for achieving this goal. Despite the schools being an educational center with only limited connections to society, teaching was also directed toward nature and the community in order to enhance and enrich learning.

The U.S. Congress considered that the schools had failed in their attempts to produce experts for a science- and technology-oriented society as required by capitalist ideology. The National Defense Education Act of 1958 (1958) asserted that the defense of the United States depended on the revival of science and technology, which, on the other hand, was related to the progress of education. For this reason the federal government allocated considerable funds for the specific development of educational programs, teaching methods, and instructional materials in the natural sciences, mathematics, and modern foreign languages as well as for teacher in-service training. School premises and teaching equipment were to be modernized. Vocational education programs and science information services were to be improved. In order to increase the number of science and technology experts, the testing, guidance, and counseling of gifted students had to be developed. Particularly skilled students in higher education were granted study loans and scholarships (National Defense Education Act, 1958, Sections 101, 204, 303, 503, 701, 801, 901). Emphasis was to be placed on academic knowledge instead of on the life preparation of progressive pedagogics.

Within the context of this comprehensive change in the national educational policy, many specialists in education and pedagogues began to develop programs and pedagogical procedures for outdoor education (see, e.g., Donaldson & Donaldson, 1958; Freeberg & Taylor, 1961, 1963; Smith et al., 1963; Hammerman & Hammerman, 1964; Gabrielsen & Holtzer, 1965; Hug & Wilson, 1965; Garrison, 1966; Mand, 1967). Likewise, teacher training in the field was promoted and national conferences were arranged (see, e.g., Smith, 1958; Conrad, 1961; American Association for Health, Physical Education, and Recreation, 1963). Based on publications from the period, the federal government's determined demand can be seen to have increased the number of experts, particularly in science, thus inevitably strengthening the procedures employed in the school-centered pattern of outdoor education.

Hammerman and Hammerman (1964) considered that the school is a center for studying, which also includes the planning and follow-up of outdoor education. Outside the school, the class extends to an outdoor laboratory where study can last from a few minutes to a week or longer. The aim and content of the curriculum, as well as the location of the school itself, influence the choice of outdoor setting. Activities taking place in the schoolyard and at different field trip locations are conducted with either one major curricular objective or several goals aiming at a variety of skills. In the resident outdoor settings, an extended program of learning activities related to the curricula of certain subjects is the norm (pp. 8–11, 78).

Hammerman and Hammerman (1964) interpreted that nearly all areas of the curriculum can be complemented with appropriate learning experiences in an outdoor laboratory. The outdoor classroom can be a schoolyard, a nearby park, a forest preserve, or some other outdoor school site. The teaching method used to combine the outdoor experience with the curriculum can be highly organized and structured or, alternatively, quite informal and unstructured. The individual teacher can determine the quality of the instruction, the amount of time and the place available, and the purposes to be achieved. Connections can be made between experience obtained out of doors and the different subjects in the curriculum (e.g., science, arithmetic, languages, art, and music), either in problem-solving situations outside of school or later in follow-up activities in the classroom (p. 20).

At the same time, the skills and abilities acquired through experience become integrated with the learner's positive attitudes and values that are transferred up to adulthood after completing school. In this manner, as Donaldson and Donaldson (1958) wrote, "Outdoor education is education *in, about, and for* the outdoors" (p. 17). The teaching and learning process of outdoor education takes place *in* out-of-school settings related to real life, deals with subject matter *about* life out of school, and prepares students *for* life outside of school (cf. p. 17). The procedures for this kind of school-centered outdoor education varied considerably from region to region and from school to school. The quality of activities also varied in accordance with the teacher's interests. Moreover, outdoor learning activities naturally depended on the students' abilities.

Seven years after the passage of the influential National Defense Education Act of 1958 (1958), the Elementary and Secondary Education Act of 1965 (1965) was passed. It promised financial support for supplementary educational centers and services to promote the further development of educational programs for students interested in studying advanced scientific subjects, foreign languages, and other academic subjects which are not taught in the local schools or which can be provided more effectively on a centralized basis (Sections 301, 303). In order to enhance and enrich school teaching, the Americans wanted to initiate innovative and exemplary educational programs and establish year-round educational service centers. Moreover, existing programs and facilities were supplemented (Office of Education, 1966b, p. 18; Office of Education, 1966c, pp. 1–2). Projects to Advance Creativity in Education (PACE) programs of this type were widely initiated in different parts of the country during the late 1960s. The content of these many programs emphasized the study of the natural sciences outside of school (for the PACE programs more closely, see, e.g., Schmierer, 1969, p. 7). The following exemplifies how these centers were organized in Connecticut, Delaware, and Florida in the late 1960s:

> In Avon, Connecticut, a mountaintop science center was established that included a planetarium, an observatory, and a meteorological station, as well as seismographical equipment. The center primarily served elementary- and secondary-school students in the eight local school districts. At a park area in Newark, Delaware, an outdoor laboratory consisting of nature trails was developed. It offered the schools guided field trips, instruction, and teaching materials. In Sarasota County, Florida,

plans were made for an educational enrichment center particularly intended for those in the community with special needs. The center was to have a marine research laboratory, a mobile field laboratory, a pedagogical greenhouse, ponds, and a wildlife campsite (for more details, see Office of Education, 1966a, p. 25; Office of Education, 1967, pp. 8, 253–254; Office of Education, 1968, pp. 6–7).

In this manner, a new boom period for science-centered active learning was initiated once again in the United States. The school reform offered a familiar perspective that had already been developed over the years by the teachers and administrators in many school districts. The following description provides an example of a revised resident outdoor education program as it was implemented at Camp Cuyamaca in the mid-1960s:

> The revised school camp program of the public schools of the City and County of San Diego, California, for the year 1966 contained science studies in addition to traditional camp activities. At this stage, Camp Cuyamaca also had a science laboratory and the necessary equipment, for example, for the study of organisms in the pond. The sixth graders of the schools stayed for 1 week in the camp and acquainted themselves with the ecology of the field, forest, and water. The students listened to the sounds of animals, examined their tracks, identified plants, measured the radioactivity of rocks, studied soil erosion control, and observed stars and changes in the weather (Schramm, 1969, pp. 9, 27, 59, 79, 88, 117, 127–128, 193).

Just a few years later, the Environmental Education Act (1970) funded the development of curricula and educational programs in environmental studies as well as the preparation of training programs and projects for educational personnel. The planning of outdoor ecological study centers was also supported (Section 3). Nevertheless, environmental education was not an altogether new issue for American teachers, since many of the existing environmental education programs and centers had already participated in the national PACE program (for some environmental education programs, see, e.g., Helgeson et al., 1972, pp. 25–34). Additionally, many outdoor education programs at the time were intended to be environmental education programs.

According to a national survey by the National Education Association (1970), about half of the environmental education programs implemented in large public schools at the end of the 1960s were called "outdoor education." The programs most often covered the natural and applied sciences, with the most popular being conservation, ecology, biology, insect study, geology, botany, general science, or weather study. Most commonly, the students studied in sites close to nature, these being forests, woodlands, ponds, lakes, recreation areas, or wildland natural areas (National Education Association, 1970, pp. 5–6, 9–10, 13). The following exemplifies the pedagogical applications of environmental education carried out at schools in North Carolina in the early 1970s:

> In Beaufort, North Carolina, the environmental education program at Carteret County Schools for 1970 familiarized its students with marine ecology. The fourth to 12th graders in the coastal schools made field trips to an open beach, an offshore island, a salty marsh, a port terminal, and a seafood-processing plant. With their teacher, the students examined the adaptation of animal communities, wave erosion, utilization of the sea, and consequent problems, as well as other conditions related to nature and life in coastal areas (Helgeson et al., 1972, pp. 35–37).

During the 1970s, environmental education became the primary theme and core content of the pedagogical programs of many schools. Numerous curriculum guides, manuals, and handbooks related to environmental education programs were published (see, e.g., Montana State Department of Public Instruction, 1972; Regents of the University of California, 1972; Van Matre, 1972, 1974, 1979; Humboldt County Office of Education, 1975; American Forest Institute, 1975, 1977). Some programs prioritized experience-centered learning strategies, with the stress placed on a sensory and conceptual approach in which ecological issues were studied at camp in similar conditions (see, e.g., Van Matre, 1972). Such programs approached interaction with nature from a reflective and personal perspective (see, e.g., Van Matre, 1974). The following summary, based on Van Matre's earth education program *Sunship Earth* (1979), depicts a comprehensive learning process in camp conditions, with activities characterized by an atmosphere of magic and adventure:

> The five-day camp program consists of acclimatization walks, concept paths, immersing experiences, discovery parties, and interpretive encounters. During the program's orientation phase, the students can be presented with a message about saving the planet. The students are seated in a dimly lit octagonal room, with slightly eerie music playing in the background. During the course of a ceremony consisting of several phases, a drawing of a Native American chieftain in a starkly natural setting appears on the wall facing them. In the distance, an image of the planet gradually takes shape. A deep, resonant voice can be heard from behind the drawing: Chief Seattle's helper welcomes them aboard

and tells them that the sunship has been speeding in space for billions of years and that its voyage has become more difficult. Eventually, the voice echoing from behind the drawing explains what the students will be doing at the study station during the coming week so that they can begin working to save the sunship before it is too late. Suddenly the lights go out and the voice disappears (Van Matre, 1979, pp. 32–35, 39–48).

Nevertheless, most environmental education projects offered outdoor learning activities that could help students develop the knowledge and skills needed to study environmental issues in the school area or its immediate surroundings. At the same time, an emphasis was placed on awakening environmental awareness. The activities stressed the study of the natural sciences, but they also tried to integrate other subjects (see, e.g., American Forest Institute, 1977). For example, *Project Learning Tree*, an environmental education program from 1977, offers exercises for first to sixth graders based on seven perspectives: (a) environmental awareness, (b) diverse functions of the forest, (c) impact on cultural contexts, (d) societal perspectives on forests and the environment, (e) management and interdependence of natural resources, (f) life support systems of our planet, and (g) evaluation and modification of personal lifestyle (American Forest Institute, 1977, p. VIII). The following description exemplifies the perspective of awakening environmental awareness through the activity of *Adopt a Tree*:

> The very first exercise can be an activity that has the students adopt their own tree near the school. As the learning process continues, the students study the life of the tree during the different seasons, guided by their own observations. Initially, they keep track of the animals and birds visiting the tree, draw and paint the shapes and the color shades of the tree, and sow its seeds and plant the seedlings that develop from them. In the upper grades, they can study increasingly demanding natural scientific phenomena, such as the effect of temperature on the buds, flowers, and leaves of a plant. Their exercises have the students classify, compare, assess, and interpret observations made at different times (American Forest Institute, 1977, pp. 2–6, 83, 112–114, 120–121).

It can be said that American teachers began to determinedly implement programs and projects in environmental education in their own work at school. For the most part, the teachers even compiled their own instructional material. Childress's (1978) national survey of the environmental education curriculum in public schools described that the instructional material principally used in many of the programs and projects in the late 1970s had been developed by the teaching staff. Additionally, these curricula utilized the material offered by resource agencies and commercial organizations. The sources that the teachers used least were textbooks in environmental education, curricular programs, materials developed by school and systemwide committees, and materials from state education agencies (Childress, 1978, pp. 8, 10). According to the survey, most of the programs and projects made use of multidisciplinary and interdisciplinary curricular organization, the most popular being biology, geography, mathematics, and history. The factors exerting the most influence on the selection of curriculum content were student and teacher interests, the personal and social needs of students, and local environmental problems and concerns. Involvement in environmental education programs and projects at public schools was at its greatest in upper elementary schools (Grades 5 and 6) and senior high schools (Grades 10, 11, and 12). The teachers utilized a variety of instructional strategies, with the most frequently used methods being small group projects, class discussions, field trips, or community resource visits (Childress, 1978, pp. 7–8, 10).

4.2.1   Challenges

It can generally be noted that the American teachers of the essentialist school should have had more financial support, time for planning, professional training, and interdisciplinary instructional materials for the pedagogy of environmental education in the 1970s. Even though a wide range of instructional materials for environmental education already existed, most of it was not interdisciplinary and often lacked the approach of the social sciences and humanities. There was a particularly acute lack of material suitable for an urban environment (Roth, 1974, p. 393). For example, according to a survey Hamm and Spear (1978) conducted in 1975 in the state of Indiana, high school teachers did not have an interdisciplinary textbook for environmental education that provided adequate coverage for all areas of environmental education. The teachers used a textbook in a specific topic area or, for the most part, utilized a textbook only infrequently in their teaching (Hamm & Spear, 1978, pp. 12, 35).

The implementation of programs in environmental education at schools was not entirely without its problems. Teachers were confronted with constraints and barriers at several levels when formulating their courses and projects. Childress's national survey (1978) revealed that the primary limitations in teachers' curriculum work were inadequate funding at all levels and lack of time to develop curricula. The teacher's insufficient preservice and in-service training was also felt to be a primary constraint (Childress, 1978, pp. 9–10).

Subjective restrictions of this type were probably exacerbated in urban school systems, particularly in their large combined programs (National Education Association, 1970, pp. 71–72).

4.3   The Neo-Essentialist School

During the 1980s, outdoor learning programs and projects were being implemented at American schools in a still increasing and varying form. Teachers most often applied nature study and science content in their instruction, but at the same time they made an effort to teach other subjects outside of school. Organizing outdoor learning activities and associated pedagogical planning and follow-up work generally took place on school premises, such as in a classroom, laboratory, or library. The schoolyard, vegetable patch, garden, and nearby environment were the outdoor learning settings, especially in the primary grades. Thus, the real-life situations for problem-solving available in the immediate vicinity of the classroom provided an environment where previously acquired knowledge could be interpreted in practice.

The students mostly worked in pairs or in groups under the teacher's guidance, while their learning was based upon themes included in the curricula of specific subjects. The students studied plants, insects, types of soils and rocks, observed the shapes of objects and their shadows, and estimated the heights of trees and buildings. They drew, painted, and built spatial models in the schoolyard. In the garden, they took care of their plants. In the school environment, they did orienteering by means of photographs or maps and solved problems marked along self-guiding trails (for more details, see the programs implemented in selected schools, e.g., Brasgalla, 1989, pp. 7–9; Ford, 1981, pp. 144–150; St. Preece, 1980, pp. 12–13; Wilburn, 1983, pp. 157–162). The following brief description illustrates outdoor learning activities at a school in Illinois:

> The students of Independence School in the city of Bolingbrook, Illinois, built a drainage model in the schoolyard. The first and second graders of the school dug lakes, rivers, and channels; constructed valleys and mountains; and studied the water cycle, flood formation, and erosion effects (Lennert, 1981, pp. 12–14).

During field trips the students most often gained direct knowledge of nature and, as far as possible, studied subjects included in the curriculum. The field trips could last anywhere from less than an hour to a full day, but pedagogical planning and preparation, as well as follow-up at school, were essential components. The teacher's professional planning was also emphasized. The teacher organized the events, which included selecting the field trip location, preparing the route and rest stops, arranging for transportation, collecting the equipment and other essentials, and obtaining the required permission from the school principal and the students' parents (Ford, 1981, p. 186).

The teacher naturally also planned the outdoor learning activities to be implemented and the instructions for students according to their abilities. The studies focused on a wide variety of sites, such as fields, forests, mountains, parks, seashores, creeks, gardens, zoos, and nature and visitor centers. The students made notes, drawings, and maps; studied plants, animals, and types of soil and rocks; observed space in a planetarium and life in an aquarium. The students also carried out projects connected with using a map and compass, estimating distances and heights, and recognizing rare plants. They carried out small-scale studies of the human impact on nature and wrote accounts of their excursions to the distant summit of a hill (for school-specific field trip programs, see, e.g., Christopherson, 1981, pp. 7–9; Parisio, 1986, pp. 32–33; Wood, 1986, pp. 26–27). The following describes a program for young students that emphasizes the Scientific-Technical Dimension in the learning environment during various field trips to beaches, dunes, and salt marshes in Georgia:

> The first and second graders from Tybee Island, Georgia, learned during their various field trips that the sandy soils and wetlands are worth studying. The teachers had planned a set of outdoor activities to help the young students focus on continuous changes in the state and understand that these processes permanently exist in this type of environment. The field trips to beaches, dunes, and salty marshes encouraged students to find a succulent plant, pick a leaf and lick it, and decide if the plant is soft or woody like a tree. They looked for grasslike plants growing above the high-tide mark, described these plants (called sandspur and salt grass), and compared them to the plants found growing on higher dunes. The students noted that on the dunes where sea oats grew the vegetation was thicker and closer together than in the places where sandspur and salt grass were plentiful. The teachers helped the young students learn that different plants thrive in different growing environments (Butler & Roach, 1986, pp. 34–36).

Field trips were also oriented toward the community and its business and commerce sector, with destinations being not only museums, libraries, and theaters, but also such places as streets, cemeteries, railway and bus stations, airports, and harbors. Instruction was arranged at community locations such as hospitals, churches, shopping centers, workshops, farms, and industrial plants. During their field trips, the students familiarized themselves with a variety of occupations, tools, methods, and the bases of the economy. They studied peoples' living habits and different stages of humankind, examined practical architecture and environmental planning, and the influence of urbanization on nature (for the field trip program of one school in detail, see, e.g., Bischoff, 1987, pp. 202–204). The following illustrates the manner in which the students applied the Sociocultural Dimension in their learning environments during a field trip in Buffalo, New York:

> Three teachers decided to take their nine students from the emotionally handicapped classes of Orleans-Niagara BOCES on a special field trip in Buffalo. This field trip took place at night and travel was by a small yellow school bus. The first stop was the Central Buffalo Police Headquarters, where the students met someone from the Community Relations Office. Under his guidance, the students visited different offices, such as a booking and printing center and the Emergency 911 System. This tour ended in a discussion with the chief detective of the Juvenile Bureau. The second stop was the Erie Basin Marina, a small boat harbor. A guard allowed the bus to enter the marina so visitors could experience the sights and sounds of the harbor. Although it was after midnight, the boats were brightly lit, with many people on board. Then they took a short trip through several ethnic neighborhoods, which was followed by a stop at an Italian restaurant. Students were eager and enjoyed these new experiences. The field trip ended at Buffalo General Hospital, where the head nurse gave them a tour through the different emergency rooms and explained how they functioned. The hospital tour ended at 2:30 a.m., as a weary group boarded the school bus for the long ride home (Cook, 1980, pp. 29–31).

In resident outdoor schools, students spent at least a few days acquainting themselves with the natural, built, or created surroundings. The resident outdoor program could last 2 days for the fourth grade, 3 days for the fifth grade, and 5 days for the sixth grade. In the junior high schools it could last from 10 to 12 days, and in high schools and higher education institutions for more than 2 weeks. The school districts most often rented their outdoor school facilities from residential sites that were chiefly maintained by state governments, youth-serving agencies, and other private organizations. Recreational areas, public parks, and urban districts functioned more rarely as outdoor settings (Ford, 1981, pp. 158–159, 194). The resident program could be broken down into blocks of time lasting for an hour, 1 and a half hours, or 3 hours, depending on the number of activities and student groups, and the teacher's flexibility (Hammerman et al., 1985, pp. 139–140). The following description further clarifies how the pedagogical applications of environmental education were carried out in a residential site. This shows how teachers and their students were involved in a resident outdoor education program in the early 1980s at an education center in New York:

> In Geneva, New York, the resident outdoor education program of the Geneva Public Schools for the year 1982 offered science studies at Rogers Environmental Education Center in Sherburne, New York. The outdoor school program for sixth graders lasted for 2 and a half days, providing studies dealing with shores and forests. The students worked in groups under the guidance of a natural scientist in the center's laboratory and on the shore of the nearby pond. A well-equipped laboratory afforded them the opportunity to study the abundant plant and animal life of the pond and marsh in detail. They also acquainted themselves with using a map and compass, and with the principles of forestry. Likewise, play and the games related to the evening program were associated with nature (Mitchinson, 1982, pp. 5–7).

In the resident outdoor schools, student groups made field trips and carried out study projects and generally concentrated on natural sciences, often in conjunction with physical education, art, music, history, and mathematics. In addition, they sometimes studied subjects related to agriculture, trade, and industry (for the teaching procedures in one resident outdoor school in detail, see, e.g., Robertson, 1987, pp. 24–27). Outdoor learning activities were quite similar to those made during field trips. Activities organized to be as consistent as possible were used to solve problems connected with nature and culture. Thus an effort was made to have the learner involved in experiences that would allow for independent discovery and, furthermore, a profound understanding of the phenomena to be studied (Hammerman et al., 1985, pp. 25, 28; for some resident outdoor education programs, see, e.g., Liston, 1982, pp. 6–13; Smith & Stahl, 1981, pp. 14–15; Taloumis, 1980, pp. 16–18). The following summary describes the manner in which the pedagogical applications of environmental education were carried out when teachers and their students were active in a resident outdoor education program in California in the late 1980s:

> At Dana Point, California, the resident outdoor education program for the year 1986 developed by the Orange County Marine Institute acquainted elementary and middle school students with nature's five ecosystems. During the three-day program, the students engaged in such activities as studying the California foothill (*chaparrall*), streamside (*riparian*), and oak woodland ecology in the Santa Ana Mountains. They studied

the interaction and interdependence of specific plants and animals, the supplies of natural resources, and the overall health of the ecosystem. In this manner, they also examined how the ecosystem has shaped the local Indigenous culture, such as the life and history of the vanishing tribe, the *Juaneños* (Rigby, 1986, p. 20).

Many school camps and field trips continued to emphasize old camp traditions; the integration of different subjects and environmental education followed the content of the curriculum and emphasized the natural sciences; the programs of school-based service-learning were linked to social studies and emphasized community spirit; and special education programs provided opportunities for a wide variety of different groups to study outside of school. Compared to the programs previously described, adventure education programs constituted yet an additional approach following quite different processes for teachers' work outdoors. Adventure education was not in itself a completely new approach; rather, it had been gaining prominence since the 1970s. Programs in adventure education were part of the learning experiences aimed at self-discovery in natural wilderness or in built and created environments, such as obstacle courses involving adventure ropes courses with high and low challenge facilities (for adventure education programs implemented at some schools, see, e.g., Rheingold, 2007, pp. 155–156; Rohnke, 1989, pp. 141–146, 155–168). The following is a more detailed description of the adventure education program at a Connecticut school in the late 1980s:

> In West Redding, Connecticut, the Project Adventure program at the John Read Middle School in 1989 aimed at promoting the students' self-esteem, their sense of responsibility, and initiative. The program contained warm-up activities, games, orienteering, and rock climbing, as well as indoor and outdoor rope courses. The students also kept a log of their exercises, assessing what they had learned and reflecting on their experiences (Rohnke, 1989, pp. 147–153).

In the early 1990s, the National and Community Service Act of 1990, amended in 2009, yielded yet another popular approach in American education, providing financial support for implementing school-based service-learning programs, including teacher training and the development of service-learning curricula for integration into academic school programs (National and Community Service Act of 1990, 2009, Sections 111–112). A national survey on youth volunteering and civic obligation conducted by Spring et al. (2006) indicated that more than a third of young people ages 12 to 18 (N = 3,178) had participated in community service organized at their school either at the time of the study or previously. About three-quarters of these students had taken a course with a service component either at the time of the study or the previous year. The study showed that more than three-quarters of students who had ever been involved in school-based services had participated in at least one aspect of the teaching and learning process. They had helped plan a service project, written about their service experiences, reflected on them in class, and/or implemented community service for at least one semester (Spring et al., 2006, pp. 1, 10).

American teachers innovatively implemented community service and service-learning programs and projects in their schools. The most popular curriculum areas that integrated service-learning were social studies, first language, character-building, and science. Service-learning projects consisted mostly of teaching and mentoring activities, community service activities, work on the environment, or administrative volunteering. In addition, there were various projects related to the pursuit of common concerns, public safety, or common campaigns, such as the promotion and construction of housing conditions (Scales & Roehlkepartain, 2004, pp. 15, 17).

Students worked under the teacher's guidance as a whole class or in small groups in various community service and service-learning activities at school and in the community. Students in lower grades performed simple service activities at school and in the surrounding area according to their abilities. For example, they tidied the school playground, organized garbage collection days in a nearby marshland, or made baby blankets for young mothers living in an emergency shelter for the homeless near the school (for different school service-learning programs, see, e.g., Roberts, 2002, pp. 38–39, 58–59, 88). High school students participated in increasingly demanding service events and processes in the community in which they taught community members how to use computers in the school computer class; assisted special students in schoolwork, cooking, and exercising; or participated in community service by serving on boards, committees, and local councils (for school service-learning programs, see, e.g., George, 1997, pp. 167–168, 171; Hill & Pope, 1997, pp. 188–189).

The Sociocultural Dimension was an essential component in instances when, for example, students helped at local centers for the elderly, nursing homes, and homeless shelters as part of their service-learning, or when they studied local history by gathering abstract and concrete material in the community as part of their outdoor education (for service-learning projects, see, e.g., Johnson, 1996, pp. 32–33). The following documents these practical efforts to enhance pedagogy at one school concerning the Sociocultural Dimension of its learning environment:

The teachers and their students at the Rabun Gap-Nacoochee School in Rabun County, Georgia, were engaged in community-based fieldwork for the purpose of firsthand observation and study in order to become acquainted with their community's past as well as its current economy and culture, special regional problems, and needs. The Appalachian Cookery Project, started in the 1980s, aimed to familiarize students with their community's cooking traditions. The students visited homes, where they observed cooking and discussed housekeeping and homemaking. They collected recipes by interviewing and photographing residents as well as trying the recipes out. Later, the students wrote and published a cookbook of the Appalachian people (McKay et al., 1991, pp. 165–172).

In the 1990s, environmental education continued to prevail as the strongest American educational approach, orienting instruction outside of school. The development of environmental education was reinforced by the National Environmental Education Act (1990) and, subsequently, by the John H. Chafee Environmental Education Act of 1999 (2000). These were intended to provide funds for developing curricula and programs related to environmental education, training educational professionals, and supplementing library services and collections, as well as funding for international activities involved in conferences, seminars, and teacher exchanges (National Environmental Education Act, 1990, Section 5504; John H. Chafee Environmental Education Act of 1999, 2000, Section 5). Furthermore, many documents on the state and resources of environmental education aimed at reforming community-based education, especially in the direction of environmental studies (see, e.g., Environmental Education Division, 1996; National Environmental Education and Training Foundation, 2002a, 2002b). The following shows how teachers and students at a school in Denver, Colorado, were involved in an environmental and community service-learning program:

At the end of the 1990s, the environmental and community service-learning program at Cole Middle School aimed at identifying and solving environmental problems in the community. The program included creating a community environmental inventory, defining the problem, studying the policies to follow and the options available to the students for influencing policy and practice, and drafting and implementing a plan of action, along with reflecting on and assessing the research and action process. The seventh graders at Cole decided to study the poor quality of the community water supply. They interviewed experts in the community, conducted tests on the water's pH and chlorine content, and studied plumbing in houses. Finally, the students drafted an action plan recommending a cooperative venture with the weatherization project in low-cost housing. They expressed their hope that water-filtration components would be installed in homes with high levels of water impurities (Boston, 1998–1999, pp. 66–69).

It is quite natural that environmental education exerted a considerable influence on the pedagogical content of the instructional programs. A national survey on the state of environmental education conducted by Ruskey et al. (2001) indicated that in the late 1990s, guidelines for environmental education curricula had been established in 20 states and development work was underway in 10 states. In some states, the guidelines for environmental education were included in the curricula of various subjects, such as science and social studies; in other states, independent environmental education standards or guidelines were created to cover all grade levels. Many states required guidelines for school districts, curriculum coordinators, and teachers in their options concerning, for example, curriculum development work and students' activities. A coordinated in-service teacher training program was implemented in 30 states, and a relevant program was developed in four states. In addition, 18 states had state-run environmental education centers (Ruskey et al., 2001, pp. 7–9).

Teachers carried out their student-centered environmental education quite pragmatically, although they also incorporated traditional teaching methods, for example, presentation-explanation models combined with discussions based on textbooks and other learning materials. McCrea and deBettencourt (2000) showed through their national survey on the state of teaching environmental education that the teachers (N = 920) used a variety of practices and teaching methods in their work. The most common methods were instructional discussions on environmental issues (about 90%) and practical activities or projects (80%). Problem-solving exercises, field trips, and study projects were quite common. Teaching methods varied by grade level, as, for example, teachers who worked in lower grades (pre-Grade 8) were much more likely to take advantage of field trips and practical activities than their counterparts in upper grades (Grades 9–12). Similarly, teachers who worked in Grades 5–8 were more likely to use study projects based on independent work or group work in their teaching than teachers who worked in all other grades (McCrea & deBettencourt, 2000, pp. 25–26). In light of this study, it can be seen that as the 20th century closed, American teachers of environmental education were striving to implement teaching practices based on active learning, where possible. Many teachers wanted to present their students with situations of active engagement that could focus on problem-oriented, exploratory, and experiential learning.

Many environmental education programs offered activities that could help students develop the knowledge and skills necessary for studying environmental issues in the school area. Provasoli (2020) described that studying minor environmental problems can develop K–5 students' confidence so that they can (a) select a sustainability problem, (b) form study groups to share research materials, and (c) construct a final project. At the same time, an emphasis was placed on developing environmental awareness (p. 15). The following shows how young students studied environmental issues in their science lessons:

> Students at the Manhattan School for Children studied environmental issues under the guidance of their science teacher. The first- and second-grade students included one new fact in their topic, while the third graders as a group contributed three new facts. In the fourth grade, each student in a group took notes on three facts, but the project could include a total of three new bits of information. In the fifth grade, the final project included three unique facts per person in each group. Then, each student group maintained a folder with the title, their brainstorming sheets, and printed materials that could help them later in their presentation. At the final meeting, the student groups presented and explained their project ideas, and participated in discussions with other students in the audience (Provasoli, 2020, pp. 14–15).

The early experiences of young students in a new learning environment can offer teachers and their students an opportunity to expand their overall awareness concerning environmental issues and values. Despite the emphasis on ecological matters, a desire was also expressed in the learning environment to simultaneously maintain the Naturalistic Dimension when participating in such activities as the day camp program at the state park, or studying nature at the laboratory of the resident outdoor education center or along the shore of a nearby pond or river. The following summary describes what educators and their young students felt while they studied a little creek:

> The educators and their young students went to see the little creek. The students walked around and, upon smelling the water, were disappointed at how dirty the water was: "This is so nasty." Later, the educators put in small aquatic plants and left them for a month. They all went back later and easily noticed the difference. The students were excited: "Look at the clarity of the water. We are not smelling the smells that were here

a month ago. That's amazing." After these experiences, the students were eager to get some aquatic plants and help to clean up other water bodies around the school (Nesmith et al., 2020, p. 183).

This explains why both the Ecological and Scientific-Technical Dimensions started to become more significant features in the learning environments of community-based learning. The relationship between organisms and their environment became the key issue within environmental education, thus replacing traditional approaches focused on the ecological impact of environmental changes. Gradually, environmental education was expected to include "a socio-critical component that encourages students to question how their actions and those of their society impact on the environment" (Taylor et al., 2009, p. 319). Such a course of thinking is evidenced by examples such as students familiarizing themselves with the living organisms that inhabit a pond in a residential site, studying the well-being of the ecosystem in a mountainous area near a research station, creating an outdoor laboratory in the semiarid foothills to study the changes in landscape, or exploring the utilization of the sea and its problems on field trips (for one environmental education program, see, e.g., Gutierrez & Sanchez, 1993, pp. 176–178). The following overview exemplifies the pedagogical applications carried out at one school regarding the Scientific-Technical Dimension of their learning environments. This involves the teachers and their students at a high school in Illinois who were active in an interdisciplinary research project in which soybean oil was made into car fuel through a unique hybrid diesel-electric system:

> For several years, biodiesel fueled the fires of learning at Oak Forest High School in Oak Forest, Illinois, after teachers of plant science, chemistry, physics, and technology started an interdisciplinary research project on the use of soybean oil as a fuel. When the first crop was planted behind the school, the science students became hands-on agronomists in their own laboratory, experimenting with seed varieties, fertilizers, and cultivation methods to increase yields. Each fall, they harvested their crop by hand, dried the soybeans, and pressed them to extract the oil. The raw soybean oil was then taken to a chemistry laboratory, where the students synthesized and purified it into a methyl ester (biodiesel). In an effort to increase the quantity and quality of the fuel, the students learned advanced procedures in chemical analysis, such as gas chromatography. To test the fuel's performance, the physics students designed, with the industrial technology students, a unique hybrid diesel-electric system for a 1999 Volkswagen Beetle that was donated to the project. The bean-to-Beetle accelerated curricula in several subject areas, such as industrial

technology, biology, and economics. Other students wrote articles for local newspapers, made presentations to community groups, and helped write grant applications (Littlejohn, 2009, pp. 216–217).

An important part of the Earth Community School (E.C.S.) model is the application of earth literacy to school activities. Teachers with their students could develop procedures to ensure the efficient use of water, energy, paper, and other resources. If students were involved in cleaning classrooms and other areas of the school, it would make them more responsible for the school's physical environment (Verhagen, 2009, p. 213). These types of learning environments can offer students an opportunity to practice shared responsibility. The following program at a Michigan high school shows that students have the chance to broaden their knowledge and develop their abilities, both of which are necessary for studying ecological questions and evaluating alternative methods for resolving problems:

> The students of Beecher High School in Mt. Morris, Michigan, made field trips for water testing, plant identification, and constructing a nature trail, including a bird sanctuary, butterfly houses, and native plant species. The students selected which native plants to buy and where to plant them. They pulled tires from the pond to use in the vegetable garden and removed dense reeds to create a space that had a positive human impact. Students also visited Kalamazoo, Michigan, to see the effects of an oil pipeline spill, completed water-quality testing, and reported their findings at a summit in Flint, Michigan. Moreover, the students worked on installing irrigation to improve the productivity of their vegetable gardens (Hammond, 2012, pp. 16–17).

This study provides evidence that, especially since the 1990s, the Scientific-Technical Dimension was increasingly emphasized in many pedagogical programs of community-based learning. Outdoor education could include the application of mathematical and physical principles, as was the case with a bridge-building project at a resident outdoor school. Service-learning could cover a survey of the developmental needs of the community using modern methods of data collection. Environmental education could include the use of laboratory instruments to study impurities in the community drinking water (for the teaching procedures in one school, see, e.g., Boston, 1998–1999, pp. 68–69). Some programs made intensive use of computer-based systems during the investigation of the natural and built environments (for the teaching procedures used at some schools, see, e.g., Coulter, 2000, pp. 55–61; Lauer, 2007, pp. 203–204; Thompson et al., 2000, pp. 47–54). Despite attempts to teach various subjects outdoors, with other areas and entities also being explored, environmental education was nevertheless emphasized in the means, content, and settings of many instructional programs (for the teaching procedures in some schools, see, e.g., Corcoran & Pennock, 2005, pp. 20–23; Roberts, 2002, pp. 58–61, 98–99; Rulison, 2007, pp. 13–17). The following summary exemplifies the pedagogical applications carried out at one school regarding the Scientific-Technical Dimension of its learning environments. This involves the students at a school in New York who were active in an environmental project that concerned a wastewater treatment plant:

> At Darrow School in New Lebanon, New York, a rural high school in the Berkshire Mountains, students established a wastewater treatment plant in the greenhouse located near the school building. The teachers integrated environmental sustainability into the curricula of different subjects, with much work done through in-house faculty education. The ultimate goal was to prepare the students for college and life. Students monitored the dissolved oxygen in the tanks, kept track of the daily flow, and fed the fish that lived in the display pond at the end of this Living Machine. The students studied environmental science, while they took water-quality tests, represented daily flow data graphically, and studied photosynthesis in the cells of the tropical plants. Teachers required students to give a formal presentation at the end of each course. The school also hosted many visits by elementary school children, high school science classes, college students, and interested parties from other communities (Riker, 2009, pp. 221, 223–224).

4.3.1   Challenges

The neo-essentialist school in the United States had access to considerably more economic, intellectual, and physical resources at the turn of the millennium than the progressive school had during the 1920s and 1930s. Despite this, when comparing the implementation of community-based learning, the neo-essentialist schools continued to be confronted with many problems.

In American metropolises, a major migration toward the suburbs ensued after the Second World War. Poor inner-city areas inhabited primarily by minorities gradually increased, establishing communities with complex patterns of social and educational inequality. During the 1980s, a critical educational policy led to utilizing standardized school achievement tests to monitor the work performed by teachers. The early 2000s also saw environmental education and service-learning topics giving way to increased emphasis on curriculum standards and the tests based on them (for justifications for not teaching environmental or service-learning studies, see, e.g., McCrea & deBettencourt, 2000, p. 31; Scales & Roehlkepartain, 2004, p. 25).

Many American teachers felt that the new school reforms were incapable of supporting their work in the community-based parts of the curricula. They came to this conclusion because the teaching and learning process, which focused on academic knowledge and learning, actually emphasized the teacher-directed transmission of knowledge. In the United States, the preservice and in-service training of teachers was considered insufficient. The instructional material used in environmental education lacked an interdisciplinary and social approach, and there was a particular lack of material suitable for the urban environment. Similarly, insufficient economic resources limited practical efforts to develop community-based learning. The opportunities for acquiring teaching material or financing for field trips were limited. Many schools did not even offer the appropriate equipment, furniture, or work premises (for a closer examination of the barriers to teaching environmental education, see, e.g., Mastrilli, 2005, p. 24; Mayeno, 2000, p. 14).

CHAPTER 3

Ideals for Learning in Communities in the Republic of India

Abstract

The aim of this chapter is to analyze the foundations of community-based learning with a focus on the philosophical views, educational aims, and associated value dimensions in India. In addition, the aim is to examine the changing nature of the pedagogical activities of community-based learning and their authentic learning environments in India. The analysis concentrates particularly on the activities of community-based learning and their central pedagogical approaches in a context of social change. This chapter shows that in India the philosophical tradition of such learning is related to the ideas of neo-traditional education and relies on a tradition that insists on truth included in the philosophy of *satyagraha*. The chapter shows that in the late 1930s India started to focus efforts on expanding learning environments from schools to the real world outside of schools. This tradition gave particular importance to sociomoral aims and socioethical and universal values, while the primary focus is on vocationally productive education. The chapter reveals that in the 1960s development in India started to stress school-centered intellectual aims and science- and technology-related values, while community-based learning allowed experts to be trained for an advanced society in which mental work was to be performed in modern production. This chapter also demonstrates that community-based learning can take place in a variety of learning environments prioritizing the Sociocultural, Productive, Scientific-Agricultural, or Scientific-Technical Dimensions, in accordance with the general direction of political, economic, and social development. During the past six decades, pedagogical approaches and their learning environments have increasingly given special importance to the use of technology-based applications. The study concludes that approaches to community-based learning could provide a way for schools to integrate instruction into students' lives and communities and help them apply what they learned at school to practices in their daily life.

Keywords

philosophy – aims – values – practices – community-based learning – neo-traditionalism – neocolonialism – postcolonialism – pedagogical activities – pedagogical approaches – learning environments – vocationally productive education – India

1 Satyagrahaism and Pedagogical Neo-Traditionalism

India was developing a philosophy of education based on an inherited philosophical tradition at the same time that the Indigenous inhabitants of the American continent were building their societies in what is now the United States. Indian philosophical tradition is generally understood to have arisen from the original Indus Valley culture, which flourished between 3000 BC and 1500 BC, as well as from the Indo-European culture that later spread into India over a long period of time (for a closer examination of the peoples speaking Indo-European languages, see Doniger, 2009, pp. 81, 90, 92). The roots of the written sources in the philosophical tradition extend to the *Vedas* (from approximately 1500 to 1200 BC) and the *Upanishads* (from approximately 800 to 600 BC).

The *Mimamsa* school, one of the earliest trends in Indian philosophy, based its thinking directly on the *Vedas*, in particular, on the first two parts of each *Veda* (Raju, 1992, p. 40). According to Raju (1992), the adherents of this school believed that the purpose of life is unending activity; a person performs tasks and enjoys their fruits in a continually alternating process in this life and the next (pp. 82–83). The *Mimamsa* doctrine concerning the validity of knowledge (*pramanyavada*) is based on the assumption that every piece of knowledge or a process relating to cognition can reveal only its own truth and the falseness of some other cognitive process. Pragmatic action can confirm the truth of a cognitive process that has already revealed its apparent truth. It has also been claimed that the meaning of every word or sentence is associated primarily with action (Raju, 1992, pp. 75–77).

The *Mimamsa* texts (from approximately the 400s BC) and their later elucidations (from the early AD 700s) offer interpretations that can be compared to the aforementioned basic ideas of pragmatism when analyzing the connection between meaning and action, even though they differ with respect to their philosophical foundations. The earliest Indian philosophers have been characterized as focused primarily on the human ego—as the Indian philosophical tradition is ultimately based on religious practice—rather than on the material world (for more on the earliest philosophical schools in India, see, e.g., Doniger, 2009, pp. 504–505).

The tradition of Indian philosophy is based on religious practice and thus differs from Western traditions. The earliest Western philosophers focused their attention on the material world, external to humans, and its explanation, but the first thinkers of the *Upanishads* experienced the actual human ego as being identical with the universe. As capitalists create luxury goods for society and Marxists believe that economic changes will bring about a happy society,

Indians focus their attention primarily on the actual human (Tähtinen, 1984, pp. 16–17). The aim is a philosophy of life based on meditation applicable to practical experience.

Millennia of Hindu tradition have also left their unique mark on Indian social behavior. According to Hindu social philosophy, the ideal social system is based on the caste system. Historically, the Hindu caste system consisted of four main groups, or *Varnas* (Brahmana, Kshatriya, Vaishya, Sudra), each of which had a specific functional status in India's hierarchical society. Another group, the untouchables (*Dalit*), was even lower than the lowest main group. Over time, each class's specific responsibilities became more defined. Thus the *Varna* system developed into numerous professional subgroups (*jati*), which diminished flexibility between the main groups (Kinsley, 1993, pp. 153–156).

Kinsley (1993) described that, according to tradition, transition from one *Varna* to another can only take place through reincarnation. Life is ruled by a cycle in which birth, death, and reincarnation follow one another (*samsara*). The moral consequences of previous actions (*karma*) are transferred from one life to another, determining a person's reincarnation and its conditions. Moving from a *Varna* may thus require several lives of appropriate activity. The ultimate goal is nevertheless liberation (*moksha*) from the cycle of *samsara* and the merging of the soul (*atman*) with the supreme reality (*Brahman*) (pp. 85–86).

In addition to the ancient philosophical tradition, Indian school reformers were deeply influenced by the various peoples who had conquered the country over the centuries. After the long period of Islamic rule (1206–1858), European colonial policy (starting in the 16th century) eventually brought the country under the subjugation of Great Britain (1858–1947). The expressed goal of the British administration was to instill Western culture in the Indians, including their educational philosophy. Among those who utilized various syntheses of Western and Indian ideas was philosopher Rabindranath Tagore (1861–1941).

Tagore based his thoughts concerning the freedom of the mind and will, that is to say, the world of human intelligence and morals, on Indian tradition, but he also wanted to derive benefit from Western culture and some of its educational practices (Tagore, 1917, pp. 82–85; Tagore, 1961, pp. 222–223). At *Brahmacharya Ashrama*, his boarding school in *Shantiniketan*, Tagore combined music, excursions, nature study, and sports in his teaching in the British sense; the esthetic and religious piety of festivals; and activity in the surrounding community (see Pearson, 1917, pp. 16–53). Western progressive educational ideas also made their way to India. Documentary evidence demonstrates that many schools were already following Parkhurst's Dalton Plan in the early 1920s (Olsson, 1926, p. 46).

The first decades of the 1900s witnessed a struggle for independence in India that was also connected with the national reform-pedagogical trend. This struggle arose in response to the further consolidation of British power and the consequent spread of Western culture. Compared to the revolutionary processes in the early Soviet Union, India chose a different path for its social development after Hindu lawyer Mohandas Gandhi (1869–1948) became the leading figure in the struggle for independence.

1.1   *Mahatma Gandhi on National Education*

Gandhi's social reformist ideas must be seen within the context of Indian cultural historical tradition, along with his sociopolitical activity, first in South Africa and then in India under British rule. During Gandhi's efforts in South Africa to achieve social and political improvements for the Indian minority, he developed a nonviolent form of civil resistance, literally the idea of "insistence on truth" (*Satyagraha*) (Gandhi, 1928/1950a, pp. 109–110). This ideal was inspired by the Bhagavad Gita's (400–100 BC) phrases in Hindi that Gandhi had long remembered, on the message of the Christian Sermon on the Mount, and on the ideas of Lev Tolstoy's book *The Kingdom of God Is Within You* (1894) (Gandhi, 1927, pp. 58, 75; Tolstoy, 1894; Fischer, 1951/1982, pp. 124–125). Satyagraha was highly characteristic of the struggle for independence in India and involved aiming for self-sufficiency through truth (*satya*) and nonviolence (*ahimsa*). This was the basis for a national program of self-sufficiency, a program that eventually also included a national basic school system.

The development of a national school system was crucial to the idea of obtaining independence from the British raj, which was not only invincible but also benevolent in offering its Indian elite a Western education considered superior to anything India could offer. Urban and Wagoner (2009) reported that a comparable context had prevailed in the United States between the 1890s and the 1930s, when government programs attempted to assimilate Native Americans by moving their children from reservations to boarding schools. There, the children were openly taught to despise their traditional Native American cultures, including the languages, customs, and values, since these were all seen as inferior to European culture (p. 244).

From this viewpoint, such a government process that forced Native Americans to abandon their ideals and beliefs was so the conquerors could maintain their domineering relation toward the Native inhabitants. The different imperialistic educational views in India and the United States were deeply contradictory, as they were linked to different life-sustaining value objectives and associated conceptions of being human. In this context, we can understand that national educational thought in India naturally formed a vital cornerstone for the independence struggle, as its philosophical background of education relied on the national legacy of Indian traditional society. The following summary provides background on Gandhi's thoughts on nonviolence and self-sufficiency:

Mahatma Gandhi, the father of Indian independence, is universally known and renowned as a proponent of nonviolence. Gandhi's convictions must be seen within the context of both Indian cultural tradition and his own sociopolitical activity in South Africa and India. After qualifying as a lawyer in England and failing in his career in India, Gandhi traveled to South Africa in 1893 to practice law. Experiencing firsthand the oppression to which nonwhites were subjected in South Africa, he gave up his law office and embarked on a struggle to improve the social and political rights of the local Indian minority (see Gandhi, 1927, 1928/1950a). Realizing that efforts to work in the midst of the Indian population were futile, Gandhi developed a nonviolent form of civil resistance, literally the idea of "firmness of truth" or "adherence to the truth" (*Satyagraha*), from the old Hindu phrases, the discourse of Jesus of Nazareth, and Tolstoy's writings (Gandhi, 1927, pp. 58, 75; Gandhi, 1928/1950a, pp. 109–110; for the letters, see, e.g., Gandhi, 1909/1991; Tolstoy, 1968, pp. 21–26). As a base for his social and political activity, and encouraged by the ideas of John Ruskin (1819–1900) on work, Gandhi first established the Phoenix Settlement and, later, the Tolstoy Farm, which attracted many members. In this work center (*ashrama*) devoted to a common goal and household, Gandhi edited a newspaper, worked on handicrafts, cultivated land, and ran a school (see, e.g., Gandhi, 1928/1950a, pp. 236–242; Gandhi, 1927, pp. 250–252, 280; for Gandhi's biography in Africa, see also Fischer, 1951/1982).

Gandhi returned to India as a well-known social reformer in 1915. Within 3 years he became a religious, social, and political reformer, a national leader to whom people turned for help with a wide variety of problems. After determining that India's most difficult problem was its status as a colony, Gandhi began his public struggle for independence in 1916 using the philosophies of truth in action and nonviolence as his weapons (see Tähtinen, 1964, pp. 11–16; Tähtinen, 1979, pp. 83–96; Tähtinen, 1982, pp. 47–50). He established *Satyagraha Ashrama* for his activities, in which the existence of a traditional religious settlement was combined with political activity. In 1920, nationwide nonviolent opposition to cooperation with the British authorities began. Boycotting everything foreign as a means of achieving self-sufficiency was an essential element of Gandhi's campaign. The boycott covered imported products, schools, and the legal system as well as the law and the power that it granted. People held meetings and strikes in different parts of the country in addition to fasting and praying. Gandhi reformed traditional village industry and offered everyone a simple spinning wheel so that the villages could attain self-sufficiency (see Gandhi, 1948c, pp. 73–74).

Gandhi believed that putting himself at the disposal of politics and business was his moral responsibility. He maintained that political and economic institutions could include violence and exploitation. In his view, centralized heavy industry is immoral because, in becoming mechanized, it furthers the interests of only a few people and necessarily results in the exploitation of the working class (Gandhi, 1954, pp. 38, 42, 45). Industrialism results in unnecessary needs, unemployment, social alienation, and moral degeneration (Datta, 1953, pp. 113–114). Social freedom is based on decentralizing political and economic power. Social justice prevails in a decentralized economy: the individual can influence economic decision-making by monitoring the system and refusing to cooperate (see Gandhi, 1947, p. 7; Gandhi, 1948b, p. 35). This natural law, truth, which is above laws and social systems, is to be achieved without violence. A requirement for truthfulness is harmony between thought and deed, thus doing away with all exploitation (see Gandhi, 1948a, p. 14; Gandhi, 1948b, pp. 33, 35). Democratic decision-making is possible only in an economically self-sufficient society, the ideal being a self-sufficient village community, the economic basis of which is handicraft production (see Gandhi, 1954, pp. 36, 45; for more details on Gandhi's economic strategy, see Tähtinen, 1970, pp. 94–95; Tähtinen, 1986, p. 27). Such a program for self-sufficiency was also firmly linked to the Indian basic school.

Gandhi's thinking on education can be seen to have been influenced by Tagore's views on education as practiced at his *Shantiniketan* School (*Shantiniketan Vidyalaya*). They were both guided by a shared view of the kind of independent future into which India should be led (for the relationship of Gandhi and Tagore, see their letters, e.g., Bhattacharya, 1997). The Gandhian reform-pedagogical ideal was related to the tradition of Indian philosophy and thus formed the national philosophical foundation for Indian approaches to community-based learning. The present study sees Gandhi's educational thinking as being founded on a tradition in the theory of truth, that is to say, the philosophy of truth in action, *Satyagraha*. Gandhi (1947) noted that social freedom in the form of self-government is achieved by acquiring the ability to resist authority when it uses its position wrongly (p. 7). This ability to resist is internal strength that is achieved by character-building, which includes developing the courage, resilience, virtue, and unselfishness that are needed in goal-directed activity (Gandhi, 1948d, p. 254). Consequently, the central function of education is to change the heart. It is essential to learn to feel what the soul is and what hidden powers it contains. Equally essential is internalizing the fact that, in the struggle of life, hate may be conquered by love, lies by truth, and violence by one's own suffering (Gandhi, 1954, p. 140). Such a process of spiritual awakening should also be part of the development of the body and mind.

A balanced education requires the holistic integration of physical, moral, and intellectual activity, which is best achieved through teaching handicrafts. For this reason, a central responsibility of the school is to offer students the opportunity to develop attributes of personal character through handicraft production or other lines of work available in the area. The students familiarize themselves with the vocational activities required in the community, such as spinning, carpentry, and agriculture. They undergo in-depth studies concerning the fundamentals of these crafts and the different phases in the relevant working processes (Gandhi, 1948d, pp. 257–259; Gandhi, 1962, p. 59). They develop themselves holistically in vocational work, the results of which they use to finance their education; the knowledge they derive from education they use outside the school (Gandhi, 1937/1950b, 1951, 1953). Gandhi (1948d) believed that vocationally productive education provides practice in being responsible for doing one's own share and ushers in the silent revolution. This will do away with the contradictions between social classes, thus laying the foundation for a just social order in a traditional Indian society (pp. 259–260).

1.2   *Aims and Values*
Within the context of an approach to neo-traditional education, rooted in satyagrahaism, community-based learning could be said to draw attention to life-centeredness in pedagogy. This constituted the neo-traditional approach of craft-related education, which was a means of searching for ways to link school education as closely as possible to practice in real-life learning environments. The purpose of craft-related education was to integrate instruction into students' lives and communities, their local productive work, and crafts. The aim was to help them utilize what they learned at school in practice to their daily life in order to promote self-sufficiency and independence in a preindustrial agrarian community.

Gandhian economics can be seen as related to spiritual and socioeconomic principles. Economic values were prioritized in education by stressing schools' self-maintaining activities and instruction without books, even though the teachers tried to correlate all of the various subject curricula around work. However, guided by social and traditional values, the most essential thing was the attempt to break down the prejudice between manual and intellectual workers in order to help implement civil rights and duties in a cooperative community. Character-building was a means for achieving the various virtues needed in goal-directed activities, such as courage, resilience, and unselfishness, that arise from universal values. The ultimate end of education related to socioethical values was to contribute to societal development without violence in order to attain a democratic social order that accentuated solidarity between the people.

The Zakir Husain Committee report (1938) was based on the final resolutions made at the highly esteemed Wardha National Education Conference in October 1937 and thus conformed with Gandhi's thoughts on education. The conference accepted the plan and passed the following resolutions:
- Free and compulsory education should be provided for 7 years on a nationwide scale.
- The medium of instruction must be the mother tongue.
- Education should center around some form of manual and productive work. Similarly, all other activities and training given should be integrally related to the central handicraft with due regard to the environment of the child.
- This system of education will cover remuneration for the teachers (Zakir Husain Committee, 1938, p. 3).

The report proposed that teaching should be closely connected with local productive work, since this was seen to be the best means of effecting integrated, diversified education. Some local craft, such as spinning and weaving, carpentry, agriculture, fruit and vegetable gardening, or other work belonging to the life of the community, was to be chosen as the basis for craft-related education in the school (Zakir Husain Committee, 1938, pp. 12–14, 19). Based on the 1938 report, craft-related education aimed to:
- create a uniform curriculum for the entire school through handicraft;
- provide all students with vocational training in handicraft in order to enhance national self-sufficiency;
- teach respect for manual work in order to break down the prejudice between manual and intellectual workers;
- teach democratic civil action, that is, to carry out responsibilities and use civil rights in a cooperative community;
- promote social development without violence, that is, work to achieve solidarity between people and democracy in the various areas of culture; and
- integrate into the child's life teaching about one's own community and its local productive work and crafts (pp. 12–17, 19).

India's educational efforts in the 1940s and 1950s rested upon traditional cultural values. Gandhi based his ideas of basic education on the traditional values of India found in truth and nonviolence. Indian education was thus organized within the country's cultural traditions and its value dimensions. Such an emphasis on these types of values strengthened the transactional role of education, in addition to abolishing the boundary between a school and society. Concerning this, the society-centered pattern of community-based learning can be seen as emphasizing the physical and sociomoral aims that endeavored to educate spiritually and morally fortified citizens for a preindustrial agrarian society. In this manner, physical, sociomoral, and intellectual education were intentionally integrated. The aim of neo-traditional education, based on the Gandhian theory of truth, was to apply universal life values in developing attributes of personal character, that is, character-building, in order to train self-sufficient, independent citizens for a traditional society. The ultimate goal associated with socioethical values was national reconstruction through Gandhian basic schools.

The Indian educators were willing to work with Prime Minister Jawaharlal Nehru (1889–1964), the leader of the Congress Party, in the new Republic of India established in 1950. Independent India started to implement neutrality and nonalignment in its foreign policy. With respect to its domestic affairs, India embarked on an approach referred to as a nondogmatic socialism based on Western parliamentary democracy as well as socialism and secularism. Despite the uneven division of capital, the economy was geared toward the Western style of industrialization with socialism as the goal. The aim of the integrated planning of the national economy was to develop agriculture, the energy economy, and irrigation systems (1951–1956), to expand heavy industry (1956–1961), and to advance education (1961–1966) (Planning Commission, 1953, pp. 70–71; Planning Commission, 1956, p. 51; Planning Commission, 1961, p. 36).

The purpose of the ideal Indian school was to be self-sufficient and to essentially be seen as a spinning and weaving institution with a cotton field attached to it. Gandhi (1948d) described that the instruction that it provides should be wholly linked to village handicraft production or other lines of work, since a person can develop best within a village community in which a balance exists between individual and social development (pp. 258–259). A school of this type, based on Indian tradition, sought to familiarize students with the vocational activities required in the community, such as spinning, carpentry, and agriculture. Here, in-depth learning of different ways of working and the phases involved could lead to a higher level of development of the body, mind, and soul (Gandhi, 1951, p. 11; Gandhi, 1962, p. 59). Teaching was to progress scientifically, emphasizing the interpretation of the bases of the work processes (Gandhi, 1948d, p. 257). The following outlines the essential nature of the aims

of community-based learning in light of the pedagogical trend inspired by Gandhi's ideas. This form of community-based learning aimed to:
- correlate the curricula of the school's various subjects with the world of work;
- provide training in a craft or other local work;
- make learning without books possible so as to decrease educational expenses;
- promote the beneficial use of what is learned at school in practice to every-day life;
- teach respect for manual work in an effort to erase the inequality between manual and intellectual work as well as between workers;
- increase self-sufficiency and thus do away with unemployment;
- promote social development, that is, raise the morals of the nation and work to nonviolently achieve a democratic social order; and
- combine teaching with the village community, its traditional means of live-lihood, and manual occupations (Gandhi, 1948d, pp. 259–260; Gandhi, 1937/1950b, pp. 30–31; Gandhi, 1951, pp. 11–12, 65, 89; Gandhi, 1962, p. 193; Gandhi, 1953, pp. 36, 44–45).

The dawn of Indian social modernization saw that community-based learning remained society-centered in accordance with Gandhi's views until the mid-1960s, with continuing emphasis on physical and sociomoral aims. This was implemented in the *First Five Year Plan* (1951–1956), which established the basic school as the model for the new education system (Planning Commission, 1953, p. 534). The syllabus for teaching in basic schools (1950) aimed at a productive and creative craft-related education that was to be firmly linked to the child's physical and social environment (Ministry of Education, 1950, p. 5). The handbook for teachers at basic schools (1956b) suggested that productive, creative, and socially useful work was to be the core of teaching, since the schools were to offer education for, as well as through, life. This would make the achievement of a nonexploitative and nonviolent society possible (Ministry of Education and Scientific Research, 1956b, p. 6). The syllabus for post-basic education (1961) held that the purpose of education was to further the construction of a new and just social order that presupposed the integration of education into the crafts pertaining to the village community's handicraft pro-duction and agriculture (Education Department, 1961, pp. 42, 44). The follow-ing describes the role of craft-related education in the pursuit of a righteous society. As a part of this process, craft-related education aimed to:
- integrate teaching in the school's various subjects through the crafts;
- develop the ability to coordinate sensory activities and apply such experi-ence in real situations;

- lead to investigation of the processes, tools, and arrangements relevant to some craft;
- enable higher education by continuing to practice a craft in a self-reliant manner;
- help attain a livelihood through the craft after schooling;
- provide the opportunity to become a good guide in the development of the crafts practiced by the community; and
- advance the development of the school and the community, that is, to make the school a center for comprehensive social service and reconstruction for the community, as well as to make the latter as self-sufficient and cooperatively functioning as possible, as an example for the surrounding region (Education Department, 1961, pp. 43–46; Ministry of Education, 1950, p. 7).

1.2.1   Summing Up

The conceptual features of Gandhian neo-traditionalism can be examined from the perspective of community-based learning by applying Hlebowitsh's (2007) classification. Neo-traditionalism interprets the ideal student as being self-reliant, community-minded, spiritually and morally strong, and adamant about truth, while also being familiar with the vocationally productive activities needed in the community and participating in social service. The ideal educational program is built around craft-related productive work linked to the child's entire social and physical environment. The student is oriented toward an ideal democratic society, the citizens of which live in self-sufficient village communities, where they work on traditional crafts and agricultural production.

Such a philosophical trend in education undoubtedly represented an exceptionally radical idea about education and its practices with regard to a society based on tradition. Since productive crafts were assigned to the lowest groups in the caste system of colonial India, the argument has been presented that Gandhi's reform reversed this hierarchy, thus causing conflict between the social classes (Kumar, 2005, p. 179). However, Gandhi's philosophy also justifies the opposite interpretation. Neo-traditional, vocationally productive education that is aimed at making one responsible for doing one's own share could bring about a silent revolution that could eradicate the contradictions between social classes and provide a setting for a just social order in a traditional Indian society. Therefore, school education had to be integrated with work and life in the surrounding community.

Since the mid-1950s, the principles of the educational policies have been aimed at modernizing India. Although the basic school was purposely established, with notable progress being made, many educational and social factors resulted in the failure and rejection of the basic system of education in the newly independent India. To begin with, administrative difficulties, insufficient teacher training, and the small amount of research devoted to teaching methodology constituted serious obstacles in the path of development. Economic resources were also modest.

India's efforts to attain independence also deepened the conflicts between Hindus and Muslims, which eventually resulted in serious violence after the Second World War. When a constitutional future for a united India, the majority of whose inhabitants were Hindus, proved to be impossible, two large areas, Pakistan and East Bengal, whose inhabitants were mostly Muslim, were partitioned and made independent in August 1947. The separation required large-scale evacuations of the population and resulted in catastrophic dissension and violence; possibly as many as one million people perished (Brown, 1994, pp. 337–339). Gandhi's fasts were influential in ending the violence. A supporter of nonviolence and brotherhood between Muslims and Hindus during the independence struggle, Gandhi was murdered by a Hindu extremist in January 1948 (see, e.g., Khan, 2007, pp. 178, 180). Gandhi's death in 1948 ushered in a simultaneous weakening in thinking concerning basic education (Sinclair, 1980, pp. 56–59).

Aside from these factors, school authorities and the students' parents preferred traditional education as a consequence of the influence of private schools, for instance. In actual fact, they regarded the academic abilities of basic school students, such as their mastery of English, to be insufficient, particularly with respect to the higher levels of study (see, e.g., Naik, 1975, pp. 32–33). It was also evident that teachers considered that the primary function of higher secondary schools was to prepare a relatively small number of students (approx. 17% of the 14-to-17 age group) for tertiary-level institutions (Ministry of Information and Broadcasting, 1970, p. 63). In the final analysis, the strategy-based economic reforms of the Central Government were perhaps the most significant obstacles to retaining the basic school, particularly with the start of the *Second Five Year Plan* (1956–1961), whose goal was Indian industrialization and urbanization (Planning Commission, 1956, p. 28).

2 Indian Modernization and Educational Reform

2.1 *Philosophical Views*

Over the course of time, the national philosophical traditions of the countries discussed in this book have been influenced by the international currents of ideas that have also been applied to educational practices. This has been particularly true when a country's political situation has been receptive to ideas from other countries. Such a philosophical turn in education took place in India, as the education system was being urged to help accelerate the country's extensive modernization process, particularly since the *Third Five Year Plan* (1961–1966). Guided by Western specialists, the Indian government intensified national modernization with the help of an education system that would now include work education based on materialistic values (Ministry of Education, 1966, pp. 210–216). The present study indicates that, in light of Indian social modernization, the philosophical background of community-based learning was built on the ideas of neocolonial work education. This interpretation was ultimately consistent with the view of dialectical and historical materialism.

Particularly after the Russian Revolution, socialist political movements found support in many Latin American and Asian countries that had been subjected to Western rule. The national leaders of former colonies hoped to escape imperialistic policies through social reforms like those being applied in the Soviet Union. Among these national leaders, Jawaharlal Nehru sought a solution for India's national future.

While residing in Europe in 1926 and 1927, Nehru familiarized himself with ideas that differed from the options British authorities offered. He was introduced not only to Western parliamentary democracy and British socialism but also to Marxism and its radical ideas. He visited the Soviet Union and, subsequently, China. Nehru believed that socialism could eventually offer the means for solving India's post-independence poverty issues and state of abasement, if a large majority of Indians wanted it (Gopal, 1975, pp. 210–213). However, socialism, which would reflect Marxism-Leninism, represented different underlying value objectives from those promoted in the social, economic, and political practices of the India that was then gaining independence. This contradiction was further intimately linked with diverse views regarding the direction in which society should develop.

In 1950, the independent Republic of India started to implement a domestic policy in accordance with Prime Minister Nehru's thinking. Referred to as nondogmatic socialism, this approach was based on ideas taken from Western parliamentary democracy as well as from socialism and secularism. Despite its uneven distribution of capital, the Indian economy was geared toward Western-style industrialization, with socialism as the goal. Starting with the *Second Five Year Plan* (1956–1961), modernization was seen as the goal of societal development. Many Indians shared the belief that this could be achieved by investing in sectors such as steel production, engineering, and the chemical industry. The model of economic development tied to socialism also included protecting the Indian economy by impeding or limiting imports of foreign goods and services.

India also chose a rather eclectic approach to developing the country's educational and cultural life. In 1966, the authoritative Kothari Education Commission recommended that, in addition to the national tradition, one should also "draw upon liberalizing forces that have arisen in the Western nations and which have emphasized, among other things, the dignity of the individual, equality and social justice, e.g., the French Revolution, the concept of the welfare state, the philosophy of Marx and the rise of socialism" (Ministry of Education, 1966, p. 20). The purpose of vocationally productive education was now to emphasize a neocolonial approach, which was basically rooted in dialectical and historical materialism. The Kothari report presented as models exemplary Soviet programs of polytechnical work education, which were adapted to the types of work-experience programs introduced as an integral part of Indian vocationally productive education (Ministry of Education, 1966, pp. 210–216). An increase in vocational orientation was set as a new goal for education, particularly in the upper secondary schools. Moreover, in addition to containing academic studies, school curricula at all levels were supplemented with programs of science- and technology-based work.

2.2   Aims and Values

India entered a new phase in the 1960s, giving precedence to education over aims connected with theoretical values. We can suggest in the spirit of the Kothari Commission report (Ministry of Education, 1966) that the neocolonial school emphasized intellectual aims in an effort to integrate physical, sociomoral, and intellectual education within community-based learning. The purpose of such a preference was, consistent with dialectical and historical materialism, to train experts for a modern society of secularism and social equality. Specifically, procedural knowledge was rated highly among the aims of neocolonial work-experience education; that is, knowledge about how to do something, which was a prerequisite for applying modern technology and science to production processes. Even though social values were still promoted in teaching, the significance of science- and technology-related values, in particular, was now underlined in order to enable students to understand modern technology and its scientific principles.

The Education Commission, under the chairmanship of Daulat S. Kothari (1906–1993), demonstrated that achieving India's national goals depended on the social, economic, and cultural transformation of society. This, in turn, was connected with a restructuring of the educational system. The commission's report argued that a modern, developed, and technology-based society needed intellectually capable workers. For this reason, school curricula were to be supplemented with programs of work-experience education implemented both inside and outside the school. The productive processes of these programs were to combine industrialization with the application of science and technology (Ministry of Education, 1966, pp. 7–8). In relation to this, *The Curriculum for the Ten-Year School* (1975) aimed at reforming teaching using work-experience education, since the technological development of a modern society presupposed familiarization with new types of working skills and processes (National Council of Educational Research and Training (NCERT), 1975, p. 18).

The Kothari Commission report (1966) defined work-experience education as "participation in productive work in school, in the home, in a workshop, on a farm, in a factory or in any other productive situation" (Ministry of Education, 1966, p. 7). It elaborated the programs of work-experience education:

1. Work experience that involves participation in some productive work found in real-life situations should be introduced as an integral part of education at all stages.
2. In the lower classes of the primary school, work experience may begin as simple handwork. This intends to train children and helps their intellectual and emotional growth.
3. In the upper classes, it may take the form of "learning a craft," which develops technical thinking and creative capacities in the students. Some work experience can be provided in real-life situations, such as work on farms at harvest time, sowing, or in a family production unit.
4. At the lower secondary stage, work experience can take the form of workshop training, as a proposed workshop is to be attached to every school or a group of secondary schools in a phased program spread over the next 10 years.
5. At the higher secondary stage, work experience should be made available in school workshops, on farms, and in industrial and commercial establishments (Ministry of Education, 1966, pp. 201–202).

This type of school education appeared to be school-centered, with particular emphasis on intellectual aims when specifically examining work-experience education and socially useful productive work. An effort was made to use intellectual aims to prepare experts for a modern society characterized by secularism and social equality through the integration of physical, sociomoral, and intellectual education. On the basis of the documents presented above, work-experience education aimed to:

– develop the knowledge, skills, and attitudes that are useful in the productive work of a modern society;
– lead to an understanding of the need for and usefulness of modern labor-saving devices and tools and to understand the underlying scientific principles and the techniques involved in their use;

- advance social and national integration, that is, improve the appreciation for intellectual and manual work with new technology, thus reducing class differences, particularly concerning the elite and the masses; and
- offer programs of work-experience education inside and outside the school (NCERT, 1975, p. 18; Ministry of Education, 1966, pp. 7–8).

Nevertheless, in social and national service consistent with the Kothari Commission report (1966), the physical and sociomoral aims were still being emphasized in the vast Indian territory. The report held that the academic instruction given in the schools was to be complemented by programs of social service implemented in the schools and the surrounding community. In this manner, social and national integration could be enhanced (Ministry of Education, 1966, pp. 9, 11–12). *The Curriculum for the Ten-Year School* (1975) urged students and teachers to participate in the life, work, and activities of the community to effect a reduction in the distance between it and the school (NCERT, 1975, pp. 52–53). The following list, based on the Kothari Commission report, indicates that social service aimed to:

- develop work habits;
- strengthen respect for manual labor;
- develop character, discipline, and social responsibility;
- improve relationships between the educated class and other segments of society, that is, strengthen the sense of social purpose and self-confidence, and increase the desire to participate in the life and activities of the community; and
- offer programs of social service at school and in the surrounding community (Ministry of Education, 1966, pp. 11–12).

2.2.1   Summing Up

If Hlebowitsh's (2007) classification is used to analyze the specific conceptual features of neocolonialism presented in the Kothari Commission report (Ministry of Education, 1966) from the more general perspective of community-based learning, one could conclude that the ideal student is an intellectually capable and technologically literate individual who is being introduced to the changing activities and processes of vocationally productive work in society. The ideal curriculum embodies work-experience programs containing vocationally productive units of study based on the application of technology and science in and outside the school. The student is oriented toward an ideal democratic society that relies on secularism and social equality, the citizens of which work in scientifically and technologically advanced production.

Despite this determined school reform, it soon became evident to many educational experts that modest vocational work experience in production was insufficient to integrate the teaching and learning processes. For example, less than 10 percent of the primary and secondary schools offered their students work-experience activities. Gutek (2006) explained that in addition to criticism directed at the schools, fierce resistance also arose at that time to the new economic policy planning, as critics wanted to avoid the problems typical of Western countries, such as environmental pollution and social exclusion (p. 88).

3 Resistance to Educational Change in India

3.1 *Philosophical Views*

India chose an entirely different approach to developing its education system compared to the Western principles in China outlined later. The neocolonial educational policies and Westernization strategy can be said to have gradually come into conflict in India. Gutek (2006) wrote that a group of Indian educators criticized their country's educational policy, which was based on a modernization theory, because it was considered to represent a neocolonial Westernization strategy. The critics maintained that education and society could be modernized by discovering ways based on traditional Indian cultural values instead of materialistic ones (p. 88). In essence, such dissimilarity in values and ideals in India at the time could be associated with conceptual systems pertaining to the human experience. These are more broadly linked to the values that guide societal and individual life as well as to beliefs related to the world.

In 1977, Western-inclined neocolonial educational policy in India eventually became inconsistent as the Congress Party's long period in power came to an end and domestic policy took a more fundamentalist direction. A desire arose to utilize Indian traditional cultural values to find solutions to reform education and society. That same year, the Patel Review Committee published a plan that approached the issue from the standpoint of the Gandhian philosophy of basic education, but with a new, unexpected connection. The Patel report (1977a) implied that the philosophical background of community-based learning rests on separate, even contradictory, views. The report's conclusions could suggest that socially useful productive work is based on the ideas of postcolonial work education—ideas that respect the Gandhian philosophy of basic education but that are closely linked to the philosophical views of rationalism (Ministry of Education & Social Welfare, 1977a, p. 6). From the perspective of rationalism, knowledge is primarily based on reason instead of experience, whereas the basic ideas of Gandhi's *Satyagraha* maintain the importance of harmony between thought and deed. This kind of syncretistic view relied on the idea of promoting economic and technological reforms by breaking away from the colonial tradition and integrating the practices of work education with the national cultural tradition and its work and customs.

3.2   *Aims and Values*

Since the late 1970s, the intellectual aims of community-based learning in India became increasingly connected to promoting theoretical values, as shown by the prevailing school-centered patterns of such education. At the time, India again aspired to detach itself from the tradition of a colonial educational philosophy and develop its own national educational thought. In the postcolonial school, in accordance with the Patel Committee report, the government attempted to integrate work with instruction by applying scientific principles to work processes, particularly in the community's physical and social environments (Ministry of Education & Social Welfare, 1977a). The familiar neo-traditional education was, arguably, now being developed intentionally in a more academic direction in the spirit of rationalism, while being more effectively embedded in the instruction of natural sciences and other academic subjects. The ultimate contributor to this syncretistic view was the political decision that India needed economic and technological reform if it was to overcome the problems of underdevelopment.

This postcolonial pedagogical approach to socially useful productive work emphasized theoretical values associated with intellectual aims, while trying to develop students' ability to understand the needs of a technology-based society, as well as their problem-solving skills, at various stages of the learning process. Socially desirable values, attitudes, and beliefs were put forward, particularly in social service and community work programs. However, it was most noteworthy that, guided by theoretical values, teachers tried to resolve the problems of the community surrounding the school, as well as those of its members, in order to narrow the gap between education and work, between school and community, or between well-off and underprivileged community members. Simultaneously, fostering in students virtues arising from rationalism and an empirical, scientific attitude was seen to be desirable.

In the late 1970s, many people in India believed that the small number of vocationally productive work experiences for students was incapable of integrating the teaching and learning process. The Patel Committee approached the problem from the standpoint of the Gandhian philosophy of basic education. The committee's report emphasized the social usefulness of productive work offered by schools providing general education. It supported the view that socially useful productive work aimed at understanding the needs of a progressive, technology-based society. The learning process was to proceed by means of problem-solving that, at different stages, made use of observation, inquiry, experimentation, and practice (Ministry of Education & Social Welfare, 1977a, pp. 11, 13). The following points, as referred to in the 1977 report, illustrate that socially useful productive work aimed to:

- guide the planning, analysis, and detailed preparation of every phase of work;
- help understand the scientific principles and processes connected with various forms and settings of work in different physical and social environments;
- lead to the use of modern tools, materials, and techniques;
- promote equal opportunities for work and learning, that is, to narrow the gap between education and work, to eliminate the separation between school and the rest of the community, and to build a connection between affluent and disadvantaged members of the community; and
- offer economic and social programs inside and outside the classroom (Ministry of Education & Social Welfare, 1977a, pp. 11–13).

In the early 2000s and later, postcolonial education was also relevant to Indian education, which had a Hindu nationalist orientation and sought ways to adapt to both neoliberal social change and associated globalization efforts. In essence, the development was linked to the view that economic growth was possible through multinational enterprises and the technological innovations these possessed. Emphasizing economic values allowed for an enhancement in the usefulness of education and an increase in national prosperity. These values were related to the ideas of postcolonial educational aims, the grounds of which primarily supported the needs of a technology-based society.

At the same time, however, official reports continued to emphasize Gandhian educational aims and their value dimensions. Of these, a 2016 report by the Committee for Evolution of the New Education Policy argued that value education must be an integral part of the Indian education system. It stated that the essential purpose of value education is to promote equity, social justice, tolerance, and national integration into society. The core values for a well-established education system are truth (*satya*), righteous conduct (*dharma*), peace (*shanti*), love (*prem*), and nonviolence (*ahimsa*). Teachers, parents, and community leaders should have a crucial role in educating children and young people to respect these values. This should enable students to become responsible citizens of India in a globalized world (Ministry of Human Resource Development, 2016, pp. 169–170).

Indian work-related, community-based learning remained school-centered at the turn of the second millennium, and later, when intellectual aims continued to be emphasized in step with the ideology of social modernization. Using work experiences and socially useful productive work, educational authorities attempted to train experts for a technologically developing industrial society (see, e.g., NCERT, 1986, 1988a, 2000, 2005, 2009). Based on existing national curriculum documents, this form of education aimed to:

- develop the knowledge, skills, and attitudes that are connected to productive work in a modern society;
- help understand the facts, concepts, terms, and scientific principles linked with different forms and conditions of work;
- promote abilities needed for productive efficiency, that is, to acquire the skills of recognition, selection, planning, and development required to master both innovative methods and materials, as well as the skills of observation, dexterity, and participation needed for work practice;
- lead to an understanding of the use of tools and equipment in production and service processes, as well as to comprehend one's own role in productive situations; and
- offer work education programs inside and outside the school (NCERT, 1986, p. 18; NCERT, 1988a, pp. 28–29; NCERT, 2000, pp. 69–71, 95; Central Board of Secondary Education, 2004, pp. 5–6).

3.2.1   Summing Up

The conceptual features of postcolonialism presented in the Patel report (Ministry of Education & Social Welfare 1977a) can be examined from the perspective of community-based learning, again applying Hlebowitsh's (2007) classification. Doing so shows that, according to a postcolonial view, the ideal student is an observing, investigating, and experimenting problem-solver being introduced to the activities of vocationally productive work necessary in the community and participating in social service. The ideal curriculum embodies programs of socially useful productive work, with the vocationally productive units of study based on the application of scientific and technological principles and processes in and outside the school. The student is oriented toward an ideal democratic society that aims at secularism and social equality, the citizens of which work in scientifically and technologically advanced production.

This kind of postcolonial work education was also associated with education consistent with Hindu nationalist ideology at the beginning of the 21st century. Then, India attempted to adapt to neoliberal social change and related globalization aspirations. This economic and technological reform was guided by a neoliberal social doctrine that was realized as part of the World Bank's adjustment program (Kumar, 2004, pp. 116, 125). International neoliberal thinking continued to be seamlessly associated with globalization efforts.

Such an international economic order also required educational reforms that would allow it to maximally exploit the neoliberal economy. Efforts were taken to harness the school system to serve the needs of both international competition and increasing economic prosperity in society. Educators were expected to help students cope with the new challenges, threats, and opportunities resulting from this type of globalization process (Boers, 2007, pp. 109–110; Kamat, 2004, pp. 281–282). The new direction gave support to conservative thinking, similar to the United States outlined previously. This meant that the measurable success of the school and human capital growth were both linked to economic productivity and growth.

The following section deals with the essence of community-based learning in India in a more concrete manner. The nature of activities is studied from the perspective offered by central pedagogical approaches and their dimensions of the learning environment. The primary focus is on vocationally productive education.

4 Community-Based Pedagogical Ideas in India

4.1 *The Neo-Traditional School*

During the late 1930s, community-based learning in the Indian school included several kinds of pedagogical activities established in craft-related lessons and vocational activities within the school; working and social service in and visits and excursions to surrounding communities; and participation in local markets and festivals. The schooling was connected with real-life situations associated with the community's crafts and means of livelihood. The nature of this specific form of education showed considerable variation in different schools owing to such local and structural factors as conditions, preferences, and school types.

The Indian basic school had a strong presence, especially from around 1937 onward, when community-based learning emphasized a society-centered pattern with physical and sociomoral aims. Gandhi (1948d) regarded the ideal self-sufficient school as essentially a spinning and weaving institution with a cotton field attached to it. The instruction that it gives is connected on all levels with handicrafts, agriculture, or other possible lines of work provided by villages (Gandhi, 1948d, pp. 258–259; Gandhi, 1953, p. 36). Gandhi (1951) described that the entire work process in a school such as this—growing, picking, carding, spinning, and weaving cotton—was designed to train students in the specific abilities and methods for achieving a particular objective. During the various phases of the work, questions connected with the subjects were to be discussed in different ways. For example, elementary arithmetic was to be correlated with spinning and weaving so that the length of the spun thread was measured in yards, the correct number of threads was determined using hanks as the unit of measure, or the number of cross threads was calculated in the warp of a specific cloth (pp. 11–12). In this manner, basic school students familiarized themselves with different types of work methods, tools, and raw materials (Gandhi, 1937/1950b, p. 31; Gandhi, 1953, p. 35). They acquainted themselves with the traditional vocational activities required in the community, the bases of their procedures, and the different phases involved in the work processes (Gandhi, 1948d, p. 257; Gandhi, 1962, p. 59). At the same time, students developed the vocational abilities for earning their living (Gandhi, 1953, p. 36).

The Zakir Husain Committee report (1938) that came out of the Wardha Conference was centrally based on Gandhi's ideas concerning education. This report proposed that more than 3 hours of the 5-hour workday be available for individual and social practice for the work to be done in local handicrafts or agriculture. According to the report, every school is to choose a craft that is part of the life of the community, such as spinning and weaving, carpentry, agriculture, fruit and vegetable gardening, leatherwork, or other local work, as the basis of its instruction. The instruction is to be connected with the community's crafts and means of livelihood. The child's entire social and physical environment is to revolve around work. The various subjects in the curriculum are also to be correlated with the school's practical projects: social studies, natural sciences, mother tongue and Hindustani, mathematics, music, and drawing. In the same manner, schoolwork includes social service, excursions, and festivals (Zakir Husain Committee, 1938, pp. 16, 19–30, 40, 44, 48–49, 203).

A reform-pedagogical process paralleling that of the United States began in India in the 1940s when the neo-traditional school attempted to comprehensively integrate education and other social activity by utilizing the occupations and means of livelihood within the community. In addition to connecting teaching with the child's social and physical environment, it was also linked specifically to the community's traditional handicrafts and agriculture (see Zakir Husain Committee, 1938, p. 203). The students of the basic school worked under the supervision of a teacher in the local production offered by the school. In cotton-growing areas, the students spun yarn, wove cloth (*khadi*) and carpets, and sewed items of clothing. They made paper, books, and other paper products. In areas where leatherwork was possible, they made belts, purses, ladies' bags, cigarette cases, and slippers (*chapals*). In agricultural areas, the students worked in gardens and vegetable plots. They dug, leveled, and manured the soil; sowed seeds or planted seedlings; kept the ground moist; pulled up weeds; and destroyed harmful insects, in addition to bringing in and selling the harvest (for the learning activities in selected schools, see, e.g., Gandhi, 1962, p. 94; Kulkarni, 1940, pp. 126–128; Kulkarni, 1949b, pp. 97–99; Ministry of Education, 1956b, p. 29).

Indian words for handicrafts are *hastkala*, *hastshilp*, *dastkari*, and *karigari*. These all mean handiwork, but these also refer to objects made by craftspeople. Handicraft items are seldom merely decorative. Their true purpose is served when they are both useful and have nice forms (NCERT, 2008a, p. 7). The Ministry of Education and Scientific Research (1956a) defined basic education as "productive, creative and socially useful work in which all boys and girls may participate, irrespective of any distinction of caste or creed or class" (p. 2). This type of education is an education for life and through life. It intended to create a social order free from exploitation and violence (p. 2). The following brief summary, based on the government publication *Experiments in Primary and Basic Education* (1956b), further clarifies these different pedagogical activities. It shows how teachers and students in junior basic schools in the former state of Hyderabad in the late 1940s engaged in local crafts or other traditional work:

> In Hyderabad, junior basic school instruction was linked to local handicraft production. Gardening and growing vegetables were also typical areas of expertise. At Subzimandi Junior Basic School, spinning and weaving were chosen as the main crafts, with gardening as the auxiliary craft. Pottery was selected as the main craft at Kunta Road Junior Basic School. At Somjiguda Junior Basic School, the main crafts were sewing and making artificial flowers. At Adikamet Junior Basic School, carpentry was the main area, but since small boys were unable to carry heavy tools, cardboard work was taught in addition to carpentry. At Nala Kunta Junior Basic School, basket making was chosen as the main craft. At Choodi Bazar Junior Basic School, the main area was leatherwork (Ministry of Education, 1956b, p. 13).

The daily program of the basic school was to accord with the needs of the child and of the community. Solanki (1958) explained that the daily model program at the school encompassed comprehensive periods of work and study. In the morning, the students occupied themselves with handicrafts or some other manual work, such as a kitchen garden or agriculture. A period of work was followed by a period of integrating knowledge based on the processes and activities of the preceding work. In the afternoon, the students assembled for community spinning, which in turn was followed by a period of drill, review, and expressional work in accordance with the needs of each student (pp. 146–150).

The correlation formed the procedural core of the educational processes used at the basic school. The correlation techniques were composed of specific pedagogical fundamentals, even though they varied considerably at different institutes. Kulkarni (1949a) wrote that the local craft or the child's social and physical environment were taught in a multilateral correlation, thus a specific activity or item was arranged to correlate with as many other items as possible in the study of academic subjects. For example, on a rainy day when a child was carding with a bow and catgut, the catgut could break due to the humidity. This humidity-related incident was taken as the topic of instruction in the natural sciences, social studies, and arithmetic. In a unilateral correlation, the activity or circumstance of the local craft or the child's social and physical environment was correlated with one item in the curriculum, as, for example, when catgut breaks in humid air. The activity and the acquisition of knowledge took place simultaneously in a collateral correlation. For instance, when children wound yarn, they also counted its rounds. In this manner, learning and doing progressed in parallel (pp. 174–176).

The correlated craft-related activities naturally varied according to the students' readiness. As early as the lower classes, students learned to pick and clean cotton, gin and card, spin a simple manual spindle (*takli*), and, later, use a spinning wheel (*charkha*) according to the production process. When they were spinning, the students practiced poetry, sang songs, and listened to stories. After they finished spinning, they improvised plays and produced drawings dealing with spinning. They tended their plots and patches in the kitchen garden, measured their length and breadth, or studied geometric forms. In the upper classes, the students spun, wove cloth, and sewed garments in addition to carrying out more demanding horticultural and agricultural tasks. In conjunction with the work, they practiced the multiplication tables for the cardinal numbers and applied these skills to practical measuring. They wrote the most important information about their craft-related work and other school activities in their notebooks (for the learning activities in selected schools, see, e.g., Dutta, 1949, pp. 110–112; Pandit, 1949, p. 121; Salaamat-Ul-lah, 1949, p. 108). The following demonstrates the correlated craft-related processes in the basic schools of a district in Bihar in the 1940s:

> The basic schools of the village communities in the Champaran District chose spinning as their main craft. The students participated in the entire spinning process: cleaning the cotton, ginning, opening up the cotton, preparing it for spinning, carding and preparing slivers, as well as spinning on the *takli* and the *charkha*. They learned the names of the raw materials, the equipment used, and the finished products, and practiced

recognizing the count, strength, and evenness of yarn. They estimated
the maximum and minimum speed of spinning in class on a daily basis,
and calculated the average speed for the whole class for a day, week, fort-
night, month, and year, in addition to comparing the average speed of
the class with the speed prescribed in the syllabus. Likewise, they calculated the cost of the raw materials and supplies used as well as the daily,
weekly, and monthly earnings from spinning.

When they were spinning, the students sang songs about cotton, the
carding bow, the *takli*, and their work. After the period spent spinning,
they often presented short plays about the different phases of the work
or drew pictures of the equipment used during the work. They wrote in
their diaries what they had done or learned, and read what they had written to each other and to the teacher. The class monitor organized the
necessary equipment and supplies. At the end of the day, the students
cleaned their cupboards (*almirah*), their classroom, and the entire school
compound (Prasad, 1949, pp. 136–139).

Characteristics of the pedagogical activities included community-
centeredness and real-life content and themes, in addition to actively practicing
craft-related processes. The curriculum was based on correlating the subjects
and integrating the teaching, which meant that community-centeredness and
real-life content and themes, in addition to actively practicing craft-related processes, were characteristics of the pedagogical procedures. Within the school
context, the curriculum benefited from projects carried out independently or
cooperatively, from work-related lessons and vocational activities, and from
on-premises work and cultivating land near the school as forms of teaching
and learning. The projects carried out by basic school students were also oriented toward life outside of the school. During visits and field excursions,
the students could observe the activities of the surrounding community and
natural environment. They familiarized themselves with work in handicraft
workshops, at the bazaar, and at plantations. Similarly, they observed life in the
woods, fields, and plains.

The students took notes and compiled small-scale reports; studied the special features of clothing, food, hygiene, and housing; examined the development of cultivated plants; and observed the influence of the seasons on the
harvest. Project assignments were related to local history, marketing, and different kinds of productive processes; students participated in the traditional
festivals of the community and had the opportunity to acquaint themselves
with the fascinating multiplicity of the tribes inhabiting the Himalayas (for
the learning activities in selected schools, see, e.g., Prasad, 1949, pp. 142–144,

147–148; Subbarao, 1958, p. 85). The following overview exemplifies the pedagogical applications of field excursions that basic school students made in the
Poona District, Maharashtra:

> The students of the Tilak Maharashtra Vidyapith Basic School, in the
> Poona District, Maharashtra, familiarized themselves with the natu-
> ral environment, sources of livelihood, and the life of the villages. They
> observed the behavior of birds and animals in nature, acquainted them-
> selves with agriculture in the fields, and studied the traditional customs
> and festivals of the villagers. During their field excursions, they had the
> opportunity to learn not only the characteristics of the laws of nature but
> also about the regularities of life more comprehensively (Sardal, 1949, pp.
> 114, 116–117).

Work and service activities, study visits, field trips, and festivals were the
main pedagogical approaches included in the out-of-school context. Using
these methods, the neo-traditional school integrated itself with society in a
planned and coordinated manner. Its function can thus be seen as the process
of social transformation. Students became familiar with using local traditional
methods, work tools, and raw materials in order to strengthen the entire Indian
preindustrial agrarian society. The properties of such procedures were justified
by the Gandhian idea of truth (*satya*) and nonviolence (*ahimsa*). This comprehensively encompassed the systems of concepts referring to humankind
and, more widely, the values guiding the lives of the individual and society,
and beliefs concerning the world. Schools made efforts to raise the vocationally productive work processes of community-based learning and associated
meanings, especially emphasizing traditional Indian cultural values rather
than material values as a strategy for helping India attain social and economic
self-sufficiency.

Social service activities within the school curriculum also targeted, at their
best, social transformation, with attempts at raising the quality of housing,
health, and hygiene; stimulating economic life; or promoting literacy (for the
pedagogical activities in selected schools, e.g., see Arunachalam, 1949, p. 103;
Devi, 1940, pp. 183–185; Salamatullah, 1970, pp. 38, 71–72). For example, the
basic school students in the villages of the Champaran District, Bihar, studied
local housing conditions under the guidance of their teacher. They discovered
that the local houses were mostly made of bamboo, with thatched roofs and no
windows, and lacked any planned layout or systematic arrangement of the inte-
rior. During this learning process, they realized that the houses easily caught
fire, but that they could be protected during the hot season from dangerous

east-west winds by building them in a north-south direction (Prasad, 1949, p. 143). Thus, the students, besides understanding that simple innovations could prevent the houses from catching fire each year, also understood how changes affecting the whole society could be based on Indian national cultural values and customs. This type of social service was intended to benefit the school and community in many ways. The following illustrates some of the pedagogical applications of social service that teachers and their students carried out in selected schools in Gujarat, Bihar, and Rajasthan:

> The students of the Thamna village school in Gujarat were responsible for the cleanliness of the school building and the surrounding community, in addition to arranging evening prayers and telling the participants the news of the day (Parikh, 1940, pp. 178–179). The students at Mihijam Senior Basic School in Santhal Pargana, Bihar, constructed soak pits for sewage removal and trench latrines for preparing manure in the nearby villages, in addition to explaining the importance of manure to the villagers. The students at Gram Vidyalaya School in Suwana, near Bhilwara, Rajasthan, took part in various kinds of postal services: acquiring postcards, envelopes, and money order forms for the public; writing letters for the villagers who were illiterate; and ensuring that everything to be sent was taken to the Bhilwara post office (Salamatullah, 1970, pp. 10, 71).

The Productive Dimension of the learning environment characteristic of craft-related education was accentuated in pedagogical activities in which students worked at the school's spinning and weaving facilities; in the leather, pottery, and other workshops; at the cowshed (*goshala*), dairy, or its store; and areas under cultivation. For example, the students of the national school in Rajkot, Gujarat, ran a dairy and produced nutritive foodstuffs, such as hand-ground flour, hand-pounded rice, pulses, and pure *ghani* oil (Gandhi, 1962, pp. 93–94), and the students at Gram Vidyalaya School in Suwana, Rajasthan, worked in the school's cowshed, store, and bank (Salamatullah, 1970, pp. 69, 72).

The Sociocultural Dimension was particularly prioritized when the students were acquainted with work linked to the processes of craft-related education at the community bazaar and plantations, or when they were involved in social service at the local markets and festivals, or within such contexts as the sanitation program and construction projects (for pedagogical activities, see, e.g., Prasad, 1949, pp. 143–144). Such emphasis could still be seen with the establishment of the first multipurpose higher secondary schools in the mid-1950s, when the modernization process was launched in India. Even if cooperation between the multipurpose school and the community tended to be modest in scale (D'Souza & Chaudhury, 1965, p. 121), there were Indian schools that were in contact with the local culture, attempting to promote its traditions and means of livelihood. The following clarifies the manner in which the Sociocultural Dimension was emphasized in the pedagogical activities of social service at one multipurpose higher secondary school in Rajasthan:

> In 1959, a multipurpose higher secondary school was established in the town of Rajgarh. The students of the school participated in community activities, developed the conditions at the school, and supplied articles produced by the craft-related courses to commercial outlets for sale. In the community, they ran the drinking water huts at the Jagannathji fair (*Jagannathji mela*), guided pilgrims, and maintained general order. The school orchestra played in the fair chariot (*mela rath*) and at various events arranged by the rural local government (*panchayat samiti*). In the school area, the students participated in constructing roads and an open-air theater, in addition to assuming responsibility for the cleanliness of the playgrounds. They bound books, dipped candles, and produced articles for sale in handcraft and tailoring classes. In the evenings, they held literacy courses for the inhabitants of the community (Salamatullah, 1970, pp. 62–65).

4.1.1   Challenges

Despite the fact that neo-traditional schools were developed in many places in the various Indian states, with the activities of community-based learning discussed in the preceding being implemented in many schools, the country has probably had a large number of such schools at which the correlation-based, craft-related instruction was at a low level or primarily followed traditional methods of instruction (see, e.g., Subbarao, 1958, pp. 145, 154; Thomas, 1970, pp. 240–241). The problems associated with teaching were the consequences of the low level of teacher education and the inadequate teaching facilities and equipment (see, e.g., Subbarao, 1958, pp. 13–15, 154). The Assessment Committee on Basic Education (Ministry of Education, 1956a) observed that the aims of basic education in prevailing school practices were not realized either, this being a consequence of deficiencies in teaching material, equipment, and buildings. Insufficient teacher training also played a part in the fact that most instruction was teacher-centered. The old-style primary schools continued as such but were named basic schools (pp. 20–23). Serious difficulties in comprehensively realizing neo-traditional education resulted from such factors as insufficient curriculum planning and implementation, the rise of new national economic strategies, the alienating impact of urbanization, and the overall weakening of neo-traditional educational thinking. With such starting points, according to Holmes and McLean (1989) the implementation of neo-traditional education encountered the following obstacles:

- The neo-traditional schools, most of which offered only 5 years of instruction, were unable to change their curriculum in the direction of vocational education. At the same time, the students finishing school at the age of 11 lacked the maturity to begin working for a living.
- The broad economic strategy-based reforms of the central administration weakened the local self-reliant activities of the rural areas to which the neo-traditional education could have been linked. Many of the manual occupations associated with craft-related education, such as spinning and weaving, actually seemed irrelevant from the perspective of economic development.
- The extension of neo-traditional education from the rural areas to the city and from children to young adults was an insurmountable challenge. In particular, various demographic segments in large cities felt no connection with Gandhian neo-traditional education, as it was based on a rural mode of life.
- The teachers and other academics were broadly opposed to the neo-traditional school curricula. Basic education in particular was considered to be only preparation for the secondary and higher education that would offer better opportunities to access salaried occupations (pp. 156–157).

4.2   The Neocolonial and Postcolonial Schools

In the mid-1960s, India implemented changes in pedagogy comparable to those taking place in the United States. This shift had a strong impact on the quality of the methods used in community-based learning. Starting specifically with the *Second Five Year Plan* (1956–1961), the new thinking about India's economic policy attempted to initiate a phase whose goal was to industrialize and urbanize the country, essentially following the model provided by the Soviet Union (see Planning Commission, 1956, p. 51). Neocolonial and postcolonial forms of education were required to participate in accelerating a scientific and technological developmental path in order to increase the productive capacity of the national economy. This might mean that overcoming such an exceptionally difficult challenge could require an effort to make schools into learning centers with only limited contact with society.

For the purpose of accelerating Indian modernization, the country's social and educational goal was to prepare intellectually capable workers for a modern society characterized by secularism and social equality. In order to reorient the craft-related programs of the basic school, the authorities responsible for educational planning wanted to develop work-experience programs, the productive processes of which were to be based on the application of science and technology, ultimately for the industrialization of the country (see Ministry of Education, 1966, pp. 7–8). The strong requirement to educate intellectually capable workers for a society utilizing new technology and science naturally also reinforced the procedures of a school-centered pattern of community-based learning.

The Kothari Commission (1966) proposed that work experience should be an integrated part of education at all stages. Work experience is productive work that can be arranged at school, at the school workshop, at local farms, or in industrial and commercial establishments. The work-experience activities assume a higher degree of diversity and difficulty in accordance with the students' abilities. At the same time, work, to an ever-increasing degree, moved to real-life situations outside the school, to locations such as farms when harvesting and sowing, family production units, or later to vocational activities in agricultural and industrial production at the secondary stage. Although productive work-experience education can continue to be constructed around agriculture in rural areas, and an attempt can be made to provide schools with gardens in urban areas, the report considers reorienting work education programs that utilize science and technology to meet the needs of a changing society to be essential. Thus the schools should make an effort to implement programs favoring industry and simple technology closely associated with the spirit of an advanced stage of development and modernization (Ministry of Education, 1966, pp. 7, 201–202, 613).

The Curriculum for the Ten-Year School (1975) was based on the educational ideas presented in the Kothari Commission report. According to this curriculum, work-experience programs should be included in teaching in order to effect the educational modernization of the ten-year school. These would deal with the various processes, modern techniques, and tools, as well as with the underlying scientific principles, involved in the technological development of modern society. Work experiences should be integrated into the entire curriculum so that five periods of 30 to 40 minutes a week are available in Grades 6 to 10 for work-experience education. The curriculum also stated that the areas of work included are to be guided by local needs, and they should be selected on the basis of a community survey. Local experts, such as artisans and mechanics, would provide input to the realization of the program (NCERT, 1975, pp. 18–19, 30). The procedures to be used in a school-centered pattern of community-based learning of this type varied considerably in different schools, not only according to local conditions but also depending on whether the schools had the necessary teaching equipment and materials, or appropriately trained teachers.

Work-experience programs began to be implemented gradually and in an uncoordinated manner in the Indian schools providing general education. In some states the Departments of Education required the schools to include work-experience programs in their teaching. In some areas of the country, the schools began their work-experience programs with no set guidelines. Programs were adapted to other teaching and were also arranged outside the school, even during summer vacation. The programs usually lasted from one to 3 hours a week. Primary and middle school students in particular were most often involved in indigenous craft-related activities: spinning and weaving, clay work, gardening, and agriculture. Only in a few primary and middle schools did they take part in more modern work-experience activities, such as repairing electrical and mechanical equipment, printing, or food preservation. Some activities were restricted to specific areas, for example, the students at the schools in Haryana made ink, those at the schools in Goa, Daman, and Diu made laboratory equipment, while those at the schools in Karnataka produced printed materials (Ministry of Education & Social Welfare, 1977b, pp. 9–10, 12).

A firm belief developed that Indian society could become a modern industrial society only if students worked within an environment that applied technological processes, where they could become familiar with the use of modern tools, devices, and materials. This justified the manner in which the Scientific-Technical and Scientific-Agricultural Dimensions to community-based learning were also emphasized in the learning environment. For example, in work-experience education, the students could work in school workshops that made laboratory supplies and ink, or they could familiarize themselves with the latest techniques and scientific achievements at the community's experimental farm (for work-experience activities, see, e.g., Ministry of Education & Social Welfare, 1977b, p. 10). Even though science- and technology-centered work-experience programs were still rare in the mid-1970s, there were schools in India where an effort was made to incorporate productive processes, modern tools, techniques, and the scientific principles underlying them. The following summary demonstrates how teachers at Buharu School accentuated the Scientific-Agricultural Dimension in work-experience education programs in Ajmer District, Rajasthan:

> During the mid-1970s, the teachers of the Buharu School encouraged their students to study characteristics of plant habitats. The students planted different species of trees in the area of the village, took care of them, and tried to protect them from damage caused by animals. They examined why certain trees did not grow in the area and what influence the trees might have on the climate. An expert visited the school and presented

various techniques for testing the soil and water, demonstrating in practice the necessity of testing for agricultural production. The students brought samples of soil from the land that their parents were cultivating to take to the laboratory at Tilonia. They familiarized themselves with the latest agricultural techniques and scientific achievements, such as hybrid varieties of maize and millet (*bajra*) on the village experimental farm. The teacher and other experts guided them in a meticulous study of the reasons why Rajasthan was becoming semiarid and the measures to take to arrest this development (Roy, 1980, pp. 369, 373–374, 376).

About a decade after the publication of the comprehensive Kothari report (Ministry of Education, 1966), the Patel Committee report (Ministry of Education & Social Welfare, 1977a) published its influential document assessing education. This report further provided a detailed examination of the nature of community-based learning in light of the Gandhian philosophy of basic education, although now from a new school-centered approach emphasizing problem-solving. The Patel report recommended that socially useful productive work should be given a central position in the curricula for all levels of school instruction. This would ensure that the content of academic subjects would, as far as possible, be related to the procedures of work-centered instruction. Social service is also to be allied with productive work. From Grades 1 to 4 (or Grade 5), 20 percent of the teaching time is available for socially useful productive work. From Grades 5 (or Grade 6) to 10 or 6 hours a week are to be used for socially useful productive work and community service. Additionally, from Grades 8 (or Grade 9) to 10, the arts, such as music, dancing, and painting, can be replaced with 2 hours a week of studies in subjects such as home economics, agriculture, and commerce (Ministry of Education & Social Welfare, 1977a, pp. 7–8).

The Patel Committee (1977a) proposed that work-centered instruction be based on community-based project activities that become more difficult and more diversified as the grade level increases. The projects of productive work and services would be selected from among six areas: health and hygiene, food, shelter, clothing, culture and recreation, and community work and social service. Work situations could be at home, in the school, and in the community, but the teaching programs had to be based on local conditions (Ministry of Education & Social Welfare, 1977a).

Nevertheless, program planning was not only the teachers' responsibility, but appropriate district and local committees were to provide the schools with plans and programs as well as consider their feasibility in practice. However, it was essential that the learning process for socially useful productive work proceed through problem-solving: (a) First the students explore the world of work through observations and inquiry, (b) then they experiment with various materials, tools, and techniques, and (c) finally they participate in work practice. During this process, the students should be aware of their own needs and the problems related to them when they try to solve the required task under the teacher's guidance. For this reason the schools should establish an evaluation system that can help the students improve their performance and which the teachers can utilize when assessing learning (Ministry of Education & Social Welfare, 1977a, pp. 11–15).

The students of schools worked under the guidance of the teacher and most often in pairs or in groups in the different situations of socially useful productive work and community service at home, at school, and in the community. In the lower grades, they mostly helped with work-centered activities, handling simple materials and tools; in the first-grade classes especially the activities could be based on creative expression. In the upper grades, they studied increasingly challenging activities, in which case the programs also followed the contents of the subject-matter areas of the curriculum more closely. The students worked in the school office, library, medical room, workshops, garden, and areas under cultivation. They offered repair services to the community for electronic devices and electrical gadgets, made teaching aids for nonformal education centers, and drew up exhibition materials on nutrition, sanitation, and health for the slums. The students adapted modern methods and processes for plant care on the cultivated lands. They helped at the local schools, hospitals, institutes for the visually disabled, and nonformal educational centers.

The Sociocultural Dimension of the learning environment was significant in both of these approaches, as students became familiar through work-experience education with such functions as working at the community clinic, temple, or village council, as well as when helping in socially useful productive work at the community's special education institutes, nonformal educational centers, and slum areas, or in social service with construction projects and festivals (for the pedagogical activities in one school, see, e.g., Kumar, 1991, p. 122). The following summaries exemplify the pedagogical applications of work-experience education that were carried out at the Buharu village school in Rajasthan and social service that was carried out in Ramakrishna Mission Vidyalaya Secondary School in Tamil Nadu. These descriptions show two different ways in which the teachers applied the Sociocultural Dimension in their community-based educational programs:

The students of Buharu School in Ajmer, Rajasthan, studied the structure and functioning of the village council (*panchayat*). Aided by a teacher, the students sought information about the village council, including its structure, electoral terms, and voting procedures. They interviewed the secretary of the village council, who visited the school and explained the council's taxation practices, how it implemented decisions, and its general responsibilities and functions. Additionally, as a digression, the students became acquainted with historical changes in the administration of the village. They studied the pre-independence methods of the local and regional administration when Rajasthan was still governed by a king and its villages governed by his representatives. Finally, using this information, the students wrote a study in which they analyzed the number of representatives in their constituency, the number of adults eligible to vote in their own families, the strength of the particular group representation, and voting turnout. The study was later utilized in their own election process at school (Roy, 1980, pp. 374–375).

In the mid-1970s at Ramakrishna Mission Vidyalaya Secondary School, located near Coimbatore, Tamil Nadu, the educational program emphasized social service. The Vidyalaya students participated in repairing the damage caused by storms and floods in the vicinity of the school. They built a new road as well as inexpensive housing for members of the casteless (*harijan*) colony inhabitants. They also dug a pond for storing rainwater that could percolate into the surrounding wells. Every year, the students participated in arranging and coordinating the Sri Ramakrishna Festival. Because this religious and social celebration attracted more than 30,000 visitors to the locality, it offered many kinds of work experiences and service activities for several months (Tillman, 1976, pp. 44–46).

Despite the emphasis on science and technology in the learning environment, the government's educational policy also favored the Scientific-Agricultural Dimension. This was particularly evident in socially useful productive work, such as undertakings in scientific cultivation projects. Sometimes the schools could apply this type of instruction to production at the camps for work or social service (for a school-specific program, see, e.g., Singh, 1998, pp. 15–16). The students at a village school in Kaira District, Gujarat, were involved in work in an environment that applied technological processes and that used modern tools, devices, and materials. The following overview illustrates the pedagogical applications of a scientific cultivation project carried out at this village school in the late 1970s in which the teachers created an authentic work and production learning environment where students could cultivate plants using scientific processes:

The educational program in the late 1970s at Vallabh Vidyalaya School in the village of Bochasan, near Borsad Taluka, emphasized work-centered education and community service. The core of the school's educational program comprised socially useful productive work that took up more than 25 percent of the teaching time. The secondary school students studied the cultivation of eggplant (*brinjal*) in their agricultural studies. They first set objectives for the eggplant-growing project, made plans for its various phases, and used the relevant literature to familiarize themselves with the different plant varieties. In the practical cultivation work, they applied scientific cultivation techniques for the 13 different varieties they grew from seed, utilizing modern fertilizers and pesticides. In their notes, they documented the measures that they took and their experiences. The project ended with the students, under the teacher's direction, assessing the degree to which the set objectives had been achieved (Buch & Patel, 1979, pp. 107, 109–113).

The camps for work and social service offer a different type of application of the Sociocultural Dimension compared to what was previously described. The following summary exemplifies the activities of the camping program for work and social service in some urban schools in Rajasthan in the late 1980s. Here, the attempt was to link vocationally productive work experiences to socially useful productive work as well as to the relevant curriculum content areas. The students made surveys and reports on such topics as handicrafts, home industries, and local agricultural products:

> In the late 1980s, the Ajmer city schools' camp program, which was based on work experiences and socially useful productive work, included not only community service but also studies in the authentic environment related to nature and culture. The Board of Secondary Education proposed a camp program for the schools with a specific schedule each day as well as detailed instructions for items such as materials, the campsite, and forming student groups. The students from Grades 9 and 10 stayed at the camp for 5 days, in which the program's themes entailed community service, surveying and collection work, a national integration project, and cultural and recreational activities. In the survey and collection work, the students studied nature and culture in small groups or individually. They conducted surveys and prepared reports about issues concerning the environment, social problems, and the local sources of livelihood, such as handicrafts, home industries, and agricultural products. They collected many kinds of objects—plant leaves and roots, insects, and bird feathers and nests—as well as different types of stones to supplement the school's natural science collections (Srivastava, 1991, pp. 100–102).

With the onset of the 1990s, the new trends in national education policy continued to emphasize the experiential nature and social usefulness of the work education offered by the general education schools. Several documents from the late 1980s and the early 2000s provided input for the compilation of improved curricula and syllabuses (see, e.g., NCERT, 1986, 1988b, 1988c, 2000, 2001, 2005, 2006b). Additionally, guides, textbooks, and instructional materials were published (see, e.g., NCERT, 1988a, 1989, 2008b; Patel, 1988; Tynan, 2009). In 1986, about a quarter of primary and secondary schools in India offered their students work-experience activities. About 10 percent of the secondary schools had vocational courses in Grades 11 and 12. A small number (approx. 4%) arranged on-the-job training (NCERT, 1992, pp. 833, 1272–1273). Less than 10 years later, possibly as many as a third of the primary schools and, correspondingly, almost 70 percent of the secondary schools offered activities that consisted of work-experience education and socially useful productive work (NCERT, 1998, p. 303).

A national longitudinal study (Yadav, 2011) investigated the implementation of the ten-year school curriculum during this reform period. This study showed that in 15 states the work education programs implemented at the secondary stage were termed "work experience" and in the other 12 states "socially useful productive work." In Uttarakhand, they were known as "work experience and entrepreneurship." In Tamil Nadu, these programs were called "life-oriented education" and in Chandigarh both "socially useful productive work" and "work experience" (pp. VIII, 96).

The most popular work-experience activities were in Delhi's sample schools (N=90), for instance, gardening, meal planning, and commercial arts (Sehgal, 2001, pp. 55, 74–75). The new trends evident at the turn of the present century included computer-assisted programs (see, e.g., Central Board of Secondary Education, 1991, 2004), but an effort was also made to use traditional methods for orienting teaching outside of school (see, e.g., N.C.E.RT., 2006a, 2008a), where teaching was connected with practical work and activities within the crafts and life of the surrounding community, thus reflecting Gandhian educational thinking.

This chapter has shown that programs familiarizing students with socially useful productive work outside the school most often included service-centered activities and emphasized the Sociocultural or Productive Dimensions (for the service-centered activities in one school, see, e.g., Chowdhury, 2005, p. 3; Kuthiala, 2007, p. 3). However since the 1990s, the science- and technology-centered programs of socially useful productive work held an alternative dimension in their pedagogical procedures. These programs prioritized the Scientific-Technical Dimension when students worked in school shops repairing electronic devices and electrical equipment, doing electrical jobs, or producing computer-aided publications (for the Socially Useful Product Work [SUPW] programs in one school, see, e.g., Narayanan, 2001, p. 88). This overview provides an example of a program of socially useful productive work in Dehradun, Uttarakhand, in the early 21st century. The teachers and students of one boarding school worked with modern computers and computer-controlled devices in the new learning environment:

> The program in the early 2000s for socially useful productive work at Doon School contained a comprehensive alternative for publishing activities. The secondary school students participated in the entire publication process nearly independently: they wrote, reported, and published. Although only working 2 hours a week, they produced many types of printed matter using modern computers and computer-controlled devices. Computer programs enabled them to draw tables and graphic designs as well as to edit photographs. A desktop publishing program allowed them to transform the layouts on the computer display into different types of publications, ranging from simple announcements to full books. In addition to producing a conventional yearbook, the students also produced other periodicals, such as the school's special publications: *The Doon School Information Review, The Academic Journal*, and the biannual scientific *Prayas, Arpan, The Echo*, and *Cosmos*. The school's weekly magazine, *The Doon School Weekly (DSW)*, which has been published since 1936, now also appears in an international Internet version (Dhillon, 2006, p. 1; The Doon School, n.d., pp. 2, 15–16, 19).

4.2.1   Challenges

Despite the fact that the Indian neocolonial and postcolonial schools had access to more resources than the neo-traditional school had during the 1940s and 1950s, the turn of the millennium witnessed the most difficult contextual issues facing the country, specifically rapid population growth and persistent poverty. Even with the existence of large cities, the majority of the Indian population continued to live in the countryside, which was also reflected in huge disparities in education and income. Government guidelines for a new economic policy started to favor an urban way of life. This kind of thinking tended to marginalize work-experience education and socially useful productive work in the themes covered at school, with emphasis being placed instead on textbook-centered teaching, year- and term-end entrance examinations, and specific school levels (for the time allotted for work-based education, see, e.g., Yadav, 2011, p. 121).

From the 1980s, the economic and technological reform that India attempted to implement was connected to the reorganization of the world economy, being undertaken as a component of the World Bank's structural adjustment program. This is partly why the Indian school institutions started to be harnessed to international competition and the pursuit of economic wealth, particularly since the turn of the present century. The educational policies based on a businesslike operational culture have also faced opposition in India (see, e.g., NCERT, 2005, pp. 9–10, 125). The new educational policy developed in the context of a neoliberal social doctrine, intertwining global economic, political, and ecological issues.

Strongly accelerating globalization has created new challenges for education policy in India. Globalization is confronting the national school systems with a wide range of serious and intertwined problems, including commercialization, competition, brain drain, cultural diversity, inequality, social exclusion, and loss of resources (see, e.g., Neubauer, 2007, pp. 36–48). Kubow and Fossum (2007) pointed out that among many other responsibilities, an important challenge for a school system is helping students understand both the common cultural, social, economic, and political convergence of the globalizing environment and its divergence (p. 295).

Many Indian teachers felt that the new school reforms were incapable of supporting their work in the community-based parts of the curricula. As American teachers earlier, they came to this conclusion because the teaching and learning process, which focused on academic knowledge and learning, actually emphasized the teacher-directed transmission of knowledge. The curriculum development for socially useful productive work proved to be inadequate because the schools lacked qualified teachers. Untrained teachers were also incapable of motivating students to engage in long-term activities. Similar to the United States, insufficient economic resources limited practical efforts to develop community-based learning. The opportunities for acquiring teaching material or financing for field trips were limited. Many schools did not even offer the appropriate equipment, furniture, or work premises (for a closer examination of the barriers to teaching work-experience education, see, e.g., Ruhela, 2006, p. 98; Sehgal, 2001, pp. 212–213).

CHAPTER 4

Ideals for Learning in Communities in the Russian Empire

Abstract

The aim of this chapter is to analyze the early foundations of community-based learning with a focus on the philosophical views, educational aims, and associated value dimensions in the Russian Empire. In addition, this chapter aims to examine the nature of the pedagogical activities in the Russian Empire, while the primary focus is on tsarist education. This chapter suggests that the ideas of society-centered education in Russia are founded on the educational writings of Peter the Great. The ideal educational program of the Petrine Revolution included training for various occupations, which develops students' character and improves the centralized tradition of the society. This chapter shows that Vissarion Belinsky, Alexander Herzen, Nikolay Chernyshevsky, Nikolay Dobrolyubov, Konstantin Ushinsky, and Leo Tolstoy were the most prominent political and social Russian thinkers who influenced school education in society. This chapter demonstrates that tsarist education emphasized sociomoral and intellectual aims and accentuated Western European ideals and their value dimensions. These values were prioritized together with economic and martial principles and their value dimensions. Traditional values provided by the Orthodox Church were also essential in the governmental life of the tsarist culture of the time. This type of tsarist school had a tendency to emphasize the Sociocultural, Practical-Agricultural, and Horticultural Dimensions of its learning environments in community-based learning. The study concludes that the mid-19th-century school reform provided an opportunity to develop not only school education but also teacher training and tried to make the Russian education system solidify social structure.

Keywords

philosophy – aims – values – practices – community-based learning – pedagogical activities – pedagogical approaches – learning environments – tsarist education – Russian Empire

1   Philosophical Views

Vissarion Belinsky (1811–1848), Alexander Herzen (1812–1870), Nikolay Cherny-shevsky (1828–1889), Nikolay Dobrolyubov (1836–1861), Konstantin Ushinsky (1824–1870), and Leo Tolstoy (1828–1910) were the most prominent political and social Russian thinkers in the 19th century who influenced school education in society. Belinsky suggested that education and life, school and society, and knowledge and experience should be intertwined. Herzen stated that the primary function of education is to educate a human and free individual who, with an interest in society, strives to change it. Herzen can be considered the most notable pre-Marxist philosopher of dialectical materialism (Zajda, 1980, pp. 3–5).

Feuerbach's materialism, Rousseau's rationalism, and English utilitarianism influenced Chernyshevsky's and Dobrolyubov's education ideas. In their view, upbringing must make use of work, the basis of all human activity. Cherny-shevsky believed that humane moral, psychological, and social characteristics are shaped mainly by the environment. Dobrolyubov amplified the importance of appreciating, understanding, and taking into account the child's personality, character, and abilities (Zajda, 1980, pp. 6–7). Ushinsky (1975) opposed abstract and theoretical pedagogies that were not connected with real life. Instead, he argued that labor is important for human physical, mental, and moral development. This type of true education combines learning, knowledge, and life. Ushinsky's educational ideas provided the basis for the teaching methods in the early Soviet school (Ushinsky, 1975, pp. 216, 232). Tolstoy accentuated free-dom, independence, and creativity in school education in general and in labor education in particular. In 1859, he opened a one-room school for peasant chil-dren at his Yasnaya Polyana estate. In 1861, he set up a three-room school and employed a few teachers to help him. Cohen (1981) describes Tolstoy's educa-tional ideas on freedom:

> On the door of his school, Tolstoy hung a sign "Enter and Leave Freely."
> He demanded total freedom for the pupil, out of respect for the person-
> hood of small children. In his words, there is no other way to influence
> children except through an understanding of their minds, their talents,
> their characteristics and personalities. Such an understanding can come
> about only when children are given freedom of movement and expres-
> sion, so that they can explore their inner world in a spontaneous man-
> ner, through work and activity out of free choice and self-awareness.
> (p. 243)

1.1   *Aims and Values*

Russia's earliest educational history was related to the Eastern Orthodox Church and its Moscow Patriarchate tradition. The church did missionary work and developed the literacy of church officials. Outside the Orthodox Church, the brotherhood schools, for instance, were founded in western Russia and maintained by urban citizens (Hans, 1963, p. 5). Hosking (2011) reported that in 1685 the Slavic-Greek-Latin Academy was opened in the Zaikonospassky Monastery in Moscow. Its curriculum included Latin, Greek, grammar, rhetoric, poetry, physics, and theology (p. 177).

The ideas of society-centered education in Russia may well be found in the educational writings of Peter the Great (Peter I) (1672–1725). The reform-minded emperor regarded education as vocational training, the aim of which was the social use of scientific, military, and technical skills (Zajda, 1980, pp. 1–2). In 1714, Peter I ordered the opening of "numbers schools," which provided technical programs (Shevchenko et al., 2018, pp. 227–228). We can interpret that this kind of thinking promotes exceptional views on the role of education in society and on the nature of the interrelationship between education and society at that time.

It would be correct to call Peter I the founder of the Russian educational tradition, as he began Russia's scientific and practical school system. Hans (1963) wrote that after Peter I returned from England in 1700, he directly subordinated the church to the secular government, founded the School of Mathematics and Navigation in Moscow in 1701, and established a medical school in Moscow in 1707 with a five-year course to train physicians and surgeons. Moreover, in establishing the secular and scientific school system, Peter I combined common European features with Russian ones. The synthesis of European culture with the Russian national character later developed into the Russian tradition in education (pp. 6–7).

Peter I had difficulties finding students who were literate enough for his schools and who would not waste their time on something other than learning. However, as elements of culture and social grace penetrated the curriculum, schools became more accepted. The nobility especially understood that education and culture were a way out for the lower social classes. The establishment of the Cadet Corps was an extension of this tendency. The Cadet Corps centered on school, regiment, state service, and landed estates (Hosking, 2011, p. 207). Hosking (2011) describes the benefits of these schools in detail:

> The graduates spoke French and were ready to become full-fledged European diplomats, to assume command in the army, or to supervise a whole district administration. To supplement their qualifications, some young

nobles where sent abroad to study, usually at German universities, from which the more serious-minded brought back German attitudes to learning and public service, at first on Pietist, later on post-Kantian idealist models. (p. 207)

Peter I also opened Russia's first public library and first museum in Saint Petersburg. Similarly, he sponsored expeditions to remote regions to prospect, make maps, and report on natural resources (Hosking, 2011, p. 208). Tsarist education of this kind aimed to:

- educate students to learn European languages, sciences, and mathematics;
- train students for such occupations as navigators, physicians, surgeons, clerics, engineers, civil servants, teaches, and craftsmen; and
- combine European culture with the Russian national character (Hans, 1963, pp. 6–7; Hosking, 2011, p. 177).

This type of tsarist education emphasized sociomoral and intellectual aims in the integration of physical, sociomoral, and intellectual education. Through these aims, the tsarist education accentuated Western European ideals and their value dimensions by favoring European educational institutions and their curricula. These values were prioritized together with economic and martial principles and their value dimensions. Traditional values provided by the Orthodox Church were also essential in the governmental life of the tsarist culture of the time. The ultimate goal was related to socioethical values that would contribute to the development of a Western European societal order that would accentuate a scientific and practical school system. It was intended to break down the prejudice between manual and intellectual work so that well-educated people would become Western European citizens who could achieve the virtues needed in goal-directed activities, such as courage and resilience that arise from universal values.

Price (1977) explicated that in the late 1700s, Empress Catherine the Great (Catherine II) (1729–1796) created a parallel state school system based on the Austrian education system. Gymnasiums (high schools) led to the universities, while other schools provided training for lower-class work in industry and agriculture, with the different tracks being separated from each other (p. 76). Catherine II reigned over Russia for more than 30 years (1762–1796), and during that time increased Russian involvement in the political and cultural life of Europe. From the moment she took power, Catherine II demonstrated an interest in education.

In 1763, Catherine II appointed I. I. Betskoy (1703–1799), who had visited educational establishments abroad, as her principal adviser on education. On March

12, 1764, Betskoy presented the *General Plan for the Education of Young People of Both Sexes*, which Catherine II approved and published. The principles of this plan were to be applied in all Russian educational institutions. The aim was to create a new kind of person, which "could only be achieved by isolating the child completely from the age of five to twenty-one from the harmful influences of parents and an illiterate, brutal and corrupt society" (De Madariaga, 1979, p. 376). Schools were to emphasize the creation of good citizens and humans, not professional and vocational training. Two years later, Betskoy presented a follow-up plan that focused on the physical in educating children from birth to youth. The instruction was to focus on such aspects as hygiene, simplicity, fresh air, loose clothing, and low-heeled shoes, regulations that were intended to accentuate didactic matters. These educational plans were distributed to all relevant government offices in the country and to the Eastern Orthodox Holy Synod. In reality, it was difficult to implement these plans in such a vast country, as Catherine II had earlier admitted that it was impossible for the state to provide universal education (De Madariaga, 1979, pp. 373, 375–376).

Alston (1969) noted that Catherine II was the first Russian monarch "to devote attention to the systematic education of the rulers themselves" (p. 15). Alston describes Catherine II's efforts toward public education through developing projects:

> In the first decade of her reign Catherine II exploited what opportunities were available for organizing the education of Russia's ruling class. The peasant mass, however, was fatally neglected. The sovereign herself remained sensitive to the need for introducing the prerequisites of civilized life into the outlying villages and back country communes. From the 1760's to the 1780's the rough drafts of her many scholastic schemes contained provisions for offering elementary opportunities to the countryside. For a moment, a first step seemed possible in connection with the legislative commission. In 1770 a subcommittee on schools devised a plan, based on the Prussian model, for establishing obligatory instruction for all male peasants. The localities would pay the expenses and the clergy would furnish the teachers. The program was minimal but not impractical, and it came from the people themselves. Nevertheless, it was filed away and forgotten. In the ensuing decades the rural masses sank out of the ranks of the educable. (pp. 15–16)

Under the 1801–1825 reign of Alexander Romanov (Alexander I) (1777–1825), parochial schools were established in 1803. However, by 1828 only about 600 parochial schools existed in the Russian Empire, since the local communities could not maintain these schools (Shevchenko et al., 2018, p. 228). Alexander I, who was also the Grand Duke of Finland from 1809 to his death, intended to form a comprehensive school in the country. Hans (1963) reported that universities were established, in addition to Moscow and Vilna, in Dorpat, Kharkov, Kazan, and Petersburg. Gymnasiums were founded in all the provincial capitals of European Russia. However, parochial schools were mostly founded in towns, and teacher training was especially difficult for all stages of the new school system. The struggle with Napoleon in 1812 and the burning of Moscow increased Russian patriotic fervor. Caught up in this movement, Alexander I became more patriotic and religious and promoted the teaching of the Russian national character in schools (Hans, 1963, pp. 21, 23). Nevertheless, under the reign of Nicholas Romanov (Nicholas I) (1796–1855), higher education remained the prerogative of the upper classes (for the school system in Russia before the revolution, see, e.g., Price, 1977, p. 78).

Kelly (2007) described that in the late 1800s intellectual narrow-mindedness became the focus of wide criticism, which was supported by hygienists and psychologists, who emphasized the excess of demands made on schoolchildren. Critics wrote about the "exhaustion" that secondary school children in particular experienced. Kelly pointed to a cluster of suicides in 1914, which were linked to the fact that these occurred during the time when students were taking their examinations and were stressed about whether they would pass. These types of crises were inspired by the educational ideas of Tolstoy or by overseas experimental projects. She continued that the state school curriculum was child-centered only in the limited sense before 1917. Educational reforms included, for instance, subjecting the secondary schools to strict scrutiny by Ministry of Education officials. They could impose severe disciplinary sanctions on teachers, up to dismissal. Alongside this, many teachers were committed to academic values. Revolutionary upheavals in 1905 also generated complications, which saw schoolchildren all over the Russian Empire involved in strikes and protests (Kelly, 2007, pp. 32–33).

1.1.1   Summing Up

Alexander Pushkin (1799–1837), who studied Peter I's regime, named it the Petrine Revolution, which included the accelerated Europeanization of the tsarist society. Peter I's educational campaign was simultaneous with military improvements, which allowed Russia to become a European superpower (Alston, 1969, pp. 3–4). However, after Peter I's regime, higher education especially remained a privilege of the upper classes.

The conceptual features of the Petrine Revolution in the Russian Empire can be interpreted from the perspective of community-based learning by applying

Hlebowitsh's (2007) classification. This kind of Petrine Revolution sees the ideal student as being a scientifically oriented Russian citizen who studies Western European languages, sciences, and mathematics, and synthesizes the European culture with the Russian national character. The ideal educational program includes training for various occupations, which develops students' character and improves the centralized tradition of the society. The student is oriented toward ideal societies, the citizens of which work in a Europeanized economy and are respected in its new fields.

A secret "cook's circular" was issued on June 18, 1887, that ordered certain types of secondary schools to stop admitting children from peasant and lower urban classes. The primary significance of the circular was that only the most privileged children could attend urban day schools, with the classical high school (gymnasium), for instance, officially leading to university education. The gymnasium's curriculum included compulsory Latin and, from 1902, also Greek. The gymnasium was intended to serve the nobility, while the children of service-class workers remained involved in the service classes (Kelly, 2007, p. 29).

The following section deals with the essence of community-based learning in the Russian Empire in a more concrete manner. The nature of activities is studied from the perspective offered by central pedagogical approaches and their dimensions of the learning environment. The primary focus is on tsarist education.

2   Community-Based Pedagogical Ideas in the Russian Empire

Between 1700 and 1914, Russia created a state system of general education. It was equipped with Western European academic standards, instilled with the national spirit of the Orthodox Church, and focused on imperial goals. Alexander I promulgated the Education Act of 1809. Alston (1969) suggested that the active principle of the 1809 act could be increasingly operative in socially and economically different countries. The act clearly undermined any elite based on anything but personal competence that could be assessed academically across the country. At the same time, the act was beneficial for the country's external security and internal stability (pp. 243–244).

2.1   The Tsarist School
The French Revolution's ideas of freedom spread through most European countries in the early 19th century. However, Russia's vastness meant that large portions of the population were unaware of these new liberal ideas. Kirchner (1991) wrote that this "new period was more in line with the spirit of Europe

than any other in modern Russian history, and it was marked by a series of progressive steps" (p. 160). Only the Grand Duchy of Finland, mainly in the territory of the present Finnish state, was an autonomous part of the Russian Empire from 1809 to 1917. It was the predecessor of the current independent Republic of Finland, which already met many of the criteria of an independent state. Alaska also belonged to the Russian Empire until it was purchased by the United States in 1867. In the early 1840s, a colony of Europeans settled in Alaska with a Finnish governor, who obtained permission from the Russian emperor to establish a Lutheran congregation in Sitka, as nearly a third of the colony's officials were Lutherans. Finnish clergyman Uno Cygnaeus (1810–1888) held the office of colonial priest there from 1839 to 1845.

Shortly after returning to Finland, Cygnaeus began to develop the school system and teacher training in the autonomous Grand Duchy of Finland. He was commissioned to study domestic and foreign public education between 1858 and 1859 and to draw up a proposal on how Finnish public schools and teacher training should be organized. He went on an extensive exploratory trip through Nordic countries and Central Europe to become acquainted with the development of school education in Sweden, Denmark, the Netherlands, Switzerland, and Austria (Haikari & Kotilainen, 2016, pp. 58, 62–63). Cygnaeus was particularly influenced by the development of handicraft teaching based on the ideas of Fröbel and, especially, by the development of normal schools based on the work school of Georg Kerschensteiner (1854–1932). Kerschensteiner believed in a school that included as much manual work as possible in the curriculum (see, e.g., Haikari & Kotilainen, 2016, p. 53; Iisalo, 1999, p. 219).

A teacher seminary (teacher college) was established in Jyväskylä in Central Finland in 1863 and a model schools for boys and girls in 1864. When public education was reformed in the 1860s, Cygnaeus emphasized the importance of handicraft in teaching. He viewed that school handicrafts had to develop the student's skills, strengths, habits, and willingness to work, while at the same time develop physical and mental abilities (Cygnaeus, 1910, p. 31). Cygnaeus' texts from the 1860s, published in 1910 in the collection *Uno Cygnaeuksen Kirjoitukset*, include separate Curriculum and Rules of Procedure for the seminary students, for kindergartens and infant kindergartens, and for both boys' and girls' model schools (pp. 235–285). The curriculum for model schools contained a detailed explanation of various subjects, including religion, Finnish language and its grammar, reading, writing, mathematics, music, history, geography, science, freehand and metrological drawing, modeling, handicrafts, gymnastics and sports, health care, and childcare (pp. 275–285).

This type of tsarist school had a tendency to emphasize the Sociocultural Dimension of its learning environments in community-based learning. This was evidenced in such activities as making furniture, household items, and tools usually needed in the society at the time. The Practical-Agricultural Dimension was also prioritized when students helped the seminary brothers in fields, meadows, and woods. The following summary shows how the upper-class students in the boys' model school applied the Sociocultural and Practical-Agricultural Dimensions in their learning environments in step with the curriculum for model schools:

> Students in the boys' model school practiced the use of a carpenter's, turner's, and blacksmith's tools in order to learn how to make furniture, household items, and tools needed in a typical peasant home and in field, meadow, and haulage work. Likewise, they were taught to use simple machines and mechanical tools, and to do simple shoemaker and saddler work. In addition, all the boys of the model school were obliged, under the direction of the brothers of the seminary, to supply all the indoor chores that were not too heavy for the children, such as cleaning rooms, chopping logs, and carrying wood to the rooms. Furthermore, students in the upper classes were allowed to assist the seminary brothers in all work outdoors, such as in fields, meadows, and woods (Cygnaeus, 1910, pp. 284–285).

The upper-class students of the girls' model school emphasized the Sociocultural and Horticultural Dimensions in their learning environments. This was shown in the making of various handicrafts and helping the seminary sisters in the garden in order to practice the skills needed in the society at the time. The following overview explains how the upper-class students of the girls' model school accentuated the Sociocultural and Horticultural Dimensions in their learning environments in accord with the curriculum for model schools:

> Students in the girls' model school took part in chores in the kitchen, bakery, laundry room, and barn under the guidance of the sisters of the seminary. They had to do their best to clean the rooms. They also had to practice cutting linen and garments, and sewing suits and linen. Students also practiced spinning, weaving, knitting socks, crocheting, and many other handicrafts that could be considered necessary. All activities had to be frugal and clean. Moreover, the girls had to help the sisters in garden work (Cygnaeus, 1910, pp. 284–285).

The curricula required that school and seminary students be provided with their own garden benches, which they were allowed to care for as their own and to which they could apply their knowledge in agriculture and horticulture (Cygnaeus, 1910, p. 285).

2.1.1   Challenges

Between 1721 and 1917, the Russian Empire extended across Eurasia, and the awakening of national identity caused major changes in the country. Russia had fought a victorious war against Sweden between 1808 and 1809, as a result of which a large area of eastern Sweden was annexed to Russia as the autonomous Grand Duchy of Finland, with its own language, religion, customs, post, money, and central government. Inland waterways and a railway network were built, with the tax revenues collected from Finland used for its own benefit; estates could nominate their candidates to the governmental council. In 1816, the name of the council was changed to the Finnish Senate and, in 1906, the unicameral parliament was born. During this long process, a large-scale national awakening grew in Finland. During the First World War (1914–1918), and especially after the Bolshevik coup in Russia in 1917, Finland's full independence began to seem even more likely. The parliament approved Finland's declaration of independence on December 6, 1917.

Figes (2015) describes in detail the unfortunate events from the end of the 19th century that caused a deepening revolutionary crisis in Russia:

> After a year of meteorological catastrophes the peasants of south-east Russia faced starvation in the summer of 1891. The seeds planted the previous autumn had barely time to germinate before the frosts arrived. There had been little snow to protect the young plants during the severe winter. Spring brought with it dusty winds that blew away the topsoil and then, as early as April, the long dry summer began. There was no rain for one hundred days. Wells and ponds dried up, the scorched earth cracked, forests turned brown, and cattle died by the roadsides.
>
> By the autumn the famine area spread from the Ural mountains to Ukraine, an area double the size of France with a population of 36 million people. The peasants weakened and took to their huts. They lived on "hunger bread" made from rye husks mixed with goosefoot, moss and tree bark, which made the loaves turn yellow and bitter. Those who had strength packed up their meagre belongings and fled wherever they could, jamming the roads with their carts. And then cholera and typhus struck, killing half a million people by the end of 1892.
>
> The government reacted to the crisis clumsily. At first it buried its head in the sand, speaking euphemistically of a "poor harvest," and warned newspapers not to print on the "famine," although many did in all but

name. This was enough to convince the public, shocked and concerned by the rumors of starvation, that there was a government conspiracy to conceal the truth. (pp. 7–8)

Figes (2015) shows how "Russian society was politicized by the famine, and from 1891 it became more organized in opposition the government" (p. 8). The tsar was unable to cope with the tasks of ruling the vast empire in a deepening revolutionary crisis. As Figes (2015) explains:

> Here, then, were the roots of the monarchy's collapse, not in peasant discontent or the labor movement, so long the preoccupation of Marxist and social historians, nor in the breakaway of nationalist movements on the empire's periphery, but in the growing conflict between a dynamic public culture and a fossilized autocracy that would not concede or even understand its political demands. (p. 10)

In the end, this revolutionary crisis caused the February Revolution in March 1917, resulting in the overthrow of the imperial government. Unpopular Nicholas Romanov (Nicholas II) (1868–1918) relinquished his crown in favor of his brother Michael Romanov (1878–1918), who further handed over power to the interim government. However, since this interim government was not effective, the October Revolution of 1917 eventually transferred power to the Bolsheviks, who established the Soviet Republic of Russia. Bolshevik revolutionaries, under Yakov Yurovsky (1878–1938), on the night of July 17, 1918, killed the Russian imperial Romanov family—Emperor Nicholas II, Empress Alexandra Feodorovna (1872–1918), and their five children.

CHAPTER 5

Ideals for Learning in Communities in the Soviet Union

Abstract

The aim of this chapter is to analyze the foundations of community-based learning with a focus on the philosophical views, educational aims, and associated value dimensions in the Soviet Union. In addition, this chapter aims to examine the changing nature of the pedagogical activities of community-based learning and their authentic learning environments, the primary focus being on productive labor education. This chapter shows that Marxism-Leninism was the official philosophical doctrine in the Soviet Union. From the time of its founding, the philosophical tradition of community-based learning was related to the tradition of dialectical and historical materialism. Educational policies intended to emphasize moral-political and polytechnical aims and their value dimensions and integrate physical, mental, and polytechnical education. This chapter also demonstrates that community-based learning can take place in a variety of learning environments prioritizing the Sociocultural, Productive, Horticultural, Scientific-Agricultural, or Scientific-Technical Dimensions, in accordance with the general direction of political, economic, and social development. The chapter shows that during the experimental period from 1921 to 1931 and again in the mid-1950s, the Soviet Union focused efforts on expanding learning environments from schools to the real world outside of schools. The study concludes that in the 1970s, development in the Soviet Union started to stress school-centered intellectual aims and science- and technology-related values, when community-based learning allowed experts to be trained for a socialist society, and the citizens of which worked in a modern national economy and, if there were societal or personal changes, they could work in new fields of production. Since the 1970s, pedagogical approaches and their learning environments increasingly gave special importance to the use of technology-based applications. The study concludes that approaches to community-based learning could provide a way for teachers to prepare students to help community members through socially useful work.

Keywords

philosophy – aims – values – practices – community-based learning – revolutionism – pedagogical activities – pedagogical approaches – learning environments – productive labor education – Soviet Union

1   The Narkompros Years

1.1   *Philosophical Views*

The first concepts about dialectical materialism were formulated in central Europe a few decades before Harvard University in the United States developed basic ideas about pragmatism. Dialectical and historical materialism, represented by German philosophers Karl Marx (1818–1883) and Friedrich Engels (1820–1895), is an integral part of socialist social theory and its philosophical basis and foundation. This doctrine of social development also provides the basis for a socialist conception of the people. The theory concentrates on political economy and the development of society and, doing so, intends to offer a revolutionary alternative to capitalist ideology. Marx and Engels developed a theory in which dialectics expresses the functioning of economic development and, consequently, the regularities of all other historical development. The theory Marx and Engels expounded combines Georg Hegel's (1770–1831) conception of dialectical change in society with Ludwig Feuerbach's (1804–1872) view of materialism, so that a society's historical development is seen within the context of its materialistic conditions (Gutek, 1997, p. 232). In terms of its starting point, Marxism represents a material counterpart to Hegel's absolute idealism. From the perspective of materialism, reality is objective, notwithstanding the observer's experience.

Critical to the dialectical and historical materialism of Marx and Engels is the assumption that historical conflict in society reflects the struggles between social classes. Here, the classes and their mutual contradictions are fundamentally determined by the degree of development in economic conditions as well as by the prevailing mode of production and the respective method of exchange (Engels, 1852/1926, p. 22). This radical theory of social development was also associated with the idea of polytechnical education that Marx and Engels originally presented in the late 1840s. In Marx's writings, the term *polytechnical education* can be understood as referring to instruction in the general principles of productive processes as well as in the methods and instruments of work utilized in socially useful labor (Marx, 1866/1968, p. 195).

The goal of polytechnically combining work and education is to provide individuals with all-around skills and knowledge for a new socialist society in which the nature of work and its duties change as a consequence of technical development (Marx, 1867/1974, pp. 436, 438–439). Marx (1932/1978) observed that all human activities are determined by the general laws of economy. This view stresses the essential importance of training young people to understand and evaluate phenomena in accordance with the social laws in the prevailing economic relations (Marx, 1932/1978, p. 250). It is thus logical that polytechnical work education, which was later applied in China, called for integrating theory and practice, school and life, teaching and production.

Georgy Plekhanov (1856–1918) was the forerunner of Russian dialectical materialism. Inspired by the works of Engels and Marx, Plekhanov formulated his own Marxist principles. Many Sovietologists have interpreted that views on dialectical materialism, militant nationalism, socially useful labor, and polytechnical education were prevalent in Soviet educational philosophy after the Russian Revolution (see, e.g., Zajda, 1980, p. 2).

In 1898, the intention was to unite the revolutionary organizations of the Russian Empire into one party, the Russian Social Democratic Labor Party (RSDLP). The party later split into two groups: the majority Bolshevik bloc and the minority Menshevik bloc. In 1917, about the same time that Gandhi was launching the struggle for Indian independence, the Bolsheviks successfully carried out a revolution in Russia. Soon after obtaining power, the Bolsheviks formed the Communist Party. The Union of Soviet Socialist Republics (U.S.S.R.) was established on December 30, 1922, along with its first constitution (U.S.S.R., 1925, p. 3). A direct consequence of adopting the Marxist materialistic view of history in the U.S.S.R. included productive labor in the Soviet school curriculum and developing activities for political-ideological youth organizations.

According to Marxist dialectical and historical materialism, a continuous process of change and development based on economic contradictions determines the development of society. In the same manner, all other human activity is subject to the general law of the development of economic relations (Marx, 1932/1978, p. 250). For Marx (1867/1974), the function of education is to produce individuals with all-around skills and knowledge for whom the various social duties are but different modes of activity in the new society (pp. 436, 439). In a process of this type, the interpretation of phenomena is guided in accordance with the prevailing social laws in economic relations (Engels, 1852/1926, p. 22; Marx, 1932/1978, p. 250). Since in Marxist philosophy, education is based on the dialectical laws of material life, the mission of socialist schooling and education is to eliminate the differences between nature and humans on the one hand, and between a state of existence and human consciousness on the other.

The aim of the labor school was to be a collectively oriented synthesis between school and life, learning and work. Such socialist education stressed the ideas of labor-related education, also referred to as revolutionary labor education, when analyzed in the context of community-based learning.

Vladimir Lenin (1870–1924), the Bolshevist leader who rose to power after the Russian Revolution in 1917, emphasized Marx's belief in the tight bond between the three areas of education: mental, physical, and polytechnical. Lenin (1929/1966a) argued that the essential function of a school is to provide young people with profound knowledge of scientific disciplines and, in this process, to educate them in the spirit of communist ideology and morals (pp. 533–534). Polytechnical education in this type of labor school consists of practical teaching about the principles of current industries and agriculture (Lenin, 1920/1966b, p. 289).

Lenin's spouse, Nadezhda Krupskaya (1869–1939), the organizer of the People's Education Program in the early Soviet Union, further developed the pedagogical ideas of the polytechnical labor school. Krupskaya (1927/1957b) pointed out that the most important aim of education is to guide students in working for the benefit of society (p. 121). The central element of schoolwork is polytechnical education in socially meaningful activities that combine school and labor. Krupskaya (1930/1957a) stated that all school subjects should be integrated with work-related activities that allow students to experience the various phases and to perceive the entire processes of industrial and agricultural production. In this manner, the polytechnical school transmits appropriate knowledge to students and teaches them to apply it in the different fields of production (pp. 189–191). The ultimate idea is to train citizens in a wide range of skills and abilities to become members of the collective, not individuals seeking their own benefits, as in Western schools (Krupskaya, 1927/1957b, pp. 119–120). The purpose of this type of labor school was a collective-based synthesis of school and life, learning and work.

Along with these Soviet processes, ideas from American educational reformers also influenced European educators. Just as American progressives utilized European ideas when establishing educational practices, American ideas soon inspired followers in Europe. For example, Georg Kerschensteiner (1854–1932) in Germany and Pavel Blonsky (1884–1941) in the early Soviet Union developed their own activity-based work school in the spirit of reform pedagogy (Danilchenko, 1993, pp. 114, 121–122; Darling & Nordenbo, 2003, p. 292).

Ballantine and Hammack (2009) argued that the writings of progressive educators "have been interpreted, misinterpreted, and modified, but they have influenced all movements in education since the turn of the twentieth century" (p. 49). Similarly, copies of the pedagogical works of such Western reform educators as Kerschensteiner, John Dewey (1859–1952), and Ellen Key (1849–1926) were widely distributed in the Soviet Union after the Russian Revolution (Mchitarjan, 2000). Soviet Russian school reformers visited Europe and the United States in the early 1900s (Brickman, 1960). Dewey himself visited the Soviet Union in 1928, discussed progressive ideas in education with Soviet educators, and learned about the aims and teaching methods used in the Soviet school system (Dewey, 1929a). Krupskaya became familiar with the writings of Western reform pedagogues during her time as a refugee in the United States before the revolution (Skatkin & Tsov'janov, 1994, p. 50).

The 1920s witnessed a major educational reform in Soviet Russia that was firmly connected with the international reform-pedagogical trend. This reform arose after the Russian Revolution in response to wartime turmoil and the traditional Russian culture. The different views on education and society before and after the revolution were deeply contradictory, as they were linked to different life-sustaining value objectives and associated conceptions of being human. The international reform-pedagogical trend in Russia provided basic methods for national educational reforms using Marxist ideas during this difficult time. Hans (1963) describes these educational processes in detail:

> Lenin's conception of polytechnic education was elaborated by Blonsky in his book. Yet both Shatsky and Blonsky retained in their ideas and practice some remnants of Tolstoy's teaching of free education. Their demand for children's self-government was at first accepted by Lunacharsky and Krupskaya, and Blonsky was a member of many Soviet committees. Krupskaya herself was influenced by Tolstoy, and wrote that his educational views have "undoubtedly left an indelible stamp on Russian educational thought." (p. 161)

These important school reformers were supported by the People's Commissariat for Education (*Narkompros*). Hans (1963) reported that Stanislav Shatsky (1878–1934) and Blonsky were the two Tolstoyans and the most important representatives of the labor school idea on the Narkompros. They worked under the protection of Krupskaya and Anatoly V. Lunacharsky (1875–1933) (p. 161). Shatsky (1981b) developed his own labor school in the proletarian spirit of the early Soviet Union. Like Krupskaya, Shatsky emphasized Tolstoy's Rousseauean idea of education, which was combined with student autonomy in the collective spirit. He founded a children's labor center near Moscow in 1909, where he applied Tolstoy's ideas on education in the principles of productive work by children (Shatsky, 1981b, pp. 26–27, 29–30). One of the most important advocate for polytechnical labor school during the revolutionary reform was Pavel Blonsky.

1.2 Pavel Blonsky and the Revolutionary Movement

Blonsky was one of the most influential psychologists and educators during the revolutionary reform. He actively served as one of the school reformers on the Narkompros. He developed his own unified labor school, which followed Western reform-pedagogical ideas in the Marxist spirit. These included active-learning methods of instruction, experiential learning processes based on problem-solving, practical and everyday activities for learning, and teaching self-reliance during educational processes (Blonskij, 1919/1973, pp. 70–71, 78–79, 220–221). The following summary provides a background for Blonsky's thoughts on education and pedagogy:

> Pavel Blonsky, born in Kyiv in 1884, was first educated at a classical high school and then at Kyiv University, where he graduated from the School of History and Philology. In the years preceding the Russian Revolution, Blonsky's had conflicting views of life due to the influence of different currents of thought, but his practical teaching activities, which dictated his interests and research, played a major role in shaping his scientific views. From 1908, Blonsky taught education and psychology in various Moscow schools. After obtaining his master's degree in 1913, he became a tutor at Moscow University, where he was appointed professor of philosophy in 1918 after the revolution.
>
> Blonsky became a proponent of the new socialist school and an active participant in its creation. He also combined a wide amount of practical teaching with theoretical work in education and psychology. His research at the Institute of Scientific Education, the Institute of Nationalities, and the Institute of Polytechnical Education was of great importance. He wrote his theory of the polytechnical school in *Trudovaya Shkola* (1919) and his educational theory in *Pedagogika* (1921) and *Foundations of Pedagogy* (1925).
>
> For the last 10 years of his life, Blonsky worked at the Institute of Psychology, where he directed the thought laboratory and trained specialists in psychology (Danilchenko, 1993, pp. 113–114; Hans, 1963, pp. 161–162).

Blonsky's well-known *Trudovaya Shkola* advocates for young students' productive labor and Tolstoy's ideas on free education. Blonskij (1919/1921) viewed labor as a process between humans and nature through which humans subordinate nature to their will and force it to serve their human needs. He regarded labor education as the processes in which students perform purposeful activities in a planned and organized manner. Through these processes, it is possible to produce objects that are useful for humanity. While students freely enjoy this type of education, they are gradually able to develop as humans who know how to employ nature to serve humanity's needs. This kind of labor education can be seen as educating humans to master nature (p. 9).

While Blonsky served on the Narkompros, he participated in school reforms, the main focus of which was to orient the school to society and life. Blonskij (1919/1921) held that the labor school should not only implement abstract "labor-related processes," but be connected with a concrete production taken as a whole and in its context. The labor school, like the working life of humans, starts from comprehensive life duties. These could be their concrete life needs in terms of housing, clothing, and so on. The connection between labor and knowledge is nowhere so clear and obvious as it is in industry. The highest level of vocational training is therefore industrial. So the essential importance of labor education is that students develop their abilities to use tools, equipment, and methods while familiarizing themselves with a variety of occupations. This is how the labor school would be a group of students involved in labor-related processes (pp. 9–12).

Blonsky considered that the school should be the young student's whole life and future. Through their instruction, teachers would abolish the dichotomy between the school and life. Blonskij (1919/1921) defined the elementary labor school as the first school level to serve as a young student's labor group. This labor group develops by performing domestic work and is organized during the division of labor in order to achieve a common goal more successfully. He suggested that the division of labor should include, if possible, a process for designing and adapting labor for everyone involved in the labor group. This type of student labor group develops students by raising their interest in performing labor. Domestic work can be any work that is of interest to students and is practiced in their homes, including housekeeping and working on household gadgets (p. 21).

Blonsky was Tolstoyan, influenced by Rousseau, and believed in the free development of young students. Blonskij (1919/1921) argued that the educational starting point is the drive to perform productive labor associated with students' interests in business, the success of which depends on the tools and the work method, since typically students' interests are instrumental and closely linked to their activities. He indicated that the content of elementary education would gradually develop the tools and methods of work to achieve maximum productive labor. It is obvious that such a view precludes the possibility of transforming a student's work community into a commercial school while doing household chores. Then tools, objects, and working methods should proceed from work not only to knowledge of nature and its natural objects but also to social culture based on progress in the means of production (p. 21).

Blonsky's main contribution to the Marxist theory of education was *Pedagogika*, his major pedagogical work. Blonski (1921/1927) relied on Marx's ideas of education that combine teaching with work, and practical technical education with theoretical technology. The development of socialist education demands rejecting the bourgeois method of teaching, which contrasts mental and physical work. Instead of this, proletarian or socialist education combines both forms of work into one integrated teaching. Blonsky also shared the ideas of anarchist communist Peter Kropotkin (1842–1921) and argued that, for the sake of science, industry, and society as a whole, every citizen, regardless of social status at birth, must receive scientific education alongside vocational training. When human education combines science and practicality, it is also essential that teaching be systematically versatile and provide students with the basics of science and related working methods (pp. 118–120).

In the early 1920s, the primary aim of the school was to help students find socially valuable labor that they could effectively perform. Blonski (1921/1927) stated that proletarian education has to be integrated with productive labor in order to promote societal production and provide people with comprehensive skills and knowledge (p. 117). Such instruction must require students to familiarize themselves with the basics of science and the use of working methods so that they want to become useful citizens along with others in society. Modern students should move from books to working with others at factories. Students under the age of 14 or 15 should be provided with extensive knowledge of nature and humanity along with the ability to apply the technical knowledge and research they have acquired (pp. 120–121).

The reform-pedagogical school Blonsky introduced eventually gave way in the 1930s to the new Stalinist school. Even though the present study suggests that progressive and Marxist educational ideas have the same basis, if they are viewed as material counterparts to Hegel's absolute idealism, progressive pedagogical ideas can be seen as inevitably in contradiction with Marxist ideas, as implemented in the early Soviet Union. There, they represented different views regarding the direction in which society should develop, along with the underlying values and ideals. As Ballantine and Hammack (2009) stated, "Education is but one of the institutions in society, and the educational pendulum reflects broad social trends" (p. 421). This was also the breakdown of Western reformist educational practices during the early decades of the Soviet Union.

While Blonsky was developing his labor school, experiments in a Soviet educational method that was the opposite of Blonsky's reform pedagogy were taking place at an orphanage for delinquent youth close to Poltava and, later, near

Kharkov, in the Ukraine. The creator of the new method was Anton Makarenko (1888–1939), director at the Maxim Gorky Colony for juvenile delinquent war orphans between 1920 and 1927 (Jackim, 2016, p. 172). Makarenko (1949/1965) used a collective educational approach based on combining theoretical teaching with productive and practical labor in the Marxist spirit. One of the central features of Makarenko's educational collective was strict discipline obtained through education, with collectives organized on a military model. The pedagogical collective consisted of both primary collectives and permanent or temporary labor and recreational collectives. Representative bodies were established to develop independent initiative and self-government and to strengthen the structure of the organization (pp. 50–53, 88–89, 91, 97).

Combining education with productive labor was the most essential element in the functioning of Makarenko's collective for juveniles. Makarenko (1949/1965) combined education with everyday life and activities; in addition to studying, youngsters worked in different phases of agricultural and industrial production. For example, they obtained vocational skills by being involved in agricultural activities on farms and manufacturing cameras and electrical equipment in production plants (pp. 128–129).

1.3   Aims and Values

Soviet Russia implemented educational policies in the 1920s that intended to emphasize moral-political and polytechnical (intellectual and moral-political) aims and their value dimensions in the Marxist spirit. Such an educational consciousness was in accord with the view of dialectical materialism. In this manner, physical, mental, and polytechnical education were integrated. This type of society-centered pattern of community-based learning intended to train vocationally capable citizens for a revolutionary socialist society.

The aim of revolutionary labor education was to train a socialist citizen through polytechnical and socially useful labor. Krupskaja (1922/1965) wrote that an essential element of polytechnical education is social education, which includes activities to develop one's social instincts, awareness, and customs (p. 145). Krupskaya (1927/1957b) stated that the aim of a Soviet upbringing is to educate young people with the help of collectives that operate with knowledge of communist morals (pp. 119–120). This thinking was based on ideas about an ideal society where physical, mental, and polytechnical (intellectual and moral-political) education is integrated through productive labor. Since work itself was considered to have great value, all learning rested upon labor. The aim of education was to train true constructors of a socialist society who have internalized Marxist socialist theory. The intention was to abolish the old cultural values and accept the new proletarian values.

Prioritizing work was intimately intertwined with moral-political values, which served to accentuate loyalty for a socialist system following communist ethics. This is a doctrine of morality derived from Marxist philosophy that brings together or forces apart individuals. Work processes requiring intellectual effort also placed vital importance on mental values, as when students worked in the various phases of industrial and agricultural production and understood the entire process. Cultural and productive values were emphasized during work processes to help students develop mentally in attaining a consciousness in learning based on the Marxist polytechnical tradition. Moreover, this was based on a sense of students' collective identity, including their attitudes, beliefs, and sensitivities, and thus considered characteristic of a person and group. This was to maintain the country's moral-political unity. The highest degree of legitimation was represented by the Soviet ideological system, called the *symbolic universe*, which was manifested in the central role of the socialist consciousness, an essential element of which was *orthodox Marxism* that referred to the methods of historical and dialectical materialism.

In step with these ideals, Blonskij (1919/1973) considered the labor school a school for labor education. This kind of polytechnical instruction proceeds from theoretical generalizations through to knowledge of working methods and tools, and mechanisms and movements of machines. The instruction must also be based on scientific applications, since the productive processes offer an opportunity to learn about the interaction between a human and nature. The labor school thus provides students possibilities for obtaining comprehensive skills and knowledge through polytechnical education (pp. 9, 12–15, 141–142).

Russian education underwent major reforms after the Russian Revolution. In the Soviet Union's highest executive unit, the Council of People's Commissars, all the commissars were members of the Bolshevik Party and subject to its discipline. Lunacharsky, the well-known author and politician, was appointed to the first People's Commissar for Education (Pipes, 1990, p. 500). He served at the Narkompros with Krupskaya and Blonsky in the 1920s. The All-Russian Central Executive Committee adopted the critical Unified Labor School statute on October 16, 1918 (All-Russian Central Executive Committee of the R.S.F.S.R., 1918/1947). According to the statute (1918/1947), the unified labor school was to consist of two teaching programs: the 5-year course for 8- to 13-year-olds and the 4-year course for 13- to 17-year-olds. Both programs included general education and polytechnical instruction. School life had to be based on socially useful productive labor and polytechnical education, which also had to cover the cost of maintaining education. The labor school had to be adapted to the local conditions, where the school had to be intimately connected with life around the school (Articles 2, 12–13). Based on this statute, this type of community-based learning aimed to:

- advance inner discipline and the sense of responsibility toward labor;
- develop instruction and training so that school programs would be creative and nonviolent;
- make school work processes and their divisions of labor an important part of education;
- evaluate work procedures so as to systematically utilize the required energy for the work;
- educate students for living in a socialist society; and
- connect the school commune's labor intimately with the community around the school (Articles 12–13).

The decade following the Russian Revolution saw a range of school experiments, and in this era of reform pedagogics, the unification of the country's dispersed school system into a polytechnical labor school (*trudovaya shkola*) was planned with the support of the New Economic Policy (1921–1928). Holmes (1991) wrote that between 1919 and 1920 the Narkompros undertook several labor school experiments that followed the freedom pedagogical principles in terms of the content and timing of studies and students' independent initiative and self-governing in the Marxist spirit (pp. 9, 32–35). Löfstedt (1980) reported that by 1925 these school experiments had been established as a 7-year factory school, from which it was possible to continue studies in apprenticeship training at factories and in technical schools (*teknikum*). This type of school provided students general and polytechnical education and therefore involved socially productive labor in school workshops, local plants, and factories (p. 54). According to Löfstedt (1980), socially productive labor aimed to:

- instill in students the habits of socialist labor conduct;
- advance group spirit and social purposefulness;
- further conscious work discipline; and
- develop the sense of the organization of the student collective (p. 54).

The early Soviet Union intended to carry out educational policies in the 1920s that rested upon Marxist values. The society-centered pattern of community-based learning primarily emphasized moral-political and polytechnical (intellectual and moral-political) aims and their value dimensions in order to train vocationally capable citizens for a revolutionary socialist society. In this process, physical, mental, and polytechnical education were integrated. The goal of revolutionary labor education, based on the Marxist socialist theory of society, was to abandon the old cultural values and combine the activities of experimenting with the proletarian spirit. Blonski (1921/1927) stated that physical, mental, and intellectual labor should be integrated in instruction. As Blonsky indicates, this type of integrated labor education aimed to:

- develop the arts and sciences;
- erase the inequality between physical, mental, and intellectual work;
- encourage respect for labor and laborers;
- increase citizens' self-esteem; and
- advance common well-being and prosperity in the society (pp. 120–121).

The basic type of polytechnical labor school became consolidated in 1925 when the 7-year factory school was established. Labor education at the factory school primarily emphasized moral-political and polytechnical (intellectual and moral-political) aims and their value dimensions. The shared goal of these moral-political and polytechnical aims and the integration of physical, mental, and polytechnical education was to train citizens to be working-class-minded proletarians equipped with all-around skills and knowledge. This type of labor education aimed to:

- provide training in manual labor or other work locally;
- teach respect for manual labor;
- help to see that it is possible to learn through performing labor;
- encourage understanding of the lives of peasants and laborers and their proletarian way of life;
- bring students closer to proletarian needs and points of view;
- instill the ideology of communism; and
- connect the school intimately with life, labor, and the working classes (Pinkevitch, 1929, pp. 225–226).

1.3.1   Summing Up

The conceptual features of the Narkompros's revolutionism can be interpreted from the perspective of community-based learning by applying Hlebowitsh's (2007) classification. This kind of revolutionism sees the ideal student as a communal citizen who is becoming familiar with the various phases of industrial and agricultural production and is involved in ideological and political studies dealing with communist ideology and morals. The ideal educational program is incorporated into productive labor within polytechnical principles; during labor processes, the student performs group work on brigade-laboratory or *synthetic* projects utilizing Marxist socialist ideas. The student is oriented toward an ideal socialist society, the citizens of which work in units of agricultural and industrial production.

The prominent pedagogy shows that in the 1920s the unified labor school tried to break the social isolation of Russian academic schools. Students spent more time working in local productive units and made more excursions and field trips within their community than in academic schools. Similarly, they were more involved in projects and political campaigns. The collegium at the Narkompros was keen to find new ways to study and work, and they quickly adopted foreign educational ideas and applied them to collective labor education. However, the factory school, for instance, did not become widespread primarily due to administrative, economic, and social difficulties as well as inadequate teacher training. These were intertwined with broader contextual obstacles that came with the rise of a conservative political trend and its demand for far-reaching changes in society. The reform-pedagogical Soviet school faced the following obstacles:

- The new Soviet federation was in extreme economic, social, and political crisis. Millions of people had died from war, hunger, and disease. Even if the New Economic Policy was adopted to overcome these difficulties, there was no relief from the prevailing poverty. The school systems or local economic units could not provide enough pens and books, not to mention facilities— chairs and tables, equipment and gear, and school meals—to provide for proper schooling.
- The mass of Soviet teachers at regular schools were unmotivated about either ideology or a reform pedagogy. Similarly, the link between teaching and the social and economic structure was weak. Related to this, Zepper (1960) reported that Krupskaya had argued that "if a teacher is not politically trained, does not gain an understanding of problems in economics, and does not understand natural phenomena, of course he will be helpless" (p. 269).
- Although the unified labor school was established by the mid-1920s, the school could not provide proper vocational training for further studies. For example, Whyte (1974) stated that it was possible that the work-based projects stressed a positive attitude toward labor and manual skills more than it actually provided in vocational training (p. 118).

The thesis of the 1920s was soon followed by a time of antithesis. U.S. educator Helen Parkhurst's Dalton Plan as well as the project and complex methods were banned in the early 1930s, abolishing the reform-pedagogical progressive trend.

2 Joseph Stalin and the Totalitarian System

2.1 Philosophical Views
Joseph Stalin (1878–1953) achieved power in the Soviet Union through the Communist Party during the first Five-Year Plan in 1928 and his regime lasted

until 1953 (Acton & Stableford, 2005, pp. 261, 446). Gutek (1997) wrote that totalitarian systems exist in one-party social systems. In these countries, education is used "to reinforce the dictator's cult of personality and to mimic the state-sponsored ideology" (p. 254). Totalitarian regimes seek to suppress divergent opinions, use highly emotional slogans, and divide people into groups of them and us. In the Soviet Union, totalitarianism started with Lenin and was consolidated under Stalin. This type of communist totalitarianism had tragic consequences (pp. 254, 256).

In this kind of learning environment, students and teachers had to accept their school's order and discipline, and students' interests were rarely incorporated. Politics, curricula, and textbooks regulated teachers' work, and whole-class instruction and limited instructional strategies dominated. Hoffmann (2003) discussed how, at the same time, the Soviet elite received special services:

> The Party elite had always enjoyed higher living standards than average citizens. ... The Party elite, as well as secret police and military officers, had special supply networks, stores, and dining halls that ensured that they received the best food, clothing, and manufactured goods. ... But material possessions also served to legitimate the elite. (p. 141)

Between 1929 and 1941, the Soviet Union was transformed from a mainly agrarian state into an industrial one. The new concept of a planned society was chosen as the useful base on which to build the country's heavy industry. Davies (1989) noted that the Soviet regime understood that, despite the backwardness of the economy and unskilled labor, industrialization must be based on advanced technology. A wide range of new industries were established so that the Soviet economy would become self-sufficient. The 1926–1927 economic year saw major advances in planned industrialization. Industrial production increased more than 20% and exceeded the 1913 level. Net industrial investment was higher during the 1926–1927 year than in 1913 (pp. 47, 50). Nove (1992) noted the following:

> Still wilder figures were dealt with in 1931. Stalin himself spoke on 4 February 1931 of fulfilling the plan "in three years in all the basic, decisive branches of industry." In the same speech he declared: "It is sometimes asked whether it is possible to slow down the tempo somewhat, to put a check on the movement. No, comrades, it is not possible. The tempo must not be reduced! On the contrary, we must increase it. ..." It was then that he made the justly famous prophecy: "We are fifty or a hundred years

behind the advanced countries. We must make good this distance in ten years. Either we do so, or we shall go under." (p. 190)

Davies (1989) reported that in May 1930 production of large-scale industry was 35.5% higher than in May 1929, and even more remarkable was the increase in capital investment. Moreover, he indicated that the increase in industrial production was accompanied by a decline in quality, which was not observed in the production statistics. The problems with work quality were due to (a) many untrained and inexperienced workers whose productivity was low, (b) most capital projects being incomplete when they were put into production, (c) factories suffering from the inability to obtain resources, and (d) payment difficulties and disorganization in agriculture leading to a decrease in important raw materials. These challenging problems resulted in a serious crisis in the industrial economy in the summer of 1930. Inflationary pressures increased urban food prices on the market by nearly 80% between June 1 and October 1 (Davies, 1989, pp. 474–475).

2.2   Aims and Values

After Lenin's death in 1924, Krupskaya and Lunacharsky began to lose influence, leading to the collapse of Western school reforms in early Soviet Russia. Stalin became the paramount leader of the country in 1928 (Acton & Stableford, 2005, p. 261). The Stalin regime abandoned the New Economic Policy and switched to an economic planning that involved centralized investment decisions along with five-year plans. The goal of the Soviet Union's first Five-Year Plan (1928–1932) was to increase production through the collectivization of agriculture and the systematic industrialization of the country (State Planning Commission of the U.S.S.R., 1933, pp. 4–5). The second plan, for the years 1933–1937, continued with similar objectives.

The power-related value dimension was central in the processes of the leading educational work, especially from the late 1930s. The endorsement of power-related values emphasized preserving a dominant position in the social system. The main socialist values of the Stalinist regime strove to ensure that competing value ideals did not undermine the balance in the country's values. The regime required that the basic values of socialism were to be ingrained into all Soviet people so that the Soviets could maintain them in order to improve society through constant control. Because Soviet administrators completely oversaw all areas of life, citizens became aware of the degree of coercion being applied for their own benefit.

This social and economic reorganization also required school reform, the goal of which was to provide compulsory education for the new society. The statute of July 25, 1930, accelerated the transition to general compulsory primary education (Central Committee of the All-Union Communist Party, 1930/1974c), and the statute of August 10, 1930, gave directions for implementing this type of compulsory education throughout the U.S.S.R. (Councils of Workers, Soldiers, and Peasants, 1930/1974).

From 1931 to 1936, nearly all aspects of previous school reforms under the Narkompros were renounced. Holmes (1991) wrote that on August 25, 1931, "the Central Committee of the Communist Party began to dictate school policy. It condemned the Narkompros and its curriculum for their neglect of subjects and content" (p. 137). Holmes (1991) describes this new policy in detail:

> The Central Committee declares that by a large margin the Soviet school does not meet the huge demands placed before it. ... The school's *fundamental defect* at the present time [is] its failure to provide a sufficient level of general-educational knowledge and an unsatisfactory preparation for technicums and higher education of fully literate people who have mastered the fundamentals of science (physics, chemistry, mathematics, native language, geography, etc.). ... It is necessary to wage a decisive struggle against thoughtless scheming with methods ... especially against the so-called project method. (p. 137)

The statute of August 25, 1931, intended to identify new general duties for the schools and to improve their methodological work. Its introduction appealed to Lenin's statement from 1920: the polytechnical issues must not be observed abstractly, but must be resolved firmly with concrete tasks. It was understood that Lenin's words referred to occupations and their teaching. Therefore, the statute stressed detailed guidelines for school staff, elementary and middle school material foundation, and school administration and management (Central Committee of the All-Union Communist Party, 1934/1974b, pp. 156–161).

The statute of August 25, 1932, provided rationale and guidelines for teaching and school management: how to develop teaching programs, organize teachers' instruction, strengthen school management, guide teaching staff, and reorganize the upper grades of the middle school. The statute (1934/1974a) emphasized that despite accepting polytechnical education, subject-specific teaching programs were to be required by teachers in elementary and middle schools. Schoolwork had to be based on the national curriculum and its procedures, such as lesson-based timetables, exams, grades, degrees, textbooks, and teacher-led and subject-based methods. School educators and principals were also required to combat student disorder and transgression. Students who violated regulations and rules set by the school administration and educators would be expelled from school for 1 to 3 years. Teachers were encouraged to teach students the basics of science, guide them in conscious discipline, and instill in them a communist relation to study and work (Central Committee of the All-Union Communist Party, 1934/1974a, pp. 162–164).

The Great Patriotic War (1941–1945) interrupted the development of education between 1939 and 1945. The war was also criticized for such problems as low academic standards, poor school discipline, and impaired overall morality. The Stalinist school began, especially after 1939, to implement rigorous discipline conforming to socialist standards of right or just behavior. The Stalinist regime considered that through strict and uniform discipline it was possible to morally educate a new socialist human for a socialist society. General obedience to authorities was the basic virtue that allowed the use of power-related values to legitimate the communist system of administration. The highest degree of legitimation was represented by the Soviet ideological system, called the *symbolic universe*, as manifested in the central role of socialist consciousness in Soviet society.

This type of atmosphere influenced the work of teachers in the late 1930s. Ewing (2002) reported that examinations, for instance, became sites of struggles over accountability. Since teachers recognized that this threated their autonomy and job security, some of them tried to avoid this pressure (p. 175). Ewing (2002) reveals how former teachers experienced situations involving written examinations:

> In the question of giving examinations all of us teachers were well trained. Each had his own method for increasing the percentage of good students. For example, I corrected with two pens, a red one for mistakes and one of blue ink to change the students' answers so as they would appear correct themselves. We had to give the students as much "leeway" in these things as possible. Some instructors gave the examinations out in advance, although this practice was one in which I never engaged. In other classes the students had their books open on their knees and the teacher looked the other way. Each teacher pretended not to see what was going on in his room and if by chance he should be speaking with another instructor, each would pretend that nothing out of the ordinary was in progress. On such occasions the speech between the teachers took on the aspect of a comedy on the stage. (pp. 175–176)

In the context of ongoing processes, school education can be seen as implementing traditional teaching and learning, the center of which was ideological

and political work rooted in dialectical materialism. The goals of this form of education were included in the constitution of 1945, according to which the Soviet regime gave particular importance to:
- providing universal compulsory education in elementary education;
- supplying free education to cover the entire education system, including higher education;
- affording school education in the mother tongue;
- awarding state scholarships to higher education institutions; and
- arranging free training in production, technology, and agronomy for workers in factories, Soviet farms, machine and tractor stations, and collective economies (U.S.S.R., 1945, Article 121).

2.2.1   Summing Up

In 1931, the Communist Party Central Committee instructed teachers to start conventional classroom-based instruction with textbooks, curricula, and examinations (for more detail, see, e.g., Ewing, 2002, pp. 7–8). Therefore, the conceptual features of socialist revolutionism under Stalin can be interpreted from the perspective of Stalinist education and learning by applying Hlebowitsh's (2007) classification. This type of revolutionism sees the ideal student as being a socialist-minded citizen who studies basic sciences in whole-class situations, is familiar with norms and values of the society, and has internalized the school's disciplinary function in the spirit of proletarian order, speech, and manners. The ideal educational program provides students knowledge with an atomistic orientation, teachers who are responsible for the production of learning arising from their skills, and teaching methods based on didactic materialism that include lecturing, questioning, and routine exercises. The student is oriented toward an ideal socialist society, the citizens of which work in agricultural and industrial production.

Maybe no one could predict what would happen after the Central Committee overturned a decade of experimentation and turned to whole-class instruction. Now teachers had to make lesson plans that included both subject content and political and ideological content. This meant that teachers had to incorporate certain ideological and political views to go perfectly with subject content in each of their written lesson plans. Ewing (2002) wrote that "approximately three-quarters of respondents in the Harvard Project on the Soviet Social System complained about excessive political content in lessons and the use of schools to spread communist ideology" (p. 4). After Stalin died in 1953, educational reforms were mainly concerned with improving academic standards and the polytechnical principles of Krupskaya and Makarenko.

3   Nikita Khrushchev and Educational Reform

3.1   *Philosophical Views*

After Nikita Khrushchev (1894–1971) became Soviet leader in 1953, he spoke strongly against the theoretical schooling that undermined vocational training and polytechnical principles. He called for polytechnical education to be established in order to produce qualified professionals for the new communist society. He also dealt with the fact that some young people did not want to work in industry or farming and he spoke against the social differences between manual and intellectual workers. This situation is reminiscent of the later political rhetoric in China in the 1960s during the Great Leap Forward and the Cultural Revolution.

Khrushchev presented the Program of the Communist Party of the Soviet Union (CPSU) at the 22nd Congress of the CPSU on October 18, 1961. He viewed that socialism and communism are two stages of the same social and economic form, the stages of which differ in terms of economic development and the maturity level of social relations. The economy provides the basis for a change both in social relations and human consciousness. The construction of a new society includes the following elements:

– A communist worldview with a deep belief in the ideals of communism; a conscious attitude to social responsibilities, socialist internationalism, and patriotism; loyalty to the homeland; and a willingness to lay down one's life to defend it.
– Through work education, a citizen internalizes a communist attitude toward work and social production.
– The consolidation of communist moral principles is sought by educating citizens to follow the rules of communist coexistence.
– The development of culture includes adopting the basics of science, general and polytechnical schooling, and aesthetic and physical education (U.S.S.R., 1961a, pp. 25, 63, 73).

Understanding that the Soviet Union had already become a communist country, Khrushchev emphasized that the most essential function is communist education and the well-rounded development of the individual. He introduced the idea that the goal of such education is to teach students that work is a life-sustaining force. All the good that Soviets do, they do for the good of the entire society. A conscientious attitude to work means caring for your comrades, who likewise work for the good of all, and shows the comradeship of members of the new society (U.S.S.R., 1961a, p. 75).

With Georgy Malenkov (1902–1988) and Lavrentiy Beria (1899–1953), Khrushchev implemented a series of political reforms after Stalin's death. These reforms focused, for instance, on removing the cult of personality that had surrounded Stalin, the Stalinist political system, and the Gulag labor camp system. The following summary shows how labor camps operated in the Soviet Union:

> Khrushchev's unyielding work intended to end the long-lasting political terror, purge trials, mass executions, and exiles to labor camps in the Soviet Union. However, labor camps were not a new phenomenon in Soviet society. Hosking (1992) wrote that "the labour camps to which the arrested—those who were not executed, that is—were sent were direct descendants of the concentration camps opened on Lenin's orders in 1918" (p. 197). Later, the nature of labor camps changed. Labor Camps were throughout the Soviet Union and lasted a long time. These camps received millions of people who were not criminals, but who were considered political opponents and undesirables under the totalitarian regime. Now their purpose was to support the country's industrialism. For example, a canal stretching from the White Sea to the Baltic that opened in 1933 was built using only the forced labor of Gulag prisoners. The working conditions were particularly inhuman, because the White Sea is an inland sea in the northern European part of the Soviet Union that is part of the Arctic Ocean (see, e.g., Hosking, 1992, pp. 183–226; Ranc, 2019, The Gulag—documentary examining Stalin's Gulag).

3.2   *Aims and Values*

At the turn of the 1960s, Khrushchev was convinced that the aims of the Soviet type of community-based learning should be based on Marxist socialist social theory. During Khrushchev's rule (1953–1964), the society-centered pattern of community-based learning emphasized polytechnical (moral-political and intellectual) aims and their value dimensions. These were stressed in the integration of physical, mental, and polytechnical education. The all-pervasive emphasis was on polytechnical values and the Soviet ideological system. Similarly, the power-related value dimension was prioritized in the processes of educational and societal work. The Soviet regime of the time, which harkened back to its prerevolutionary heritage, adapted imperial doctrines to its own needs while opposing tsarism. The party and its ideology, *orthodox Marxism*, represented the main virtues in education and generated obedience to the authorities in all fields. Matthews (1982) discusses school operations in more detail:

> The burden of homework was heavy—optima of one to four hours a *day*, according to class, were stipulated for the RSFSR in December 1951.

The school regulations fixed a range of permissible responses to pupils' behaviour, from the issue of a certificate of merit down to exclusion or transfer to a Borstal-type institution. Corporal punishment was, however, still banned. Control of a more social kind was the concern of "pupils' committees" which, under the terms of a statute of 4 August 1950, were elected at the level of the fifth class and above. The *Komsomol* and Young Pioneer organisations monitored activities of an ideological character. (p. 17)

Soviet Russia and its educational system experienced a new period after the war. Polytechnical education was to be the building block of the socialist school and thus an essential basis for the development of the socialist personality. Consistent use of the principles of such education required combining theory with practice, school with life, and education with production. It was understood that polytechnical education would prepare students to cope with the demands of different occupations and, when necessary, moving from one occupation to another. In this way, polytechnical education was to educate citizens who would be equipped with all-around skills and knowledge in a new communist society.

On December 24, 1958, the Central Committee of the CPSU and the Council of Ministers of the U.S.S.R. introduced a statute titled Strengthening Ties Between School and Life and Further Developing the Public Education System in the U.S.S.R. (Central Committee of the CPSU and the U.S.S.R. Council of Ministers, 1958/1974). The statute (1958/1974) emphasized that social communist reform had to be connected with the upbringing of a new citizen, which had to be in harmony with mental richness, moral purity, and physical perfection. These virtues could advance the harmonious development of a person through performing physical and creative work, strengthening the body, and elevating life activities. Moreover, the chief emphasis was on values connected with the basics of science and systematic physical work. It was believed that internalizing the fundamentals of science and systematic production would increase the benefits to and promote the values of society. Therefore, it was essential that school education be connected to productive work in the national economy, where young people by the age of 15 or 16 would be taking part in socially useful work in line with their own strengths (pp. 54–55).

The December 1958 statute was designed to connect schools with socially useful labor and, particularly, to transform schools into polytechnical ones. It established an 8-year compulsory labor school, also known as an incomplete polytechnical labor school, which provided general education. Teaching and educational work at this school was to combine the basics of science and the principles of polytechnical education. This was possible by broadly pulling students into socially useful labor appropriate to their age (Article 2). The statute indicated that young people would receive a complete secondary education during the second stage of instruction, years 8 through 11.

Polytechnical education increased in the upper grades of the 11-year *complete labor school*. This included general evening middle schools, general polytechnical middle labor schools, technicums and other special middle schools, and secondary polytechnics with production programs. Teaching was thus combined with productive labor so that all students at this stage could participate in productive and socially useful labor. Instruction was to be performed at the closest productive plants, student brigades of collective and state-owned farms, experimental units in agriculture and industry, and at schools' productive workshops. Political-ideological education was also increased in the schools (Articles 3–4, 6). Based on the December 24, 1958, statute, this type of community-based learning aimed to:

- teach general and polytechnical knowledge;
- increase support for labor and appreciation for laboring people;
- advance students' abilities and readiness for socially useful labor and activities; and
- combine teaching with the community, its plants, farms, units in industry, and their occupations (Articles 2, 6).

The intention was to train vocationally capable citizens for a new communist society. Concerning this, the 22nd Congress of the CPSU adopted the Communist Party program of the Soviet Union on October 31, 1961. Based on this program, general and polytechnical education aimed to:

- teach polytechnical basic skills and knowledge;
- advance students' scientific and technical basis so as to improve the prevailing production;
- provide labor and political training in accord with the rising level of science and engineering;
- advance skills and abilities for socially useful labor to build a communist society;
- instill the ideology of communism and a communist worldview in the spirit of proletarian internationalism;
- train communist-minded people who are harmoniously developed members of society; and
- ensure that public education is combined with life and productive labor (U.S.S.R., 1961b, pp. 111–113).

3.2.1   Summing Up

The conceptual features of communist revolutionism under Khrushchev can be interpreted from the perspective of community-based learning by applying

Hlebowitsh's (2007) classification. This type of revolutionism sees the ideal student as being a communist-minded citizen who has internalized the communist worldview in the spirit of proletarian internationalism and who is familiar with the basic sciences and the principles of polytechnical education. The ideal educational program provides students with fundamental polytechnical skills and knowledge in order to advance their scientific and technical expertise to enable them to help improve the prevailing production. It improves students' vocational competences through socially useful labor in the community's plants, farms, and factories. The student is oriented toward an ideal communist society, the citizens of which work in agricultural and industrial production.

The Khrushchev regime understood that the struggle over an educational system would continue, and that he would be commonly considered to have implemented poorly structured educational reforms. Zajda (1980) observed that the statute of December 1958 turned out to be very unpopular among educationists, teachers, parents, and students. The new 8-year and 11-year schools were too hastily instituted and organized. Educationists and those in the upper-class especially did not like that idea that students could go to university only after working at least 2 years in factories and collective farms. This reform could not bridge the gap between education and labor or between mental and physical work. The statute was revoked in 1964 (pp. 32–33). On October 15, 1964, the Kremlin announced that Khrushchev was released from all his positions (Riasanovsky & Steinberg, 2005, p. 533). However, his 1958 reforms restructured the Soviet educational system for nearly 4 decades.

4   Leonid Brezhnev and Modernization-Inclined Ideas

4.1   *Philosophical Views*
Leonid Brezhnev (1906–1982) implemented a conservative and pragmatic approach to leading the country during his regime (1964–1982). This was meant to stabilize the positions of the Soviet Union and the Communist Party. He was also careful to minimize disagreements among party members by reaching decisions through consensus. A Brezhnev-led society can be described as rigidly bureaucratic.

According to Brezhnev's policy, societal reforms are not allowed in socialist countries. This doctrine justified the use of military force against socialist states in the U.S.S.R. that attempt societal reforms. The occupation of Czechoslovakia in August 1968, for example, shocked the Western world. Although the Soviet Union was seen as a socialist superpower, the arms race became a real problem for the country. The weakening of economic growth in the Soviet Union in the second half of the 1970s meant spending an increasing share of the country's resources on the arms race. At the same time, Brezhnev's leadership began to turn into a cult of personality. His regime denied all claims of an economic crisis and declared the superiority of socialism (Jungar, 2004, pp. 482–484, 493).

The report from the 24th Congress of the CPSU, held in 1971, emphasized that the party and the people have always endorsed and will endorse Marxist-Leninist ideology. The crucial work is to find solutions to the problems of communist construction using Lenin's ideas and methods. The report confirmed that the party had experienced the consequences of the cult of personality and that subjective mistakes have positively contributed to the ideological situation in the country. As a consequence, the party will never make any concessions in questions of ideology (U.S.S.R., 1971, pp. 119–120).

Under a new Soviet constitution in 1977, the regime claimed that Soviet society had reached the stage of advanced socialism. The highest goal of the Soviet Union was to build a classless communist society. The government should create a material and technical basis for such a society, raise the material and cultural level of workers, guarantee the security of the country, establish peace, and promote international cooperation (U.S.S.R., 1977, pp. 2–3). Securing peace required the continued development of weapons. Economic stagnation deepened, and the country's economic growth weakened from the 1960s to the 1990s. Inevitably, this caused political uncertainty.

4.2   Aims and Values

The 23rd Congress of the Communist Party of the U.S.S.R. presented the directives for the Five-Year Plan for 1966–1970. This document stated that the main economic task was to secure industry growth and maintain high rates of agricultural development. This was to be achieved through the application of science and technology, the industrial development of social production, and the enhancement of efficiency and higher labor productivity. There was a strong belief that this would increase the gross domestic product by 40% and basic production assets by more than 50%, including 60% in industry and 90% in agriculture (U.S.S.R., 1966, p. 19).

Brezhnev saw that the main goal of education was to train capable citizens in a developed socialist society. The U.S.S.R. constitution of 1977 emphasized that schools should train students to become patriotic and international workers who are proud to be citizens of the U.S.S.R. Students should learn that the U.S.S.R. is the first developed socialist country in the world and understand that they are part of the international proletarian world. They should be convinced that the U.S.S.R. is a society of order, ideology, and consciousness (see U.S.S.R., 1977, p. 2).

Labor education in Soviet schools under Brezhnev primarily emphasized polytechnical (intellectual and moral-political) aims through the integration of physical, mental, and polytechnical education. Within this, the society intended to train versatile, capable citizens who could work in a developed socialist society. Emphasis was placed on polytechnical values, and the Soviet ideological system was associated with the power-related value dimension. From the late 1960s, the intention was to instruct students to apply scientific knowledge to practical purposes, and intellectual aims were therefore to be connected to promoting technological knowledge and associated theoretical values.

During these years, the main goal was to train capable citizens in a socialist society. The ninth Supreme Council of the U.S.S.R. adopted the 1977 constitution on October 7, 1977. The constitution of 1977 aimed to:

- provide free education in all forms of school;
- permit all young people to complete general secondary education;
- develop extensively technical vocational training, secondary special training, and higher education based on the relation between education, life, and production;
- arrange further letter and evening studies;
- grant state scholarships and other benefits to students, such as free textbooks;
- provide an opportunity to study at school in their native tongue; and
- create favorable conditions for self-study (U.S.S.R., 1977, Article 45).

In the 1970s, the school structure and teaching content were reformed. A school for 10-year general education was established, with the 3-year elementary school beginning at the age of 7. Since moral and political education was considered the most important issue in educational reform, on December 22, 1977, the Central Committee of the CPSU introduced a statute titled On Further Improvements in Education and Upbringing of the Secondary School Students and Their Preparation for Labor. The December 22, 1977 statute indicated that general education was to prepare young people for a working life as completely developed builders of a socialist society. This type of work-related education aimed to:

- increase devotion for work and deep appreciation for working people;
- strengthen readiness to work in the field of material production;
- establish absolute faithfulness to the homeland and the Communist Party;
- instill a readiness to defend the socialist homeland; and
- link the instruction of the basics of science more closely to life and the construction of a theory of communism (Central Committee of the CPSU, 1977/1987, Article 2).

The 1974 curriculum considered the primary classes of the 8-year school. The statute of December 22, 1977, intended to advance education of secondary school students and their training for labor. Based on these reforms, this type of community-based learning aimed to:

- develop students' character through labor;
- advance the communist viewpoint on labor and working people;
- broaden students' work experiences and their knowledge about work and technologies;
- develop labor skills, basics of work culture, and abilities to plan and organize one's own and a comrade's work;
- teach skills for working in a modern national economy; and
- provide basic information from different fields of science (U.S.S.R., 1974, p. 56; Central Committee of the CPSU, 1977/1987, Articles 2, 6).

During the 1970s, the school system was expected to train citizens to be technology-minded supporters of Soviet industry and to respect manual labor and handicraft in order to make the polytechnical principle successful. Soviet citizens should have a Marxist-Leninist worldview with a materialistic and atheistic outlook. It was essential to trust in the sciences within schoolwork, when history and social studies were to politically and ideologically strengthen the prevailing socialist society. Even though ideological values were still promoted in teaching, the significance of science and technology, in particular, was now underlined in order to enable students to understand modern technology and its scientific principles.

4.2.1 Summing Up

The conceptual features of revolutionism during advanced socialism under Brezhnev can be interpreted from the perspective of community-based learning by applying Hlebowitsh's (2007) classification. This kind of revolutionism sees the ideal student as being a citizen who is involved in physical and mental work when learning the various phases and processes of industrial and agricultural production. The ideal educational program includes polytechnical work, the processes of which provide students polytechnical basic skills and knowledge that advances their scientific and technological understanding so as to improve production. While taking part in these processes, students can learn to think economically and choose their own profession and its training within socialist ideology and morals. Students are oriented toward an ideal socialist society, the citizens of which work in a modern national economy and, if necessary, are able to change their profession to new fields of production in a developed socialist society.

During the Brezhnev years, the Soviet school intended to be a polytechnical labor-based school that had general educational worth. Education aimed to advance abilities for independent, useful work and work relations between comrades and contacts in the surrounding community in order to keep pro-mote the relation between education, life, and production. Similarly, it was important to be able to be involved in production and labor processes. The 10-year Soviet school was academically oriented, even if the process of collective socialization was different. The most difficult barrier was that school authori-ties and the students' parents preferred traditional education.

5   Yuri Andropov, Konstantin Chernenko, and the Brezhnevian Policies

5.1   *Philosophical Views*

After Brezhnev died in 1982, Yuri Andropov (1914–1984) and Konstantin Chernenko (1911–1985) carried on his politics. The most important was to keep the country going forward in consensus. There was continuing emphasis on high productivity, scientific and technological progress, and the expansion of workforce training (U.S.S.R., 1984/1987, Articles 2, 3).

Andropov (1983) emphasized that the educational task is not to purify the Marxist-Leninist doctrine but, on the contrary, to struggle for its purity and creative development. This is how it is possible to comprehend and solve new problems. Such an approach could meet the traditions, the spirit, and the needs of the communist movement so that (a) a large amount of manual labor, which accounts for almost half of the industry, should not be allowed, (b) the Soviets have to accelerate scientific and technological progress and make use of its achievements, especially in areas where labor costs are high, and (c) it is similarly important to modernize work areas through the mechanization and automation of production. This was also seen to be socially and politically important (pp. 9, 15).

At a speech in 1975 at the Conference on Security and Cooperation in Hel-sinki, Finland, Chernenko (1976) indicated that the Soviets oppose confronta-tion on the battlefield but consider it inevitable on the ideological field. The confrontation is rooted in a strong determination to ensure world peace and cooperation among people. The Soviets reject ideas based on all sorts of preju-dices, doubts, and fears but support the exchange of constructive ideas. Consci-entious opponents of the Soviets know that they do not oppose the exchange of information, ideas, and international contacts. The Soviets oppose destruc-tive and nationalist ideas that divide peoples and nations and set them against each other. The Soviet Union and other socialist countries favor a stable and consistent way of transforming the agreements of the Helsinki conference into a policy of peace and mutual understanding between peoples (pp. 27–28, 32).

The Brezhnevian economy continued stagnating during the Andropov (1982–1984) and Chernenko (1984–1985) periods. Foreign observers also found that the pace of the rigidly centralized economy of the Soviet Union slowed through the 1970s and into the 1980s. It was observed that the Soviet regime had little chance of implementing radical reforms that could improve the Soviet economy. While average GDP growth could be as low as 2%, no improvement in economic performance was expected without major policy changes. The Soviet economy would wane due to serious inefficiency and irrationality (C.I.A. sees stagnation, 1983, p. 1).

5.2   Aims and Values

Andropov and Chernenko continued Brezhnev's educational policies. On April 12, 1984, the Supreme Soviet of the U.S.S.R. approved a statute titled Guidelines to Reform General Education and Vocational Schools. This act regulated the school system for general and vocational education and secured young people's general middle school education as well as work and vocational training. The school system was organized as follows:
- primary schools included Grades 1 to 4;
- incomplete middle schools included Grades 5 to 9; and
- general and vocational middle schools included general school Grades 10 and 11 as well as vocational schools and vocational middle schools (U.S.S.R., 1984/1987, Article 4).

The April 12, 1984 statute emphasized that all areas of the national economy must benefit science and technology, implement extensive automatization of production, guarantee a significant increase in labor productivity, and produce the best products in the world. Achieving these goals required young citizens to have as modern an education as possible, a high level of intellectual and physical development, a deep understanding of the scientific and technological basis of production, and a conscious and creative relationship with work. Work education must be seen as (a) the most important factor in the development of an individual's personality, and (b) a means of responding to the labor needs of the national economy (Article 2).

Realizing that this type of educational reform faced many challenges in accordance with advanced socialism, the April 12, 1984 statute required the government to:
- raise the standard of teaching by strengthening mastery of the foundations of science and by developing work education, ideological-political education, and moral education;

- reform curricula, educational programs, textbooks, and materials;
- expand the training of the highly skilled workforce by improving work arrangements, vocational training, and career guidance; and
- increase student responsibility for the quality of their studies and adherence to work and study discipline (Article 3).

The most important aim of the April 12, 1984 statute was to train socialist-minded citizens who would be able to work in a developed socialist society. Education was to be based on polytechnical (intellectual and moral-political) aims in integrating physical, mental, and polytechnical education. The emphasis was on polytechnical value dimensions and associated intellectual, moral-political, and power-related values. Such a school system of polytechnical education aimed to:

- teach respect for work and workers;
- familiarize students with the basics of modern transportation, industrial and agricultural production, and the building and service sectors;
- instill work habits and skills through teaching processes and socially useful work;
- guide students in choosing their own profession and its training; and
- teach students to be careful and frugal when handling common property (Articles 21, 24).

5.2.1   Summing Up

The conceptual features of revolutionism under Andropov and Chernenko can be interpreted from the perspective of community-based learning by applying Hlebowitsh's (2007) classification. This kind of revolutionism sees the ideal student as a patriotic and international citizen who is familiar with the various phases of industrial and agricultural production within socialist ideology and morals. The ideal educational program includes polytechnical work, the processes of which provide students the basics of modern transportation, industrial and agricultural production, and the building and service sectors. Through this, students can choose their own profession and its training. The student is oriented toward an ideal socialist society, the citizens of which work in a modern national economy and, if there are societal or personal changes, they can move to a new field of production.

The far-reaching implications of Brezhnev's policies gave confidence to the privileged in the Soviet Union bureaucracy, the members of the Central Committee, and the directors of its departments. However, at the same time, the economic slowdown was leading this vast socialist country into a dangerous situation.

6   Mikhail Gorbachev Reforms with Perestroika and Glasnost

6.1   *Philosophical Views*

Mikhail Gorbachev (1931–) ideologically adhered to Marxism-Leninism, although by the early 1990s he had moved toward social democracy. Gorbachev began to implement reforms with perestroika and glasnost through his period (1985–1991). Perestroika was a political movement that referred to the restructuring of the Soviet political and economic system and was associated with the policy of glasnost, which aimed for a more open, consultative government and wider dissemination of information. Iivonen (2004) summarizes Gorbachev's reforms as follows:

> Had Gorbachev moved aside at the end of 1990, he would have remained one of the greatest statesmen in history in the 20th century. In less than six years he had:
>
> – put an end to the Communist Party's monopoly in the Soviet Union and set aside the old guard that had led it for decades;
> – renounced state atheism and granted freedom of action to the Orthodox Church founded a 1,000 years earlier and to certain other denominations;
> – brought the previously lacking transparency into the country's cultural life;
> – renewed the country's history from the unknown periods;
> – granted greater economic and political freedom to both the Soviet republics and the regions;
> – abandoned the state's economic monopoly and restored private property and entrepreneurship;
> – reduced the Soviet armed and security forces, and brought them under more democratic political control;
> – allowed the countries of Eastern Europe to choose their own path; and
> – took a number of disarmament initiatives and normalized the country's relations with the United States and Western Europe. (p. 523)

6.2   *Aims and Values*

In the late 1980s, the Soviet Union attempted a more far-reaching and fundamental restructuring. Gorbachev's campaign of perestroika and glasnost aimed to democratize the Soviet society. He came to the conclusion that many Soviet citizens supported perestroika and glasnost and was convinced that these would lead to new thinking and make the prevailing socialist society more democratic. During this time, the school-centered pattern of community-based learning emphasized intellectual and moral-political aims and their value dimensions. These were stressed in the integration of physical, mental, and polytechnical (intellectual and moral-political) education. The pervasive emphasis was placed on intellectual values within the Soviet ideological system.

The 27th Congress of the CPSU, held in Moscow in February and March 1986, adopted the Communist Party program of the Soviet Union. According to this program, general and polytechnical education aimed to:

- strengthen communist attitudes toward work, including respect for labor and a sense of responsibility, as well as creativity, collective cooperation, and the ability to take the initiative;
- educate students to become conscious and knowledgeable citizens capable of both physical and mental work, and who actively participate in the national economy in various spheres of social and state life, and in the fields of science and culture;
- prepare citizens for an independent working life;
- integrate general education and vocational training; and
- contribute to the socioeconomic, scientific, and technological development of the country and to the development of communism (U.S.S.R., 1986a, pp. 92, 97–98).

However, the 27th Congress also observed the slowdown in national economic development. The attempts to increase production were weak as was the restructuring of production processes, the administration of the regime, and the management of the economy. These problems led to disruptions in societal essentials and achievable production levels, demands for material items, and difficulties meeting the country's food needs (U.S.S.R., 1986b, pp. 10–11). These difficulties were caused by the following:

- New industrial equipment and production methods introduced far too slowly.
- The technical level and quality of many products, such as consumer goods, fell short of modern requirements.
- Breaches in contractual obligations in delivering products.
- The failure of some republics, ministries, combinations, and companies to reach five-year plan goals in terms of production volumes, labor productivity, product and labor costs, saving on material resources, and starting up production units.
- Politicians who felt compelled to further efforts to maintain the country's defense capabilities.

A major school reform meeting was held in the plenary session of the CPSU Central Committee in February 1988. The following, from Gorbachev's speech at the session, explicates the manner in which he reviewed the Soviet Union's past:

> In all 70 years, our party and our people have been inspired by the ideals of socialism and built socialism. But for both external and internal reasons, we have not been able to fully implement the principles of Lenin's new social structure. It was severely hampered by a personality cult, in the 1930s command mentality-based management developed, bureaucratic, dogmatic, and voluntaristic distortions, arbitrariness, as well as in the late 70s and early 80s lack of initiative and procrastinating phenomena that led to stagnation. (U.S.S.R., 1988b, p. 9)

Yegor Ligachyov (1920–2021), the secretary of the CPSU Central Committee, presented at the 1988 Congress the guidelines for reforming primary, secondary, and tertiary education as well as the functions of the party in its implementation. He also dealt with the aims and associated procedures of small-scale organizational and educational reforms within perestroika:
- Increase the responsibility of students for their studies and the responsibility of teachers for the level of their teaching.
- Strengthen the connections of higher education institutions to production and science. Concerning this, the authorities started to establish the branch departments of university chairs, research laboratories, and other joint sub-units in production facilities, combinations, and research institutes.
- Have technical vocational schools train more multi-occupational workers, and have higher education institutions participate in the work of scientific and technical institutes in various fields (U.S.S.R., 1988a, p. 48).

The 28th Congress of the CPSU, held in Moscow in July 1990, turned out to be the last Congress of the Communist Party of the Soviet Union. According to Kalashnikov (2016), between 1986 and 1990, Gorbachev had initiated a perestroika-focused reform program, leading to a bitter struggle within the party regarding some of his reforms. The Congress was important in rebuilding consensus between the centrist group, the liberal democratic group, and the conservative Marxist group. Although the negotiations at the Congress did not succeed, the party's strategic direction in the form of the party program was delineated (pp. 35–36). The CPSU resolutions stated that:
- Through asserting human rights, free elections, and a multiparty system, the entire political structure was being altered, and becoming more democratic.

- The CPSU was being revamped to become more openly competitive and cooperating with other parties, elections, and parliamentary activities.
- The political situation was complicated by the decline in discipline at both state and labor levels; the increase in crime and violence; the presence of corruption, profiteering, drunkenness, and drug addiction; and the decrease in moral standards.
- The party committees, party branches, and all communists were encouraged to actively consolidate party properties and effectively utilize financial and material resources in the new conditions of the CPSU.
- The principle of a phased transition to a market economy was supported for foods and agricultural raw materials, and the guaranteed provision of resources enabling state orders to be fulfilled.
- The Congress intended to democratize education by giving greater independence to educational institutions and developing international cooperation in educational fields (U.S.S.R., 1990, pp. 96, 98, 99, 107, 109, 114).

6.2.1   Summing Up

The conceptual features of revolutionism under Gorbachev can be interpreted from the perspective of community-based learning by applying Hlebowitsh's (2007) classification. This kind of revolutionism sees the ideal student as being a citizen who is a supporter of perestroika and glasnost, and who is capable of physical and mental work in the fields of science and culture and in various spheres of economic, social, and state life. These well-educated people are creative and have respect for work and collective cooperation, a sense of responsibility, and the ability to take the initiative. The ideal educational program includes polytechnical work, the processes of which students are able to involve in the projects that prepare them for an independent working life. The student is oriented toward an ideal socialist society, the citizens of which work in a modern national economy and, if there are societal or personal changes, they can work in new fields of production.

The Soviet Union experienced many types of problems, but it seemed unable to repair its socialist country, and all of Gorbachev's reforms weren't enough to save Soviet socialism. One after another, reforms failed or remained incomplete. Many opponents, including the old guard and elite, did not want to give up their interests. The country's GDP and labor productivity continued to decline and the Soviet Union was unable to balance its budget. Legislative reforms were too slow, and Gorbachev's proposal in November 1990 for a new union treaty, for instance, was too late. However, an inescapable problem came in the form of political awakenings. In April 1991, a new Soviet constitution was adopted, which included the election of a president by a direct referendum.

It is obvious that many officials recognized the problems in education. There was a gap between the prevailing state of primary, secondary, and tertiary education and the atmosphere that was spreading widely across the country. Many people in the society were convinced that reform was stuck due to numerous problems. Similarly, there were noticeable signs that progress in schooling was slowing down compared to international schooling levels (see U.S.S.R., 1988a, p. 49).

Gorbachev was an ardent defender of perestroika and glasnost. After Stalin died, he was a keen proponent of the de-Stalinization reforms of Khrushchev. His work was also noticed by foreign observers. The Norwegian Nobel Committee, crediting that Gorbachev played a leading role in bringing the Cold War to a peaceful end, awarded him the Peace Prize in 1990. Eventually, however, Gorbachev resigned as president on December 25, 1991. The following day, the Soviet Union was formally dissolved.

Why did the Soviet Union break up? The following quotation, based on Lord John Dalberg-Acton's (1834–1902) letter to an Anglican bishop in 1887, speaks to this: "Power tends to corrupt, and absolute power corrupts absolutely." Even though reforms were strictly forbidden in the Soviet Union, the collapse was possible due to an internally rigid system and other associated internal and external factors. The monolithic regime could not solve its many problems, and the system began to quickly and uncontrollably disintegrate (Iivonen, 2004, p. 531). Iivonen (2004) summarized the reasons for the breakdown into five factors:

1. Deficiencies in the Soviet political system and the internal crisis of the Communist Party.
2. A widening gap between the decision-making and privileged political elite and ordinary citizens.
3. The collapse of the Soviet economy.
4. Exacerbation of national conflicts within the country.
5. The Soviet Union's unfavorable international position (p. 531).

It can also be interpreted that the rigid political system eventually drove the state into chaos. As Iivonen (2004) described, within the party and in society as a whole, a strong hierarchy was established, with the lower level submitting to the higher level. The power of the Communist Party leadership was not divided between the lower party bodies and the parliamentary bodies. No one wanted to relinquish power, making the leadership stagnant and even more incapable of meeting new challenges. It was very difficult for new ideas to emerge in such a system. The Soviets had created a one-party system in which a small group of privileged people enjoyed freedom and the majority of the population was subjugated (pp. 531–532).

The following section deals with the essence of community-based learning in the Soviet Union in a more concrete manner. The nature of activities is studied from the perspective offered by central pedagogical approaches and their dimensions of the learning environment. The primary focus is on polytechnical education.

7   Community-Based Pedagogical Ideas in the Soviet Union

After years of turmoil in Soviet Russia (1918–1922)—after the Russian Revolution and Civil War, the Allied intervention during World War I, the war with Poland in 1918, and national independence movements—the Bolshevik Communist Party led by Lenin came to power. The Fifth All-Russian Congress of Soviets adopted the first Soviet constitution, which went into effect on July 10, 1918. The constitution established the Russian Soviet Federated Socialist Republic (R.S.F.S.R.). On December 30, 1922, the Union of Soviet Socialist Republics (U.S.S.R.) came into being as a federation of Russia, Belarus, the Ukraine, and Transcaucasia. In the late 1920s, three Central Asiatic republics also received the status of Union Republic. The new federation was in extreme economic, social, and political crisis. Millions of people had died from war, hunger, and disease. To overcome these difficulties, the New Economic Policy was adopted (Riasanovsky & Steinberg, 2005, pp. 466–477).

Teachers in this vast country implemented labor education in school programs. This type of education included work lessons, communal work at the school, and labor-related activities in school workshops and in certain parts of the community. Implementation varied with local conditions and the prevailing social trends. The following examines community-based pedagogical ideas in the Narkompros School and in the years following the Narkompros, particularly during the regimes of Stalin, Khrushchev, Brezhnev, and Gorbachev.

7.1   The Narkompros School

The writings of the Western reform pedagogues impacted the educational ideas of the school reformers at the Narkompros, in addition to Marxist polytechnical education and Tolstoy's Rousseauian child-centered pedagogy. Brickman (1960) reported that "Shatski, Blonski, Albert P. Pinkevitch, Anatol Lunacharski, and other educators of the first decade of Soviet existence made frequent mention of Dewey in their writings and made use of his ideas" (p. 84). Shatsky's (1981a) Tolstoyan labor school was a combination of physical and intellectual work, games, artistic activities, and social life. He believed that work training was most important, especially when students regard it as essential for their collective (*kolkhoz*). Therefore, he was convinced that work training should be integrated not only with communal labor but with the economic conditions and the cultural aspects of the region, since socially useful labor would be the crucial method for socialist education (Shatsky, 1981a, pp. 35–36, 190).

During this innovative era, the All-Russian Central Executive Committee published several educational documents. One of them is the well-known statute of the Unified Labor School of October 16, 1918. The statute (1918/1947) viewed that such progressive ideas as self-governing, individual needs, group work, and group divisions were to be common in Soviet educational thinking after the Russian Revolution. These ideas and methods were to be used in projects in which socially useful productive labor and polytechnical education were intimately combined with instruction. It was forbidden to give homework to students. Similarly, all degrees and penalties were abolished (All-Russian Central Executive Committee of the R.S.F.S.R., 1918/1947, Articles 12–13, 17–20, 27).

During the experimental period from 1921 to 1931, Soviet educators applied various kinds of methods to collective instruction within the revolutionary society. Pinkevitch (1929) wrote that educators also applied a system of student parliaments and courts, presented by educator Wilson L. Gill (1851–1941), to their instruction (p. 214). The educational policymakers changed Western methods by omitting individual assignments. Educators utilized Parkhurst's Dalton Plan in the brigade method as the *synthetic* method with Marxist ideas. Pinkevitch (1929) held that the synthetic method "should be understood as the pedagogical expression of the dialectic method" and includes "a general philosophic theory underlying all the work of our school" (p. 304).

Educators also applied Kilpatrick's project method to integrated teaching as the *complex* method for students 8- to 12-years-old. According to Pinkevitch (1929), this term refers, to "a certain method of organizing the materials of instruction" when implementing group work on projects (p. 313). Parkhurst's Dalton Plan was utilized for students older than 12 in the brigade-laboratory method that included group work on projects. Fitzpatrick (1979) wrote that by 1931 the Narkompros had also recommended this method to universities, where students worked under the supervision of a professor. The practice of collective testing (*kellektivnyi uchet*) replaced formal examinations (p. 191). Fitzpatrick (1979) describes the difficulties in organizing this type of method at the Plekhanov Economics Institute:

> Each brigade, consisting of five or six persons, had its own study plan and its own timetable. All this required a colossal number of separate

classrooms. The supply of auditoria was completely inadequate. A breakdown of classes occurred.

No account was taken of the student's allocation of time. There were a large number of gaps between classes. In testing knowledge, it was difficult to establish the individuality of each member of the brigade. The more competent students, on whom fell responsibility for the success of the whole brigade, carried an enormous workload. (p. 191)

Schools could pursue active and social pedagogical ideas of the content and timing of study, children's freedom, and common life. Degrees, certificates, and grades were eliminated. Textbooks were replaced with exercise booklets in accordance with the statute of October 16, 1918. The elementary school teaching program (for 8- to 12-year-olds) was grouped around three main cycles: nature, labor, and society. Students were involved in the labor life of the village or city block in which they lived, or they studied the economics of a local region. They also took part in a certain amount of self-governing in the school. The teacher acted with the students as an instructor, organizer, assistant, or older comrade (Pinkevitch, 1929, pp. 202, 305).

Students worked on projects and became acquainted with nature as well as social and working life in accordance with the 1923 curriculum. At elementary schools, students became familiar with the basics of the surrounding community, including its nature and labor life, as well as the economy of the Russian Republic and other Soviet countries. Teachers guided students in writing and talking about such topics as the labor life of their community or the economics of their local region. During the first year of secondary school, students explored organic and inorganic nature, the use of natural resources, and social life. Teachers could design a project on such topics as the struggle of peasants against landowners or an autocratic regime (Pinkevitch, 1929, pp. 305–306).

Under the Narkompros in the 1920s, the basic type of polytechnical school for general education became consolidated in 1925. The students of the unified labor school could participate in socially productive work, school workshops, factory shops, and plants. By working, they familiarized themselves with the habits of socialist labor conduct, social purposefulness, organization, and conscious work discipline. After this type of labor school, students could be accepted into factory apprenticeships or technical schools (Löfstedt, 1980, p. 54). The unified labor school strove to maintain the Sociocultural Dimension of its learning environment, when students made needed items from wood and metal and simple supplies for school use. The following presents how students prioritized the Sociocultural Dimension in their learning environment at a factory school in the district of Sormovo in the city of Nizhny Novgorod, Central Russia:

> The Edison School of Industrial Workers was founded in 1922 in the district of Sormovo. It provided students with general education and a vocational qualification. The school was located in one of the oldest buildings in the factory section. The facilities included two large classrooms, a small storage room, two workshops, and a small auxiliary workshop. One of the workshops was for metalwork and the other for woodcraft. The school, which admitted students continuously, could have as many as 65 students. This school was intended for factory workers' children who were 15- to 17-years-old and had already passed elementary school. School instruction included theoretical lessons that were common to all. In practical work, students were divided into wood- and metalworking groups. Teachers implemented different methods: some of the lessons were lectures, some were homework assignments, and some of the lessons utilized the insight method. Students also made simple supplies for school use. Carpenters made trash cans, ladders, and guardrails for work machines. A group of filers made angle rulers and harps (Okunkov, 1923, pp. 95–98).

There was increasing emphasis on electrical training. In 1934, the Central Committee of the All-Union Communist Party enacted a statute that emphasized students learning electrical techniques: they made plans for electrical works, applied electrical techniques in the processes of mechanical production, and become acquainted with the electrical systems of stations, construction sites, and state farms. Middle school students also had to be taught how to handle wood and metal (Central Committee of the All-Union Communist Party, 1934/1974a, p. 162). One school in Shuya had implemented electrical training earlier in the 1920s when the content and nature of work-related teaching varied in different areas according to the needs of the community and society. The following two summaries show how teaching was organized in two different schools, one in the town of Shuya and the other in the city of Saratov, Russia:

> The Shuysky School in the town of Shuya in the city of Ivanovo-Voznesensk began as early as 1925 to teach electrical works because of the growing need for electricians in the area. This decision was also supported by the fact that the school had a well-equipped physics class that made it possible to teach this occupation. Despite emphasis on the

Scientific-Technical Dimension of the learning environment in which students performed electrical installations, teaching also accentuated the Sociocultural Dimension of the learning environment through financial benefits for the school from their work. The school independently developed the following electrical technique curriculum:

- An in-depth course in the theory of electricity. Teachers prepared the program (4 hours a week).
- An electrical technique work plan drawn according to engineer Valentin A. Alexandrov's (1909) textbook (6 hours a week).
- A course program that included geometric drawings, projections, and technical drawings (2 hours a week).

As no internships were available for students, the school organized an internship workshop. All students at the school were required to complete a month-long summer internship. After the internship, the students could attend a workshop for paid work, for which the school contracted with a maintenance company. Some of the students' pay was transferred from workshop operations to the school. With this money, the school purchased three used lathes, a drill, five different vises, and various files. The school received the materials partly from the employer and partly from the workshop. The electrical tools were used in work starting in 1927. From May 1927 to October 1928, the students did the electrical installation in a new secondary school building for free. This work was valued at 1,500 rubles at the time. However, the school could earn 17,685 rubles from large projects, such as repairing the town's electrical grid in 1927 and 1928, making electrical grid repairs and improvements, installing electrical systems in new buildings in Shuya, working on electrical and engine installations at the new water station and at the new hospital, and performing other work ordered by the Economic Committee of Shuya (Ryabtsev, 1929, pp. 32–34).

Students may have been trained in a particular occupation or given different vocational titles. The following summary shows how teaching was organized in a school in the city of Saratov:

The Saratovsky School was located in the city of Saratov, along the Volga in southeastern Russia. In the fall of 1918, the regional Public Education Committee *Gubotnarob* decided that all elementary and secondary schools should spend 4 hours a week on occupational training. Work process instructors were appointed in all schools, and teachers of general subjects also taught in workshops. Schools provided the tools, work machines, and essential materials. During these processes, the Sociocultural Dimension was an essential component when, for example, students performed drama on the stage or did knitting work. Similarly, the Productive Dimension was most likely prioritized in the learning environment when students were producing mugs and buckets.

One teacher at this school had previously worked in Moscow and taken a course that dealt with the ideas of Blonsky's system. Now his school undertook an experiment in Elshanka, which was famous for its school palace. Students were divided into groups focused on different labor, such as of housework, handicrafts, the arts, making equipment, and performing certifications. For example, students in the handicraft group did knitting and braiding work, students in the art group published a magazine and performed drama on the stage, and the certification group did different kinds of work, such as the census. Some schools started to do productive work, such as teaching students to create mugs, buckets, and boxes according to orders. One teacher worked with straw, as the local conditions were favorable for braiding and making supplies from straw (Lonzinger, 1921, pp. 15, 20–21).

In Soviet schools, labor was not a separate subject—it was the axis of the entire pedagogical process (Pinkevitch, 1929, p. 268). Whyte (1974) wrote that Soviet schools aimed to be operationally connected to the activities of a farm, factory, or other institution in the community, and which provided materials, equipment, tools, and part-time teachers. Therefore, the school and a community site could form an integral part of the whole (Whyte, 1974, pp. 117–118). The Productive Dimension was emphasized most strongly in these two learning environments when students worked in the factory during winter and in the large state farm *Uspenskoe* during summer. The following describes how students applied the Productive Dimension in their learning environments at the Narkompros Secondary Polytechnical School when they worked at the factory and the state farm:

> The Secondary Polytechnical School located near Moscow had 35 students who were 12- to 16-years-old. The school year was divided into two periods: the winter period from October to March and the summer period from April to September. During winter, students worked in the factory and during the summer in the large state farm *Uspenskoe*. After a medical examination and consultation between school doctors and the

factory, students were allowed to work at the factory 2 hours a day 4 days a week. Students could work in the winding, warping, pressing, pleating, and filing departments, and at the electric and thermal stations, but were not allowed to work in the weaving, rinsing, and dyeing departments. During the summer, students worked on the large state farm, about 35 versts (23 miles) from Moscow. The students performed all kinds of agricultural work according to their abilities. The Secondary Polytechnical School also had a Polytechnical Middle School at the farm, where its students studied and worked year-round (Pistrak, 1922, pp. 48–49, 51).

Teachers aimed to integrate instruction with the life and activities of the community and its people. During these processes, the Sociocultural Dimension was the first priority when the students and their teacher enhanced well-being in the community, such as equipping the school's electric station to light the school and the local premises. The following shows how a Narkompros experimental school maintained the Sociocultural Dimension in its learning environment when the school benefited its community:

The Khotkovsky Experimental School of the Narkompros was established in 1919 in the city of Khotkovo, near the city of Yaroslavl, northeast of Moscow. This secondary school was located in the house of the former manor owner and had a few small cottages, a greenhouse, a field, and a vegetable garden with hotbeds. Students' activities in the school community can be divided into three separate but interrelated forms of education: general, vocational, and agricultural. Within a few years, the school arranged workshops for wood- and metalworking in the old stable and equipped its own electric station for lighting the school and neighboring premises. During years of difficult growing conditions, cultivating new varieties of seeds proved to be important. The school distributed plant seedlings to local residents and taught them how to grow plant species. The local residents grew various cabbage species and other plants for food from school seedlings (Dukhovskoy, 1923, pp. 63, 65).

Students often worked for their school and supported their community. With their teachers, students took care of school maintenance, prepared teaching aids, and performed other school-related activities, such as helping community members, either on their own or collectively. The students of the school in Shatura accentuated the Sociocultural Dimension of their learning environment when they made teaching aids the school needed. The following describes how the students of the local school in Shatura benefited their school and community:

> The Shatursky School, established in 1919 in the town of Shatura in the Moscow region, intended to implement the principles of the labor school. In the beginning, the school had only eight students, but gradually the number of students increased to 250. During the first year and a half, the school had to move from one temporary space to another and had to build fences and a henhouse, and dig occasional wells and compost pits. The students made teaching aids, procured necessary raw materials, cleared the woodland, prepared a vegetable garden, searched for old furniture, repaired or built new furniture, and made decorations, costumes, and stage properties for school celebrations. Moreover, the students built the workshops for sewing, shoemaking, and woodcrafting. Students also helped local people with such jobs as firefighting, harvesting, and planting potatoes (Radchenko, 1922, pp. 43–45).

Pinkevitch (1929) wrote that the school should provide: (a) a workshop for simple repairs of school furniture and equipment, (b) an opportunity to work in various productive activities in a vegetable garden, field, and factory, and (c) the introduction of manual work as a method of teaching different subjects (p. 259–260). The students of the school in Mologa accentuated the Scientific-Agricultural Dimension in their learning environment when they carried out experiments on fertilizer and plant species. The following describes how the Narkompros experimental school in the town of Mologa implemented gardening and beekeeping in their studies:

> The Botanical and Beekeeping Experimental School operated in the town of Mologa, at the confluence of the Mologa and Volga Rivers in the Yaroslavl region. The 1923 program of this 7-year school offered, in addition to general education, courses in gardening and beekeeping for rural students. At the beginning of the school year, there were 22 boys and 19 girls who were 15- to 19-years-old, while at the start of spring work, there were only 18 boys and 10 girls, since the others were helping their parents. The school grounds had a mansion, garden with apiaries, vegetable garden, nursery garden, compost, hotbed, flower bed, maintenance area, and an experimental plot. The school also used a field outside the city where students and teachers cultivated hay for the school's animals: six workhorses, 12 cows, one bull, 30 chickens, and rabbits. The students built a well from which water could be obtained for irrigation and other purposes. This helped students in their watering work. The beehives had an

educational purpose, and the students took care of the garden with 17 apiaries. If work on the vegetable garden did not go as well as the most enthusiastic students wanted, the work on the experimental plot went better. Tests with fertilizer and plant species were carried out on the experimental site in order to determine which plant species were best suited to the area (Karelskikh, 1923, pp. 121–125, 127).

Some schools offered rural students an opportunity to get vocational training alongside general educational studies. Pinkevitch (1929) wrote that students could organize agricultural projects, work in the field, and take care of their own garden. This offered labor processes with various productive facts, relations, processes, and principles (pp. 258–259). During these processes, the Sociocultural Dimension was prioritized in the learning environment when students repaired vegetable garden tools for school use. The Horticultural Dimension was also emphasized in the learning environment when the student groups took care of their own vegetable garden. The following explains how the students at a school in the city of Petrograd accentuated the Sociocultural and Horticultural Dimensions in their learning environment while working in the school's vegetable garden during the summer:

The Petrograd School was accustomed to providing a theoretical perspective on students' new physical work. In 1919, work that was started on a vegetable garden was used to illustrate science teaching. Initially, students were divided into groups. Each group had to collect stones and trash from their own vegetable garden, turn beds, make rows, sow seeds, take seedlings from hotbeds and transplant them to the vegetable garden, and irrigate, weed, and harvest the crop. Work started in mid-May, with good results achieved due to good care and good weather conditions. The school was invited to a vegetable garden exhibition in early October, where they were awarded a diploma.

In 1920, this school began preparing for the spring season as early as the end of March. The school's garden tools, such as shovels and rakes, were repaired; rusted watering cans were soldered; new stretchers were made; and fences and broken sides of hotbeds were repaired. All of this work was done with teachers of different subjects during the handicraft lessons. The school's summer program also included work in the vegetable garden and excursions (Chelyustkin, 1922, pp. 52–53, 55).

7.1.1   Challenges

After the Russian Revolution of 1917, the Soviet school curriculum included productive work in line with Marx's ideas. Soviet school reformers Krupskaya,

Shatsky, and Blonsky were also influenced by the educational ideas of Western school reformers. Central to the New Economic Policy-based society was party affiliation, on the one hand, and experimentation and self-confidence, on the other. The goal was a Soviet society that took into account the needs of society and where manual labor was performed in agricultural and industrial production. The Soviet schools faced the following obstacles:

- Davies (1980) documented that, according to a 1929 survey, the majority of rural teachers were of peasant origin and a considerable number of rural teachers were reluctant to implement the new educational policies (p. 53).
- Whyte (1974) reported that teachers at regular schools did not have the necessary training, and therefore they had great difficulty in putting new educational programs into practice. It ended up that "students were supposed to be given a fair amount of responsibility in planning, carrying out, and evaluating these complexes" (p. 118).
- Educational policymakers tried to make schooling more interesting and relevant, especially for children from worker and peasant families. This resulted in situations in which courses and projects were implemented in accordance with ideological principles, not academic ones (see, e.g., Whyte, 1974, p. 119).

7.2   *The Stalin School*

In the 1930s, the Stalin regime retreated from earlier innovations regarding education. Instead of the ideas of Western education, the Soviet regime emphasized hard work and discipline in educational processes. In 1931, Makarenko became the most important pedagogue of Soviet education. His main principle of instruction was collective education and training.

Makarenko (1949/1965) considered that labor education outside productive conditions is impossible because "labour which does not aim to produce values is not a positive element of education" (p. 119). He was convinced that labor has no educational significance unless it does not go alongside of general, social, and political education. This meant that unless students do not join social and political life, their work is a mere neutral process (p. 35). For studies and political-ideological upbringing, Makarenko had a labor commune composed of 500 children where all educational processes were organized, and every member had to uphold and value the interests of the collective (p. 43–44). This type of commune aimed to train students to be conscious and responsible in their studies, labor, and all activities that benefited their collective.

Makarenko (1951) believed that the special role of productive work in the development of human consciousness is based on the production process, which seeks to fulfill complex production plans and develops individual responsibility for collective work (pp. 103–104). While he opposed tying the school curriculum to work processes, he understood that the division of labor is essential in producing products. This also meant that Makarenko did not consider the teaching of a craft occupation important; he saw no need for a master who could make an entire chair, only carpenters who could plan and lathe parts of the chair (p. 115).

Makarenko (1951) viewed that the school's learning phase and the production of products determine an individual's development, as they erase the differences between physical and mental work. Through this, students would be able to develop into highly skilled people. In Kharkov, for instance, he met a girl who was studying at a higher education institution and, simultaneously, was grinding lenses in the sixth grade. He understood that such activities would also be beneficial. The Dzerzhynsky labor commune in the Ukraine, for instance, operated for 8 years, however, for the last 5 years its factory, dormitory, food, clothing, and school were self-sustaining, and it earned the state 5 million rubles a year. It is said that after 6 years, this commune had the best factory in the Soviet Union, valued at tens of millions of rubles (pp. 113, 115).

During work processes, the students applied the Sociocultural Dimension in their learning environment when they benefited the school by renovating the old building in Makarenko's colony near Poltava. The students also accentuated the Productive and Scientific-Technical Dimensions in their learning environments when they produced many things in the workshop and made power tools at the factory in the Dzerzhynsky labor commune. The following describes how the students worked in the colony and the labor commune:

> In 1920, Makarenko was invited to create the Gorky Colony for juvenile offenders near Poltava. In the same year, the colony gained access to a villa at Trepke on the banks of the Kolomak River, near Poltava. The students of the colony spent 4 years renovating the villa, at a cost of 14,000 rubles and 20,000 working hours. The colony was home to 130 boys and 10 girls aged 14 to 18. The colony included a vegetable garden, lawn area, park, and an orchard. They also had seven horses, four cows, seven calves, 30 sheep, 80 pigs, and one rented steam mill (Makarenko, 1925, pp. 217–218).
>
> In 1927, Makarenko was appointed to head the Dzerzhynsky labor commune, named after Bolshevik revolutionary F. E. Dzerzhynsky (1877–1926). Ukrainian Chekists founded the Dzerzhynsky commune in the Kharkov city area. The commune had 100 communards, a small school, and a modest workshop where a variety of products were made, from panties to pine furniture. In 1931, a new factory was established to produce power tools, such as electric drills and electric welding equipment.

The factory's products were exported throughout the Soviet Union. The communards, most of whom were from 13- to 16-years-old, studied in their own work school. Almost all the communards had been homeless children found living in the streets or in the train station (Makarenko, 1933, p. 199).

7.2.1   Challenges

One of the central features of Makarenko's educational collective was strict discipline obtained through education organized according to a military model, which fit with the system of school discipline throughout Stalin's regime. In reality, teachers in the Stalin schools of the 1930s faced several obstacles.

Ewing (2002) noted that a survey of 60 elementary teachers in 1931 showed that three-quarters of them found preparing for lessons was difficult due to the lack of methods, literature, textbooks, and programs. Moreover, one teacher with almost 30 years of experience recommended that "stabilization" of the curriculum, textbooks, and instructional materials would improve the schools. In 1933, a survey of teachers in Astrakhan found that only a minority read educational journals and newspapers and, most practically, none had read any pedagogical articles or textbooks published after the 1931 Central Committee repudiation of "leftist" and "rightist" methods. However, teachers continued in many cases to read "instructional materials advocating a variety of methods other than those sanctioned by Stalinist educational policies" (p. 179). When asked about a method for teaching young children to read, inexperienced teachers did not understand why they needed a method when teaching in the elementary school. One teacher asked: "Do you really need to prepare lessons for a first-grade class" (p. 179)? In the Stalingrad region, one teacher refused to read pedagogical literature and commented: "I am my own methods. I have worked in schools for twenty years" (Ewing, 2002, p. 179).

7.3   *The Khrushchev School*

After the Soviet Union launched a small satellite, *Sputnik*, into orbit around the earth in 1957, the regime realized that students must learn about the construction of the simplest machines and how to use them. This was based on the idea that if students are working with electric tools and devices, they could acquire knowledge and skills within modern industry and agriculture. In 1959, the Khrushchev regime introduced an 8-year school program in the U.S.S.R. that doubled the weekly load of labor training and manual work. This program required that the students in Grades 1–2 should be involved in manual training 2 hours a week. Students in Grades 3–4 should be involved in manual training and socially useful labor 4 hours a week, and students in Grades 5–8 should take part in these types of activities 5 hours a week. Moreover, the students in Grade 5 should participate in socially useful production practice for 18 hours over 6 days, in Grade 6 students should perform this type of practice for 24 hours over 6 days, and in Grades 7–8 students should practice as much as 48 hours over 12 days (U.S.S.R., 1963, p. 36).

In addition to subject-based classroom instruction, students worked according to their abilities in school workshops or community factories and farms. The students in Petrozavodsk emphasized the Productive Dimension when they produced many things in the factory or when they performed agricultural work. The students also applied the Sociocultural Dimension in their learning environment when their work provided financial benefits for the school. The following summary reveals how students prioritized the Productive and Sociocultural Dimensions in their learning environment in the polytechnical labor school of Petrozavodsk:

Polytechnical Middle School No. 9 in Petrozavodsk conducted an industrial and agricultural internship for the ninth-grade students in the tractor factory in Onega and at the school's own workshop. Half of the students took part in an internship at the factory, which provided a training area in the mechanical works department equipped with seven machines: three lathes, two millers, and two drills. The students with their machines were divided into two groups working under the supervision of a factory master. Students made bolts, nuts, levers, and shaped and drilled blocks; they earned 5,000 rubles for the school. Half of the students completed an internship in a school workshop under the guidance of a mechanics teacher. The school had a mechanical workshop equipped with six lathes, three drills, one planer, and an electric grindstone. During the internship, the students produced various blocks and products, valued at 2,500 rubles. The school also had an internship under the guidance of three biology teachers. The students were divided into four student brigades. They fertilized the land, pulled up weeds in five acres of land, and sowed beetroots, carrots, and radishes (Fradkov, 1960, pp. 18–20).

Vasyl Sukhomlynsky (1918–1970) was a Ukrainian educator in the Soviet Union who served as the principal of a combined primary and secondary school in the village of Pavlysh from 1948 until his death in 1970. At this school, students applied the Productive Dimension in their learning environment when they cultivated the land. During the construction of buildings to benefit the school, students also accentuated the Sociocultural Dimension in their learning environment. Soloveychik (1988) described that almost everything was done by the students, from the workshop building to the tools and machines. Alongside the simple work done by younger children was the demanding work done by older students (pp. 120–121). The following exemplifies the nature of industrial vocational training in the Middle School of the village of Pavlysh:

> The Middle School in the village of Pavlysh, Soviet Ukraine, intended to implement holistic vocational education. Students at the age of 7 or 8 sowed tree seeds on the slopes of ravines, took care of small trees grown from the seeds, looked after the nursery garden, planted shelter forests, and grew fruit trees. At the age of 8 or 9, students grew wheat, sunflower, sugar beet, and corn hybrid varieties, or they joined groups to look after young cattle and provide them with feed. Many older students designed radio receivers, assembled working models of machines and devices, learned how to control an internal combustion engine, and worked with a metal cutting machine. When students were from 10- to 12-years-old, they knew how to cultivate the land, prepare it for a wheat crop or feed, reserve fertilizers and sow them in the soil, and grow fruit trees. They were also able to control an internal combustion engine, work with a lathe, and a drill. When the students were at the age of 14 or 15, they were not afraid to drive a car or a tractor. The youngsters at the age of 16 or 17 were not afraid to use the tractor, but also plowed, sowed, and fertilized by the tractor. All students participated in physical work, especially unpleasant one. All together fertilized the soil with local fertilizers, exterminated plant pests, and constructed buildings for the farm (Sukhomlinskiy, 1980, pp. 294–295, 297–298).

7.3.1   Challenges

The Khrushchev regime was convinced that school should be combined with work experiences in factories and farms, while educators and students' parents thought that this type of school would train young people to an excessively high level in some industry or trade. This thinking implied that the 2 years of work in factories and collective farms before higher education were unnecessary. It was also understood by the regime and other communists that Soviet society had diverted too far from Marxism. In addition, there were many discussions concerning whether there should be 8-year or 11-year schools in Soviet Russia. During this time, polytechnical education took diverse forms in different regions, with students working in factories and farms. Even many experimental schools appeared in the Russian Soviet Republic which connected school education to production.

G. I. Zelenko, director of the Labor Reserves Administration, voiced the following criticisms in the September 10, 1958, edition of the newspaper *Komsomolskaya Pravda* about the plans for vocational training:

- Modern industry demanded highly trained technicians, while a program that allowed only a few days of work in factory brigades could not provide highly skilled workers.
- The students who graduated under the age of 18 from the first phase of the program were too young to receive training in industry.
- Many communities had a single specialized industry with no facilities for training in other specialties.
- Experimental schools tended to shift vocational training to industrial enterprises.
- Students could occupy the places of skilled workers for years while the interests of the enterprises were not well served.
- Economic planning for workforce distribution, training, and placement became too complex (Rapacz, 1960, pp. 36–37).

7.4   *The Brezhnev School*

The Brezhnev regime understood that schools should train students to be patriotic workers who are proud to be citizens of the U.S.S.R. (U.S.S.R., 1977, p. 2). The constitution of December 22, 1977, held that it was necessary for schools to prepare young people for work in material production. Similarly, efforts had to be focused on providing concrete and effective assistance to schools in advancing work education and developing training in socially useful work. Students had to be provided with effective training and career guidance, taking into account production plants, collective farms, and state farms close to the school. The participation in socially useful work had to be implemented according to the age of the students. Eighth graders, for example, had to choose their place of further education in vocational training. In addition, curricula, instruction programs, and textbooks should be changed to include sciences similar to the subjects studied in schools. This would support the prevailing technical work and educational approach of the subject content (Articles 1, 3, 6). The following presents how the Sociocultural Dimension was emphasized in the learning environment when students built drawing desks and arranged classes at an urban school in Leningrad:

> Between 1980 and 1982, the students of Leningrad School No. 159 organized two literature classes, separate classes for history, mathematics, biology, and chemistry, wardrobes for lower and upper school students, and a

gymnasium dressing room. Students built drawing desks with adjustable lids and a teacher's desk equipped with a special device that allowed movies to be played without a darkened room. Students also focused on equipping the workshops and their layout. It was discovered that students who participated in furnishing the school felt that the school property became more valuable (Malkovskaya et al., 1983, pp. 104–105).

During these years, vocational education was organized in several schools using student school brigades. In Soviet Kyrgyzstan, for example, the first student school brigade was established in the Osh town area as early as 1958. The Kyrgyz students prioritized the Scientific-Agricultural Dimension in their learning environment when they tried to determine what corn species could survive. The following summary shows the organization and methods for agricultural studies for students in the work brigade in Soviet Kyrgyzstan:

At the Michurin Middle School in the village of Suzak, Soviet Kyrgyzstan, a work brigade of students in Grades 7 to 10 became acquainted with methods of growing new agricultural species, learned to use modern techniques, and performed experimental work. During the agricultural science classes, the students familiarized themselves with the biological properties of field species, fertilizers, and crop rotation. For example, in 1976, members of the school brigade studied the survival of corn species in difficult climatic conditions. The school also considered it important for students to learn to use agricultural machinery. To this end, the school sought to provide opportunities commensurate with the level of modern agricultural development: well-equipped classrooms, five tractors, a harvester, and a variety of other agricultural machinery. During the summer seasonal work, the state farm also provided the school with the necessary technology. In the winter, theoretical knowledge of tractors, the basics of agriculture, and practical work with a tractor using a simulator were introduced. It was crucial to learn how to start a tractor and how to control it (Dzhantakova, 1980, pp. 97–98, 101).

At another school brigade in Soviet Uzbekistan, the students applied the Productive Dimension in their learning environment when they performed productive work in large cotton fields. The following summary exemplifies the organization and methods for agricultural studies for students at brigades in Soviet Uzbekistan:

Soviet Uzbekistan had more than 2,000 operating work brigades in 1977, including nearly 60,000 students in Grades 7 to 10. The students played an important role in carrying out the work of state and collective farms. Students participated in productive work in cotton fields and, at the same time, learned the skills necessary to be a machine operator and a mechanic. Knowledge related to driving machines and tractors were considered most important because they were perceived to combine technological information and skills. When determining the guidelines governing the activities of student work brigades, the specialization of cotton farms in the area and statistical data on the operation of village schools over many years were taken into account. This determined the field areas for brigade members: 0.2 hectares for seventh- and eighth-grade students and 0.395 hectares for ninth- and 10th-grade students. These recommendations were introduced in many Uzbek schools (Davlyatov, 1977, pp. 8–9, 12).

7.4.1   Challenges
In the 1960s, Brezhnev viewed that moral and political education should be the major concerns in educational reforms. The teachers worked diligently in their schools and carried out socialist education to the best of their ability. While school programs were filled with hundreds of lessons in academic subjects, polytechnical education took diverse forms within different regional demands. Training often included helping community members through socially useful work, such as having students to organize classrooms and wardrobes, make drawing desks and teaching equipment, and furnish workshops. Older student brigades performed productive work in cotton fields during the summer and studied the survival of corn species in difficult climatic conditions.

However, the annual economic growth of the Soviet Union declined from the early 1960s to the early 1980s, while the Soviet government was still declaring the supremacy of socialism and refuting all allegations of economic crises. Therefore, efforts were made to exploit new areas in Siberia, the Far East, and Central Asia. The ninth Five-Year Plan (1971–1975) prioritized the consumer goods industry. Related to this, Jungar (2004) reported that living standards rose significantly, although consumer goods production did not meet the growth in purchasing power and demand. Suspicions aroused during the Cold War of the increasing militarization of Soviet society, with military education starting in schools (pp. 484, 486, 488, 491). Jungar (2004) crystallizes the intimate connection between political propaganda and human consciousness in more detail:

Soviet society never abandoned the assumption, close to the Marxist point of view, that a change in the social system, a transition to socialism, would change human consciousness. Therefore, political propaganda in education, in different areas of culture, and in the media withheld its important role in the transition of "advanced socialism." The work to create a new person continued. Ideological work was closely linked to efforts to develop the economy and raise living standards. (p. 488)

7.5   The Gorbachev School

Throughout his regime, from 1985 to 1991, Gorbachev was convinced that a good Soviet citizen was to be an advocate of perestroika and glasnost, with the combination of these approaches expected to make the Soviet Union more democratic. This new thinking would also accelerate the teaching of information technology in schools, if Soviet administrators and teachers accepted it. The change occurred when a course titled *Fundamentals of Informatics and Computer Technology* was introduced into all U.S.S.R. schools in September 1985. This stimulated great excitement for computers and related technologies in schools, and many teachers started teaching the course even without an actual computer (Pearson, 1990, p. 396).

Long and Long (1999) wrote that "educators have always accepted new technologies with great reluctance" (p. 196). However, in a 1997 interview with a Russian responsible for developing information technology courses for students in teacher education, the interviewee believed that computers could supplement teachers' work: "Teacher educators have a great responsibility to prepare teachers who not only know computers, but also know specifically how to use them to increase their teaching effectiveness" (p. 196). The following reveals how students applied the Scientific-Technical Dimension in their learning environment when they studied information technology in the city of Novosibirsk, Russia:

> The teachers and administrators in Novosibirsk understood that one of the most important developments in educating young people was strengthening knowledge related to using computers. Experimental Schools No. 130 and No. 166 had been doing such work for more than 10 years. From the second grade onward, students became acquainted with using a personal computer and studied information technology and the basics of programming. In School No. 166, the seventh and ninth graders studied the basics of programming and the use of PC s through a special program (Kolesnikov, 1986, pp. 39–40).

During these years, students also continued studying polytechnical labor in many rural areas. Atutov and Kalney (1987) reported that in the Zarinsk

School in the Kemerovo region, for example, the students' work benefited the school kitchen so that it could have its own vegetables and other agricultural products (p. 188). The following summary shows how students emphasized the Sociocultural Dimension in their learning environment when they performed artistic wood handling in the workshop for handicrafts and how the students prioritized the Horticultural Dimension in their learning environment when they took care of the school's greenhouse. The students favored the Productive Dimension in their learning environment when they produced barrels of different sizes. They also accentuated the Scientific-Agricultural Dimension when they performed experimental work on sheep under the guidance of experts. The following summary explains how activities were organized in a rural school in the region of the city of Ivano-Frankovsk in the Soviet Ukraine:

> The Yavorov Middle School created a high-quality work center together with its associates, the collective farm (*kolkhoz*), called *40-Richya Zhovtnya*, the forestry society of the Yavorov city, and the art and design factory in the city of Kosov. In addition, teachers, students, and their parents participated in this project. The work center included well-equipped workshops: for primary school classes; for woodcraft, where students learned the artistic handling of wood, such as decorative cutting and firing; for metalwork; and for the installation of tractors. In addition to the workshops, there was a greenhouse run by the students, an experimental farm used for training, and a cattle farm with 30 pigs and 200 sheep.
>
> In the workshop for lower-grade students, they made toys for kindergartens and packaging cases for artistic products for the combine in the city of Kosov. The students marked and colored the cardboard, after which they joined the parts of the cases together using handheld machines. They also took care of rabbits and lambs in the school and farm shelters, worked in the greenhouse, and collected medicinal plants and waste paper. The fourth- and fifth-grade girls specialized in making wool felts of different colors that were filled according to *gutsuly* style. This was taught to them by a master who was paid by the farm. Young woodcutters made decorative engraved cases and decorative plates. The productive work of the fourth to eighth graders was arranged according to their interests and capabilities. The boys made wood products according to orders from the farm. They also made barrels of different sizes under the direction of the farm master. The girls sewed work clothes and knitted wool pants. The boys in the upper classes, who were completing

their third-class tractorist-miller degree, manufactured a wide variety of custom machine parts for the farm workshop.

The sixth- and seventh-grade boys herded a large flock of sheep at the collective farm throughout the summer. The students performed experimental work on sheep under the guidance of farm experts and a scientist from the research institute. They practiced intensive fattening of lambs with the aim of achieving quality standards in the first year. They also bred black wool sheep, which was necessary for the production of blankets of different colors. Between 1981 and 1985, a total of 307 students graduated from the Yavorov Middle School, with 187 of them beginning work in the agriculture, industry, or service sectors. The rest continued their studies, mainly in occupations related to agriculture (Losyuk, 1988, p. 5).

Education and training were intimately connected with productive work. It was understood that this connection positively impacts the quality of the teaching process and, consequently, enriches physics, chemistry, and social science lessons. Similarly, education was seen as being connected to other cultural and human activity and thus intimately linked to society and its economic and political power structure. For example, the students of Moscow School No. 67, Leningrad School No. 159, and Chelyabinsk School No. 81 performed productive work and increased industrial production (Atutov & Kalney, 1987, p. 188). The following overview shows how one Siberian school accentuated the Productive Dimension in its learning environments when it combined instruction with factory work:

> The students of Middle School No. 47 in the city of Tomsk combined their studies and work at a bearing factory, where they became acquainted with production processes, technology, economics, and work organization. The factory had a separate two-story school especially built for the middle school. This building had work departments and, in particular, a continuous production line equipped with work machines made for this purpose in Leningrad. The bearing factory offered a workplace for 100 students in the upper grades, a workplace for 100 students in Grades 4 through 8, and a work department for students in the lower grades. Before working in the factory, the physics, chemistry, and mathematics teachers taught how the continuous production line operated, the structure of the machine, and the operating principles, as well as described the product's quality and properties and the bearing production technology (Kolesnikov, 1986, p. 38).

7.5.1   Challenges

The Gorbachev regime understood that despite the fact that the Soviet Union was the most developed socialist society in the world, Soviet teachers had to work long days through difficult economic times, knowing that they were paid less than factory workers. Additionally, teachers who worked in elementary schools had to complete a 5-year teaching diploma.

Westbrook (1994) found that during perestroika, for instance, such publications as *Izvestiya, Pravda,* and *Literaturnaya Gazeta* enumerated the difficulties and shortcomings in Soviet schools. These included inadequate heating, sewerage, and water supplies in 50% of the schools; overcrowded schools that required split shifts for 25% of students; serious health and nutritional deficiencies in schoolchildren; a shortage of teachers; the absence of modern textbooks and teaching resources as well as parental participation in the schools; and a decline in funds allocated in the schools (p. 105).

Although Soviet teachers had high social status, a shift in the ideology with socioeconomic changes could contribute to people's views, attitudes, and values. This situation would be more difficult for modern and aware teachers, especially when being criticized for educational failures, as previously described in the December 1977 reform (see, e.g., Zajda, 1980, pp. 245–246). Long and Long (1999) explain in more detail the difficulties during this time:

> Just as emphasis on the human factor was considered the key to unleashing the energies of the masses to implement *perestroika,* so was it the key to revitalizing the school system. What was wrong with society at large was what was wrong with education: the development of the human personality was stunted because of the command-and-administer system, whereby those in positions of authority made all [the] decisions for their subordinates and insisted that they be carried out obediently without any consultation. ... In Moscow only 10 percent of the graduates of the general education school continued to work in the specialty that they acquired in school. ... Nearly 40 percent of the country's pupils had no desire to attend school and 50 percent were not satisfied with the knowledge that they acquired in school. (pp. 86–87)

CHAPTER 6

Ideals for Learning in Communities in the Russian Federation

Abstract

The aim of this chapter is to analyze the foundations of community-based learning with a focus on the philosophical views, educational aims, and associated value dimensions in the Russian Federation. In addition, this chapter aims to examine the changing nature of the pedagogical activities of community-based learning and their authentic learning environments, while the primary focus is on active learning pedagogics. This chapter shows that the ultimate goal of education is to lead students to a free, humanistic, and democratic society. A post-Soviet school of this type aims at familiarizing students with the skills and courses of action needed in a new society. The school-centered pattern of community-based learning emphasizes intellectual and sociocultural aims and their value dimensions. These are stressed in the integration of intellectual, mental (spiritual and moral), and sociocultural education. The all-inclusive emphasis is on intellectual values within the Russian societal system. This chapter also demonstrates that community-based learning can take place in a variety of learning environments prioritizing the Sociocultural, Practical-Agricultural, or Scientific-Technical Dimensions, in accordance with the general direction of political, economic, and social development. The study shows that the community-school movement, developed in Russian schools during the sociopolitical and economic crisis of the 1990s, was intended to strengthen the civic base of educational activities in schools. The movement was based on three training components: democratization of schools, school-community partnerships, and volunteerism. The study concludes that approaches to community-based learning could provide a way for teachers and students to strengthen the relationship between schools and their communities.

Keywords

philosophy – aims – values – practices – community-based learning – pedagogical activities – pedagogical approaches – learning environments – active learning pedagogics – Russian Federation

1   Implications under Boris Yeltsin

1.1   *Philosophical Views*

Boris Yeltsin (1931–2007) served as the first president of the Russian Federation from 1991 to 1999. At the beginning of 1992, the Russian regime radically reformed the national economy by reducing restrictions on prices, removing subsides, and privatizing state property, which Yeltsin had long sought. However, as Yeltsin did not have a transitional economic and political program, this transformation of Russia's vast socialist state economy into a capitalist market economy ended with economic collapse and hyperinflation (Iivonen, 2004, p. 539). The Central Bank of the Russian Federation (2013) discovered that "the post-Soviet period of 1992–98 was characterized by overall economic and financial instability combined with hyperinflation (1992–1994) and high inflation (1995–1998)" (p. 294).

Efforts were also made to reshape the administration of the new country. The Constitution of the Russian Federation was adopted by a national referendum on December 12, 1993. The first meeting of the State Duma of the Federal Assembly of the Russian Federation was held on January 11, 1994, with a term that lasted until January 15, 1996.

From 1992 to 1993, the Western trend in Russian foreign policy was represented by Andrey Kozyrev (1951–), the Minister of Foreign Affairs, whom Yeltsin initially supported. They defined Russia as a country liberated from totalitarianism with the aim of creating a democratic society based on a market economy. They sought to integrate Russia into Europe's key political and economic structures, thus developing cooperation with the United States and Western Europe. Russia also attended meetings of the Group of Seven (G7), an organization of leading industrialized countries. Russia was able to secure extensive Western financial assistance, which it received not only from bilateral arrangements but also from the World Bank and the International Monetary Fund. However, controversy arose in Russia over the many financial assistance and loan commitments. Although bilateral cooperation continued, more political disagreements began to emerge (Iivonen, 2004, p. 538).

1.2   *Aims and Values*

On July 10, 1992, the Yeltsin regime adopted the Law of the Russian Federation, titled On Education (1992). This law gave educators more independence and freedom than before to develop new programs, and students had to become cooperative specialists. As a result, new types of schools began to emerge across Russia: gymnasiums for talented students and various alternative schools. Gymnasiums emphasized the humanities, including the study of foreign languages in Grades 5 to 11. Sometimes these grades formed the elementary school, with Grades 8 to 11 the actual gymnasium. Lyceums taught mainly natural sciences and mathematics. Both of these institutions had entrance examinations. Of the alternative schools, for example, the popularity of Steiner schools increased. The alternative schools could be independent schools or part of the state school system, similar to gymnasiums and lyceums. Leontovich (2002) reported that in 1998–1999, Russia had 66,700 general education schools with more than 21,100,000 students. Alongside regular secondary schools, a network that included 2,547 lyceums and gymnasiums had 1,700,000 students (pp. 1139, 1141).

The Law of the Russian Federation (1992) rejected the idea of unified education and contradicted compulsory secondary education. In addition to the state, the founders of educational institutions could be local governmental bodies, domestic and foreign companies or nonprofits and their associations and unions, public associations, religious organizations, and private citizens (Article 11). The educational programs could be in the form of full-time, part-time, family education, self-education, and external education. Combinations of different forms of education were also allowed (Article 10).

The ultimate goal of education was to lead students to a free, humanistic, and democratic society. A post-Soviet school of this type aimed at familiarizing students with skills and courses of action needed in the new Russian society. The most important was training scientifically minded citizens to be cooperative specialists who use their own initiative and creativity and are thus able to work in the changing labor needs of a market economy. The school-centered community-based learning was to be centered on intellectual aims within the integration of cooperative, mental (sociomoral and intellectual), and creative education. Integrating school education with activities in the school and society was consequently a prerequisite for free and humanistic education. The emphasis was on humanistic values, meaning emphasizing universal value dimensions and associated freedom, humanism, and creativity-related values, which also represented a desire for socioethical values related to the individual's sense of responsibility, fellow citizens, and national spirit.

The new educational regulations transferred more administrative responsibilities for education and training to regional and local administrations. The educational institutions, for instance, had freedom to choose their own programs and pursue a wide range of goals, not only polytechnical education. The law On Education (1992) aimed to:
- prohibit the activities of political parties or organizations in schools;
- keep education secular in public and municipal schools;
- emphasize freedom and pluralism in education;

- increase educational institutions' autonomy;
- ensure the protection and development of national cultures and regional cultural traditions and features; and
- present a humanistic nature of education, prioritizing universal values, human life and health, and free personal development (Article 12).

The new educational regulations gave schools the right to establish contacts abroad. Russian universities soon developed to follow Western European systems. For example, in Saint Petersburg, the Herzen State Pedagogical University of Russia founded a Department of Humanities. The rector of the university indicated that their intention was to reform the new 6-year teacher training so that students graduate with a bachelor's degree. During the first 2 years of studies, students became acquainted with the basics of their chosen field of study, and during the second 2 years, they immersed themselves in special studies, after which, they had completed a bachelor's degree. The final 2 years emphasized students' greater independence in acquiring knowledge and using scientific methods. Teaching internships began in the first year of study in neighborhood schools. In addition to the schools' own teachers, the internships were also supervised and evaluated by university teachers. During the last year of study, a 3-month period of independent teaching was arranged (Kimonen & Nevalainen, 1993, p. 58). This type of teacher education aimed to:
- train students to be professional, independent, and free teachers;
- guide students to develop their teaching methods through their own initiative and creativity; and
- guide students to adapt themselves to the changing labor needs of a market economy.

The Karelian State Pedagogical Institute, founded in Petrozavodsk in 1931, had eight departments at the start of the Russian Federation. The purpose of the institute was to train teachers in elementary schools and other public educational institutions in the Republic of Karelia. The activities of the institute show how Soviet education and traditional teaching were still important. The teachers of the institute recounted how, during the Soviet era, a good teacher guided children toward communist thinking, as ideology was paramount. A good teacher was not only a well-trained specialist, but a balanced personality. When the Soviet Union was dissolved, some programs of foreign language teaching were added to the structure of the 4-year teacher training. However, the status of work education in Petrozavodsk schools did not change. The teaching internship organized by the institute took place in schools where the study was closely connected with productive work. The schools' joint

productive training center, for instance, provided instruction to upper-class students in about 20 alternative occupations, such as radio mechanic, chauffeur, cook, and typist (Kimonen & Nevalainen, 1993, pp. 58–59). This type of teacher education within productive work aimed to:
- guide students to be scientifically oriented, sophisticated teachers who love children and have high morals;
- emphasize subject-based knowledge; and
- teach mastery in communication skills.

1.2.1   Summing Up

The conceptual features of democratization under Yeltsin can be interpreted from the perspective of community-based learning by applying Hlebowitsh's (2007) classification. One could conclude that this kind of democratization sees the ideal student as being a civilized citizen who is scientifically oriented, has high morals, and develops occupational methods through their own initiative and creativity. The ideal educational program includes general and occupational training that improves students' economic, legal, and industrial competence as well as their ability to adapt to the changing labor needs of a market economy. The student is oriented toward an ideal post-socialist society, the citizens of which have an independent working life in a modern market economy and who are free to move to new occupational fields.

Throughout the 1990s, educational change in Russia was a complicated and challenging process. Development work was hampered by Russia's multidimensional problems caused by the country's transition to a market economy, even though the old and rigid centralized system was still in place. Successful changes also depended on how teachers were able to implement a new approach to their work, as the On Education (1992) law as a whole was questioned. Moreover, realizing deep changes was hindered by the country's weak economic situation, partly because the Soviet Union had left Russia with great economic and social problems. On, December 31, 1999, President Boris Yeltsin announced his resignation as president.

2   Implications under Vladimir Putin

2.1   *Philosophical Views*

Vladimir Putin (1952–) served as president of Russia from 1999 to 2008 and then from 2012. During this time, Russia's social policy thinking placed the state in the most prominent position, and Russia no longer sought to adhere to Western values. Van Herpen (2014) indicates that Putin's Russian ideas contain the following three elements: (a) the status of state power externally, (b) a strong state internally, and (c) patriotism, which refers to citizens' pride in external and internal state power (p. 111). The following from Putin (2000) describes the status of a strong state power, an internally strong state, and patriotism:

> Strong State. Russia needs a strong state power. I am not calling for total-itarianism. History proves all dictatorships, all authoritarian forms of government are transient. Only democratic systems are lasting. What-ever our shortcomings, humankind has not devised anything superior. A strong state power in Russia is a democratic, law-based, workable federal state. I see the following steps in its formation:
>
> - streamlining state agencies and improving governance; increasing professionalism, discipline, and responsibility amongst civil servants; intensifying struggle against corruption;
> - reforming state personnel policy through selection of the best staffs;
> - creating conditions that will help develop a full-blooded civil society to balance out and monitor the authorities;
> - increasing the role and authority of the judicial branch of government;
> - improving federative relations (including budgetary and financial);
> - launching an active and aggressive campaign against crime. (p. 215)

> Statism. Russia will not become a second edition of, say, the U.S. or Brit-ain, where liberal values have deep historical traditions. Our state and its institutions and structures have always played an exceptionally import-ant role in the life of the country and its people. For Russians, a strong state is not an anomaly to be gotten rid of. Quite the contrary, it is a source of order and [the] main driving force of any change. ... Russians are alarmed by the obvious weakening of state power. The public looks forward to a certain restoration of the guiding and regulating role of the state, proceeding from Russia's traditions as well as the current state of the country. (p. 214)

> Patriotism. This term is sometimes used ironically and even derogatorily. But for the majority of Russians it retains its original, positive meaning. Patriotism is a feeling of pride in one's country, its history and accom-plishments. It is the striving to make one's country better, richer, stronger, and happier. When these sentiments are free from the tints of nation-alist conceit and imperial ambitions, there is nothing reprehensible or bigoted about them. Patriotism is the source of our people's courage,

staunchness, and strength. If we lose patriotism and the national pride and dignity that are connected with it, we will no longer be a nation capable of great achievements. (p. 214)

2.2   *Aims and Values*

With the support of the Putin regime, the Ministry of Education introduced the Federal Law of the Russian Federation of December 29, 2012, titled On Education in the Russian Federation (2012). The Russian educational authorities sought to establish a humanistic education system. The Federal Law on Education (2012) suggested that a patriotic citizen should be a well-educated and independent person who works in fields that are in accordance with the spiritual, moral, and sociocultural values of the society and nature (Articles 3, 12). Concerning this, the school-centered pattern of community-based learning began to emphasize intellectual and sociocultural aims and their value dimensions. These were stressed in the integration of intellectual, mental (spiritual and moral), and sociocultural education. An all-inclusive emphasis was placed on intellectual values within the Russian societal system. The Federal Law on Education (2012) aimed to:

- support the humanistic nature of education so that human life, health, rights, personal freedom and development, and patriotism were prioritized, in addition to respect for nature and the environment;
- strengthen the independent and accessible nature of education by seeking to ensure the autonomy of educational organizations, academic rights, and freedom for teachers and students; freedom to choose the forms of education and training as well as the organization carrying out educational activities; and the right for lifelong education in accordance with individual needs, abilities, and interests;
- emphasize the democratic nature of education management by giving teachers, students, parents (legal representatives), and minor students the right to participate in the management of educational organizations; and favorable conditions for integrating the education system of the Russian Federation with education systems of other states on an equal and mutually beneficial basis; and
- maintain the secular nature of education and the secular approach in all state and municipal organizations that carry out educational activities (Article 3).

2.2.1   Summing Up

The conceptual features of democratization under Putin can be interpreted from the perspective of community-based learning by applying Hlebowitsh's

(2007) classification. This type of democratization sees the ideal student as being a patriotic citizen who supports the guiding and regulating role of the state, and who advocates for a strong state power based on Russia's traditions and the prevailing state of the country. The ideal educational program includes freedom to choose the forms of education and training and the organization that carries out educational activities, the training of which improves the students' rights for lifelong education in accordance with individual needs, abilities, and interests. The student is oriented toward an ideal society, the citizens of which have an independent working life in a modern market economy.

Most educators know that traditional schooling and education is accepted and successful around the world. Shmis et al. (2020) examined the situation at Russian schools and the teaching methods used in classrooms. Their findings confirmed the prevalence of traditional practices in Russian schools and the lack of diverse approaches to teaching and learning. The researchers suggested the following three elements to policymakers:

1. Nationwide analysis and development of school infrastructure:
   - Reviewing and documenting the prevailing stock of school buildings.
   - Promoting flexible educational methods in the many Russian schools that have traditional learning facilities.
2. Improvement of school leadership:
   - Targeting efforts to improve the learning outcomes of students with a lower socioeconomic status.
   - Addressing bullying, which is a problem that affects both safety and learning outcomes.
   - Focusing on educational success, which is directly connected to academic achievement and teacher job satisfaction.
3. Analysis and improvement of class practices:
   - Expanding the understanding of teaching and learning in the classroom in Russia.
   - Developing the strong relationship between students' academic achievement and teaching styles (pp. 31–32).

3   Community-Based Pedagogical Ideas in the Russian Federation

The Yeltsin regime sought to increase schools' freedom and authority, with the goal of providing an opportunity to establish different types of schools. The aim was to emphasize humanistic and pluralistic education, and the autonomy of school institutions was intended to ensure the preservation of national and local cultural traditions. Leontovich (2002) reported that new types of schools, such as professional colleges and lyceums, combined general and professional training with improving students' economic, legal, and industrial competence (p. 1143).

3.1   The Yeltsin School

In the early 1990s, the Russian Ministry of Education under Yeltsin provided general curriculum guidelines, which teachers were to supplement and develop into curricula that took into account regional and local conditions. This type of situation would need teachers capable of developing students as learners who can construct their own conceptual structures during the active learning processes that Russian teachers would be implementing. The following summary describes how teachers developed their curriculum at School No. 80 in the city of Saint Petersburg:

> Teachers at School No. 80 strove to develop their curriculum based on their experiences. Political-ideological education at the school was transformed into esthetic education in which the orthodox tradition of worship was also integrated. Such teaching was largely carried out as an extracurricular activity in the centers of esthetic education, that is, in the former Young Pioneer Palaces. This teaching was implemented through such events as a puppet show in early education (Kimonen & Nevalainen, 1993, p. 57).

In active learning situations, teachers are primarily advisors, organizers of active situations, and evaluators of the students' learning process. Teachers guide students in their search and processing of knowledge, direct them to learn initiative, and help them to become self-reliant, and thus self-regulating. Teachers should be able to create secure learning environments and be capable of utilizing modern technology (Olkinuora, 1994, p. 68). Active learning is a creative process guided and encouraged by the teacher, who seeks to inspire with positive encouragement. In large cities such as Moscow, some schools developed new curricula and innovative programs. During these processes, the Sociocultural Dimension was accentuated most strongly in this learning environment when students were involved in visual and performing activities in the school's pioneering child-centered programs. School principals could implement successful new curriculum programs by utilizing their previous work experiences in the field of education. The following reveals how the K-to-11 school in Moscow organized an alternative program:

> The principal of a Moscow school participated actively in the national reform movement in Russia. The school had 120 teachers and more than 1,000 students from kindergarten to Grade 11. This school was designed for students who would respect student creativity, cooperative learning,

student-centered instruction, and an unstructured curriculum. The principal designed an alternative program based on the former "Young Pioneer" camp program, in which he had been involved before being appointed to this school. The program was initiated just before the dissolving of the Soviet Union in response to the nation's political chaos and difficult economic conditions. The school chose creative and flexible methods, which allowed it to survive in a modified form, and the teachers intended to carry on an innovative child-centered program focusing on the visual and performing arts (Polyzoi & Nazarenko, 2004, pp. 68, 73–75).

During these times, the schools felt that parents should be more involved in school practices, and Russian society should more adequately meet the needs of challenged students. Amid these ideas, teachers realized that students could work together with other students on projects or on other open-ended creative activities, or all students could work on the same activity. The following shows how teachers and their students prioritized the Sociocultural Dimension of their learning environment when teachers taught at a blacksmith workshop or at a theater. This overview explains how the principal removed all gaps while educating special needs students in Moscow:

> A group of parents founded a community school in Moscow in 1992 in which 80% of the students were special needs, although the principal declined to use this kind of labeling. The school acquired a state-funded school building that included well-equipped classrooms and special facilities for its many programs. Through their instruction, the teachers provided a stable environment in the school while teaching in a blacksmith workshop, theater, gymnasium, physical therapy facility, or kindergarten (Polyzoi & Nazarenko, 2004, pp. 68, 73).

Many educational institutions planned their new educational programs in the same areas as before. In many places across Russia, schools implemented teaching practices in parks, recreational areas, and experimental farms. The students had a tendency to emphasize the Practical-Agricultural Dimension in their learning environment when they were active in work processes at an experimental farm under a teacher's guidance. The following summary examines how students were involved in active learning processes while helping at an experimental farm in Saint Petersburg:

> Saint Petersburg was home to a training and experimental farm in connection with the Youth Organization Palace. The farm area was about two hectares in size with greenhouses, a fruit garden, collection and vegetable

department, and shelter for animals. Under the guidance of the teachers, the students grew and took care of flowers and vegetables such as cucumbers, tomatoes, onions, and carrots. They also became acquainted with the feeding and care of poultry and other animals (Lipchin, 1991, p. 62).

3.1.1 Challenges

The Yeltsin regime understood that teachers in the Russian Federation were professionals who could enhance education according to the new principles and ideas. However, the country's transition to a market economy and more stable economic and social conditions took more time than expected. Iivonen (2004) wrote that the disintegration of the Soviet Union was followed by 8 years of the national economy deteriorating further in the new Russia. Economic development stopped or slowed. Food supplies were left to spoil and commodities rusted away in storehouses (Long & Long, 1999, p. 86). During this time, the Russian population suffered, and Russia sank into a kind of nuclear weaponized third-world country, a former superpower with only memories of its former greatness (Iivonen, 2004, p. 549).

Teachers in post-Soviet Russia had enormous material difficulties. Schools experienced serious problems, including unpaid teacher salaries, unrenovated schools, and deficient teaching equipment and materials. Bacon (2006) explains in detail:

> Whilst debates about curriculum reform occupied many specialists, schools were undermined by salary arrears, equipment shortages and lack of teachers. The teaching profession in Russia became so unattractive in the 1990s that by the end of the decade only about half of those graduating from teacher-training institutions went on to teach in schools. The difficulties in attracting teachers were felt especially in remote regions, as the Soviet practice of requiring teachers to work in designated schools on qualification was discontinued. At the tertiary level, Russian higher education became more and more expensive and open to corruption. (p. 66)

3.2 *The Putin School*

During the Putin regime, Russian scientists and educators actively took part in reforming the field of special education. N. N. Malofeyev, Director of the Institute of Special Education of the Russian Academy of Education, and N. D. Shmatko, Head of Special Education, presented the following types of integration to utilize in educational processes in preschool and regular educational institutions that have traditional classes, groupings, and special education subdivisions:

- Combined integration. One or two students with psychological, physical, and speech development challenges are educated in appropriate large group classes close to their age level. Within the large group setting, special needs students receive continuous special assistance from a teacher or a specialist in mental or physical challenges.
- Partial integration. One or two children who are not fully capable of functioning in a regular class are brought into the larger class for part of a day.
- Temporary integration. Children from the special education class, depending on their psychological, physical, or speech needs, are combined with regular class students several times a month for a variety of activities that are specifically designed to foster character development.
- Mixed integration. Preschool institutions suffering from reductions in educational and general staff create mixed classes with a proportionate ratio of not less than 2:1 in groups of regular students and special needs students. With this type of group integration, the special education teacher works as a specialist leader in the educational processes (Borisova, 2011, ch. 11–12).

The following summary describes how the educators of one school in Moscow organized their integrated teaching of special needs students:

> The Kovcheg School in Moscow was created as an integrated school. For many years, it has applied the concept of integration, since the prerequisites for the development of an inclusive education process did not exist. As a result of integration, all students in the school received instruction that utilized new approaches. The special needs students were in a class that offered full-time or part-time learning with additional support according to an individualized education plan. The regular classroom teacher was responsible for the special needs students placed in the class.
>
> The school educated 446 students. Among them were students demonstrating regular development, students with diverse differences in development, and special needs students, including some not officially identified as such. Most of these students demonstrated development that fell into various categories of emotional disturbance, including those on the autism spectrum, hyperactivity syndromes, attention deficit disorders, and a series of other issues, for instance, organic disturbances of the central nervous system.
>
> The school had three distinctive types of classes: (a) integrated general education classes, (b) general education classes with special instruction, and (c) individual or small group instruction at home. The third subdivision was for special needs students who were instructed on the basis of

their particular medical diagnoses. Instruction was conducted in diverse forms, yet still in accordance with the general education program. The students were instructed both at home and in school. The form of instruction (in a small group or individualized) for a particular student was chosen in a meeting of the school medical-educational team. The average class size for general education classes was 21 students, special education classes had 11 students, and small groups in a home or school had two to eight students. Altogether 58 students received individual or small group instruction at home, seven were instructed individually at home because of their health conditions. The remaining students received individual instruction at school. The Kovcheg School operated on a single-shift, full-day schedule with some extended-day groups in the elementary and main school grades from 1 to 11. The school had a system of clubs, activities, and studios to supplement academic education that all students could utilize, regardless of their form of instruction (Borisova, 2011, ch. 14–16).

Many Russian teachers and their students have also been actively involved in environmental education projects, even cooperating with international institutions. Some Saint Petersburg schools, for example, implemented different forms and methods of community-based learning. One of the most successful programs was called North Palmyra: Parks and Gardens of Saint Petersburg. This program focused on historical, scientific, exploratory, and environmental content and guidance. Piskaryovsky Park and the Piskaryovsky Memorial Cemetery were chosen as research areas for students. This vast area was built in honor of the townspeople who died during the Second World War. The teachers at one Saint Petersburg School felt that this type of program was important and it principally guided their work to:
- help students attain an integrated world outlook;
- create an environmental culture that is deeply connected with devotion to their native country and hometown;
- develop students' knowledge and understanding of environmental education;
- teach students investigative skills and guide their creative initiative;
- lead to realizations about the processes that change the natural environment as a result of human interaction;
- guide students in practical ways to use and protect the environment; and
- assist students and community residents in understanding the different views in the field of protecting nature (Maslukova, 2000, p. 118).

The use of metacognitive abilities is essential in a reflective teaching and learning process. The active role of learners is concurrently emphasized: learners must experience themselves as participants. The pedagogical challenge thus includes motivating students to adopt goals that are characteristic of reflective activity. It is important to understand what the student is learning and doing and to see learning as a way to be aware of one's own actions and the whole world. Along these lines, the students of the Saint Petersburg Lyceum prioritized the Scientific-Technical Dimension in their learning environment when they investigated, for example, the quality of air. The following describes the processes of students' active investigations in Saint Petersburg:

> At the Saint Petersburg Lyceum, students from Grades 7 and 9 actively studied Piskaryovsky Park, with the student groups selecting their own topics. Using informational material, one group decided to research the history of settlement in this area. They investigated the ancient forests and marshes to learn how the land's current appearance came to be. Another group explored the ecosystems of flora and fauna in the park utilizing different methods. The students determined the level of degradation of the environmental system and the air quality through lichens and the conditions of the pines. They also calculated the amount of pollution caused by vehicles on the nearby streets. Their results were combined with current information for establishing a nature trail around Piskaryovsky Park for schoolchildren in Grades 3 to 5 (Maslukova, 2000, pp. 118–119).

The community-school movement developed in Russian schools during the sociopolitical and economic crisis of the 1990s. The Krasnoyarsk Center for Community Partnership (KCCP) was organized in 1997 as the center for community-school development in Russia. The KCCP started its activities in 1998 with a program for educators in the city of Krasnoyarsk, the territory of Krasnoyarsk, and the Republic of Khakassia. Called the Training Program for Democratic Teachers, it was intended to strengthen the civic base of educational activities in schools. History, civics, and English teachers were required to initiate democratic change in their schools. The Russian community-school model was based on three training components: democratization of schools, school-community partnerships, and volunteerism. Teachers and school administrators (24 participants and 12 schools) participated in the Training Program for Democratic Teachers (Fomina, 2020, p. 47).

Fomina (2020) presented how the community-school movement grew in Russia at the end of the 20th century and into the early 21st century (Table 1, p. 49). In 1999, 20 schools in four Siberian regions (Krasnoyarsk Territory, Tomsk, Novosibirsk, and Irkutsk) were involved in the training program. In the third year of training, another four regions in Siberia (Altai Territory, the Altai

Republic, and the regions of Omsk and Kemerovo) were added. During these processes, the enthusiastic attitude among the Siberian schools gave birth to the community-school movement (p. 48). In 2000 and 2001, 80 schools from nine other regions joined the community-school movement: the Amur and Tyumen regions, Yekaterinburg, Perm, Voronezh, Samara, Penza, Taganrog, and Arkhangelsk. During 2001 and 2002, as many as 210 schools from six more regions joined this movement, including Volgograd, the Republic of Tatarstan, Ivanovo, the Moscow region, Sochi, and Sakhalin Island. In 2013, there were 653 adapted community schools in 42 regions of Russia (p. 49). Fomina (2020) found that community schools sought to:

- improve the understanding of social issues and their approaches;
- give young people a greater understanding of culture;
- provide better knowledge on youth legislation;
- share new ways to combat conflicts between young people and community groups, and improve civic skills;
- strengthen the relationship between schools and their local communities;
- establish and strengthen links between community schools and local people, and draw common plans for improving community life;
- conduct valuable experiences through community activities and provide positive results for young people who volunteer during these activities;
- create a positive attitude toward socially significant activities; and
- develop responsibility and a desire to be socially active while acquiring qualities such as tolerance, respect, kindness, and compassion (p. 53).

Experiential learning encompasses many teaching traditions and covers a wide range of learning methods. These methods may include project work, problem-solving, action learning, active learning, and independent learning. The community schools that applied activity learning methods had a tendency to emphasize the Sociocultural Dimension of the learning environment during processes of community-based learning. This was evidenced in such activities as projects devoted to improving the environment at a summer camp, taking part in interregional sessions and festivals, and entering essay writing contests, in addition to participating in community development, volunteer initiatives, and establishing school–community partnerships. The following summary describes how community schools carried out projects and festivals in the Altai Republic and the Chuvash Republic:

> The School No. 1 for orphans in the city of Gorno-Altaysk, Altai Republic, conducted a project titled the Cradle of Friendship and Green Miracle. This project was aimed at improving the environment of the *Cheryomushki*

summer camp and the orphans' house. The secondary school in the village of Chemal began an ecological project, titled Clean Mountain-Clean Planet. In the Chuvash Republic, the festival celebrating the republic included a series of interregional training sessions on community education development. Moreover, the first festival of community schools was organized in 2009 in the Chuvash Republic (Fomina, 2020, p. 52).

In 2007, the KCCP set up a Coordinating Committee, which would become the legal successor to the KCCP Working Group. Fomina (2020) described that the committee's main function was to provide information to the people who interacted with it, discuss existing problems, and find solutions where possible. It also organized annual events to attract schoolteachers and other staff to feel part of the wider movement (p. 52). Community-school events were seen as important because they supported interactions between schools in different regions and allowed for more effective use of the valuable experiences of community schools (p. 53). The following overview shows how students prioritized the Sociocultural Dimension in their learning environment when they took part in activities during International Community School Day:

> International Community School Day was first celebrated on March 1, 2009, and is observed every year across Russia and Eastern Europe. The project Community Schools through the Eyes of Children included 78 schools across 16 Russian regions, the Republic of Armenia, Poland, and Ukraine. The schools shared student drawings, essays, and photographs, which helped create connections between regions by sharing ideas and information about each other's community schools. In the 2010 student essay competition, titled Hand in Hand with My Teachers: A Story of One Activity, young people wrote about the role of teachers in their development and described what they did together with their teachers. The competition received 83 essays from 19 regions of Russia, and the authors of the best essays were given diplomas and awards (Fomina, 2020, p. 52).

3.2.1   Challenges

The difficulties continued in Russian schools during the Putin regime. Today's instruction is supposed to include: (a) group work with smaller groups for discussions and joint work, (b) individual work with more self-paced learning, (c) instruction with a team of teachers working with a large group of students, and (d) instruction in various community settings (see Shmis et al., 2020, p. 22). In reality, Russian teachers were less likely to carry out group and individual work with poorer students, although this work is especially necessary for students from lower-income backgrounds. Normally it is important for teachers and other staff to respect their working environment because their perception about their schools is directly linked to student learning outcomes. The issue of bullying was also a complex problem in Russian schools that related to safety and security, learning outcomes, and equity.

Problems in Russian schools echo problems in schools throughout the world. Learning environments were traditional and, in most cases, teachers did not teach outside the classroom. Shmis et al. (2020) documented that "95 percent of teachers said that they use direct instruction every day or at least two to four times per week" (p. 22). Teachers rarely performed team teaching. Even though Russian teachers had movable furniture in their classrooms, they did not take advantage of the teaching possibilities. Similarly, although schools had technological equipment, teachers reported that they used them infrequently (Shmis et al., 2020, pp. 9, 13, 21–22).

Nikandrov (2014) has analyzed Russian education and its reformation since the disintegration of the Soviet Union. During the 1990s, innovative changes were burdened with many challenges and problems. The contemporary trends in the Russian Federation include, for example, introducing education standards, keeping and widening access to quality education, and improving teacher training and school facilities (p.29). Nikandrov (2014) argues that "all this will be possible if financing education is kept stable and gradually increased and if evolutionary change is accepted as general practice with no more revolutionary upheavals" (p. 29). Nikandrov (2014) wrote:

> There have certainly been important achievements in the education system though they are all coupled with challenges. There is much more freedom in society and much more choice in education—but it is often misused. Access to education has never been so easy—but it has contributed to poor quality in many educational institutions. Teachers are free to experiment with the content and methods of instruction—but the teaching load is too high and some teachers leave schools for better salaries and less stress. There are many initiatives by educational authorities to change things for the better—but teachers and specialists in education are not always consulted. There is accountability of schools and competition among them to get more and better students—but it does not always help to maintain social justice. People demand good quality education—but that means more lessons, more study and poorer student health. Monitoring the quality of education is important and necessary—but the principles, methods and the practice itself is hotly debated and severely criticized. (p. 36)

CHAPTER 7

Ideals for Learning in Communities in the People's Republic of China

Abstract

The aim of this chapter is to analyze the foundations of community-based learning with a focus on the philosophical views, educational aims, and associated value dimensions in China. This chapter also aims to examine the changing nature of the pedagogical activities of community-based learning and their authentic learning environments, while the primary focus is on productive labor education. This chapter shows that the Chinese philosophical tradition of community-based learning is rooted in the ideas of revolutionary education, which rely on the radical social theory of dialectical materialism. This tradition in China gave particular importance to moral-political aims and values. In addition, this chapter demonstrates that community-based learning can take place in a variety of learning environments prioritizing the Sociocultural, Productive, Economic, Martial, Scientific-Agricultural, or Scientific-Technical Dimensions, in accordance with the general direction of political, economic, and social development. The chapter indicates that in the late 1940s, China had started to focus efforts on expanding learning environments from schools to the work-related contexts outside of schools. Since the 1980s, pedagogical approaches and their learning environments have increasingly given special importance to the use of technology-based applications. The chapter concludes that development in China started to stress school-centered intellectual aims and science- and technology-related values, and community-based learning allowed experts to be trained for an advanced socialist society in which mental work is performed in modern production.

Keywords

philosophy – aims – values – practices – community-based learning – revolutionism – postrevolutionism – pedagogical activities – pedagogical approaches – learning environments – productive labor education – China

1　　　Confucianism and Pedagogical Revolutionism

Chinese educational philosophy is related to Confucianism. Although more than two millennia old, the Confucian school tradition has had a strong influence on the Chinese and on Chinese educational philosophers. The philosophical foundations of Confucius (551–479 B.C.) and his followers are set out in the *Four Books*, which for centuries contained the basic writings of Chinese teaching and education. One of the *Four Books*, the *Analects*, includes a collection of thoughts and dialogues attributed to Confucius. The *Analects* has been one of the most widely read and studied books in China for the last 2,000 years, and it continues to have a substantial influence on Chinese thinking today (Collinson et al., 2000, pp. 217–218, 221). Confucius believed that social reform could be implemented through education, and he aimed to create an ideal social order by cultivating ideal individuals. In his ideal society, which is the state of Great Harmony, both individual and social rights are perfectly developed and harmonized (Chen, 1990, p. 459).

The *Doctrine of the Mean*, another of the *Four Books*, allegedly written by Confucius's grandson, elaborates the way of harmony. The goal of the Mean, or the Middle Way, is to maintain balance and harmony by directing the mind to a state of constant equilibrium (Collinson et al., 2000, p. 218). The Confucian *harmony* is a philosophy that can be understood as defining the relation between the self and others and among the elements of the unity. It is a way of living and behaving that leads to modesty and flexibility. Furthermore, it is a moral process starting from the self and reaching the Mean. The way of harmony is not only theoretically important to Confucian philosophy but also practically significant for Chinese culture, and it gradually became central to the doctrinal foundation on which all philosophical schools operated (Yao, 2013, pp. 252–268).

As early as possibly 1000 B.C., Chinese philosophers formulated a dualistic belief system that examines the universal interplay of two opposing forces, yang and yin. Each of these cosmic principles represents the whole of certain characteristics. Yang is a masculine principle that makes itself known in everything that is active, radiant, hot, vigorous, strong, and aggressive. Yin is a feminine principle that is expressed as passive, moist, cold, docile, yielding, and gentle (see, e.g., Liu, 2006, p. 7). Yang and yin together gave birth to the heaven of the universe, which mainly has yang characteristics, and the earth, which is reigned by yin characteristics (see, e.g., Zhang, 2002, p. 88). According to this interpretation, these two opposing forces are in permanent conflict with each other, which leads to constant struggle and change.

The Chinese view of nature is based on the interaction of yang and yin as well as on the certain systematic connection between five elements: water, fire, wood, metal, and earth (Zhang, 2002, p. 96). Chinese tradition considers this interplay as creating the Great Harmony, a part of which also includes humans (see, e.g., Liu, 2006, pp. 37–38). This belief is especially evident in Confucianism, in which ethics, ideology, and the sciences all belong to a vision of a common mental foundation. According to Western philosophy, humans are the actual goal of the creation of the world and the master of nature, but in Chinese philosophy humans are only a part of the world process. Where Western individuals aim to subjugate nature to be their servant, the traditional Chinese have tried to live in harmony with the universe.

The influences of international ideas in China were comparable to that of India and the U.S.S.R., especially during the first decades of the 20th century. In addition to the Confucian philosophy, Chinese school reformers were influenced by ideas from many European countries, Japan, and the United States. Innovative ideas were introduced by Chinese who had studied abroad and by foreigners, mostly American missionaries. Additional influences also came through translated literature. Berry (1960) mentioned that Chinese intellectuals became acquainted with the ideas of Tolstoy, Darwin, Spencer, and Rousseau. Knight (2015) reported that a significant number of works by Marx, Engels, Lenin, and other Marxists became available in China in the 1920s and early 1930s.

Dewey, invited by Chinese students, visited China from 1919 to 1921 (see Keenan, 1977). In addition to progressive ideas on education, Dewey gave lectures in universities on Western political philosophy and radical empirical philosophy. Several of his works were translated into Chinese, among them *How We Think*, *Schools of To-Morrow*, and *Democracy and Education* (see Berry, 1960). Olsson (1926) documented that hundreds of experimental schools following Dewey's and Parkhurst's progressive educational ideas were founded in the country (p. 46).

As indicated previously, progressive principles were applied in school experiments in the early Soviet Union in the 1920s. Similarly, pedagogical progressivism also became popular among some circles in China after Dewey had visited and lectured there. Xu (1992) reported that Dewey's ideas on education were applied intensively in school experiments in various parts of revolutionary China. School programs emphasized learning, which was connected with activities and immediate experiences, and ultimately aimed at the social reform of the local area. In 1927, for example, Tao Xing-zhi established the Xiao Zhuang Normal School in the countryside outside Nanjing for his education experiments. The school aimed to offer not only teacher training but also to reform the village community surrounding the school. Although the school experiment lasted only for 3 years, it strengthened the dialogue concerning the status of progressive education in China (Xu, 1992, pp. 58–60).

This study shows that many countries also started to vigorously oppose the influence of international educational currents, even after their ideas had been in practice for several years. Related to this, Xu (1992) documented that, from the Guomindang (Nationalist Party of China) administration's standpoint, this progressive work-based inclination was seen to be increasingly connected to revolutionary factions and was considered a political threat. It decided that the progressive, communal school experiment had to be discontinued. The GMD government at the time may have feared its influence on the society at large (Xu, 1992, pp. 116–117). Xu's research (1992) elucidates Tao Xing-zhi's school experiment in more detail:

> Xiao Zhuang Normal School started with thirteen students. In order to train them as teachers and educators, the school set up a central elementary school for the peasants' children to enable students to learn teaching in the real-life practice. As the Normal School expanded, it established four kindergartens for preschool education training, eight elementary and secondary schools for basic teacher training, evening schools for adult education, and a hospital, a carpenter workshop, and a tea house for vocational education. Besides teaching to teach in real school settings, the school also required students to immerse themselves in the rural life by having them work with the peasants, so as to transform their outlook and adapt them to the village life for village reconstruction. (p. 59)

The school's involvement in educating village children and participating in village life, together with its vocational branches, soon claimed it an important role in the village. In order to help village's development, the school also taught peasants agricultural skills, organized self-defense leagues, proposed road building projects, and assisted in the village administrative decision-making. For instance, when the scarce water supply became a problem, the school suggested that the villagers hold a town meeting, and the students participated as an advisory committee. A solution was reached after a democratic discussion and vote. During the process both students and peasants learned problem-solving by doing (pp. 59–60).

After the Great Qing Empire (1611–1911), the Guomindang party ruled the Republic of China (1912–1949). China also experienced the Chinese Civil Wars (1924–1949), along with new international ideals. Many different schools competed with each other until several useful alternatives were seen in the political practice of the Russian Bolsheviks. After the unsettled era of the Guomindang— after the power struggle between the Nationalist Party of China, the Communist Party of China (C.P.C.), and Japanese intruders—the Communist Party, led by Mao Zedong (1893–1976), rose to power. In 1949, the People's Republic of China was founded (see, e.g., Moise, 1986).

The Western reform pedagogical ideas and school experiments had to move away from the ideas of the communist revolution and its socialist education. The revolution began after the Second Sino-Japanese War (1937–1945) that is known in China as the War of Liberation. Mao Zedong was the well-known leader of this revolutionary movement.

1.1   *Mao Zedong and the Revolutionary Movement*

National philosophical thinking on education can be strongly influenced by international currents of thoughts concerning society as well as by educational trends connected to them. These new ideas can lead to radical national reforms that include periods of major pedagogical shifts, meaning that development proceeds in a contradictory manner. Such radical education reform was associated with the communist revolution in China, which began in 1946 and was the culmination of the Communist Party's drive for power since its founding in 1921.

The successful Bolshevik Revolution and its implications strengthened Marxist-Leninist thinking in China. Soviet advisers were invited to the country to help organize a revolutionary program and activities and to provide guidance in founding the C.P.C. in Shanghai in 1921. Chinese socialist literature was as yet largely reformist instead of revolutionary, and the works of Marx and Engels had not been completely translated into Chinese. The ideas of socialist thinkers were difficult to understand in China because its cultural history differed so greatly from that of the West. To alleviate the situation, Marxist study groups were founded; one participate was Mao Zedong, future Communist Party leader (see, e.g., Grasso et al., 2004, pp. 87–89). The following is a brief account of the main development steps in Mao's system of political beliefs:

> Mao Zedong's ideas concerning the function of an ideal society developed within the context of the Chinese philosophical tradition and a Marxist materialistic view of history as well as the social crisis that took place in China during the early decades of the 20th century. After studying at the First Provincial Normal School in Changsha from 1913 to 1918, Mao moved to Beijing, where he worked as a library assistant at the Peking University Library. At this point, he had been strongly influenced by the ideas of Li Dazhao (1889–1927) and Chen Duxiu (1879–1942), the future founders of the C.P.C. After also familiarizing himself with the social views of Hegel, Marx, and Lenin, Mao started to develop his own philosophy based on dialectical materialism. Between 1940 and 1945, the Chinese form of Marxism-Leninism began to crystallize, with Mao as its originator. At the first

plenary session of the seventh Central Committee of the c.p.c. in 1945, Mao's thinking was canonized as the leading ideology of the Communist Party (see, e.g., Collinson et al., 2000, pp. 307–308, 310; Pantsov, 2012, pp. 340–341, 583). His speeches and writings have been published in many collections; probably the most well-known volume is the *Mao zhu xi yu lu*, which is often called the Little Red Book (Mao, 1964). In October 1949, Mao proclaimed the foundation of the People's Republic of China, which he led until the end of his life (for Mao's biography, see, e.g., Pantsov, 2012).

The influence of traditional Chinese philosophy on Mao's ideas is perhaps best expressed by the similarities that exist between the views of Confucianism and dialectical materialism regarding the concept of conflict and its importance in the development of society. Mao (1937/1966a) argued that social development requires a continuing revolution because conflict is inherent in society, both between different classes and between forces and production relationships. The development of these conflicts propels society forward and provides the driving force for replacing an old society with a new one. Conflicts are the prerequisite for all existence and development (Mao, 1937/1966a, pp. 26–27). The function of a school in this battle is to serve the proletarian politics and the socialist model of production.

In addition to the Chinese philosophical tradition, Mao's philosophical thinking on education is based on Marx's dialectical and historical view of materialism and Lenin's practical educational thinking. Marxism is for Mao (1938/1965) a means of solving problems: he studied Marx's and Lenin's theories in order to adapt them to China's conditions and circumstances. He put his ideas firmly into practice and applied the Marxist-Leninist theory to China's current conditions (Mao, 1938/1965, pp. 208–210). In the battle for social equality, Mao (1948/1961) believed in the power of the masses because an individual can easily make a mistake, whereas the nation and the party as a whole never can (pp. 241–242). He trusted a strategy known as "walking on two legs," which could support heavy industry along with light industry and agriculture (for more details, see, e.g., Mao, 1956/1977, pp. 284–285). This policy also allowed work-study schools to be established beside academic ones. Like the Soviets, Mao (1991/1998a) was convinced that a citizen develops best as a member of a collective. He proposed in 1958 that all schools should have contracts with local factories or agricultural cooperatives in order to combine theory with practice (Mao, 1991/1998a, pp. 796–797).

According to Mao (1937/1966b), human knowledge is generated during the process of consciousness, which takes place when performing practical activities. The first phase of consciousness involves sense perceptions and impressions, during which the citizen is unable to form profound concepts or make logical conclusions. The continuation of societal practice leads to a process that repeats the phenomena caused by the sensations and impressions (pp. 4–5). During the second phase of consciousness, the rational phase, the citizens use concepts when they make judgments and conclusions. Mao discovered that concepts are formed when a sudden change takes place in the human mind. This is a leap in the process of cognition. These concepts no longer reflect just the phenomenal character of things and their separate aspects and external relations but encompass the essence of the phenomenon, the phenomenon as a whole, and the various internal relations of phenomena (p. 5).

Mao (1937/1966b) interpreted that the function of consciousness is to proceed, with the help of perceptions, to the thinking phase and to gradually continue until insight into the inner contradictions of objective things occurs, along with comprehending the relationships between different processes. Logical consciousness is capable of understanding the surrounding world as a whole within an inner relation of all its aspects (pp. 5–6).

The two phases of the process of consciousness, sensory, and rational, have different qualities but are not actually distinguishable from each other when they integrate in the course of practical activities. As Mao (1937/1966b) contended, "all genuine knowledge originates in direct experience. But one cannot have direct experience of everything; as a matter of fact, most of our knowledge comes from indirect experience" (p. 8). However, theoretically, during the first phase of the consciousness process, through their senses, people are in contact with the phenomena of the external world. During the second phase, the new information associated with a sensation is synthesized, arranged, and reconstructed and is when concepts, judgments, and conclusions are created. Mao emphasized that only when sensory observations have provided detailed and comprehensive information can they be the basis for forming correct concepts and theories (p. 11).

In relation to this awakening process of consciousness, Mao (1937/1966b) argued that the most important aspect is to be able to apply this understanding of the laws of the objective world to the processes in which people can actively change the world. Consciousness begins with practice, but the theoretical knowledge acquired through practice has to return again to practice (p. 14). The following quotation from Mao (1937/1966b) describes how the dialectical and materialistic theory of knowledge could be applied to practice:

> Discover the truth through practice, and again through practice verify and develop the truth. Start from perceptual knowledge and actively develop it into rational knowledge; then start from rational knowledge and actively guide revolutionary practice to change both the subjective and the objective world. Practice, knowledge, again practice, and again

knowledge. This form repeats itself in endless cycles, and with each cycle the content of practice and knowledge rises to a higher level. (p. 20)

Mao Zedong (1937/1966b) claimed that during the process of knowledge development, when forming judgments and conclusions, people should use their prior sensory observations, with the help of the appropriate concepts. The actual function of consciousness is to discover the internal conflicts of the laws of objective things and phenomena for the purpose of achieving logical consciousness. This phase of rational consciousness must be researched through practice. Mao wrote that knowledge should be explored in all fields of practical life: production processes, class struggles, and scientific experiments. During this examination, people would become aware of the lack of relation to nature, to other people, and to themselves (Mao, 1937/1966b, pp. 4–9, 11–18). Participation in production life is thus the process of self-actualization because, according to Marxist thinking, people actualize themselves best by expressing themselves at work and in production plants (Marx, 1867/1974, pp. 168, 435).

The immediate result of adopting the Marxist theory of knowledge is the synthesis of learning and work, school and life. In doing so, school teaching should be combined with productive work and scientific research. The following from Mao (1937/1966b) illustrates how human knowledge depends on personal activity in production:

> Man's knowledge depends mainly on his activity in material production, through which he comes gradually to understand the phenomena, the properties, and the laws of nature, and the relations between himself and nature; and through his activity in production he also gradually comes to understand, in varying degrees, certain relations that exist between man and man. None of this knowledge can be acquired apart from activity in production. (pp. 1–2)

1.2   Aims and Values

After the Chinese Civil War ended in 1949, the main goal of the Communist Party was a classless society and the means to achieve it was revolutionary education. This type of education stressed the ideas of labor-related education, also referred to as revolutionary labor education, when analyzed in the context of community-based learning. Such an educational consciousness was in accord with the view of dialectical materialism. Lu (1958/1998) held that the aims of this form of education can be seen as an attempt to educate citizens to be well-rounded, politically and culturally conscious, and capable of both intellectual and manual work (p. 855). In step with revolutionary ideas, the school should train citizens to be proficient and skilled, to internalize socialist ideology, and to work efficiently in collective production. Teaching should support and advance socialist production and be subjugated to politics. The organizational center of political life was to be the Communist Party, which would also lead education and teaching.

Based on an examination of revolutionary labor education, community-based learning in the late 1950s appeared to be school-centered, with particular emphasis on moral-political and intellectual aims. This placed a prime emphasis on moral-political and mental values, while also stressing traditional and cultural values. Mao (1957/1966c) stated that the Chinese educational policy should provide students physical, moral, and intellectual education so they could become skilled workers with a socialist consciousness (p. 110). The idea behind this thinking was that a harmonious education requires the holistic integration of physical, moral-political, and intellectual activity and that such an education is best achieved through productive labor. The aim of education was to produce true builders of society who have internalized a collective sense of identity and a culture rooted in dialectical materialism. This was due to a firm belief that work has value in itself and that all social well-being can be created through human work. This view held that work is at the highest level of a value hierarchy.

Appreciation for work was intimately intertwined with moral-political values, which served to accentuate patriotism and loyalty toward a socialist system and the various virtues it represented. Work processes requiring intellectual effort also placed vital importance on mental values, which could be obtained while students were engaged in different types of work-study programs in schools. Traditional and cultural values were emphasized during work processes in order to help students develop mentally for the purpose of attaining a harmony in learning based on Confucian tradition. The intention of this was to maintain the country's political unity and cultural bases. Confucian values accepted the hierarchical arrangements and unequal power divisions of the prevailing society. The Chinese regime adapted these traditional doctrines to its own needs although opposing Confucianism. A Confucian belief regarding general obedience to authorities was the basic virtue that allowed the use of traditional values to legitimate the system of administration. The highest degree of legitimation was represented by the Chinese ideological system, called the *symbolic universe*, which was manifested in the central role of socialist consciousness in the society.

At the beginning of the Great Leap Forward campaign (1958–1961), the party confirmed the three basic principles of education, which were to be closely intertwined and mutually supportive. Mao formulated the resolutions for a new educational reform and thus started a new era for the society (Chu, 1980). Mao ordered the following pedagogical doctrines in which educators had to:

- obey half-work and half-study procedures;
- accentuate "red" before "expert," meaning that educators should teach students to be ideologically devoted before teaching them to be vocationally and technically proficient;
- take the Chinese road, meaning that it is important to think independently about teaching well in light of socialist China's needs and to shatter the shackles of all foreign dogmas;
- abolish the bourgeois pedagogical line that encourages students to be interested only in personal fame and individual gain;
- criticize bourgeois reactionary academic authority and thus abolish the rules and systems that bound students and teachers; and
- establish a "democratic" system of pedagogical affairs, which means that the party cadres, students, and teachers decide all matters concerning teaching (Chu, 1980, p. 349).

This type of education should (1) serve proletarian politics, (2) be combined with production and labor, and (3) be led by the Communist Party (Lu, 1958/1998, pp. 852, 855). During 1957 and 1958, Mao (1991/1998a) came to the conclusion that the aim of education should be a citizen who is capable of both intellectual and manual labor. He stated that these two aspects should be united: the real Chinese should be both "Red" (politically conscious) and an "expert" (skillfully competent) (p. 796). This form of community-based learning aimed to:

- enhance all-around development;
- improve the application of the subject matters learned at school to practice in the community;
- provide training in manual labor that also develops the physical body;
- erase the inequality between urban and rural areas, between manual and intellectual labor, and between workers;
- ease schools' economic difficulties and thus reduce educational expenses in society;
- increase productivity that benefits the whole socialist society; and
- teach the ideology of communism through local, productive work (Lu, 1958/1998, pp. 855–856; Ministry of Education of the C.P.G., 1998d, pp. 800–801).

The Great Proletarian Cultural Revolution was a sociopolitical movement that took place in China from the mid-1960s to the mid-1970s. Chu (1980) viewed that educational reform was part of the political movement in China, especially in the 1960s. In 1953, Mao "re-emphasized proletariat-centered pedagogy, which means teaching should implement proletariat dictatorship" (p. 350). At the beginning of the Cultural Revolution in 1966, Mao stated that students for whom study was foremost should also do other things, such as engage in ideological debates and class struggle. Moreover, he saw that an important task of the Great Cultural Revolution was to reform the old educational system and teaching methods (Chu, 1980, pp. 350–351). In 1964–1965, Mao repeatedly ordered educators to thoroughly reform teaching methods through the following directives:

- Teaching should be politicized through teaching ideological war in which class struggle is the main issue.
- Teaching abstract knowledge should start with social and productive practice, which means expanding the work-study program.
- Class teaching must be changed to shorten lectures, in particular, to at least one-third the time.
- Examinations must be abolished, and testing methods should be humane, reasonable, or informal.
- Students' study burden must be lighter.
- Students must have a role during the classwork process, for instance, they should be allowed to speak out against teachers (Chu, 1980, p. 350).

During this era, the society-centered pattern of community-based learning began to emphasize moral-political aims and their value dimensions. The goals of revolutionary education were guided by Mao's thoughts, as was life in general in the country at that time. Political ideology laid a foundation for all schooling and education, which served to accentuate moral-political values. The power-related value dimension also was central in the processes of leading educational work in the socialist revolutionary society. Values related to power emphasized the achievement or preservation of a dominant position in the social system. The main socialist values of the central administration were striving to ensure that competing value considerations did not undermine the consensus in the country's values. The Mao's regime insisted that the basic values of socialism were to be inculcated to all Chinese people so that they could maintain them in order to improve society through constant revolution. The administrators oversaw all areas of life—politics, economics, natural resources, power, and truth—on an exclusive basis. It is understandable that this movement could significantly prevent China's society and economy from functioning normally. The following quotation expresses more clearly Mao's status during the Cultural Revolution (Decision of the Central Committee, 1966):

> In the Great Proletarian Cultural Revolution, it is imperative to hold aloft the great red banner of Mao Tse-tung's thought and put proletarian politics in command. The movement for the creative study and application of Chairman Mao Tse-tung's works should be carried forward among the masses of the workers, peasants and soldiers, . . . and Mao Tse-tung's thought should be taken as the guide to action in the Cultural Revolution. (p. 11)

In the context of the ongoing revolutionary process, rooted in dialectical materialism, community-based learning can be seen as focused on productive labor in teaching and education. This type of pedagogical practice appears to refer to the revolutionary approach of labor-related education, the center of which was ideological and political work in the prevailing proletarian revolution. The goals of this form of education were also included in the constitution of 1975, according to which education should (1) serve proletarian politics, (2) benefit workers, peasants, and soldiers, and (3) be combined with productive labor (China, 1975, Article 12). We could consider that during this era the focus was on political and ideological values in which the higher education and training offered to the peasant and working classes was especially to serve proletarian politics, with priority also placed on political and economic values. These values could arise from learning processes in which general school students participated in labor-related activities that combined manual labor with ideological campaigns in collective economic production.

The nature of sociopolitical thinking during the Great Proletarian Cultural Revolution represented an exceptionally radical orientation toward education and its practices. Mao (1967/1998c) insisted that the school should respond to the needs of a Chinese revolutionary society (p. 1383). Labor-related education should gradually remove the traditional dichotomy between rural and urban areas, between workers and peasants, and between manual and intellectual labor as part of preventing the restoration of capitalism, as documented in 1965 (see C.P.C. Central Committee, 1998a, p. 1356). Such education was to make students become class-conscious citizens for the socialist society, in the process of which they could internalize the worker-peasant-soldier role. This led to a specific doctrine, according to which the real Chinese should be over-ridingly "red," a politically conscious member of the collective and people (see, e.g., Chen, 1981, p. 144). During this process, labor-related education aimed to:

- teach by performing manual labor;
- narrow the traditional dichotomies in the Chinese proletarian society;
- reduce educational expenses; and
- become familiar with fellow workers' mindset and communist ideology (see C.P.C. Central Committee, 1998a, pp. 1356–1357).

1.2.1   Summing Up

The conceptual features of Maoist revolutionism can be interpreted from the perspective of community-based learning by applying Hlebowitsh's (2007) classification. Revolutionism sees the ideal student as being a class-conscious citizen who is a brave fighter in the class struggle, who is involved in ideological and political studies within the ongoing proletarian revolution, and is also becoming familiar with the productive labor activities offered by the local commune or separate production cooperatives. The ideal educational program is incorporated into productive labor, during the harmonious process of which the ideology and politics permeate the entire curriculum and school life. The student is oriented toward an ideal socialist society, the citizens of which live in the people's communes and work in agricultural and small-scale industrial production based on manual labor.

Some of Mao's ideas discussed above can be compared to the basic Deweyan ideas of progressivism, especially when analyzing the relationship between knowledge and experience. These two ideas, however, differ sharply with respect to their philosophical foundations. In Mao's view, the process of knowledge development is based on the dialectical and materialistic theory of knowledge. Mao (1937/1966b) argued that this process is, according to Marxist materialism, "the deepening movement of cognition, the movement by which man in society progresses from perceptual knowledge to logical knowledge in his complex, constantly recurring practice of production and class structure" (p. 6).

2   Chinese Modernization and Its Educational Reforms

2.1   *Philosophical Views*

In the late 1970s, the People's Republic of China initiated a modernization process that was quite similar to that of India in the 1950s and 1960s. Such a major social shift was possible because China's political situation was open to economic reforms that were implemented in Singapore. This foreign success story is partly why the Communist Party of China was ready to strengthen the fields of agriculture and industry so as to accelerate the modernization of science and technology (see Hua, 1977, pp. 86, 88). Five years later, industry was set as the material foundation for the modernization of the whole economy (Hu, 1982, p. 22; Central People's Government, 1984, p. 72). This development gradually led to an extensive process for changing the country's entire economic system. The Chinese regime made a historic decision in 1992 to shift its highly centered, planned economic system to one that follows the principles of a socialist market economy. Deng Xiaoping (1904–1997) was the principal leader of this major social reform in the People's Republic of China from 1978 to 1989, and again in 1992. The following provides an account of Deng's road as a committed supporter of revolutionary principles:

> Deng Xiaoping is the most influential politician in China when interpreting its modernization process from the late 1970s onward. Deng was born in Paifang, Guang'an County, Sichuan Province. In 1920, 3 years after the Russian Revolution, Deng traveled to France. While traveling and working there, he took part in discussion groups and studied the basics of capitalism, imperialism, and the socialist practice in the new Soviet Union. He also participated in a meeting of young European communists, who declared their intention to unite with the Chinese Communist Youth League. After becoming a committed supporter of revolutionary principles while in France, Deng traveled to Russia in 1926 to study at Sun Yat-sen University in Moscow. He attended courses that dealt with revolutionary themes, including the works of Marx, Engels, and Lenin; the ideas of historical materialism; and the basis of the past political events of the Soviet Communist Party and the Chinese revolutionary movement. Deng returned to China in 1927 and joined the ongoing Chinese revolution. He played an integral part in the Communist Party's rise to power in China during the 1930s and 1940s (for Deng's biography above, see Vogel, 2011, pp. 15–26).

China also introduced quite significant administrative strategies, which required both an easing of central control and an expansion of market-based educational policy. This turn in social philosophy was realized when the Chinese regime made the exceptional decision to integrate the educational system with national economic reforms at the beginning of the sixth five-year period (1981–1985) (Principles for future economic construction, 1981/1991, pp. 237, 239).

In order to implement this enormous reform, some major educational documents were issued. Of these, the regime allowed the local authorities in 1985 "the power for the administration of elementary education.... They should encourage state-owned enterprises, public organizations and individuals to run schools and provide them with guidance" (Decision of the C.P.C. Central Committee, 1985/1991, p. 472). The intention was to accelerate the flow of development using local "economic and cultural resources" through required permissions from local people's authorities (p. 481). Furthermore, the regime explicitly declared in another significant educational document that private citizens and organizations should establish schools (Department of Foreign Affairs, 1994, p. 10). This document stated that school education was to be integrated with productive labor so that "each branch of society should actively provide sites for schools to carry out education through labor" (p. 22). In these pedagogical settings "education through labor must be included in teaching plans, and gradually institutionalized and serialized" (p. 22). The document argued that the most critical challenges are both the change in educational thinking and the reform of educational content and methods. As a basis of the 1994 document, the present study suggests that Chinese socialist modernization gives special importance to the view that the philosophical background of community-based learning strategies can be seen as resting upon the ideas of labor-related education, also referred to as postrevolutionary labor education. This analysis is in accord with the theory of dialectical materialism.

2.2   Aims and Values

China chose a way to change its educational future that is comparable to India and the United States. Starting post-Mao (from 1976 onward), the Chinese launched unparalleled social reforms and were willing to ensure a smooth transition from the previous social period and its conditions to the new one. The Chinese understood that they would have to quickly create an intellectual socialist workforce in order to build a modern socialist power. The period after the Cultural Revolution can be regarded as a socially transitional one and, as such, was known as the years of the Four Modernizations (1978–1982).

The post-Mao era evidenced the society-centered pattern of community-based learning gradually becoming school-centered, with more emphasis placed on intellectual aims when specifically considering postrevolutionary education. Along these lines, the components of physical, moral-political, and intellectual education were intentionally integrated. This can be understood as referring to the postrevolutionary approach of labor-related education committed to the ideology of socialism. Such an approach can be seen as a method by which the postrevolutionary school could connect students' learning with modern production in real-life learning environments for the purpose of developing a socialist society with science and technology.

The Chinese experienced that by accentuating intellectual aims they could emphasize values related to science and technology, as they felt that without improving the bases of these scientific fields in the country it would be impossible for them to develop a modern agriculture, industry, or national defense. For this reason, the intention was to promote theoretical values associated with truth, knowledge, and science. This could be achieved through learning processes in which students were engaged in productive labor-related projects based on new technology. Special importance was also given to economic values instead of traditional and cultural values.

This rapid change in the national educational policy was manifested in 1978 in the third constitution of the People's Republic of China. The constitution promulgated that the educational aims would no longer focus on worker-peasant-soldier class consciousness, but instead would more generally serve proletarian politics. The ultimate aim was the idea that a balanced education necessitates integrating physical, moral-political, and intellectual training. This form of education could best be obtained by means of productive labor in the context of the overall development of a socialist consciousness and culture (see China, 1978, Article 13).

The beginning of the Four Modernizations saw reforms initiated, policies opened up, and new educational programs developed. A true Chinese citizen was now to be a trained expert or a scholar who is committed to the proletarian ideology of socialism. The realization of the Four Modernizations required rapidly training a great number of people with skills and technical competence. This establishment of a proletarian intellectual workforce was to be crucial in China's future course of making itself a great modern socialist power (Central People's Government, 1998a, p. 1579). Based on the educational programs presented by Fang Yi in 1977, this form of labor-related education aimed to:

- accelerate a developing national economy based on new technology;
- foster a national defense equipped with modern technology; and
- significantly increase labor productivity (Fang, 1979, p. 40).

2.2.1   Summing Up

An examination of the conceptual features of postrevolutionism, using Hlebowitsh's (2007) classification from the perspective of Chinese community-based learning, suggests that postrevolutionism would see the ideal student as being a socialist and an expert, that is to say, a technologically literate, socialist intellectual who is a self-disciplined builder of an economic modernization. The ideal educational program serves a modern socialist society and embodies projects of productive labor and social practices, the units of study of which are academic and subject-centered in the school and the community. The student is oriented toward an ideal socialist society, the citizens of which work in the production processes that follow the principles of a socialist market economy.

Realization of the Four Modernization urgently required training and supporting a great number of both "red" and "expert" construction workers (Central People's Government, 1998a, p. 1579). However, China met serious challenges during this early postrevolutionary era. Moise (1986) describes various difficulties during that time:

China went on a construction binge. Whole factories were purchased from abroad; others were built with local resources. Coordination was poor; sometimes two factories were built where there were only enough raw materials, or only enough electric power, for one factory actually to function. Besides this, the range of projects being started simply ran beyond what the Chinese economy could pay for. By 1978 the frenzy for new projects reached a level that reminded some people of the Great Leap Forward. (p. 231)

3   Borrowing Educational Ideas in China

3.1   *Philosophical Views*

During the 1980s, China witnessed a growing interest in a socialist modernization process. At that time, China, as a socialist country, was ready to apply ideologies based on classical liberalism and a free-market economy to its social philosophy. This time was also characterized by an effort to harness the educational system to serve the society, the goal of which was to increase economic prosperity by means of a socialist market economy. Despite many challenges, there was a clear desire to support the teaching of technology-oriented subjects connected with industry and economics for the purpose of ensuring a professional workforce. In the same manner, the regime sought to increase the number of out-of-school and labor-related activities for students attending schools that provided a general education. In this way, an effort was made to accelerate the developmental path created by the modernization of society. The socialist regime decided to advance its national modernization with the help of a market economy system and a school system adjusted to it.

The examination of this process, in the context of a socialist market economy, suggests that these different views of the trends in societal development are deeply contradictory, as they are associated with different life-sustaining value objectives and views of human nature held in them. These are related to the fundamental cognitive orientations of worldview and outlook on life.

The ultimate change appeared when the Chinese regime officially launched the outline of curriculum reform for basic education in 2001 for the entire general education system, referred to as the *Jichu jiaoyu kecheng gaige gangyao of 2001*. It included a compulsory course on Integrated Practical Activity with such modules as Research Study, Community Service and Social Practice, Labor and Technical Education, and Information Technology Education. The reform aimed at strengthening the connections between curriculum content and life outside the school by focusing on students' own learning experiences.

The instruction could take place in real-life learning environments, such as production units, museums, and natural areas, for the purpose of gaining out-of-school experiences. The learning process was to proceed by collecting and processing information, grasping new knowledge, and analyzing and solving problems while communicating and cooperating with each other (Ministry of Education of the P.R.C., 2003, pp. 907–908).

This curriculum reform holds a syncretistic and eclectic view when observed in relation to the orientation of a socialist worldview based on the theory of dialectical materialism. This can be interpreted as meaning that these Chinese educational views and ideas may have been borrowed from Deweyan peda-gogical methods and the philosophical meanings associated with them. The progressive learner-centered teaching and learning process is based on both an experiential curriculum and an experimental education. It aims at mastery of cooperative learning and working, information acquisition and process-ing, and problem solving. The Chinese curriculum reform of 2001 could be an attempt to legitimize the adaptation of progressive views to new social needs using the idiom "walking on the old road in new shoes," the practical imple-mentation of which is to use different types of activity and socio-pedagogical teaching methods. As Guo (2012) stated, although the curriculum of 2001 introduced Western pedagogical methods, communist ideologies still remain a dominating feature of Chinese education and philosophy (p. 88).

3.2   Aims and Values

In China, the early 1980s witnessed a pedagogical turn in educational policy that was comparable to what had taken place earlier in the United States and India. Since that time, the school-centered pattern of community-based learning can be seen as placing particular emphasis on intellectual aims, especially when considering postrevolutionary labor education, which allowed economic and materialistic values to become prominent. The new industrial policies greatly advanced the significance of science- and technology-related values. The most far-reaching value dimension was related to power, which was intertwined with the desire to achieve a dominant role within the world economic sys-tem. This was evident when the Twelfth Party Congress further reinforced the advancement of socialist modernization by making industrial development a priority in 1982 (Hu, 1982, p. 22). Such a shift was due to a firm belief in the need for national economic change, which resulted in requiring the education system to accelerate the country's modernization process. Zhao (1983/1998a) emphasized that the development of education, science, and technology is the key issue when carrying out cultural and economic modernization. In order to accelerate this process, he suggested that all levels of administration must make intellectual development an important priority (p. 2098).

The regime argued in 1985 that massive socialist modernization in China requires workers who are well educated, technically skilled, and professionally competent. Similarly, China needs personnel who are equipped with current knowledge of science, technology, and economic management. All citizens should also be imbued with a pioneering spirit (Decision of the C.P.C. Central Committee, 1985/1991, pp. 465–466). The intention was to support modernization in society by prioritizing economic and theoretical values. Such values of self-actualization as effectiveness, capability, and competence were regarded as crucial. The critical purpose of education was to serve the values of the Chinese modernization process, as the following quotation from the education law illustrates: "Education must serve the socialist modernization drive and must be combined with productive labour in order to foster builders and successors for the socialist cause" (State Education Commission of the P.R.C., 1995, Article 5).

The turn of the 21st century saw fundamental educational changes in China. Of these, the regime decided in 1999 to focus educational reform on quality education. The official report stated that particular importance should be given to guiding young people in community service and community building. All aspects of society should provide the necessary conditions for schools to carry out productive labor, scientific and technological activities, and other social activities (C.P.C. Central Committee, 2003, p. 287). In 2001, the regime established important guidelines for basic education reform and development (State Council, 2003). These guidelines emphasized that schools should strengthen cooperation with their communities and make full use of community resources (p. 889).

On the basis of the documents discussed above, postrevolutionary education, following the theory of dialectical materialism, can be observed as attempting to stress the shared goals of intellectual aims and holistic integration of physical, moral-political, and intellectual education. Through these aims, the intention was to provide experts for the world's most advanced socialist society. The intellectual aims of community-based learning were seen to be increasingly connected to promoting economic, theoretical, technological, and power-related values. Even so, the most interesting fact is that, guided by these values, the regime later in 2001 issued major curriculum reform for basic education. This reform aimed to prioritize the aforementioned complex set of values in order to enhance the modernization of Chinese society. The epoch-making curriculum, *Jichu jiaoyu kecheng gaige gangyao of 2001*, showed that the values needed in a society were to arise from learning situations in which students improved their information-gathering and problem-solving skills while involved in various labor-related technology projects offered inside and outside the school (Ministry of Education of the P.R.C., 2003, pp. 907–908).

This allows for the analysis that within the context of approaching postrevolutionary labor education, the reform of community-based learning at the time constituted the postrevolutionary method of labor and technical education. The intention was to introduce students to labor-related out-of-school activities so they could study in real-life learning environments, such as local production units. The overall social goal was to make China the most modern technology-based socialist society.

China moved to a new era of education in the early 1980s. This was important for the purpose of accelerating the country's modernization in accord with the ideas of socialist ideology. The preparation of intellectually capable workers for a modern society characterized by socialism was set as a joint social and educational goal. Such views on the role of education required the postrevolutionary school to train socialist-minded experts, intellectuals who have the latitude to develop socialist modernization. The *Education Law of the People's Republic of China* (1995) specified that this should be implemented through an all-inclusive development process that encompasses moral, intellectual, and physical aspects (State Education Commission of the P.R.C., 1995, Article 5). Based on the *Jichu jiaoyu kecheng gaige gangyao of 2001*, labor and technical education aims to:

- enhance the awareness of exploration and innovation;
- foster students' sense of social responsibility;
- promote students' awareness and ability to use information technology;
- utilize various learning environments inside and outside the school;
- improve the close relationship between the school and society; and
- strengthen the ideology of collectivism and socialism (Ministry of Education of the P.R.C., 2003, pp. 907–908).

In 2017, the Chinese regime issued the curriculum outline for comprehensive practical activities in primary and secondary schools. This document attempted to integrate production with instruction by applying scientific principles to work processes, particularly in the community's physical and social environments. Similarly, it held the view that the holistic integration of teaching, production, and social practice could provide students with an in-depth understanding of the basic values of socialism (Ministry of Education of the P.R.C., 2017).

In the late 2010s, the social function of education in China intended to increase the productivity of the national economy, accelerate the developmental path of the modernization of science and technology, advance social and national integration, and maintain social, moral, and political values. Furthermore, many documents on the state of education attempted to reform the aims and practices of education, especially in the direction of active-learning pedagogics such as integrated practical activities. This pedagogical approach was to place primary emphasis on educational aims arising from students' learning activities that are based on applying knowledge to real-life situations. The multidisciplinary, integrated modules Research Study, Social Service, Information Technology, Labor and Technical Activities, and Career Experience formed a framework for teaching and learning (Ministry of Education of the P.R.C., 2017). Based on this document, integrated practical activities could aim to:

- enhance learning in the use of information technology, that is, to guide students to design and produce digital works;
- encourage innovative ideas concerning accurate explanations for the prevailing problems in the community with the intention of solving these problems;
- develop self-reliance, love of life, and the willingness to actively participate in school and community life; and
- promote a national spirit and cultivate harmonious feelings for the C.P.C.

To consider the outcomes of modernization in China, we can take the view that many people tend to emphasize more economic values in situations where materialism and prosperity become more important than previously. The Chinese interpretation of neoliberalism is characterized by the values of economic modernization, as encapsulated by the idiom "some get rich first, so others can get rich later," which openly ignores the inequality that would result from this policy. Political ideology is a powerful basis for education and, by its very nature, it emphasizes moral-political values in the process of developing a socialist society. This allows the use of moral-political values to legitimate the system of administration. The administrative and political authority is concentrated in the paramount leader, who is engaged with all the political and state activities of the country. General Secretary Xi Jinping (1953–) delivered a speech on educational policies in 2017 (Xi, 2017). The following quotation from his 2017 speech illustrates that the C.P.C. is the central body defining educational policy and its values:

> We will draw on core socialist values to guide education, efforts to raise cultural-ethical standards, and the creation, production, and distribution of cultural and intellectual products, and see that all areas of social development are imbued with these values and that they become part of people's thinking and behavior. . . . We should fully implement the Party's education policy, foster virtue through education, enhance our students' well-rounded development, promote fairness in education, and nurture a

new generation of capable young people who have a good and all-around
moral, intellectual, physical, and aesthetical grounding and are well-
prepared to join the socialist cause. (pp. 37, 40)

3.2.1   Summing Up

If Hlebowitsh's (2007) classification is used to analyze the specific conceptual
features of the postrevolutionism presented in the *Jichu jiaoyu kecheng gaige
yangyao of 2001* from the more general perspective of community-based learning, one could conclude that the ideal student is an intellectually capable and
technologically literate socialist-minded expert who is being introduced to
labor-related, out-of-school activities in the community. The ideal curriculum
embodies different forms of community service and labor- and technology-
related programs, the units of study of which are based on the application of
experiential, active-learning pedagogics in and outside the school. The student
is oriented toward an ideal socialist society, the citizens of which work in scientifically and technologically advanced production, thus following the principles of a socialist market economy.

Typical of this social development in China was a domestic policy with economic growth as its goal. Economic and technological reforms were guided
by doctrines borrowed from Western countries. Such a reorganization of the
economy also required fundamental educational changes. The reforms of 2001
reflected neoliberal educational policies and practices (Tan, 2016, p. 46; Tan
& Reyes, 2016, p. 19). Based on her study, Tan (2016) wrote that many Chinese
educators refused to acknowledge the new subjective and relativist concepts of
knowledge and, instead, they experienced that knowledge exists in the objective world and as external reality. Moreover, educators did not stand behind
the alternative evaluation procedures presented in the new curriculum, as
they thought that these were not accurate enough compared to assessments
based on standardized tests (Tan, 2016, pp. 84, 86).

The following section deals with the essence of community-based learning
in China in a more concrete manner. The nature of activities is studied from the
perspective offered by central pedagogical approaches and their dimensions of
the learning environment. The primary focus is on productive labor education.

4   Community-Based Pedagogical Ideas in China

4.1   *The Revolutionary School*

A development similar to the one in the Soviet Union in the 1930s occurred in
the People's Republic of China in the 1950s. After the foundation of People's

Republic of China in 1949, Chinese communists took the central fields of economy under their control. Agriculture and private industry were nationalized. The reconstruction of the entire economy was based on Soviet-type economic planning, which was aimed at developing heavy industry. Assisted by Soviet experts, the Chinese regime drew up a plan for a specialized and technically oriented school system in 1951 (see Central People's Government, 1998b, pp. 105–106). Price (2005) reported that higher education institutions had some 600 Soviet experts between 1950 and 1958 (p. 102).

However, during the Khrushchev era (1953–1964), the ideological conflict between the two countries intensified. Problems in Chinese productivity were warded off with the Great Leap Forward (1958–1961), the economic model of which differed from the Soviet one. The Chinese authorities attempted to create rapid industrialization and collectivization in the country by means of decentralized industry (see, e.g., Pantsov, 2012, pp. 453–454). This type of development is an indication that the prevalent Soviet socialism at that time represented different value objectives from those the People's Republic of China was supporting in its social, economic, and political practice. This conflict continued to be tied in with different ways of understanding about what direction to develop the new socialist society. This meant also reforming the educational system so that it would be based on China's own views. The authorities developed the work-study school, which was to be the main Chinese school, which would engage students with productive labor and ideological political activities (see, e.g., Chen, 1981, pp. 68–70).

During the Great Leap Forward, China implemented a major educational reform that instituted a radical change to students' studies and teachers' work. The revolutionary school intended to teach children and young people respect for the principles of socialist consciousness and culture. The means to achieve this was a course of productive labor in each school in which students would participate. Schools would run factories and farms and, similarly, industrial and agricultural cooperatives would run schools.

At the beginning of the Great Leap Forward, the work-study school was established according to the Mao's ideas in order to implement the fundamentals of education that would serve proletarian politics and be combined with productive labor. Schools were encouraged to set up factories or workshops and to create contracts with local agricultural cooperatives, factories, or different production units. The purpose was to enhance the ability of students to participate in productive labor (Mao, 1991/1998a, p. 797). Studying and performing productive labor were to be integral parts of the school program, usually consisting of half-time study and half-time work in agricultural production, the handicraft industry, or public service. The intention was to combine theory

with reality, and manual labor with mental labor (Ministry of Education of the
C.P.G., 1998d, p. 800).

Labor-related activities varied according to the grade level, from cleaning
the school premises to various activities in local villages and communes. Working and studying could also alternate on a daily and weekly basis or even longer
at harvesting time. Work-based learning took place in many kinds of settings.
It included labor courses and units of study in the school, working after school
for the benefit of the school and the community, and working in factories and
on farms at the school as well as at local cooperatives and production units. For
example, Wang et al. (1996) found out that between 1957 and 1959, the schools
in Ningbo, Zhejiang, developed their productive labor program with academic
studies. Many high school students in the old city area were engaged in building animal breeding farms on Jin'E Mountain. Jiangdong High School was the
first to build a factory and arrange for its students to work there. They studied
3 days and performed labor for 3 days a week, with 4 hours of studying and 4
hours of work a day. Later, the high school in the village of Zhangchun opened
a school farm for forestry programs, built an electric maintenance workshop, and served local farmers. Wang et al. also noted that the Young Pioneer
drug-manufacturing factory of Cang Shui Jie Primary School was considered
very profitable, and that some rural elementary schools opened rabbit farms
that offered many kinds of labor and service activities (Wang et al., 1996, pp.
290–291).

During learning processes, the students were guided by teachers, workers,
and peasants. Labor was divided among the students according to their abilities. Everyone was considered to be important and beneficial in the process of
advancing a socialist society through labor and productive work (for requirements for students' work in each grade in two schools, see, e.g., Guang ya zhong
xue, 1959, p. 9; Si ping shi yi ma lu xiao xue, 1959, p. 19). The following explains
how labor-related activities were organized at one high school in Shanghai in
the late 1950s:

> High School No. 2 in Jiading County built chemical, casting, and electric
> factories as well as factories for wood- and metalworking. The older and
> stronger students worked in the electric and chemical factories, in the
> smithy or forge, and in front of the furnace in the casting factory. The girls
> and less strong boys helped with filtering, fitting molds, and as firefight-
> ers. Often these students were, however, involved with various activities
> in experimental fields and farming. They took care of vegetable and fruit
> gardens and reaped the harvest (Jia ding xian di er zhong xue, 1959, pp.
> 13–14).

The integrated labor-related activities naturally varied according to the students' readiness and class studies. In conjunction with their courses, the students applied the subject matter learned at school to their practice in school factories or local cooperatives. Ke (1958) reported that High School No. 1, for example, had contracts with the factories, farms, and stations of the villages in Qin County, Shanxi. The teachers arranged opportunities for students to work in local production units, and their technical workers taught production skills to the teachers and students (p. 30). The relevant courses at school were closely connected with the practical activities that took place on the school premises and at local establishments. The Productive Dimension was emphasized in learning environments where the students practiced the subject matter during the production processes, when they made such tools as hammers and drills to be used at the school. They worked with cutting tools to make metal parts, shaped them with the machine, made speed changes, and stopped the machine when the work was done. The production could consist of cutting, drilling, welding, installing rivets, and other processes (for pedagogical activities at specific high schools, see, e.g., Liu, 1956, pp. 31–32). The following overview exemplifies the manner in which the Productive Dimension was prioritized in the process of combining study with work at one high school in Changchun, Jilin, at the time:

> The junior students of Shiyan High School studied zoology and botany in class and applied the subject matter when they practiced agriculture and husbandry. The first- and second-grade seniors studied mechanics and machinery during the physics course and applied what they learned to making machines and casting. In the chemistry course, the third graders studied how heat can change iron and steel from a solid to a liquid state, and they applied this knowledge when practicing iron- and steelwork. The school also organized research groups. The physics research group studied how to make a simple computer, and the biology group learned how to grow plants and make new varieties (Ji lin sheng shi yan zhong xue, 1959, p. 20).

The dimensions of the learning environment were especially connected with sociocultural values and methods when the projects students carried out were oriented toward life outside of the school. During visits and field excursions, the students could observe the activities of the surrounding community as well as participate in various activities for the benefit of the community. The Sociocultural Dimension was emphasized in learning environments where the students constructed and afforested a martyrs' cemetery, carried water to the

fields during a serious drought, or dug up sweet potatoes and harvested grain
or pulse for the village (for the pedagogical activities in selected schools, see,
e.g., Huang, 1959, p. 17; Sun, 1957, pp. 43–44). The following illustrates the pedagogical applications that were carried out at one high school in Lankao, Henan:

> The students of Lankao High School No. 2 familiarized themselves with
> work on local farms. The students took notes and studied the basic skills
> of field farming, the development of cultivated plants, and the influence
> of the seasons on the harvest. They collected documents related to local
> history, nature, and different kinds of productive processes. During their
> farm visits, the students learned about farming production methods
> and helped the farmers with their work. Yunsan Shi and Zengyu Zhang,
> for instance, taught one farmer how to plow the field, and Jinghua Yang
> taught a village woman how to grow cotton. Fude Guo helped the villag-
> ers to plant, grow, and harvest sweet potatoes and taught them how to
> grow tubers (Lian, 1958, pp. 9–10).

During the Great Leap Forward, the dimensions of the learning environment were tightly linked with the country's economic productivity, as the goal
was to save educational expenses while carrying out the principles of labor and
productive work (for self-sufficiency at all schools, see Bo, 1958/1998, p. 798).
Social reform based on revolutionary thinking was intended to promote the
adaptation of education to the new needs of the socialist society. It also aimed
to have a sudden and major impact on schooling and educators' work. This
form of revolutionary education, the efforts of which were directed toward
the society-centered transformation of knowledge, was integrated with society in an organized manner. Chen (1981) wrote that revolutionary education
"contained potent ideas of an educational program rising from the needs and
problems of contemporary society and was designed to produce immediate
changes in contemporary living" (p. 221). The conclusion can be drawn that,
from the perspective of community-based learning, the orientation of the
interrelationship between education and society was radical and contextual.
Fouts and Chan (1997) stated that "the inclusion of labour into the school curriculum was based on an ideological position held by the Communists, and
that ideology ran contrary to traditional Chinese educational thought and
practice" (p. 31).

The Productive and Economic Dimensions of the learning environments,
characteristic of productive labor education, gave importance to pedagogical
activities when the students made school tables and chairs, agricultural chem-
icals and tools, and drilling machines in the school's workshops and factories;

when they grew local crops in farms on the school premises; or worked in local cooperatives and their production units (for pedagogical activities in selected schools, see, e.g., Ke, 1958, p. 30; Lian, 1958, p. 7; Shang hai shi jiao yu yu sheng chan lao dong xiang jie he zhan lan hui, 1958, pp. 1–2). The Sociocultural Dimension was especially emphasized in learning environments where the students were involved in voluntary and social welfare work within such contexts as local construction projects and natural-disaster programs (for school-specific pedagogical activities, see, e.g., Chu xiong zhuan shu bian, 1958, pp. 6–7; Wang, 1958, pp. 35–36). The following overview provides an example of applying the Productive Dimension in the activities of labor-related education at one primary school in the area of Baicheng, Jilin:

> In the town of Taonan, Jingren Primary School started to build school farms and factories in 1958. The students participated in agricultural work according to both their abilities and the prevailing seasons. The rice-planting program for 1959 included many activities for all students. The students in higher grades turned over piles of manure; plowed, harrowed, and leveled the land; constructed irrigation canals; performed springtime sowing and summertime hoeing and weeding; transplanted rice seedlings; and did grafting. Students in the middle grades mainly selected seedlings and did weeding and pollination. All students in the school were engaged in harvesting and plowing the field in the fall (Cui, 1959, p. 21).

The Great Leap Forward was an economic and social campaign led by Mao during the second five-year period (1958–1963). The intention was to transform the country's economy through rapid industrialization and collectivization. However, it is commonly considered to have created poorly organized economic, agricultural, and industrial reforms without Soviet experts and, within the context of natural disasters between 1959 and 1961, resulted in widespread famine (for these difficulties, see, e.g., Palese, 2009, p. 30; Zhou, 1984/1998, p. 1083).

In the middle of this disastrous time, the work-study students were needed to help on the farms and save the harvest (Ministry of Education of the C.P.G., 1998e, p. 1028). Teachers were inexperienced, unqualified, and strained by the Great Leap changes (Ministry of Education of the C.P.G., 1998a, p. 1079). Consequently, school days were combined with time for rest instead of labor (C.P.C. Central Committee, 1998c, p. 989), and many rural middle schools were integrated with spare-time schools (Ministry of Education of the C.P.G., 1998e, p. 1028). Despite these difficulties, some schools intended to increase working time and production capacity as well as encourage teachers and students to improve production tools and modify techniques and skills. In many cases, the reasons for teachers' willingness to assist the society in crisis were based on how experienced a certain school community and its region was with the Communist Party's moral-political values. The following summary illustrates how teachers at one primary school in Jiutai County, Jilin, tried to serve society when working with their students:

> Shiyan Primary School improved the school's workshops and working schedule in 1960. Now the first and second graders had 1 hour for study and 6 hours for work a week. The teachers arranged for the students to take care of themselves and to collect food for the pigs and rabbits. They were shown how to do some agricultural work in local places with their third-grade mates. The school constructed the factories for sewing, and wood- and metalwork, and built a new workshop with an electric saw. A greater number of students could now make wooden boxes, sew facial masks, saw wooden plates, or make articles using a metal press for the local factory. In the school's metalworking factory, the students and their teachers also studied and developed a nut-punching machine for more efficient production and safer work (Jiu tai xian shi yan xiao xue, 1960, p. 23).

By 1963, the importance of academic schools and spare-time schools increased considerably, as Liu Shaoqi (1898–1969) had become Mao's designated successor, after the unsuccessful Great Leap Forward in 1961, and new curriculum work had begun (Ministry of Education of the C.P.G., 1998b, pp. 1202, 1204–1205). The reduction in work-study schools led to conflict in 1963 and 1964 between the adherents of work-study schools and those of academic schools (see, e.g., Liu, 1998, pp. 1253–1254). As a consequence of this conflict, Mao renewed his 1955 campaign in which urban intellectuals were resettled in rural areas to study his ideas and perform labor (Gong qing tuan, 1998, p. 1274).

In 1965, on the eve of the Cultural Revolution, the revolutionary regime organized the discussion in the Political Bureau of the Central Party Committee on urban work-study schools. Liu Shaoqi stated in his speech that work-study schools should be established in urban and rural areas and that the emphasis should be on developing lower secondary schools and institutions of higher education. The aims documented at the conference included (1) increasing farm and factory production, (2) strengthening the interaction between theory and practice in teaching, (3) decreasing parents' educational expenses, (4) settling urban students in rural areas, and (5) increasing students' motivation to study. This plan was to be implemented within 10 years after a five-year experimental period (see, e.g., Liu, 1993/1998, pp. 1369–1371). Through the era of political changes and conflicts, many schools continued to perform labor during their work-related studies. Schools were engaged in production so that they could attain the goal of self-sufficiency. Especially at rural schools, students helped the village people and, in turn, the villagers helped teachers to run the school. The following demonstrates these processes at some rural schools in Yangquan County, Hebei:

> At the Wang Jia Liang village school, the fourth- and fifth-grade students had only 3 hours for study at school. The morning and afternoon hours were reserved for working in the village. After studying the use of an abacus at school, the fifth graders taught their family members to calculate the working hours with an abacus. Similarly, the higher-grade students helped the village accountants to do food and payment calculations using this tool. The students of Shi Jia Hui School collected lime, a natural substance that improves growth, and made fertilizer by burning it. The school received economic support from peasant families for schoolbooks and tuition. About 30 village schools, such as Heiyan and Wang Jia Gou, found some local solution to the lack of schoolbooks and other things for students (Jin, 1965, pp. 25–26).

The Great Proletarian Cultural Revolution (1966–1976) was preceded by a campaign started at the beginning of the 1960s in the People's Liberation Army to promote the study of Mao's ideas. In the mid-1960s, Mao strongly criticized the inequality of both the educational system and academic leadership in higher education institutions. He condemned the exclusive attention paid to theoretical studies in the curriculum, the fact that book-centered learning was too dominant, and the burden of an examination system. He demanded that work-study schools should be standardized throughout the nation (Mao, 1967/1998b, pp. 1249–1250; Mao, 1967/1998c, p. 1383). Mao's criticism is connected with the larger social disapproval—the criticism of bourgeois ideology and revisionist thinking. Mao's school reform was part of transforming the superstructure of society, including the Party, existing administrative bodies, and production machinery. The following quotation from Mao's (1964/1990) pivotal 1964 speech included the basic elements for the upcoming educational revolution:

> Our general policy is correct, but our methods are wrong. There are quite a few problems regarding the present school system, curriculum, methods

of teaching, and examination methods, and all this must be changed. They are all exceedingly destructive of people. ... Nowadays, first, there are too many classes; second, there are too many books. ... Real understanding must be acquired gradually through experience at work. (pp. 45–46)

In June 1966, the Chinese regime directed that, in order to forward the Cultural Revolution, all lower level institutions of higher learning not take any new students (Ministry of Higher Education of the c.p.g., 1998, p. 1403). This caused the closure of all schools in the nation. In August 1966, the regime decided to start the Cultural Revolution (c.p.c. Central Committee, 1966/1998b, pp. 1406–1408). An editorial on January 22, 1967, in the *People's Daily* had an enormous effect on the masses, inspiring them to action. After this, new organizations began to take power, causing chaos throughout the country (Ren min ri bao she lun 1967–1–22, 1967/1998, p. 1411). Young people formed groups of Red Guards that freely roamed the country and destroyed everything that represented old thoughts, old culture, old traditions, and old habits. This resulted in demolishing old temples and burning books, paintings, and sedan carriages used at weddings and funerals (Han, 2000, p. 53). Primary schools gradually reopened in late 1967, secondary schools a couple of years later. Universities were closed more than 4 years during the Cultural Revolution. Academic classes were completely closed and plans for the revolutionary education started to emerge.

The Cultural Revolution regime intended to integrate labor-related work with teaching at all school levels and types according to prevailing political and social needs. Education was regarded as connected with other cultural and human activity and thus intimately linked to society and its economic and political power structure. This social reform required that ideological teaching, accompanied by book reading, was to be given in close connection with production. The means to achieve this goal was that the school and a factory, a commune, and the army should form a coherent whole. Hong (1975) described that during this era, primary schools, middle schools, and higher institutions were to function in conjunction with the local factories, people's communes, or army units. Small factories and farms were to be set up in primary and secondary schools, where workers, peasants, and soldiers were part-time teachers (p. 482).

Wang's (1975) investigation evaluating education in China at that time revealed that secondary and higher institutions set up local factories within schools for the purpose of training students in practical work and engaging them in production. Students also worked at local factories for practical training. Veteran workers were often invited to teach certain parts or aspects of their work at school (p. 763). The dimensions of the learning environment were

intimately linked with productivity, and students participated in the work processes of local factories and construction sites. Their work was valued, since
it was seen to increase productivity that benefited the entire socialist society.
Productive labor education gave importance to pedagogical activities when
the students and teachers were working in a local factory for several months.
The students learned how to use a windlass or plate roller and how to do riv-
eting and electric welding. They could learn a skilled trade, such as being a
welder, carpenter, or electrician (for industrial work-study programs in a local
factory and school factory, see, e.g., Tian jin shi si shi er zhong ge ming wei yuan
hui, 1970, pp. 58–60). The following overview exemplifies the manner in which
the Productive Dimension was emphasized in the learning environment when
the students of one primary school worked in the Xinhua Lock Factory and at
a construction site in Harbin, Helongjiang:

> Anguang Primary School intended to combine teaching with production
> in the late 1960s. The higher graders took turns working in an assembly
> workshop of the Xinhua Lock Factory. The school also invited the work-
> ers to give lectures at the school. The teachers and students wrote mate-
> rial for the Industrial Learning course, which included experiences and
> ideas about lock-assembly work. The students felt that they had learned
> a lot from the workers, could exchange their ideas with them, and were
> encouraged to apply the material learned at school to practice in the
> assembly workshop. Similarly, the school arranged for the students to
> work at a construction site. There, the workers showed them how to mix
> concrete and how to determine the proportions of cement, sand, pebble,
> and water (Har bin shi an guang xiao xue, 1971, p. 22).

During the Cultural Revolution, learning was to be intimately linked to
the economic life of the local community. This was possible since productive
work in factories and on farms formed a major part of the schools' curriculum.
Schools utilized a system consisting of an integrated curriculum that was built
around productive labor. This type of appreciation for work was intertwined
with moral-political values, which served to accentuate patriotism and loyalty
toward a socialist system and the various virtues it represented. These could
be obtained when students were engaged in different types of work-study programs in schools. Wang (1975) reported in his Chinese investigation that some
factories even established schools of their own where teachers and students
worked. It is also possible that these educational reforms, designed to achieve
economic goals, offered students more practical training and actual work
in production than the previous educational system (p. 764). The following

summary shows how teachers and students implemented labor-related education at one factory-run middle school in Lanzhou, Gansu:

> Wu Qi Middle School arranged for teachers and students to be involved in activities in the School of Lanzhou Steelworks. The school program comprised Mao's thinking, industrial and agricultural studies, and military training. About half of the teachers and students worked in the factory while about half worked on the farm. Normally, they changed places every second year. The workers, peasants, and soldiers taught with the schoolteachers. During the work, the students had an overseer to guide them. They had to learn to do certain factory work and to use certain methods on the farm alongside the workers and peasants. The military course included Mao's war strategies and general knowledge of military training (Gan su lan zhou ge ming wei yuan hui, 1969/1998, p. 1441).

In the agrarian areas, students worked in the gardens and fields together with the peasants. The learning programs included such activities as clearing unproductive lands, planting and harvesting, and helping with the construction of irrigation systems. The specific objectives depended on the particular needs of the local community (Wang, 1975, p. 763). Tchen (1977) found out that Peking Middle School No. 12, for instance, decided to set up an affiliated boarding school in a village several kilometers from the school where the students could study the entire term and work for a month alongside the peasants in the fields (p. 414). Similarly, productivity was emphasized in the learning environment when the school in Nanning, Guangxi, built an affiliated school in a rural area. Combined with their studies, the students were involved in agricultural work in the fields. They leveled the field, turned over the earth using a plow so that seeds could be planted, and improved the soil (for the pedagogical activities, see, e.g., Guang xi nan ning shi di er zhong xue dang zhi bu, 1976, pp. 42–43). The following illustrates the manner in which the Productive Dimension of the learning environment was stressed when the students of one high school worked on the school premises and on a tea farm in Wuyuan County, Jiangxi:

> Wukou Tea Cultivation High School was founded in 1965. The learning program included such areas as planning a tea farm, designing a tea factory, growing tea, and transplanting tea. The school had a tea workshop, garden, field, and regular classrooms. The busiest working time was from August to April, when the students grew tea on the Wukou tea farm, cleared marginal lands for the farm, and took care of tea bushes and transplants. The farmers and workers taught students as they performed

labor in the farm's fields. At harvest time, they picked tea and volunteered to produce tea after practicing for two months (Wu yuan xian ge ming wei yuan hui, 1968, pp. 25, 27–28).

The educational and social reform at the time required that political and ideological education be taught during learning processes in the factories, farms, and army units. The military courses were normally organized according to similar militia groups. Students took part in military activities, during which they were involved in such exercises as marksmanship, bayonet handling, and guerrilla warfare. They learned about true Chinese qualities when they studied the principles of the People's Liberation Army. They also received further political lessons, as was typical of all military training in China at that time (Ong, 1970, p. 172). The Martial Dimension was stressed in the learning environment in which the students participated in artillery measurement programs in an army unit (for the pedagogical program that included military training, and industrial and agricultural work, see, e.g., Bei jing shi di shi san zhong xue dang zhi bu, 1975, pp. 40–43). The following shows how military training was integrated with the learning program carried out by a factory, a farm, and an army unit in Lanzhou, Gansu:

High School No. 5 was transformed into the High School of Lanzhou Casting Factory. The teaching program included productive work at the casting factory, agricultural work at the Gaolan People's Commune, and military training in a local army unit. The teachers arranged the work according to the students' age and health. Some teachers and their students worked in rural areas while others worked in the factory. They changed places once a year. In small groups at the factory, the students learned how to use tools and equipment for making metal objects by melting metal and pouring it into molds under the guidance and instruction of specific workers. In the countryside, the work and study times were organized according to the farming seasons. The students were to work full-time during sowing and harvesting days, but at other times they could concentrate more on studies. At the army unit, the students engaged in similar military training, with military exercises and political lessons typical of common military training in the Chinese army at that time (Gan su lan zhou ge ming wei yuan hui, 1969, pp. 30–34).

During the Cultural Revolution, school education was connected more firmly with the life of the community outside the school than most educational systems had before. The revolutionary schools intended to attain the goals and values inherent in the neighboring community directed by the local Party organizations. During work processes, teachers and students also engaged in production in order to become self-sufficient and avoid needing the support of the local leadership body. This economic value of the work-study schools was emphasized in China, while the Central People's Government and Party maintained authority over the teachers' work and school activities. The Socio-cultural and Economic Dimensions were stressed in the processes in which the students especially benefited the school and the community. Together with their teachers, they cleared marginal lands for buildings and fields; built their own schoolhouses, factories, and farms; and helped local people, who, in turn, helped teachers to run the school (for the pedagogical activities in selected schools, see, e.g., Nei meng gu wu yuan xian min zu gong she, 1973, pp. 75–77; Liao ning sheng ge ming wei yuan hui, 1968, pp. 50–51; Zhao yuan he sui hua ge wei hui, 1971, p. 48). The following summary exemplifies the manner in which the students at the agricultural high school in Wuyuan County, Jiangxi, bene-fited their own school and nearby community members:

> The students of Wukou Tea Cultivation High School were involved in work that benefited the community and the school. Some students took part in the repair work on the road from the school to the stream. Some students of the Wukou production team helped an old woman by bring-ing water, cutting firewood, and growing vegetables for her. Some stu-dents helped farmers to draw their carts along the muddy road near the school. Apart from these, the school students and teachers made their own teaching materials, washed and repaired clothes, maintained desks and chairs, grew vegetables, and raised pigs. This made it possible for them to attain the goal of self-sufficiency (Wu yuan xian ge ming wei yuan hui, 1968, p. 29).

4.1.1 Challenges

The challenges and problems of the Chinese educational reforms were com-pletely different during the Great Leap Forward and the Cultural Revolution than in the United States and India described above. The opposite reform efforts to solve the prevailing educational problems in China caused a pendu-lum swing between revolutionary education and academic education. Chen (1981) argued that the problem with the revolutionary education was weak planning, with a lack of understanding about academic education. The revo-lutionary politicians did not know the particulars of pedagogical processes in applying theories to practice and, instead, they emphasized political dogma and wording. The ultimate purpose of revolutionary educational reform was to create an educational form based on Maoism that superseded the intellectual and cultural elites. Chen (1981) explains this in more detail:

> The ideologues-radicals fashioned a program that diminished the importance of formal schooling, threw systematic learning and the acquisition of knowledge out the window, and gave no significant role for the intellectuals to play. The management of revolutionary education was left in the hands of ... ideologues, functionaries, and cadres of limited or no educational experience, and unschooled workers-peasants-soldiers who were barely literate but had learned to repeat the dogmas and clichés and were given authority to demand that students and teachers follow their example of ideological devotion. (p. 223)

For teachers' work, revolutionary education produced many challenges, since teachers were forced to follow the Party's instructions on what, where, and how to teach students. Many factors regarding contexts and resources were beyond the teachers' authority and fell under the responsibility of people who were active in Party politics. The main obligations should have been to design and maintain a physical learning environment that would promote students' health, safety, well-being, and learning. However, in many cases, this type of educational reform did not succeed in providing learning environments that would meet at least minimum requirements. This was evidenced in such activities as working in the front of furnaces in the casting factory, where metal objects were made by melting and pouring hot liquid metal into molds. Additionally, organizing appropriate training for the teachers and workers who participated in the teaching was inadequate.

Through this revolutionary era, the school-specific studies used in this chapter suggest that it is possible that the revolutionary regime forced teachers to do their work in accordance with the all-powerful value objectives that constituted the background for the revolutionary society of that time. In this demanding situation, many teachers, guided by their practical ethics, were willing to work effectively and cooperate multiprofessionally. Chinese teachers seem to have been committed to their work despite the prevailing difficult circumstances. Han (2000) even described that teachers "learned to respect villagers and other working people.... Farmers no longer viewed the educated elite with mystic feelings because they knew the educated teachers better after working with them" (p. 116).

Chen (1981) wrote that dissatisfaction with the revolutionary education in China did not arise in a moment or accidentally. Although many people were interested in the theoretical background and concepts of this approach to education in the beginning, opposition grew, especially among those who felt that the function of education is not to transmit political ideology but to develop various skills and abilities (p. 125).

4.2   The Postrevolutionary School

In 1977, after the Cultural Revolution, the 11th National Congress of the C.P.C. began a new phase for China's development policies called the Four Moderniza-tions. Its new goal was to modernize agriculture, industry, and national defense through science and technology (Teng, 1978, p. 7). This development required educational reforms, and in 1978, the National Educational Conference drafted national education regulations (1978–1985) that restored educational policies that had been condemned during the Cultural Revolution. Basic curricula, teach-ing materials, textbooks, and teaching outlines were to be standardized. Primary and middle school instruction was to emphasize academic studies, particularly technology and science, in addition to political education and physical training. The teachers were to play a leading role in the classrooms. In addition to an aca-demic orientation, integrating work and studies was still valued, for instance, the new teaching plan allocated a similar amount of time for manual labor as the 1963 regulations (Ministry of Education of the C.P.G., 1998c, pp. 1630–1632).

During the years of the Four Modernizations (1978–1982), the overall inten-tion was to reform school pedagogics in the direction of formal teaching and methods in classrooms and out-of-school settings. The important principle was to integrate manual labor with studies in gardens, fields, and neighboring farms, providing learning environments where students could acquaint them-selves and practice the prevailing skills and procedures. Although the empha-sis was on productive processes in the learning environment, there was also a desire to prioritize the Scientific-Technical Dimension. This type of change in the nature of learning environments was especially seen when having students make test-based analyses of soil in the laboratory, perform experiments, and develop better varieties of rice and wheat, as well as when they created solu-tions for disease and pest problems. The students also shared their experiences with community members in order to benefit agricultural work (for pedagogi-cal activities on agricultural work at some schools, see, e.g., Zhang, 1980, pp. 34–36). The following illustrates how students at one primary school in Zhejiang Province applied the subject matter to real-life scientific investigations:

> Shangyang Primary School in Suichang County had an experiment field in the Wang Cun Kou Commune in the late 1970s. In their field, the students plowed and improved soil by removing weeds and using fertilizers. They transplanted rice seedlings, cut rice crop, and beat rice into flat, light, and dry flakes. The students were keen to conduct experiments through the

triple-cropping system for rice, wheat, and corn as well as interplanting sweet potatoes and soybeans. These methods enabled them to produce a far greater harvest on a small plot of land. Students also made field trips to the mountain area to pick traditional Chinese medicine for their pigs, based on advice given by the veterinarian (Liu & Rong, 1982, pp. 31–32).

According to the constitution of the P.R.C. of 1982 and the Sixth Five-Year Plan (1981–1985), the number of intellectuals would increase, since they would have an important role in contributing to socialist modernization (see China, 1983, Article 23; Central People's Government, 1984, pp. 124–125). In 1981, the *Trial Draft of the Teaching Plan for Full-Time Primary and Middle Schools in a Ten-Year System* directed that work-based education should be implemented according to local situations and needs, the conditions of the school, and the interests and aspirations of the student (Central Educational Science Institute, 1990, pp. 317–318). This type of labor-related education was arranged in certain areas of handicraft production, agriculture, and industry that were established in conjunction with schools in addition to the classroom-centered school work. The students familiarized themselves with the vocational activities required on the school premises. They created scientific innovations in labor technique education, the results of which their school used to finance its functioning (for pedagogical activities on industrial work, see, e.g., Zuo, 1986, p. 29; Wang, 1988, p. 22). The following exemplifies how the Productive and Economic Dimensions were stressed in the learning environments at the middle school in Yangjiang, Guangdong, in the early 1980s:

> Guangya Middle School in the District of Yangdong started to emphasize labor in its teaching procedures in 1958. The importance of labor rose and fell with the political climate of the times. In 1978, an academic emphasis returned, although the work-study procedures remained in the curriculum. Since the early 1980s, two school enterprises have supplemented the work-study concept and provided income for the school. One of the factories produced a mixture of metalwork, especially small components for machines and other products, which could be manufactured with small lathes. This enterprise was housed in an old building of about 700 square feet with 15 lathes used for educational purposes for students. The enterprise offered many kinds of activities for students. They learned that they could perform various operations with lathes, such as cutting, sanding, knurling, drilling, and shaping (Fouts & Chan, 1997, pp. 39–40).

In line with socialist modernization efforts, Zhao Ziyang (1919–2005), the premier of the Central People's Government, stressed at the Sixth National

People's Congress that "economic reform, revolution of technology and economic construction all urgently need a great amount of qualified personnel
who possess modern science, technology, and management knowledge" (Zhao,
1984/1998b, p. 2184). The Decision of the C.P.C. Central Committee (1985/1991)
emphasized that China needs a high-level workforce with qualified workers.
The new direction for the education policy called for improving educational
achievement and producing as many skilled people as possible (pp. 465–466).
As a result, in 1987, the State Education Commission of the P.R.C. announced
the *Teaching Plan for Full-Time Primary School and Junior Secondary School for
Compulsory Education*. This curriculum, based on an academic model, reduced
the time allocated to languages and mathematics but increased the time for
social development, nature study, arts, and labor at the primary level and, for
instance, labor technology at the secondary level. The curriculum provided a
new impetus for combining academic education, productive labor, and technological education (Lewin et al., 1994, pp. 157–159). The intention was to
transform the manual labor activities to those of science and technology in
accordance with the students' individual abilities.

The Scientific-Agricultural and Scientific-Technical Dimensions were prioritized in the learning environment when the students produced fertilizers and
pesticides and were taught by farmers how to prevent pests on a hybrid rice
field, or when they installed electrical equipment, made technical drawings,
and were involved in craft-based designing (for pedagogical activities, see, e.g.,
Liu & Dou, 1988, p. 16; Wang et al., 1991, p. 53). The following two summaries
describe the pedagogical processes at two junior high schools, one in Liaoning
and the other in Zhejiang:

> Shiyan Junior High School in Fengcheng, Liaoning, had agricultural and
> industrial experiment facilities in order to combine theory with practice.
> At the beginning of the learning process, the school offered courses on
> work-based learning. The first graders studied basic agricultural skills
> and tree growing; the second graders concentrated on crop plantation;
> the third graders learned about raising animals, carpentry, and sewing;
> and the fourth graders were to learn how to grow fruit trees and maintain
> home electrical appliances. After obtaining basic knowledge in class, the
> school's gardens, nurseries, greenhouses, farms, and factories provided
> spaces where the students could apply and practice the subject matter
> through agricultural and industrial experiments (Feng, 1988, p. 30).

Ge Yan Zhen Junior High School in Shaoxing, Zhejiang, cooperated with
the Automobile Factory No. 2. The students made excursions to the factory

and the school invited factory employees to visit the school. The activities that took place in conjunction with the factory excursions were closely linked with relevant courses at the school. The students utilized the learned information about the technology of car manufacturing when they attended the school's technical drawing course. In 1989, this course introduced basic technical drawing skills and terminology. It familiarized the students with the specific skills of sketching, geometric construction, and auxiliary drawing (Gao et al., 1992, p. 15).

Since the turn of the 21st century, educational policies in China have increasingly emphasized modernization through science and technology. Fundamental transformations in the educational system have been focusing on equality, quality, efficiency, and revitalization (Li, 2017, p. 136), as the following quotation from the basic education curriculum issued by the Ministry of Education of the P.R.C. (2003) outlines:

> Basic education is the foundational project for the rejuvenation of the country through science and education. It has a holistic, fundamental and leading role in improving the quality of the Chinese nation, cultivating talents at all levels and promoting socialist modernization. To maintain a moderately advanced education, basic education must be given priority and it should be effectively protected as a key area for infrastructure development and education development. (p. 908)

The curriculum reform for basic education in 2001 aimed to cover educational thinking, goals, content, and methods. The intention was to change teachers' professional orientation from transmitting knowledge to transforming knowledge. Tan and Reyes (2016) argued that this reform reflected neoliberal educational policies and practices such as "decentralization, school autonomy, student-centered teaching, critical and innovative thinking and real-life application" (p. 19). The emphasis of the reform is not only on increasing "scientific knowledge but developing a scientific spirit, attitude and method, as well as shaping one's worldview, value system and whole-brain ability" (p. 25). Cui and Zhu (2014) reported that the reform tried to draw attention to an integrated curriculum structure for the purpose of meeting the needs of schools and students. This reform intended to enhance active and problem-solving learning styles in order to improve such abilities as acquiring and processing information and cooperating with peers. It strove to change control of the centralized curriculum toward a joint effort between the central committee, local authorities, and schools to enhance the relevance of the curriculum to local situations (pp. 2–3).

The 13th Five-Year Plan for education (2016–2020) also emphasized accelerating modernization, promoting innovation, and rejuvenating the Chinese nation. In the future, it will be central to Chinese education to implement such pedagogical methods as social investigations, productive labor, community service, scientific and technological labor education, and integrated practical activities (State Council, 2017, para. 13, 35). In 2017, the curriculum supplement on integrated practical activities was published to improve the quality of teachers' work in Chinese schools. This curriculum proposed to enhance students' ability to gain competences in doing research, using information and communication technology (ICT), designing products, and participating in social service. These pedagogical areas emphasize comprehensively understanding, analyzing, and solving real problems. The ultimate focus is on adapting the learned information to authentic social life and the world of work (see Ministry of Education of the P.R.C., 2017, Appendix 1, para. 4).

Integrated practical studies aimed to encourage teachers and students to do research on certain topics. The Sociocultural Dimension was stressed in this learning environment when some primary school students presented museum exhibits for visitors under the guidance of their teacher. These exhibits included local history and culture, and environmental issues (for pedagogical activities, see, e.g., Efird, 2015, p. 1147). The following summary shows how students of a rural primary school were involved in a community service-learning program in Yuncheng, Shanxi:

> The teachers of Guan Ai Primary School in Yongji organized a program of integrated practical studies for the third-to-sixth graders. The goal was to investigate smoking problems in the villages around the school. First, the students talked with villagers in order to understand the smoking problem in rural areas. With their teacher's help, they decided to launch a public campaign that would focus not only on the hazards of smoking but also on the difficulties of quitting and effective methods for quitting. Next, the students collected information and materials for their campaign. They interviewed a local doctor and looked up resources online. All students participated in designing materials such as posters and calendars, and some students prepared presentations. Finally, the students delivered PowerPoint presentations at meetings in the villages where they had conducted their studies and distributed the materials they had designed (Yang & Geng, 2009, p. 9).

Innovative science and technology education was launched in 2015 for the purpose of accelerating the growth of innovation through education and training. Some researchers indicate that training students in science-related issues and helping them to keep up with the fast-paced progress of the intelligent technology era is a challenge for Chinese schools (see, e.g., Liu, Gong et al., 2017, para. 1). Ministry of Education of the P.R.C. (2017) recommended topics for the Design and Production Activities module, which is a subcomponent of Labor Technology. For example, the topic Bionic Design in Life for ninth graders gives special importance to students' understanding of the practical meaning of bionics. Its main function is to identify structures and processes in biological systems that can be applied to engineering constructions. The topic includes such activities as visits to bionics exhibitions in museums, field trips to bionic buildings, and investigating the application of bionics in life. The learning focus is on biodiversity, biological characteristics for bionic design, and improving the spirit of innovation and the ability to solve problems (Appendix 5). The following illustrates how the Scientific-Technical Dimension was prioritized in the learning environment when the students of one high school implemented this topic in Qingdao, Shandong:

> The students of Qingdao Experimental High School carried out activities based on the Bionic Design in Life topic. These activities included visits to expeditions, field trips to community sites, and camps for generating new learning. During these activities, the students encountered the latest science and technology, brainstormed with their classmates, and had more chances to find, ask, and solve life-related questions. They were able to make use of community resources and generate economic and social benefits. The Bionic Robots project, for instance, was popular because it combined many ideas. Students could conceive, design, implement, and operate their own robotic fish swimming freely on the surface or underwater to undertake assignments such as detecting pollution or exploring undersea life (Liu et al., 2017, para. 24, 32).

4.2.1 Challenges

Since opening up its market economy policies in the early 1980s, China has experienced far more difficult challenges than the policies in the United States and India. Contemporary China faces difficult contextual issues, and especially suffers from urban and rural disparity, social inequalities and instability, environmental problems, and political and legal challenges. Much has been written about the profound changes in China's educational models, forms, and content. However, educational reforms have not yet been able to adapt to the needs of comprehensive human, economic, and social development. Imbalances and problems in coordinating education still exist, as the following quotation from the State Council (2017) on the 13th Five-Year Plan for education depicts:

> The fundamental processes involved in integrating production and education and in integrating science and education have not yet been formed. Cultivating students' innovative and entrepreneurial ability needs to be strengthened. The gap between education in urban and rural areas and regions is still great. The total amount of quality educational resources is insufficient. The quality and structure of the teaching staff cannot adapt to the new requirements for improving the quality of education. (para. 11)

The central obstacle for educational reform is teachers' reluctance to give up traditional teacher-directed and book-centered teaching based on transmitting knowledge, which includes the testing of learned information. This approach, which views teachers' professional role and orientation as essentially knowledge transmitters, is in contradiction with the conception of learning and the nature of knowledge of the new curriculum of 2001 (see Tan, 2016, pp. 81–82). Its intention is to direct learning toward knowledge transaction. Rao (2013) argued that this curriculum reform emphasizes a view according to which "a teacher should not only impart knowledge, but also provide guidance, supervision, and evaluation for students in their learning lives. A teacher should be a designer who can establish a democratic, equal, and interactive relationship with students and create student-friendly learning environments" (p. 263).

Chinese teachers tend to reject the theory that all knowledge and moral values are subjective and, instead, believe that these are based on viewable or measurable facts (Tan, 2016, p. 84). An exam-oriented education system overemphasizes mastery of facts, patient listening, and teachers' authority, rather than attention that should be given to active learning pedagogics and integrated practical activities (see Bing & Daun, 2001, p. 22). Brown and Gao (2015) emphasized that the new philosophy of assessment would change teachers' thinking and practice. This led to policy pressures to manage, control, and hold schools accountable as well as to evaluate schools and teachers (pp. 14–15).

Changing teacher roles are bound to contemporary requirements for teacher education. The teachers' preservice- and in-service training has to face the following fundamental issues, as Rao (2013) revealed:

> Most of the teaching practice in Chinese preservice teacher education programs has been regarded as the process of the application of theories. There is no interaction or mutual improvement between course studies

and teaching practice. In such circumstances, the difficulty of cultivating practical competence and the ability to reflect teacher's work is not surprising. The inefficiency of in-service training programs is one of the main challenges regarding in-service training of teachers. Many teachers who have attended in-service teacher training courses have had difficulty putting their new skills into practice when they have returned to their teaching environment. (pp. 292–293)

The next section briefly discusses the properties of the activities of community-based learning in the United States, India, Russia, and China. The activities of the pedagogical approaches are compared from the perspective offered by the dimensions of the learning environment. In the United States, the primary focus is on experiential education, in India the focus is on vocationally productive education, in the Russian Empire the focus is on tsarist education, in the Soviet Union the focus is on polytechnical education, in the Russian Federation the focus is on active learning, and in China the focus is on productive labor education.

CHAPTER 8

Conclusions

Abstract

This chapter examines community-based learning in the context of social change and trends in the United States, India, Russia, and China. It compares the progressive schools in the United States during the early industrial era and the neo-traditional schools in India during its socially traditional period. The essentialist and neo-essentialist schools will be compared in the United States during its late industrial age, and the neocolonial and postcolonial schools in India will be compared during social modernization. The tsarist school in the Russian Empire is examined up until 1918. In the Soviet Union, the polytechnical school in the preindustrial 1920s and the polytechnical school in the advanced socialist society in 1980s will be compared. Russian education is examined in the Russian Federation from 1991 onward. The revolutionary schools and postrevolutionary schools will be compared in China during its revolutionary period and postrevolutionary period. In addition, this chapter describes aspects of curricula in centralized and decentralized school systems and the implications for school culture and community-based learning. Finally, the chapter makes conclusions for future reforms and challenges of education.

Keywords

comparative education – philosophy – aims – values – community-based learning – school culture – learning environments – United States – India – Russia – China

1 Comparisons

The ideas that underlie an international school of thought can be adapted or assimilated into the national philosophical tradition as they cross national borders. Phillips (2004) concluded that this kind of integration is possible if the new current of ideas is experienced as philosophically or ideologically intriguing and the national context is also receptive for political, economic, or social reasons. The specific national conditions in one country thus create the need to experimentally utilize the experiences other ones offer (pp. 56, 58). The philosophical background of community-based learning in the countries studied here can be considered to rely both on national philosophical traditions and on the reformist ideas represented by international schools of thought. The study also shows that a strong opposition to the influence of certain international pedagogical ideas has surfaced in these countries over the course of time.

This section examines community-based learning in the context of social change and trends in the United States, India, Russia, and China. We will compare the progressive and neo-traditional schools in the United States during the early industrial era (from approx. 1820 to 1940) and in India during its socially traditional period (up until the mid-1950s). The essentialist and neo-essentialist schools will be compared in the United States during its late industrial age (from approx. 1940 onward), and the neocolonial and postcolonial schools in India will be compared during social modernization (from the mid-1950s onward). The tsarist school in the Russian Empire is examined up until 1918. In the Soviet Union, the polytechnical school in the preindustrial 1920s and the polytechnical school in the advanced socialist society in 1980s will be compared. Russian education is examined in the Russian Federation from 1991 onward. The revolutionary schools and postrevolutionary schools will be compared in China during its revolutionary period (up until the mid-1970s) and postrevolutionary period (from the mid-1970s onward).

Reforms dealing with an entire society usually bring about major changes in a nation's social, economic, and political structure. Social reforms can also change educational policies and their implications, either incrementally or radically. In the United States, pedagogical progressivism developed within the context of the philosophical trend of pragmatism and the rapid social changes taking place in the increasingly industrialized country. In line with the neo-evolutionist paradigm, the reform based on pragmatistic educational thinking was intended to promote the adaptation of education to the new needs of society. The school aimed to familiarize students with the knowledge, skills, and procedures necessary in an early industrial society. In this process, the progressive school was connected with real life and the surrounding society in a purposeful manner. Based on an experimental education and an experiential curriculum, the learner-centered teaching and learning process emphasized mastery of cooperative learning and working, information acquisition and processing, and problem-solving.

The neo-traditional school in India, conforming with national educational thinking, attempted to promote the democratic attitudes and craft-related skills needed for societal developmental work during the neo-traditional era. Instruction within the neo-traditional school that was based on both a comprehensive curriculum and national education sought to cultivate students' independent initiatives. Such instruction was linked to local traditional handicraft and agriculture. In the neo-tradional school, students were encouraged to be spiritually and morally fortified, insist on truth, and be self-reliant and community-minded, while also being familiar with the vocationally productive activities needed in the community and participating in social service. The educational program was built around craft-related productive work to which the child's entire social and physical environment was linked. The students lived in self-sufficient village communities and worked in traditional crafts and agricultural production offered by their communities.

A comparison of the activities of the progressive and neo-traditional schools can be made from the standpoint of the interrelationship between education and society applying Saunders's (1979, p. 218) typology of localistic curricula. This allows the following interpretation. The progressive school was trying to make comprehensive use of the resources available in the surrounding environment in the school's activity-pedagogical processes in addition to using the environment as both the means and subject of learning. In contrast, the neo-traditional school regarded education as a societal resource that enabled the transition into a completely new culture. Here, students acquired knowledge and skills by participating in activities in the community, such as the processes of craft-related education and social service. This type of Indian neo-traditional school, the efforts of which were directed toward the society-centered transformation of knowledge, was integrated with society in a planned and coordinated manner. Comparably, the American progressive school was mainly oriented toward the society-centered transaction of knowledge. The conclusion could be drawn that, from the perspective of community-based learning, the orientation of the interrelationship between education and society was essentially radical and contextual in India, but adaptable and pragmatic in the United States.

The present study reveals that a change in educational policy and a pedagogical turn can be a response not only to an internal need for policy reform but also to a sudden external political crisis or threat. In the late 1940s, during the Cold War, the United States saw conservative social thinking become more prominent. This intensified the need for a rapid remodernization of society. Consequently, a critical discussion of education called for a reform, with educational thinking influenced by realism as its basis. Roughly a decade later, Congress passed an education act in response to what was perceived as the scientific and political dominance of the Soviet Union. This act stated that schools should increase the levels of science and technology in order to develop the national defense. To achieve this goal, instruction in the essentialist or neo-essentialist school emphasized the scientific study of the laws of the physical universe. A teacher-directed teaching and learning process based on a subject-centered curriculum stressed academic expertise, particularly in the studies of science and mathematics. The school became an educational center of structured instruction with limited connections to society.

The pedagogical approaches of the essentialist and neo-essentialist schools can be compared by applying the typology presented by Saunders (1979, p. 218) from the viewpoint of the interrelationship between education and society. This comparison allows for the interpretation that in some pedagogical approaches to community-based learning, such as service-learning, the resources of the surrounding environment could be used not only as a teaching medium but also as a means of developing social responsibility. However, most approaches, such as environmental education and outdoor education, observed the close surroundings of the school mainly as they were, with no effort made to participate in or influence them. Schools tended to utilize local content in a program-oriented manner, in the form of pedagogical support for instruction in various subjects. This could lead to the conclusion that these types of essentialist or neo-essentialist schools were mainly oriented toward the society-centered transmission of knowledge. From the perspective of community-based learning, the nature of the interrelationship between education and society can be viewed as being simultaneously pragmatic and syncretistic during this period.

The results of this work suggest that national educational reform can also be a response to the internal need for policy reform inspired by the models of social planning and the related educational reforms in other countries. Social modernization in the mid-1960s required the Indian education system to accelerate the modernization process by adapting the example of the Soviet school. The work-experience activities of the neocolonial school stressed technological processes and modern techniques. Despite these work-experience programs, the teaching and learning process that aimed at advancing academic expertise was based on a subject-centered curriculum and, in practice, emphasized the society-centered transmission of knowledge on a teacher-directed basis. The school became an educational center with only limited connections to society. This period was characterized by a deterministic belief that the social goals leading to modernization could also be achieved through educational reforms in a linear and efficient manner in economically developing countries even when implemented in cooperation with modern and economically developed societies. In the late 1970s, however, neocolonial views of modernization met with opposition. Postcolonial work education conforming to national Indian cultural values was now favored as a means of reaching modernization.

The pedagogical approaches of the neocolonial and postcolonial schools can be compared from the standpoint of the interrelationship between education and society by applying the typology presented by Saunders (1979, p. 218). The comparison allows for the interpretation that the teacher-directed work-experience programs of the neocolonial school could be described as mainly utilizing the content offered by the community as pedagogical support in the instruction of various subjects, but making only some effort to change its functioning. To the contrary, the practices of socially useful productive work and the processes of social service in the postcolonial school were potentially capable of contributing to productivity and self-confidence in the community. From the perspective of community-based learning, the nature of the interrelationship between education and society in the neocolonial school was pragmatic and syncretistic. In contrast, the interrelationship between the postcolonial school and society could potentially attain a higher level of tolerance than the aforementioned school had, with students working for longer periods in community service activities outside the school, for example, in the processes of social service. It is possible that this type of Indian school was also oriented toward a school-centered transaction of knowledge.

In the development of the societies covered by this volume, we can distinguish eras whose events and processes incrementally influenced the nation's educational policy, the development of the school system, and the whole country. For example, in the Russian Empire, the tsarist school emphasized Western European ideals by stressing European-style educational institutions and curricula. These were prioritized together with economic and martial principles. Traditional values provided by the Orthodox Church were equally essential in the governmental life of the tsarist society. The ultimate goal was to contribute to societal development in order to attain a Western European societal order that would serve to accentuate a scientific and vocational school system. It was intended to break down the differences between manual and intellectual work. These well-educated people would become Western European citizens who could achieve the virtues needed in goal-directed activities, such as courage and resilience.

The conceptual features of tsarist education can be examined from the perspective of community-based learning by applying Hlebowitsh's (2007) classification. Tsarist education interprets the ideal student as respecting Western European ideals and their value dimensions and traditional values provided by the Orthodox Church. The ideal educational program is related to socioethical values that can contribute to societal development. The aim was to accentuate a scientific and vocational school system. The student is oriented toward an ideal democratic society, the citizens of which become Western Europeans who can acquire the skills and knowledge needed in goal-directed work and activities in the prevailing society.

In the 1920s, the early Soviet Union intended to carry out educational policies that rested upon Marxist values. The dialectical-historical materialism represented by Marx considers that social conditions affect the inner life of a person. By combining work and education, educators can prepare young people for a new communist society. Such polytechnical education requires a combination of theory and practice, instruction and production, and school and life. The society-centered pattern of community-based learning primarily emphasized moral-political and polytechnical aims and their value dimensions in order to train vocationally capable citizens for a revolutionary socialist society. In this process, physical, mental, and polytechnical education were integrated. The goal of revolutionary labor education, based on the Marxist socialist theory of society, was to combine learning activities with the proletarian spirit and disconnect from the old cultural values.

The Soviet Union emphasized in the mid-1980s that all areas of the national economy must be used for the benefit of science and technology and to significantly increase labor productivity. Achieving these goals required young citizens to have as modern an education as possible, a high level of intellectual and physical development, and a deep understanding of the scientific and technological basis of production. This is how work was to be carried out in the advanced socialist society. Such polytechnical education must be seen as the most important factor in the development of an individual's personality and as a means of responding to the labor needs of the national economy within the Marxist educational ideology.

A comparison of the pedagogical approaches of the polytechnical school of a preindustrial society during the 1920s and the polytechnical school of an advanced socialist society during the 1980s can be made from the standpoint of the interrelationship between education and society applying Saunders's (1979, p. 218) typology of localistic curricula. The polytechnical school of a preindustrial society in the 1920s integrated the curriculum into polytechnical and productive work. In this process, the ideological and economic importance to society was accentuated when applying Western educational ideas to instruction in the early Soviet Union. Education was seen as a social resource and tool that helped the transition to a new culture. School education was often integrated with local production opportunities. This type of school was potentially capable of contributing to productivity and self-confidence in the community. The polytechnical school of an advanced socialist society in the 1980s prioritized all areas of the national economy be used for the benefit of science and technology and to significantly increase labor productivity. Schools used information technology and the basics of programming in their practical studies. From the perspective of community-based learning, the orientation of the interrelationship between education and society was pragmatic and syncretistic by nature in the polytechnical school of a preindustrial society in the

1920s. It is possible that this type of polytechnical school was oriented toward a society-centered transformation of knowledge and was integrated with society in a planned manner. In contrast, the students in the polytechnical school of an advanced socialist society in the 1980s acquired working skills by observing their community and participating in and influencing the operations provided by the community, which they could later relate to their subjects, general theory, and their own profession. From the community-based learning point of view, the orientation of the interrelationship between the polytechnical school and an advanced socialist society in the 1980s was pragmatic and adaptable. It is possible that this type of polytechnical school was oriented toward a school-centered transaction of knowledge.

In the Russian Federation, the theoretical foundation for society is based on social political thinking in which the state rises to a superior position. The ultimate goal of education is to lead students to a free, humanistic, and democratic society. A post-Soviet school of this type aims at familiarizing students with the skills and courses of action needed in a new society. The school-centered pattern of community-based learning emphasizes intellectual and sociocultural aims and their value dimensions. These are stressed in the integration of intellectual, mental (spiritual and moral), and sociocultural education. The all-inclusive emphasis is placed on intellectual values within the Russian societal system.

If the conceptual features of Russian education presented by Hlebowitsh (2007) are approached from the perspective of community-based learning, the conclusion can be made that the ideal students are scientifically minded patriotic citizens and cooperative specialists who work through their own initiative and creativity and are thus able to function in the changing labor needs of a market economy. The ideal curriculum embodies the integration of school education with activities in the school and society that are a prerequisite for free and humanistic education. The students are oriented toward an ideal democratic society that depends on scientific knowledge while operating in industrial production and service-based sectors.

The successful Bolshevik Revolution in Russia and its implications strengthened Marxist-Leninist thinking in China. Soviet advisers were invited to the country to help organize a revolutionary program and activities, and to provide guidance in founding the C.P.C. in Shanghai in 1921. The ideas of socialist thinkers were difficult to understand in China because its cultural history differed so greatly from that of the West. To alleviate the situation, Marxist study groups were founded—one participate was Mao Zedong, future Communist Party leader.

In addition to the Chinese philosophical tradition, Mao's theoretical thinking on education is based on Marx's dialectical and historical view of materialism and Lenin's practical educational thinking. The influence of traditional Chinese philosophy on Mao's ideas is perhaps best expressed by the similarities that exist between the views of Confucianism and dialectical materialism regarding the concept of conflict and its importance in the development of society. Mao viewed that social development requires a continuing revolution because conflict is inherent in society, both between different classes and between forces and production relationships. The development of these conflicts propels society forward and provides the driving force for replacing an old society with a new one. Conflicts are the prerequisite for all existence and development. The function of a school in this battle is to serve the proletarian politics and the socialist model of production.

In 1976, after Mao's death, China began to strengthen the fields of agriculture, industry, defense, science, and technology. In the 1990s, China started to develop its community-based learning by adopting the view of a progressive-minded postrevolutionary education. This suggested that the curriculum program embodies units of study based on Western experiential, active-learning pedagogics within and outside the school. In this manner, the present analysis sees the philosophical background of community-based learning as founded on ideas that reflect both Western and Chinese philosophies of education. The intention was to educate capable workers for neoliberal industrial production in a socialist society, applying the principles of a Western market economy, led by the Chinese Communist Party. Such views indicate the acceptance of a syncretistic doctrine when seen from the tradition of the dialectical and materialistic theory of knowledge and the Chinese orientations in worldview and outlook on life, both of which are based on the theory of dialectical materialism.

The pedagogical approaches of the revolutionary and postrevolutionary schools can be compared from the standpoint of the interrelationship between education and society by applying the typology presented by Saunders's (1979, p. 218) localistic curricula. The comparison allows for the interpretation that students in the revolutionary school were integrated into productive work in the agricultural and small-scale industrial production offered by the local people's commune. Such education placed special emphasis on political and ideological values connected to the power-related value dimension. Instead, the practices of the postrevolutionary school sought to implement activities based on Western experiential and active-learning pedagogics within and outside the school. This could lead to the conclusion that the curriculum of the revolutionary school was to be strongly integrated into productive work, emphasizing the ideological and economic significance of the curriculum for the community. Such instruction sought to promote productivity and self-confidence in the community so as to help the transition to a new culture. From the perspective of community-based learning, the orientation of the interrelationship between education and society was pragmatic and anarchic in the revolutionary school. This type of revolutionary school was mainly oriented toward a society-centered transmission of knowledge. In contrast, when interpreted from the perspective of community-based learning, the orientation of the interrelationship between education and society was pragmatic and syncretistic in the postrevolutionary school. Students also had opportunities to observe and participate in the community as well as influence community operations while they implemented community projects in agriculture, health, and environmental protection. It is possible that this type of postrevolutionary school was oriented toward a school-centered transaction of knowledge.

2 Implications of Centralized and Decentralized School Systems

There have been enduring debates regarding educational reforms about who should control curricula and make decisions in education as well as about what to teach, how to teach it, and how to assess it. Traditionally, curriculum development has been largely centralized while there have been increasing efforts to expand the role of local schools and their teachers, allowing them to exert more influence over curriculum (see Arends & Kilcher, 2010, pp. 79–81). Previous studies have identified the advantages and disadvantages of curricula in centralized and decentralized school systems (Marsh, 1997, pp. 141, 149; Nevalainen et al., 2017, pp. 209–210, 214–217). The following sections explore these aspects and their implications for school culture and ultimately for community-based learning from the perspective of the four dimensions of school culture presented by Schoen (2013, pp. 13, 29–31).

2.1 The Teacher's Professional Orientation
In the context of a centralized curriculum, the professional orientation of teachers can be called the narrow-band transmission of their meta-orientation. In compliance with this orientation, the key responsibilities of teachers include transmitting information and guiding learning. This leaves teachers minimal room for their own initiatives. Teachers thus often assume the role of mere technicians, lacking the opportunity to participate in the planning of activities at their school. In traditional school culture, teachers use a learning process that is reproductive. They react to changes in the internal and external operating environments at their schools chiefly by identifying and correcting errors. That is how they preserve the behaviorist thought and action models

that stress the external control of learning. This kind of single-loop learning actually aims at preserving the prevailing school practices and routines.

In school-based curriculum thinking in a decentralized school system, teacher professionalism rests on autonomy, while a teacher is committed to help students become active learners. An additional requirement is commitment to personal lifelong learning and cooperation with various groups. A teacher's professional orientation emphasizes a broad-band transaction of their meta-orientation. This implies that students should be provided with learning opportunities based on active learning and cooperation in different learning environments. A teacher should participate in the development of teaching and various school activities together with colleagues, other staff, and different interest groups in the community. Central characteristics of the profession would include enthusiasm and participation in continuous learning and skills improvement.

A teacher's learning process and the associated school development are closely interconnected. The transformation of a traditional school context requires teachers to critically reflect on their own operating principles and practices and to renew them, in other words, they have to create a new school context. For teachers, the change in their work and the management of change imply a holistic learning process in which the prevailing school culture is internalized and altered through externalization. A school culture based on progressive pedagogy and a constructivist idea of learning presumes transformative learning. If teachers are to change the school context, they must acquire new models for thought and action that will facilitate changing the basis of action so that it becomes a double-loop learning process for them. Transformative learning also includes reflective learning, this being based on deliberation and discussion.

American progressive schools in the late 1930s, for example, were intended to connect teaching with real life and the surrounding society. Despite difficult economic times, the 1930s produced a number of experiments in education and profoundly changed teachers' professional orientation. The learner-centered teaching and learning process emphasized mastery of cooperative learning and working, information acquisition and processing, and problem-solving. At Holton High School in Holton, Kansas, for example, students carried out a study of city planning and the prevailing housing conditions. They also surveyed the utilities in and the modern conveniences of houses on the basis of a questionnaire they had created. Drawing on this data, they created tables and graphs as well as a map that classified the city's houses according to their convenience level. Finally, the students wrote an analysis describing the execution of the study and providing the study's findings and conclusions.

Later, a group of Holton High students took part in drawing up a housing program with the city housing committee. In this work, they made use of a survey they had carried out.

2.2 The Structure of the School Organization

A homogeneous school organization that follows a centralized curriculum is highly hierarchic and bureaucratic. Its decision-making is centralized and goal-oriented and emphasizes supervision. This model does not allow for the analysis of the local needs of individual schools. The purpose of an effective and easily controllable organization is to save time, energy, and money. The organization often lacks implementation strategies, or insufficient attention is paid to them, even though the central administration monitors activities at schools and requires them to attain certain goals. These policies lead to a uniform school culture in which schools are expected to be more similar, with limited goals. This type of rational organizational model expects school staff members to be willing to implement the operating principles created by the central administration.

A school organization that follows a school-based curriculum has its own culture that can be modified and improved. This requires collegial cooperation and in-depth reflection on thought and action models. The objective is to empower teachers to influence the direction and development of reforms. However, forced cooperation to achieve externally determined goals can suppress teachers' desire to cooperate and develop school culture.

Ideal schoolwork creates organic relations with all interest groups in the surrounding community. Outcomes of schoolwork must also be utilized in areas other than facilitating learning. Teachers can, if they want, act as animators in helping community members to achieve common goals and solve problems. One village school in Hebei, China, in the early 1960s, for example, was engaged in production so that they could attain self-sufficiency. The school helped the villagers and, in turn, the villagers helped the teachers to run the school. Students assisted the peasants by collecting lime, a natural substance that improves plant growth, and burning it to make fertilizer. The school received economic support from peasant families for schoolbooks and tuition.

This book has indicated that education can use all the human, physical, and financial resources of the community's learning networks. Different groups within the community can utilize the learning networks to develop various cooperative partnerships. In the Russian Federation, for example, International Community School Day was first celebrated on March 1, 2009, and is observed every year across Russia and Eastern Europe. The Community Schools Through the Eyes of Children project included 78 schools across 16 Russian regions. The schools shared student drawings, essays, and photographs, which helped create connections between regions by sharing ideas and information about each other's community schools.

2.3   *The Quality of Learning Environments*

A centralized curriculum favors traditional learning that occurs mainly in closed environments in which studying is connected to a specific time and place. The pace of studying is strictly predetermined. Studying is subject-centered with content that includes clearly defined problems and answers that are common to all learners. Learning is primarily based on external motivation. The classroom is the dominant learning setting, where students have only little or no contact with authentic alternative learning environments. The school culture does not allow concentration on local problems.

A school culture that implements a school-based curriculum in a decentralized school system gives preference to open and contextual learning environments. Students' responsibility, inner motivation, and self-direction are emphasized, and learning is oriented toward authentic learning environments connected to the physical, mental, and cultural dimensions of the reality outside the school. Information and communications technology is frequently utilized in learning and teaching, and the school culture supports the utilization of local resources in teaching.

The chapters in this book present numerous approaches to community-based learning that are designed to meet the challenges of contemporary education. The case studies in this book show how learning is connected with authentic community environments, where learning is linked to life, experiences, and practical problems. In the late 1930s, Indian basic and postbasic schools, for example, intended to make the school a center for comprehensive social service and reconstruction for the community. The aim was to make the school as self-sufficient and communally functioning as possible. This is illustrated by the case in which the students at one school in Rajasthan took part in various kinds of postal services, such as acquiring postcards, envelopes, and money order forms for the public; writing letters for the villagers who were illiterate; and ensuring that everything was taken to the city post office.

2.4   *A Student-Centered Focus*

Centralized curriculum thinking favors teacher-led and traditional methods that guarantee continuity but hinder diversity and creativity. In some subjects, it also reduces learning opportunities. Instruction utilizes technologically advanced methods and tools and, at the national level, the methods used at different schools are mostly uniform.

A school-based curriculum provides teachers with considerable freedom to test alternative pedagogical methods. Curriculum reform favors approaches of active learning, including collaborative research and problem-solving projects, theme-based learning, inquiry-based learning, and small-group discussions of phenomena. Active learning is based on personal, action-based experiences, accompanied by reflection on them. Inner motivation and a genuine interest in exploring one's own environment are essential. Self-direction, cooperation, initiative data collection, and the ability to process data are emphasized in the learning process. Active learning takes place in an environment that is open and allows the learner to participate in planning, implementing, and evaluating the learning experience.

This book has demonstrated that the ideal school offers the opportunity to articulate reality in such a way that teaching and education are connected with situations of social reality, and learning is connected to the student's life, experiences, needs, and particular problems. Community members of various ages should also have the opportunity to be involved in mapping communal needs and identifying the resources that can satisfy these needs. Teachers could coordinate these kind of activities, if they are willing. One middle school in Colorado in the late 1990s, for example, aimed at identifying and solving the community's environmental problems. The students decided to perform a study of the poor quality of the community water supply. They interviewed community members, conducted water quality tests, and studied plumbing in homes. With their teacher, the students drafted an action plan recommending a cooperative venture with the weatherization project in low-cost housing.

3   Future Reforms, Challenges, New Pedagogics and Views

Contemporary societies are also facing social, economic, and environmental challenges. Global education reform is searching for new models in 21st-century pedagogy to meet these problems. The OECD Learning Framework 2030 (Organisation for Economic Co-operation and Development, 2018) presented a set of pedagogical aims and underlying values that can be applied to community-based learning. This document provides a detailed example of value-oriented aims:

> Education has a vital role to play in developing the knowledge, skills, attitudes and values that enable people to contribute to and benefit from an inclusive and sustainable future. Learning to form clear and purposeful

goals, work with others with different perspectives, find untapped opportunities and identify multiple solutions to big problems will be essential in the coming years. Education needs to aim to do more than prepare young people for the world of work; it needs to equip students with the skills they need to become active, responsible and engaged citizens. ... Educators must not only recognise learners' individuality, but also acknowledge the wider set of relationships—with their teachers, peers, families and communities—that influence their learning. A concept underlying the learning framework is "co-agency"—the interactive, mutually supportive relationships that help learners to progress towards their valued goals. In this context, everyone should be considered a learner, not only students but also teachers, school managers, parents and communities. (p. 4)

It is possible that future learning environments will increasingly emphasize technology-based learning. Thus, in the coming years, students will use more technological applications when participating in various activities of community-based learning. The advancement of information and communication technologies has promoted various learning paradigms, from free-tech learning to electronic technologies (e-learning), and from e-learning to mobile learning (m-learning), and on to ubiquitous learning (u-learning). U-learning aims at accommodating learners and their learning style by providing appropriate information anytime and anywhere they wish. Ubiquitous learning environments make it possible to carry out educational activities in several places at the same time, from any device, and adapt to the user's situations and needs (Yahya et al., 2010, p. 120).

However, recent technological developments cannot replace human interaction between a school and a community. Smith and Sobel (2010) argued that the real world for many young people is what happens on their computer monitors. Due to this alienation of students from the real world directly outside their schools, many of them are nature- and community-deprived. Approaches to community-based learning could provide a way for teachers and communities to prepare students to become participants in local problem-solving (p. VIII). Prast and Viegut (2015) suggested that it is important for community-based learning to increase curricular partnerships within the community, to research and use instructional techniques that help students obtain meaning from the content and improve student engagement (p. 111).

Smith (2017) described four approaches that lead to a meaningful life. Her thinking can be applied to future school education. In school learning environments, the search for a meaningful life should be a key priority. The search for a rewarding and meaningful life in the development of future learning environments could be based on the following principles of life-centered learning:

1. Relationships to life outside school: A central basic human need is a sense of belonging, as a person needs to be connected with others. School culture should support teaching and upbringing where students can connect with the lives of others through different communities, such as work assignments, research projects, and hobbies. The meanings of things and phenomena studied in open and authentic learning environments open up students' thinking and, at the same time, help students find relevance in life.

2. Purposeful learning outside of school: Many community-based learning approaches emphasize doing good things for one's own community, its nature, and people's lives. At the same time, students can develop themselves and their own important life-related principles, find a purpose in their life, utilize their strengths and gifts in nature conservation, and improve the quality of life in the surrounding community. Purposeful goals guide everything we do and involve an effort to improve the world in things that matter to us. Often, improving the world simply means the people surrounding us, whose quality of life we can influence through our own actions.

3. Reflecting experiences by writing: By reflecting on experiences gained outside of school, students can articulate the world. Writing about experiences obtained in the process of life-centered learning can help students understand what is going on in their life, how things relate to each other, and find meaning about it all. Through fictional and factual narratives based on their own experiences, students can discover new dimensions in the meaning of their life.

4. Perceiving wholes: In authentic learning environments, students can perceive wholes and experience being part of something greater, such as a campfire in the middle of quiet nature, field trips to a concert hall music event, theater play performance, an art museum exhibition, or a church devotional. These activities can act as ways to transcend themselves and thus offer students the opportunity to step outside of time and place and feel connected to something higher than themselves.

Afterword

This comparative study presents a holistic picture of the manifestation of community-based learning in the United States, the Republic of India, the Russian Empire, the Soviet Union, the Russian Federation, and the People's Republic of China. The 20th century saw extensive social changes taking place in these countries. The changes, caused by complex dialectical dynamics relating to the social, economic, and political structure, have also influenced education. Alternatively, they could simply be regarded as a reflection of changes and turnovers in leadership. This study demonstrates conclusively that new ideas concerning educational policy spread from one country to another. Reformist ideas concerning education have entered the international trends within educational theory and have been assimilated into national education thinking in these countries. However, the different views are mutually contradictory since they are linked to different background value objectives and the concepts of people that are associated with them. Furthermore, these contradictions are intimately linked with broader social changes in these socially different countries.

The subject of study demonstrated itself to be dialectical by nature. School-centered and society-centered patterns of community-based learning alternate with one another throughout the development of national educational policies. According to this study, the development has progressed toward the school-centered pattern of community-based learning, which emphasizes intellectual aims and school-centered procedures. The essential feature here now is socialization based on externalization and internalization. This, in turn, produces the experts in science and technology that a developed society requires, where intellectual work is a component of modern production.

Modern society is difficult to govern. It is also increasingly difficult to educate citizens who are able to function in this complex world. Societies that have adopted a technocratic basic principle place their trust in school-centered education and intellectual teaching, the implementation of which is largely detached from social reality. The primary duty of the schools is to train citizens for work in the modern world. However, it is apparent that overcoming the existing social, economic, and societal problems requires an understanding of new values, goals, and procedures in order to govern the globalizing world. This study argues that the articulation of entities can create the basis for understanding even a complicated society. The best context for profoundly articulating human action is social reality and life, in which people also learn to assess individual and communal choices. A person only develops into a socially functional human being in relation to other people and communal work and activity.

The ideal school offers the opportunity to articulate reality in such a way that teaching and education are connected with situations of social reality, in which learning can be connected to the student's life, experiences, and practical problems. This view holds that problem-solving requires an understanding and awareness of the whole, which can be achieved through activity. By combining work and activity with a holistic approach, a level of action can be reached that is not merely a repetition of previously learned knowledge and skills but which includes the ability to function in new situations. Therefore, previous knowledge helps to articulate an increasingly broad and complicated reality.

A report to the Club of Rome, entitled *No Limits to Learning*, suggests changing traditional, conventional learning into innovative and societal learning (Botkin et al., 1979, pp. 79–82). In the countries studied in the present volume, attempts have been made to connect learning with nature, production, culture, or other aspects of society whenever appropriate. In this close relationship, the fundamental function of community-based learning is to articulate the essence of reality and to internalize and transform its physical, intellectual, and cultural world. The objectivated products of human social activity can be viewed through the lenses of the world that produces resources, this being termed here as an *integrating world*. The main environment for secondary socialization is linked to the contexts of pedagogical processes inside the school as well as to certain physical, personal, and sociocultural contexts outside the school that are connected with these processes. In so doing, certain Naturalistic, Sociocultural, Productive, Ecological, and Scientific-Technical Dimensions are emphasized in accordance with social trends in socialization environments that focus on secondary socialization. Hence, the examination leads to the conclusion that the activities taking place in all of the subcomponents of an ideal society also enhance education and instruction. In this manner, learning is linked to its natural context, with ideal instruction being actively problem-oriented, holistic, and life-centered.

The national educational policies in the countries studied in this volume support educational practices based on active learning. The main principles of the curriculum reform currently being implemented support a school culture that stresses the autonomous control of learning. It encourages flexibility and develops interactiveness, both within the school and between the school and the surrounding community. Active learning implies that students are mentally and physically involved. They guide their own learning, invent solutions to problems, define and interpret concepts as well as reflect on their interrelations. It is important that students interact with their environment. Through active learning, students enhance their reflective thinking as well as their metacognitive knowledge and skills.

Active learning requires conditions that allow for immediate and meaningful experiences in genuine learning situations. Students create new knowledge by utilizing prior learning when they reflect on their experiences gained through concrete activities. Learning is active when the subject matter to be learned is expressed as problems and questions, for which students seek solutions guided by their inner motivation, either independently or in small groups. Of prime importance in the functioning of these small groups is the interplay between students as they participate in discussions and joint reflection. The opportunity to make choices at the various stages of the learning process is essential for empowering students as a result of the activities. In the learning process, it is crucial that students evaluate how well they have attained their own targets. They should also be able to critically evaluate the information and the development of learning skills in their group.

Curriculum development continuously requires new data documenting successful models of action and practices in schools. Schools and their associated interest groups need qualitative and contextual information that can probably best be acquired from school-based case studies. The experiences of teachers and other participants during their careers as implementers of the new curriculum should also be utilized in the preservice and in-service training of new teachers and others, such as administrative and social personnel. One important objective of this training is to develop forms of education offering those involved an opportunity for constructing internal models of action. Educators can connect different theories of learning and teaching to these models of action, to utilize later in their work. During the continuous formation of models of action, the experiences gained in practical work play an essential role as well as critical deliberation on these experiences. The goal is to learn strategies that change school practices by means of transformative learning.

References

Acton, E., & Stableford, T. (Eds.). (2005). *The Soviet Union: A documentary history: Vol. 1: 1917–1940*. Exeter, U.K.: University of Exeter Press.

Alexander, R. (2000). *Culture and pedagogy: International comparisons in primary education*. Oxford, U.K.: Blackwell.

Allport, G. W., Vernon, P. E., & Lindzey, G. (1960). *Study of values: A scale for measuring the dominant interests in personality* (3rd ed.). Boston, MA: Houghton Mifflin.

All-Russian Central Executive Committee of the R.S.F.S.R. (1947). Polozhenie o edinoj trudovoj shkole [The statute of the unified labor school]. In N. I. Boldyrev (Ed.), *Direktivy VKP(b) i postanovleniya Sovetskogo pravitelstva o narodnom obrazovanii: Vyp. 1. Sbornik dokumentov za 1917–1947 gg* [*The directives of the Communist Party of S.U. and the statutes of the Central Executive Committee and the Council of People's Commissars on public education: Pt. 1. Collection of documents for 1917–1947*] (pp. 120–127). Moskva, U.S.S.R.: Akademii pedagogicheskih. (Original work published 1918)

Alston, P. L. (1969). *Education and the state in tsarist Russia*. Stanford, CA: Stanford University Press.

American Association for Health, Physical Education, and Recreation. (1963). *Education in and for the outdoors: Report of the National Conference on outdoor education at the Kellogg Gull Biological Station, Michigan, May 2–4, 1962*. Washington, DC: Department of the National Education Association.

American Forest Institute. (1975). *Project learning tree: Supplementary curriculum guide for kindergarten through grade 6*. Washington, DC: Author.

American Forest Institute. (1977). *Project learning tree: Supplementary activity guide for grades K through 6*. Washington, DC: Author.

Andropov, Y. (1983). *Karl Marxin oppi ja eräitä sosialismin rakentamisen kysymyksiä Neuvostoliitossa* [The doctrine of Karl Marx and some issues of building socialism in the Soviet Union]. Helsinki, Finland: A.P.A.

Andrus, E. P. (1935). General procedure at Abraham Lincoln High School, Los Angeles. *The Clearing House, 9*(6), 334–339.

Arends, R. I. (2009). *Learning to teach* (8th ed.). New York, NY: McGraw-Hill.

Arends, R. I., & Kilcher, A. (2010). *Teaching for student learning: Becoming an accomplished teacher*. New York, NY: Routledge.

Armstrong, D. G., Henson, K. T., & Savage, T. V. (2009). *Teaching today: An introduction to education* (8th ed.). Upper Saddle River, NJ: Pearson.

Arunachalam, G. A. (1949). Periyanayakanpalayam Basic School: An experiment in Tamil Nad. In *Two years of work: Report of the Second Basic Education Conference, Jamianagar, Delhi, April 1941* (3rd ed., pp. 102–105). Sevagram, India: Hindustani Talimi Sangh.

Atutov, P. R., & Kalney, V. A. (1987). *Shkola i trud* [*School and work*]. Moskva, U.S.S.R.: Pedagogika.

Bacon, E. (with Wyman, M.). (2006). *Contemporary Russia*. London, U.K.: Palgrave Macmillan.

Ballantine, J. H., & Hammack, F. M. (2009). *The sociology of education: A systematic analysis* (6th ed.). Upper Saddle River, NJ: Pearson.

Ballantine, J. H., & Roberts, K. A. (2009). *Our social world: Introduction to sociology* (2nd ed.). Los Angeles, CA: Pine Forge Press.

Bei jing shi di shi san zhong xue dang zhi bu. (1975). Kai men ban xue, yue ban yue hao [A school combined with a society, a society becomes better]. *Hong qi, 18*(12), 40–43.

Bereday, G. Z. F. (1964). *Comparative method in education*. New York, NY: Holt, Rinehart and Winston.

Berger, P. L. (1969). *The sacred canopy: Elements of a sociological theory of religion*. Garden City, NY: Doubleday.

Berger, P. L., & Luckmann, T. (1967). *The social construction of reality: A treatise in the sociology of knowledge*. Garden City, NY: Doubleday.

Berry, T. (1960). Dewey's influence in China. In J. Blewett (Ed.), *John Dewey: His thought and influence* (pp. 199–232). New York, NY: Fordham University Press.

Betti, E. (1962). *Die Hermeneutik als allgemeine Methodik der Geisteswissenschaften* [*Hermeneutics as a general method for the humanities*]. Tübingen, Germany: Mohr.

Betti, E. (1967). *Allgemeine Auslegungslehre als Methodik der Geisteswissenschaften* [*The general theory of interpretation as a method for the liberal arts*]. Tübingen, Germany: Mohr.

Bhattacharya, S. (Ed.). (1997). *The Mahatma and the poet: Letters and debates between Gandhi and Tagore 1915–1941*. New Delhi, India: National Book Trust.

Bing, L., & Daun, H. (2001). *Gender and school inequalities in China: Case study in five Beijing schools*. Stockholm, Sweden: Institute of International Education, Stockholm University.

Bischoff, H. (1987). A walking tour of an ethnic neighborhood: Communities as outdoor classrooms for teaching immigration history. *The Social Studies, 78*(5), 202–205.

Blonski, P. P. (1927). *Kasvatusoppi* [*Pedagogy*] (L. Letonmäki, Trans.). Leningrad, U.S.S.R.: Kniga. (Original work published 1921)

Blonskij, P. P. (1921). *Die Arbeits-Schule* [*Labor school*] (H. Ruoff, Trans., Part. 1). Berlin, Germany: Verlag Gesellschaft und Erziehung. (Original work published 1919)

Blonskij, P. P. (1973). *Die Arbeitsschule* [*Labor school*] (Anon. Trans.). Paderborn, Germany: Ferdinand Schöningh. (Original work published 1919)

Bo, Y. (1998). Guan yu 1958 nian du guo min jing ji ji hua cao an de bao gao (jie lu) [The report of a draft plan for the national economy in 1958 (extract)]. In D. He (Ed.), *Zhong hua ren min gong he guo zhong yao jiao yu wen xian: 1949–1975* [*The important educational documents of the People's Republic of China: Vol. 1. 1949–1975*] (pp. 797–799). Haikou, P.R.C.: Hainan Publishing. (Original work published 1958)

Boers, D. (2007). *History of American education*. New York, NY: Peter Lang.

Borisova, N. V. (2011, March 1). Kovcheg: An unusual school for unusual children. *Russian-American Education Forum: An Online Journal, 2*(1). http://www.rus-ameeduforum.com/content/en/?task=art&article=1000821&iid=9

Boston, B. O. (1998–1999). "If the water is nasty, fix it." *Educational Leadership, 56*(4), 66–69.

Botkin, J. W., Elmandjra, M., & Malitza, M. (1979). *No limits to learning: Bridging the human gap. A report to the Club of Rome*. Oxford, U.K.: Pergamon Press.

Boutelle, M. W. (1937). A school experiment with integration. *Curriculum Journal, 8*(5), 216.

Bowes, C. A. (1935). The first junior high to construct a golf course. *The Clearing House, 9*(8), 500–501.

Brasgalla, J. (1989). School yard gardening reaps harvest of learning and lettuce. *PTA Today, 14*(7), 7–9.

Braund, M., & Reiss, M. (2004). The nature of learning science outside the classroom. In M. Braund & M. Reiss (Eds.), *Learning science outside the classroom* (pp. 1–12). London, U.K.: Routledge.

Bray, M. (2004). Continuity and change in education. In M. Bray & R. Koo (Eds.), *Education and society in Hong Kong and Macao: Comparative perspectives on continuity and change* (2nd ed., pp. 251–269). Hong Kong, P.R.C.: Kluwer.

Brickman, W. (1960). John Dewey in Russia. *Educational Theory, 10*(1), 83–86.

Brookfield, S. (1983). *Adult learners, adult education and the community*. Milton Keynes, U.K.: Open University Press.

Brown, G. T. L., & Gao, L. (2015). Chinese teachers' conceptions of assessment for and of learning: Six competing and complementary purposes. *Cogent Education, 2*(1), 2–19.

Brown, J. M. (1994). *Modern India: The origins of an Asian democracy* (2nd ed.). Oxford, U.K.: Oxford University Press.

Bruner, H. B. (1937). Criteria for evaluating course-of-study materials. *Teachers College Record, 39*(2), 107–120.

Buch, M. B., & Patel, P. A. (1979). *Towards work-centered education: A programme of socially useful productive work in education*. Ahmedabad, India: Gujarat Vidyapith.

Butler, V. R., & Roach, E. M. (1986). Coastal studies for primary grades. *Science and Children, 24*(2), 34–37.

Buttenwieser, P. L. (1969). *The Lincoln School and its times 1917–1948* [Unpublished doctoral dissertation]. Columbia University.

Central Bank of the Russian Federation. (2013). The history of the Bank of Russia's exchange rate policy. *BIS Papers, 73*, 293–299.

Central Board of Secondary Education. (1991). *Work experience in schools: Guidelines and syllabus* (2nd ed.). Delhi, India: Ministry of Human Resource Development, Government of India.

Central Board of Secondary Education. (2004). *Work education in schools.* Delhi, India: Ministry of Education, Government of India.

Central Committee of the All-Union Communist Party. (1974a). Ob uchebnyh programmah i rezhime v nachalnoj i srednej shkole [On curricula and administration in elementary and middle schools]. In A. A. Abakumov, N. P. Kuzin, F. I. Puzyrev, & L. F. Litvinov (Eds.), *Narodnoe obrazovanie v SSSR, obshcheobrazovatelnaja shkola: Sbornik dokumentov 1917–1973 gg* [*Public education in the U.S.S.R.: Collection of documents for 1917–1973*] (pp. 161–164). Moskva, U.S.S.R.: Pedagogika. (Original work published 1934)

Central Committee of the All-Union Communist Party. (1974b). O nachalnom i srednei shkole [On elementary and middle schools]. In A. A. Abakumov, N. P. Kuzin, F. I. Puzyrev, & L. F. Litvinov (Eds.), *Narodnoe obrazovanie v SSSR, obshcheobrazovatelnaja shkola: Sbornik dokumentov 1917–1973 gg* [*Public education in the U.S.S.R.: Collection of documents for 1917–1973*] (pp. 156–161). Moskva, U.S.S.R.: Pedagogika. (Original work published 1934)

Central Committee of the All-Union Communist Party. (1974c). O vseobshchem obyazatelnom nachalnom obuchenii [On general compulsory primary education]. In A. A. Abakumov, N. P. Kuzin, F. I. Puzyrev, & L. F. Litvinov (Eds.), *Narodnoe obrazovanie v SSSR, obshcheobrazovatelnaja shkola: Sbornik dokumentov 1917–1973 gg* [*Public education in the U.S.S.R.: Collection of documents for 1917–1973*] (pp. 109–111). Moskva, U.S.S.R.: Pedagogika. (Original work published 1930)

Central Committee of the C.P.S.U. and the U.S.S.R. Council of Ministers. (1974). Ukrepleniye svyazey mezhdu shkoloy i zhiznyu i dalneysheye razvitiye sistemy gosudarstvennogo obrazovaniya v S.S.S.R. [Strengthening ties between school and life, and further developing the public education system in the U.S.S.R.]. In A. A. Abakumov, N. P. Kuzin, F. I. Puzyrev, & L. F. Litvinov (Eds.), *Narodnoe obrazovanie v SSSR, obshcheobrazovatelnaja shkola: Sbornik dokumentov 1917–1973 gg* [*Public education in the U.S.S.R.: Collection of documents for 1917–1973*] (pp. 53–61). Moskva, U.S.S.R.: Pedagogika. (Original work published 1958)

Central Committee of the C.P.S.U. and the U.S.S.R. Council of Ministers. (1987). O dalneyshem sovershenstvovanii obuchenija, vospitaniya uchashchikhsya obshcheobrazovatelnykh shkol i podgotovki ikh k trudu [On further improvements in education and upbringing of the secondary school students and their preparation for labor]. In N. E. Golubeva (Ed.), *Narodnoe obrazovanie v SSSR: Sbornik normativnykh aktov* [*Public education in the U.S.S.R.: Collection of statutes*] (pp. 121–125). Moskva, U.S.S.R.: Juridicheskaja. (Original work published 1977)

Central Educational Science Institute. (1990). Middle school education (D. Luo & X. Yang, Trans., S. Yang, Rev.). In *Education in contemporary China* (pp. 258–329). Ghangsha, P.R.C.: Hunan Education Publishing.

Central People's Government. (1984). *The sixth five-year plan of the People's Republic of China for economic and social development 1981–1985.* Beijing, P.R.C.: Foreign Languages Press.

Central People's Government. (1998a). Guo wu yuan pi zhuan jiao yu bu guan yu yi jiu qi qi nian gao deng xue xiao zhao sheng gong zuo de yi jian [Communications by the Central People's Government on the opinions of the Ministry of Education of the C.P.G. on student enrollment in higher education institutions in 1977]. In D. He (Ed.), *Zhong hua ren min gong he guo zhong yao jiao yu wen xian: 1976–1990 [The important educational documents of the People's Republic of China: Vol. 2. 1976–1990]* (pp. 1579–1582). Haikou, P.R.C.: Hainan Publishing.

Central People's Government. (1998b). Zheng wu yuan guan yu gai ge xue zhi de jue ding [The decision of the Central People's Government on reforming the school system]. In D. He (Ed.), *Zhong hua ren min gong he guo zhong yao jiao yu wen xian: 1949–1975 [The important educational documents of the People's Republic of China: Vol. 1. 1949–1975]* (pp. 105–107). Haikou, P.R.C.: Hainan Publishing.

Chelyustkin, I. (1922). Letnie zanyatiya v odnoy iz Petrogradckikh shkol [Summer classes in one of the Petrograd schools]. *Na putyakh k novoy shkole, 1*(1), 51–61.

Chen, J. (1990). *Confucius as a teacher: Philosophy of Confucius with special reference to its educational implications.* Beijing, P.R.C.: Foreign Languages Press.

Chen, T. H. (1981). *Chinese education since 1949: Academic and revolutionary models.* New York, NY: Pergamon Press.

Chernenko, K. (1976). *One year after Helsinki.* Moscow, U.S.S.R.: Novosti Press.

Childress, R. B. (1978). Public school environmental education curricula: A national profile. *The Journal of Environmental Education, 9*(3), 2–11.

China. (1975). *Constitution of the People's Republic of China, adopted on January 17, 1975 by the Fourth National People's Congress of the People's Republic of China at its first session.* Peking, P.R.C.: Foreign Languages Press.

China. (1978). *Constitution of the People's Republic of China, adopted on March 5, 1978 by the Fifth National People's Congress of the People's Republic of China at its first session.* Beijing, P.R.C.: Foreign Languages Press.

China. (1983). *Constitution of the People's Republic of China, adopted on December 4, 1982 by the Fifth National People's Congress of the People's Republic of China at its fifth session.* Beijing, P.R.C.: Foreign Languages Press.

Chowdhury, S. (2005, October 15). Residential project. *Doon School Weekly*, 3.

Christopherson, A. M. (1981). A treasure hunt at the zoo. *Science and Children, 18*(6), 7–9.

Chu, D.-C. (1980). *Chairman Mao: Education of the proletariat.* New York, NY: Philosophical Library.

Chu xiong zhuan shu bian. (1958). *Qin gong jian xue di yi mian jing zi: Da yao zhong xue jian chi de fang xiang shi yi qie xue xiao de fang xiang [A mirror on a work-study program: The orientation Dayao High School takes is the one for all schools*]. Yunnan, P.R.C.: Yunnan People's Publishing.

C.I.A. sees stagnation in Soviet. (1983, May 31). *The New York Times*, D1.

Clapp, E. R. (1939). *Community schools in action*. New York, NY: Viking Press.

Clarke, J. M. (1951). *Public school camping: California's pilot project in outdoor education*. Stanford, CA: Stanford University Press.

Cohen, A. (1981). The educational philosophy of Tolstoy. *Oxford Review of Education*, 7(3), 241–251.

Collinson, D., Plant, K., & Wilkinson, R. (2000). *Fifty Eastern thinkers*. London, U.K.: Routledge.

Conrad, L. H. (Ed.). (1961). *Outdoor teacher education: A report drawn from the First National Conference on the preparation of teachers for carrying suitable portions of the curriculum to the out-of-doors (Lorado Taft Field Campus, September 23–24, 1960)*. DeKalb, IL: Northern Illinois University.

Cook, S. (1980). While the city sleeps. *Communicator*, 11(1), 29–31.

Corcoran, P. B., & Pennock, M. (2005). Democratic education for environmental stewardship. In T. Grant & G. Littlejohn (Eds.), *Teaching green: The elementary years. Hands-on learning in grades K–5* (pp. 20–24). Gabriola Island, Canada: New Society.

Coser, L. A. (1956). *The functions of social conflict*. Glencoe, IL: Free Press of Glencoe.

Coulter, B. (with Litz, N. & Strauss, N.). (2000). Investigating an urban watershed: How healthy is Deer Creek? In R. Audet & G. Ludwig, *GIS in schools* (pp. 55–61). Redlands, CA: ESRI Press.

Councils of Workers, Soldiers, and Peasants, All-Russian Central Executive Committee, and the Council of People's Commissars of the Russian S.F.S.R. (1974). O vvedenii vseobshchego obyazatelnogo obucheniya [The introduction of universal compulsory education]. In A. A. Abakumov, N. P. Kuzin, F. I. Puzyrev, & L. F. Litvinov (Eds.), *Narodnoe obrazovanie v S.S.S.R., obshcheobrazovatelnaja shkola: Sbornik dokumentov 1917–1973 gg [Public education in the U.S.S.R., comprehensive school: Collection of documents for 1917–1973]* (p. 111). Moskva, U.S.S.R.: Pedagogika. (Original work published 1930)

C.P.C. Central Committee. (1998a). Zhong gong zhong yang guan yu ban nong ban du jiao yu gong zuo de zhi shi [Instructions by the C.P.C. Central Committee on educational work related to partial farming and partial studying]. In D. He (Ed.), *Zhong hua ren min gong he guo zhong yao jiao yu wen xian: 1949–1975 [The important educational documents of the People's Republic of China: Vol. 1. 1949–1975]* (pp. 1356–1359). Haikou, P.R.C.: Hainan Publishing.

C.P.C. Central Committee. (1998b). Zhong gong zhong yang guan yu wu chan jie ji wen hua da ge ming de jue ding [The decision of the C.P.C. Central Committee on the Great Proletarian Cultural Revolution]. In D. He (Ed.), *Zhong hua ren min gong he guo zhong yao jiao yu wen xian: 1949–1975 [The important educational documents of the People's Republic of China: Vol. 1. 1949–1975]* (pp. 1406–1408). Haikou, P.R.C.: Hainan Publishing. (Original work published 1966)

C.P.C. Central Committee. (1998c). Zhong gong zong yang, guo wu yuan guan yu bao zheng xue sheng, jiao shi shen ti jian kang he lao yi jie he wen ti de zhi shi [The directive of the C.P.C. Central Committee and the Central People's Government on guaranteeing students and teachers are healthy and have proper work]. In D. He (Ed.), *Zhong hua ren min gong he guo zhong yao jiao yu wen xian: 1949–1975 [The important educational documents of the People's Republic of China: Vol. 1. 1949–1975]* (p. 989). Haikou, P.R.C.: Hainan Publishing.

C.P.C. Central Committee. (2003). Zhong gong zhong yang guo wu yuan guan yu shen hua jiao yu gai ge quan mian tui jin su zhi jiao yu de jue ding [The decisions of the C.P.C. Central Committee and the Central People's Government on deepening education reform and fully advancing quality education]. In D. He (Ed.), *Zhong hua ren min gong he guo zhong yao jiao yu wen xian: 1998–2002 [The important educational documents of the People's Republic of China: Vol. 4. 1998–2002]* (pp. 286–290). Haikou, P.R.C.: Hainan Publishing.

Cremin, L. A. (1961). *The transformation of the school: Progressivism in American education 1876–1957*. New York, NY: Knopf.

Cremin, L. A. (1988). *American education: The metropolitan experience 1876–1980*. New York, NY: Harper & Row.

Cuban, L. (1992). Curriculum stability and change. In P. W. Jackson (Ed.), *Handbook of research on curriculum* (pp. 216–247). New York, NY: Macmillan.

Cuban, L. (1993). *How teachers taught: Constancy and change in American classrooms 1890–1990* (2nd ed.). New York, NY: Teachers College Press.

Cui, J. (1959). Bu bu shen ru, bi bi luo shi [Make a further step and make sure it will happen]. *Ji lin jiao yu, 4*(6), 21.

Cui, Y., & Zhu, Y. (2014, June). Curriculum reforms in China: History and the present day. *Revue Internationale D'éducation de Sèvres*. http://journals.openedition.org/ries/3846

Cygnaeus, U. (1910). *Uno Cygnaeuksen kirjoitukset: Suomen kansakoulun perustamisesta ja järjestämisestä [Works of Uno Cygnaeus: On the establishment and organization of the Finnish primary school]*. Valtion varoilla toimitettu kokoelma 100-vuotispäiväksi 12 p. lokakuuta 1910. Helsinki, Finland: Kansanvalistusseura.

Dahrendorf, R. (1959). *Class and class conflict in industrial society*. London, U.K.: Routledge & Kegan Paul.

Danilchenko, M. G. (1993). Pavel Petrovich Blonsky (1884–1941). *Prospects: The Quarterly Review of Comparative Education, 23*(1–2), 113–124.

Danner, H. (1979). *Methoden geisteswissenschaftlicher Pädagogik: Einführung in Hermeneutik, Phänomenologie und Dialektik [Methods of humanistic pedagogy: Introduction to hermeneutics, phenomenology, and dialectic]*. München, Germany: Reinhardt.

Darling, J., & Nordenbo, S. E. (2003). Progressivism. In N. Blake, P. Smeyers, R. Smith, & P. Standish (Eds.), *The Blackwell guide to the philosophy of education* (pp. 288–308). Malden, MA: Blackwell.

Darling-Hammond, L. (2007, May 21). Evaluating "No Child Left Behind": The problems and promises of Bush's education policy. *The Nation*. https://www.thenation.com/article/evaluating-no-child-left-behind/

Datta, D. M. (1953). *The philosophy of Mahatma Gandhi*. Madison, WI: University of Wisconsin Press.

Davies, R. W. (1980). *The socialist offensive: The collectivisation of Soviet agriculture, 1929–1930*. The industrialisation of Soviet Russia 1. Basingstoke, U.K.: Macmillan Press.

Davies, R. W. (1989). *The Soviet economy in turmoil, 1929–1930*. The industrialisation of Soviet Russia 3. Basingstoke, U.K.: Macmillan Press.

Davlyatov, K. D. (1977). *Sovershenstvovanie trudovogo politekhnicheskogo obucheniya i professionalnoy orientatsii selskikh shkolnikov Uzbekistana* [*Improving the level of polytechnical work education and vocational guidance for students in village schools in Uzbekistan*] [Doctoral dissertation]. Scientific Institute in Tashkent.

Decision of the Central Committee of the Chinese Communist Party concerning the Great Proletarian Cultural Revolution. (1966, August). *Peking Review, 9*(33), 6–11.

Decision of the C.P.C. Central Committee on the reform of the educational structure. (1991). In *Major documents of the People's Republic of China: December 1978–November 1989* (pp. 465–484). Beijing, P.R.C.: Foreign Languages Press. (Original work published 1985)

de Lima, A. (1939). *A school for the world of tomorrow: The story of living and learning in the Lincoln School. Elementary division*. New York, NY: Lincoln School of Teachers College, Columbia University.

de Lima, A. (1941). *Democracy's high school: The story of living and learning in the Lincoln School of the Teachers College. High school division*. New York, NY: Teachers College, Columbia University.

de Lima, A. (1942). *The little red school house*. New York, NY: Macmillan.

De Madariaga, I. (1979). The foundation of the Russian educational system by Catherine II. *The Slavonic and East European Review, 57*(3), 369–395.

Demers, C. (2007). *Organizational change theories: A synthesis*. Los Angeles, CA: Sage.

Department of Foreign Affairs of the State Education Commission of the P.R.C. (1994). *Suggestion of the State Council on the implementation of the outline for reform and development of education in China*. Beijing, P.R.C.: Author.

Devi, S. A. (1940). The Segaon village school. In *One step forward: The report of the First Conference of Basic National Education, Poona, October 1939* (pp. 179–186). Segaon, India: Hindustani Talimi Sangh.

Dewey, J. (1902). *The child and the curriculum*. Chicago, IL: University of Chicago Press.

Dewey, J. (1910). *How we think*. Boston, MA: Heath.

Dewey, J. (1916). *Democracy and education: An introduction to the philosophy of education*. New York, NY: Macmillan.

Dewey, J. (1929a). *Impressions of Soviet Russia and the revolutionary world: Mexico, China, Turkey*. New York, NY: New Republic.

Dewey, J. (1929b). Matthew Arnold and Robert Browning. In J. Ratner (Ed.), *Characters and events: Vol. 1. Popular essays in social and political philosophy* (pp. 3–17). New York, NY: Holt. (Original work published 1891)

Dewey, J. (1933). *How we think: A restatement of the relation of reflective thinking to the educative process* (Rev. ed.). Boston, MA: Heath.

Dewey, J. (1938). *Experience and education*. New York, NY: Macmillan.

Dewey, J. (1940). My pedagogic creed. In J. Dewey, *Education today* (J. Ratner, Ed., pp. 3–17). New York, NY: Putnam. (Original work published 1897)

Dewey, J. (1943). *The school and society* (Rev. ed.). Chicago, IL: University of Chicago Press. (Original work published 1899)

Dewey, J. (1952). Introduction. In E. R. Clapp, *The use of resources in education* (pp. vii–xi). New York, NY: Harper.

Dewey, J. (1960). From absolutism to experimentalism. In R. J. Bernstein (Ed.), *On experience, nature, and freedom* (pp. 3–18). Indianapolis, IN: Bobbs-Merrill. (Original work published 1930)

Dewey, J., & Dewey, E. (1915). *Schools of to-morrow*. New York, NY: Dutton.

Dewey, J. M. (Ed.). (1951). Biography of John Dewey. In P. A. Schilpp (Ed.), *The philosophy of John Dewey* (2nd ed., pp. 3–45). La Salle, IL: Open Court. (Original work published 1939)

Dhillon, M. (2006). *The Doon School Weekly: Computer aided SUPW programme* [Unpublished project work]. Doon School, Dehra Dun, India.

Donaldson, G. W., & Donaldson, L. E. (1958). Outdoor education: A definition. *Journal of Health, Physical Education, Recreation, 29*(5), 17, 63.

Doniger, W. (2009). *The Hindus: An alternative history*. Oxford, U.K.: Oxford University Press.

The Doon School. (n.d.). *The Doon School: Information handbook*. Dehra Dun, India: Author.

D'Souza, A. A., & Chaudhury, K. P. (1965). *The multipurpose school: Its theory and practice*. Bombay, India: Allied.

Dukhovskoy, V. (1923). Khotkovskaya Shkola–Kommuna 2-y stupeni [On school–community relationship]. *Na putyakh k novoy shkole, 2*(2), 63–68.

Durkheim, E. (1956). *Education and sociology* (S. D. Fox, Trans.). Glencoe, IL: Free Press. (Original work published 1922)

Durkheim, E. (1977). *The evolution of educational thought: Lectures on the formation and development of secondary education in France* (P. Collins, Trans.). London, U.K.: Routledge & Kegan Paul. (Original work published 1938)

Dutta, H. (1949). A year of basic education in Gurukul Kangri: Hardwar. In *Two years of work: Report of the Second Basic Education Conference, Jamianagar, Delhi, April 1941* (3rd ed., pp. 110–113). Sevagram, India: Hindustani Talimi Sangh.

Dzhantakova, Z. D. (1980). *Trudovoe vospitanie shkolnikov: Iz opyta raboty shkol respubliki* [*Work education of schoolchildren: On work experiences of schools in the Republic*]. Frunze, U.S.S.R.: Mektep.

Education Department. (1961). *Report of the Syllabus Committee for post basic education*. Ahmedabad, India: Government of Gujarat.

Efird, R. (2015). Learning places and "little volunteers": An assessment on place- and community-based education in China. *Environmental Education Research, 21*(8), 1143–1154.

Elementary and Secondary Education Act of 1965, 20 U.S.C. § 301, 303. (1965).

Engels, F. (1926). Friedrich Engels' preface to the third German edition. In K. Marx (Ed.), *The eighteenth Brumaire of Louis Bonaparte* (E. Paul & C. Paul, Trans., pp. 21–22). London, U.K.: Allen & Unwin. (Original work published 1852)

Environmental Education Act, 20 U.S.C. § 2–3. (1970).

Environmental Education Division. (1996). *Report assessing environmental education in the United States and the implementation of the National Environmental Education Act of 1990*. (1996). Washington, DC: U.S. Environmental Protection Agency.

Ewing, E. T. (2002). *The teachers of Stalinism: Policy, practice, and power in Soviet schools of the 1930s*. New York, NY: Peter Lang.

Fägerlind, I., & Saha, L. J. (1989). *Education and national development: A comparative perspective* (2nd ed.). Oxford, U.K.: Pergamon Press.

Fang, Y. (1979). A report on the state of science and education delivered by comrade Fang Yi at the Seventh Enlarged Meeting of the Standing Committee of the Fourth National Committee of the Chinese People's Political Consultative Conference. *Chinese Education, 12*(1–2), 33–47.

Federal Law of the Russian Federation of December 29, 2012, No. 273-FZ, On Education in the Russian Federation. Moscow, Russia: Government of the Russian Federation.

Feng, D. (2006). China's recent curriculum reform: Progress and problems. *Planning and Changing, 37*(1–2), 131–144.

Feng, Z. (1988). Tan tan gai ge nong cun chu zhong de ke cheng jie gou [On the improvement of the course schedule of a rural junior high school]. *Ren min jiao yu, 39*(Z1), 30, 32.

Figes, O. (2015). *Revolutionary Russia 1891–1991: A history*. New York, NY: Picador, Metropolitan Book, Henry Holt.

Fischer, L. (1982). *The life of Mahatma Gandhi*. London, U.K.: Grafton Books. (Original work published 1951)

Fitzpatrick, C. N. (1968). *Philosophy and goals for outdoor education* [Doctoral dissertation]. Colorado State College. ProQuest Dissertations and Theses.

Fitzpatrick, S. (1979). *Education and social mobility in the Soviet Union 1921–1943*. Cambridge, U.K.: Cambridge University Press.

Fomina, E. (2020). The importance of trainers/facilitators within the community school network in Russia. *Peabody Journal of Education, 95*(1), 46–54.

Ford, P. M. (1981). *Principles and practices of outdoor/environmental education*. New York, NY: Wiley.

Fouts, J. T., & Chan, J. C. K. (1997). The development of work-study and school enterprises in China's schools. *Journal of Curriculum Studies, 29*(1), 31–46.

Fradkov, I. S. (1960). *Navstrechu zhizni [Toward life]*. Petrozavodsk, U.S.S.R.: Gosizdat Karelskoy A.S.S.R.

Frank, A. G. (1969). *Capitalism and underdevelopment in Latin America: Historical studies of Chile and Brazil*. New York, NY: Modern Reader.

Freeberg, W. H., & Taylor, L. E. (1961). *Philosophy of outdoor education*. Minneapolis, MN: Burgess.

Freeberg, W. H., & Taylor, L. E. (1963). *Programs in outdoor education*. Minneapolis, MN: Burgess.

Freire, P. (1970). *Pedagogy of the oppressed*. New York, NY: Continuum.

Fullan, M. (with Stiegelbauer, S.). (1991). *The new meaning of educational change*. London, U.K.: Cassell.

Fullan, M. G. (1993). *Change forces: Probing the depths of educational reform*. London, U.K.: Falmer Press.

Gabrielsen, M. A., & Holtzer, C. (1965). *The role of outdoor education*. New York, NY: The Center for Applied Research in Education.

Gadamer, H.-G. (1965). *Wahrheit und Methode: Grundzüge einer philosophischen Hermeneutik [Truth and method: Fundamentals of a philosophical hermeneutics]* (2nd ed.). Tübingen, Germany: Mohr.

Gandhi, M. K. (1927). *An autobiography or the story of my experiments with truth* (M. Desai, Trans.). Ahmedabad, India: Navajivan Publishing.

Gandhi, M. K. (1947). *India of my dreams* (R. K. Prabhu, Ed.). Bombay, India: Hind Kitabs.

Gandhi, M. K. (1948a). Discipline for the realization of truth. In N. K. Bose (Ed.), *Selections from Gandhi* (pp. 13–19). Ahmedabad, India: Navajivan Publishing.

Gandhi, M. K. (1948b). Fundamental beliefs and ideas. In N. K. Bose (Ed.), *Selections from Gandhi* (pp. 20–47). Ahmedabad, India: Navajivan Publishing.

Gandhi, M. K. (1948c). Industrial organization: Old and new. In N. K. Bose (Ed.), *Selections from Gandhi* (pp. 64–74). Ahmedabad, India: Navajivan Publishing.

Gandhi, M. K. (1948d). On education. In N. K. Bose (Ed.), *Selections from Gandhi* (pp. 251–267). Ahmedabad, India: Navajivan Publishing.

Gandhi, M. K. (1950a). *Satyagraha in South Africa* (2nd ed., V. G. Desai, Trans.). Ahmedabad, India: Navajivan Publishing. (Original work published 1928)

Gandhi, M. K. (1950b). Questions before educational conference. In *Educational reconstruction: A collection of Gandhiji's articles on the Wardha scheme along with a summary of the proceedings of the All India National Educational Conference held at Wardha, 1937* (5th ed., pp. 29–32). Sevagram, India: Hindustani Talimi Sangh. (Original work published 1937)

Gandhi, M. K. (1951). *Basic education* (B. Kumarappa, Ed.). Ahmedabad, India: Navajivan Publishing.

Gandhi, M. K. (1953). *Towards new education* (B. Kumarappa, Ed.). Ahmedabad, India: Navajivan Publishing.

Gandhi, M. K. (1954). *Sarvodaya: The welfare of all* (B. Kumarappa, Ed.). Ahmedabad, India: Navajivan Publishing.

Gandhi, M. K. (1962). *True education*. Ahmedabad, India: Navajivan Publishing.

Gandhi, M. K. (1991). Tolstoy on non-retaliation. In R. Iyer (Ed.), *The essential writings of Mahatma Gandhi* (pp. 73–75). Delhi, India: Oxford University Press. (Original work published 1909)

Gan su lan zhou ge ming wei yuan hui. (1969). Chang ban xiao, liang gua gou [Cooperation between a factory and a factory-run school]. *Hong qi, 12*(2), 30–35.

Gan su lan zhou ge ming wei yuan hui. (1998). Hong qi za zhi dui diao cha bao gao de an yu [Comments of the Red Flag regarding the investigative report of "A factory sets up a school: The school is cooperating with a factory"]. In D. He (Ed.), *Zhong hua ren min gong he guo zhong yao jiao yu wen xian: 1949–1975* [*The important educational documents of the People's Republic of China: Vol. 1. 1949–1975*] (pp. 1440–1442). Haikou, P.R.C.: Hainan Publishing. (Original work published 1969)

Gao, W., Wu, F., & Yuan, H. (1992). Yi xiang ju you shen yuan yi yi de jiao yu gai ge shi yan [An educational reform test in the Keqiao area of the County of Shaoxing, Zhejiang]. *Ren min jiao yu, 44*(1), 13–18.

Garrison, C. (1966). *Outdoor education: Principles and practice*. Springfield, IL: Thomas.

Garrison, J., & Neiman, A. (2003). Pragmatism and education. In N. Blake, P. Smeyers, R. Smith, & P. Standish (Eds.), *The Blackwell guide to the philosophy of education* (pp. 21–37). Malden, MA: Blackwell.

Gauvain, M., & Parke, R. D. (2010). Socialization. In M. H. Bornstein (Ed.), *Handbook of cultural development science* (pp. 239–258). New York, NY: Psychology Press.

George, F. (1997). Middle school programs. In R. C. Wade (Ed.), *Community service-learning: A guide to including service in the public school curriculum* (pp. 159–179). Albany, NY: State University of New York Press.

Gibson, H. W. (1936). The history of organized camping: Establishment of institutional camps. *The Camping Magazine, 8*(3), 18–19, 26–19.

Gibson, H. W. (1939). *Camp management: A manual of organized camping* (Rev. ed.). New York, NY: Greenberg.

Gong qing tuan. (1998). Zhong gong zhong yang pi zhuan gong qing tuan zhong yang shu ji chu guan yu zu zhi cheng shi zhi shi qing nian can jia nong cun she hui zhu yi jian she de bao gao [Report by the Central Secretary Division of the Communist Youth League on organizing urban youth to participate in the rural socialist construction]. In D. He (Ed.), *Zhong hua ren min gong he guo zhong yao jiao yu wen xian: 1949–1975* [*The important educational documents of the People's Republic of China: Vol. 1. 1949–1975*] (pp. 1274–1276). Haikou, P.R.C.: Hainan Publishing.

Gopal, S. (1975). *Jawaharlal Nehru: A biography: Vol. 1. 1889–1947*. London, U.K.: Jonathan Cape.

Gordner, I., Davis, L. J., Askins, J. H., Ipock, J., White, W. H., & Johnson, B. (1938). Active learning in a high school of North Carolina. *Progressive Education, 15*(12), 629–635.

Grasso, J., Corrin, J., & Kort, M. (2004). *Modernization and revolution in China: From the Opium Wars to world power* (3rd ed.). Armonk, NY: Sharpe.

Green, R. L. (1936). Developing a modern curriculum in a small town. *Progressive Education, 13*(3), 189–197.

Groothoff, H.-H. (1975). *Einführung in die Erziehungswissenschaft* [*An introduction to education*]. Ratingen-Kastellaun, Germany: Henn.

Guang xi nan ning shi di er zhong xue dang zhi bu. (1976). Kai zhan jiao yu ge ming da bian lun de yi xie ti hui [Some ideas based on discussions about educational reform]. *Hong qi, 19*(2), 40–43.

Guang ya zhong xue. (1959). Sheng chan lao dong tong jiao xue jie he de yi xie zuo fa [Some practices of combining productive work with teaching]. *Guang dong jiao yu, 4*(9), 9–10.

Guo, L. (2012). New curriculum reform in China and its impact on teachers. *Canadian and International Education, 41*(2), 87–104.

Gutek, G. L. (1997). *Philosophical and ideological perspectives on education* (2nd ed.). Boston, MA: Allyn & Bacon.

Gutek, G. L. (2000). *American education 1945–2000: A history and commentary*. Prospect Heights, IL: Waveland Press.

Gutek, G. L. (2006). *American education in a global society: International and comparative perspectives* (2nd ed.). Long Grove, IL: Waveland Press.

Gutek, G. L. (2009). *New perspectives on philosophy and education*. Columbus, OH: Pearson.

Gutek, G. L. (2011). *Historical and philosophical foundations of education: A biographical introduction* (5th ed.). Boston, MA: Pearson.

Gutierrez, E. D., & Sanchez, Y. (1993). Hilltop geography for young children: Creating an outdoor learning laboratory. *Journal of Geography, 92*(4), 176–179.

Habermas, J. (1970). *Technik und Wissenschaft als "Ideologie"* [*Technology and science as an "ideology"*] (4th ed.). Frankfurt am Main, Germany: Suhrkamp.

Haikari, J., & Kotilainen, S. (2016). *Opettajuuden mallia: Jyväskylän normaalikoulu 1864–2015* [*On models for teachership: Jyväskylä Normal School in 1864–2015*] (S. Kotilainen, Ed.). Jyväskylän normaalikoulun julkaisuja No. 15. Jyväskylä, Finland: Jyväskylän normaalikoulu, Jyväskylän yliopisto.

Hamm, R. L., & Spear, R. D. (1978). *Environmental education in Indiana Public Schools*. Terre Haute, IN: Curriculum Research and Development Center, School of Education, Indiana State University.

Hammerman, D. R. (1961). *A historical analysis of the socio-cultural factors that influenced the development of camping education* [Doctoral dissertation]. Pennsylvania State University. ProQuest Dissertations and Theses.

Hammerman, D. R., & Hammerman, W. M. (1964). *Teaching in the outdoors*. Minneapolis, MN: Burgess.

Hammerman, D. R., Hammerman, W. M., & Hammerman, E. L. (1985). *Teaching in the outdoors* (3rd ed.). Danville, IL: Interstate.

Hammerman, D. R., Hammerman, W. M., & Hammerman, E. L. (2001). *Teaching in the outdoors* (5th ed.). Danville, IL: Interstate.

Hammond, D. (2012, May). Environmental education in impoverished communities. *Green Teacher, 27*(96), 16–17.

Hammond, R. I. (1942). *A functional curriculum for a small high school: To formulate a plan for developing and initiating a more functional curriculum in the Castana, Iowa six-year high school* [Unpublished doctoral dissertation]. Columbia University.

Han, D. (2000). *The unknown Cultural Revolution: Educational reforms and their impact on China's rural development*. New York, NY: Garland.

Hand, H. C., & French, W. (1937). Analysis of the present status in curriculum thinking. In H. Harap (Ed.), *The changing curriculum* (pp. 1–31). New York, NY: Appleton-Century.

Hanna, L. (1940). The operation of the core curriculum in Tulsa. *Curriculum Journal, 11*(2), 66–68.

Hans, N. (1950). *Comparative education: A study of educational factors and traditions* (2nd ed.). London, U.K.: Routledge & Kegan Paul.

Hans, N. (1963). *The Russian tradition in education*. London, U.K.: Routledge & Kegan Paul.

Har bin shi an guang xiao xue. (1971). Hen zhua lu xian dou zheng, shang hao she hui zhu yi wen hua ke [Pay attention to the correct way, use socialist cultural lessons]. *Wen hua da ge ming, 5*(4), 19–22.

Harisalo, R. (2008). *Organisaatioteoriat* [*Organizational theories*]. Tampere, Finland: Tampere University Press.

Harré, R. (1978). Accounts, actions and meanings: The practice of participatory psychology. In M. Brenner, P. Marsh, & M. Brenner (Eds.), *The social contexts of method* (pp. 44–65). London, U.K.: Croom Helm.

Hawkins, J. N. (2007). The intractable dominant educational paradigm. In P. D. Hershock, M. Mason, & J. N. Hawkins (Eds.), *Changing education: Leadership, innovation and development in a globalizing Asia Pacific* (pp. 137–162). Hong Kong, P.R.C.: Comparative Education Research Centre, University of Hong Kong.

Helgeson, S. L., Blosser, P. E., Howe, R. W., Helburn, N., & Wiley, K. B. (1972). *Environmental education programs and materials* (PREP Report, No. 33). Washington, DC: National Center for Education Communication, Office of Education, U.S. Department of Health, Education, and Welfare.

Hentschke, A. C. (1935). The basic course at Eagle Rock High School. *The Clearing House, 9*(9), 555–559.

Hickman, L. A. (1996). Dewey, John (1859–1952). In J. J. Chambliss (Ed.), *Philosophy of education: An encyclopedia* (pp. 146–153). New York, NY: Garland.

Hill, D., & Pope, D. C. (1997). High school programs. In R. C. Wade (Ed.), *Community service-learning: A guide to including service in the public school curriculum* (pp. 180–196). Albany, NY: State University of New York Press.

Hirsch, E. D., Jr. (1967). *Validity in interpretation.* New Haven, CT: Yale University Press.

Hlebowitsh, P. S. (2007). *Foundations of American education: Purpose and promise.* Dubuque, IA: Kendall Hunt.

Hoffmann, D. L. (2003). *Stalinist values: The cultural norms of Soviet modernity, 1917–1941.* Ithaca, NY: Cornell University Press.

Holland, B. (1955). About our outdoor school. *Journal of Health, Physical Education, Recreation, 26*(5), 16–18.

Holland, B., & Lewis, J. (1950). The outdoor education curriculum at the secondary school level. *The Journal of Educational Sociology, 23*(9), 539–540.

Holmes, B. (1981). *Comparative education: Some considerations of method.* London, U.K.: Allen & Unwin.

Holmes, B. (1985). Trends in comparative education. *Prospects: Quarterly Review of Education, 15*(3), 325–346.

Holmes, B. (1986). Paradigm shifts in comparative education. In P. G. Altbach & G. P. Kelly (Eds.), *New approaches to comparative education* (pp. 179–199). Chicago, IL: University of Chicago Press.

Holmes, B., & McLean, M. (1989). *The curriculum: A comparative perspective.* London, U.K.: Unwin Hyman.

Holmes, L. E. (1991). *The Kremlin and the schoolhouse: Reforming education in Soviet Russia, 1917–1931.* Bloomington, IN: Indiana University Press.

Hong, Y. (1975). The educational revolution. *Prospects: The Quarterly Review of Education, 5*(4), 481–484.

Hopkins, D. (2013). Exploding the myths of school reform. *School Leadership & Management, 33*(4), 304–321.

Hosking, G. (1992). *A history of the Soviet Union: 1917–1991* (3rd ed.). London, U.K.: Fontana Press.

Hosking, G. (2011). *Russia and the Russians: A history* (2nd ed.). Cambridge, MA: The Belknap Press of Harvard University Press.

Hu, Y. (1982). Create a new situation in all fields of socialist modernization: Report to the Twelfth National Congress of the Communist Party of China. In *The Twelfth National Congress of the C.P.C.* (pp. 7–85). Beijing, P.R.C.: Foreign Languages Press.

Hua, K. (1977). Political report to the Eleventh National Congress of the Communist Party of China. In *The Eleventh National Congress of the Communist Party of China* (pp. 1–111). Peking, P.R.C.: Foreign Languages Press.

Huang, S. (1959). Ben xue qi wo ban sheng chai lao dong de an pai [The work schedule of our class for this semester]. *Guang dong jiao yu, 4*(7), 17.

Hug, J. W., & Wilson, P. J. (1965). *Curriculum enrichment outdoors*. Evanston, IL: Harper & Row.

Humboldt County Office of Education. (1975). *Green box: A kit of environmental awareness activities to be conducted on field trips*. Eureka, CA: Author.

Hungerford, H., Peyton, R. B., & Wilke, R. J. (1980). Goals for curriculum development in environmental education. *The Journal of Environmental Education, 11*(3), 42–47.

Iisalo, T. (1999). *Kouluopetuksen vaiheita: Keskiajan katedraalikouluista nykyisiin kouluihin* [Developmental trends of schooling: From medieval cathedral schools to present schools]. Helsinki, Finland: Otava.

Iivonen, J. (2004). Neuvostoliiton/Venäjän historia 1985–1999 [A history of the Soviet Union/Russia 1985–1999]. In H. Kirkinen (Ed.), *Venäjän historia* [A history of Russia] (pp. 497–549). Helsinki, Finland: Otava.

Illich, I. (1970). *Deschooling society*. London, U.K.: Boyars.

Inkeles, A., & Smith, D. H. (1974). *Becoming modern: Individual change in six developing countries*. Cambridge, MA: Harvard University Press.

Jackim, O. (2016). Anton Semyonovich Makarenko: A few Western myths debunked. In J. M. Paraskeva (Ed.), *The curriculum: Whose internalization?* (pp. 169–180). New York, NY: Peter Lang.

James, W. (1890). *The principles of psychology* (Vol. 2). New York, NY: Holt.

James, W. (1899). *Talks to teachers on psychology: And to students on some of life's ideals*. New York, NY: Holt.

James, W. (1907). *Pragmatism: A new name for some old ways of thinking*. New York, NY: Longmans Green.

Jarvis, P. (2009). *Learning to be a person in society*. Abingdon, U.K.: Routledge.

Jensen, C., & Burgess, R. C. (1952). *An analysis of the school and community camping program in Highline, King County, Washington* [Unpublished master's thesis]. University of Washington.

Jia ding xian di er zhong xue. (1959). Ba sheng chan lao dong an pai de geng hao [Make better arrangements for a work schedule]. *Shang hai jiao yu, 3*(6), 13–14.

Ji lin sheng shi yan zhong xue. (1959). Gao ju jiao yu yu sheng chan lao dong xiang jie he de hong qi qian jin [Go ahead and hold high the Red Flag of combining education with productive work]. *Ji lin jiao yu, 4*(1), 17–21.

Jin, Y. (1965). Yang yuan xian nong cun xiao xue jiao yu jian wen [Educational information about primary schools in the rural County of Yangyuan]. *Ren min jiao yu, 16*(3), 24–26.

Jiu tai xian shi yan xiao xue. (1960). Guan che jiao xue gai ge yuan ze, shi dang zeng jia lao dong [Carry out the principle of teaching reform, provide reasonably more work]. *Ji lin jiao yu, 5*(14), 23.

John H. Chafee Environmental Education Act of 1999, 20 U.S.C. § 2–5. (2000).

Johnson, J. L. (1996). The benefits of service learning: Student perspectives. *Thresholds in Education, 22*(2), 32–33.

Johnson, P. (2006). *Rakenteissa kiinni? Perusopetuksen yhtenäistämisprosessi kunnan kouluorganisaation muutoshaasteena [Stuck in structures? The integration process of basic education as a change challenge for the municipal school organization]* [Doctoral dissertation]. University of Jyväskylä.

Jungar, S. (2004). Neuvostoliitto—Supervalta [The Soviet Union—the Super Power] (A. Juntunen, Trans.). In H. Kirkinen (Ed.), *Venäjän historia [A history of Russia]* (pp. 456–496). Helsinki, Finland: Otava.

Kalashnikov, A. (2016). Interpellation in the late Soviet period: Contesting the de-ideologization narrative. *Canadian Slavonic Papers, 58*(1), pp. 23–48.

Kamat, S. (2004). Postcolonial aporias, or what does fundamentalism have to do with globalization? The contradictory consequences of education reform in India. *Comparative Education, 40*(2), 267–287.

Kandel, I. L. (1933). *Studies in comparative education.* London, U.K.: Harrap.

Kandel, I. L. (1936). Comparative education. *Review of Education Research, 6*(4), 400–416.

Kandel, I. L. (1955). *The new era in education: A comparative study.* Boston, MA: Houghton Mifflin.

Karelskikh, A. (1923). Mologskaya shkola ogorodnichestva i pchelovodstvo kak opytnoe uchrezhdenie Narkomprosa [Mologa School of Gardening and Beekeeping as an experimental institution of the Narcompros]. *Na putyakh k novoy shkole, 2*(7–8), 121–133.

Kauppi, A. (1996). Mistä nousee oppimisen mieli? Kontekstuaalisen oppimiskäsityksen perusteita [The foundations of the contextual learning conception]. In A. Kajanto (Ed.), *Aikuisten oppimisen uudet muodot: Kohti aktiivista oppimista [New forms for adult learning: Toward active learning]* (pp. 51–109). Helsinki, Finland: Aikuiskasvatuksen tutkimusseura.

Kazamias, A. M. (2001). Re-inventing the historical in comparative education: Reflections on a protean episteme by a contemporary player. *Comparative Education*, *37*(4), 439–449.

Kazamias, A. M. (2009). Comparative education: Historical reflections. In R. Cowen & A. M. Kazamias (Eds.), *International handbook of comparative education* (Vol. 22, Pt. 1, pp. 139–157). Dordrecht, The Netherlands: Springer.

Ke, R. (1958). Jie shao qin xian yi zhong de jiao xue gai ge gong zuo [*Introducing the teaching reform of High School No. 1 in the County of Qin, Shanxi*]. Ren min jiao yu, *9*(8), 30–31.

Keenan, B. (1977). *The Dewey experiment in China: Educational reform and political power in the early Republic*. Cambridge, MA: Council on East Asian Studies, Harvard University.

Kelly, C. (2007). *Children's world: Growing up in Russia, 1890–1991*. New Haven, CT: Yale University Press.

Kelly, G. P., & Altbach, P. G. (1989). Comparative education: Alternative approaches. In T. Husén & T. N. Postlethwaite (Eds.), *The international encyclopedia of education: Research and studies* (Suppl. Vol. 1, pp. 137–144). Oxford, U.K.: Pergamon Press.

Kelly, G. P., Altbach, P. G., & Arnove, R. F. (1982). Trends in comparative education: A critical analysis. In P. G. Altbach, R. F. Arnove, & G. P. Kelly (Eds.), *Comparative education* (pp. 505–533). New York, NY: Macmillan.

Kendall, G. (1939). The Norris community program. *Curriculum Journal*, *10*(3), 108–110.

Kerschensteiner, G. (1913). *Begriff der Arbeitsschule* [*The concept of work school*] (2nd ed.). Leipzig, Germany: Teubner.

Khan, Y. (2007). *The great partition: The making of India and Pakistan*. New Haven, CT: Yale University Press.

Kilpatrick, W. H. (1918). *The project method: The use of the purposeful act in the educative process*. New York, NY: Teachers College, Columbia University.

Kilpatrick, W. H. (1940). *Group education for a democracy*. New York, NY: Association Press.

Kilpatrick, W. H. (1942). The role of camping in education today. *The Camping Magazine*, *14*(2), 14–17.

Kimonen, E. (2015). *Education and society in comparative context: The essence of outdoor-oriented education in the USA and India*. Rotterdam, The Netherlands: Sense Publishing.

Kimonen, E., & Nevalainen, R. (1993). Vapaat spesialistit valtaavat Venäjän koulut [Free specialists are taking over Russian schools]. *Dixit: Opetushallituksen tiedotus- ja keskustelufoorumi*, *3*(2), 56–59.

King, E. J. (1968). *Comparative studies and educational decision*. London, U.K.: Methuen.

King, E. J. (1969). *Education and development in Western Europe*. Reading, MA: Addison-Wesley.

King, E. J. (1979). *Other schools and ours: Comparative studies for today* (5th ed.). London, U.K.: Holt, Rinehart and Winston.

Kinsley, D. R. (1993). *Hinduism: A cultural perspective* (2nd ed.). Englewood Cliffs, NJ: Prentice Hall.

Kirchner, W. (1991). *Russian history* (7th ed.). New York, NY: Harper Collins.

Knight, N. (2015). Introduction: Soviet Marxism and the development of Mao Zedong's philosophical thought. In N. Knight (Ed.), *Mao Zedong on dialectical materialism: Writings on philosophy 1937* (pp. 3–83). London, U.K.: Routledge.

Kolesnikov, L. (1986). Neotlozhnye zadachi [Urgent duties]. In *Uchitel po imeni trud* [*Teachers' work*] (pp. 33–41). Moskva, U.S.S.R.: Izdatelstvo politicheskoy literatury.

Krupskaya, N. K. (1957a). The difference between professional and polytechnical education. In N. K. Krupskaya, *On education: Selected articles and speeches* (G. P. Ivanov-Mumjiev, Trans., pp. 188–191). Moscow, U.S.S.R.: Foreign Languages Publishing. (Original work published 1930)

Krupskaya, N. K. (1957b). The young pioneer movement as a pedagogical problem. In N. K. Krupskaya, *On education: Selected articles and speeches* (G. P. Ivanov-Mumjiev, Trans., pp. 118–122). Moscow, U.S.S.R.: Foreign Languages Publishing. (Original work published 1927)

Krupskaja, N. (1965). Yhteiskunnallinen kasvatus [Social education]. In N. Krupskaja, *Kasvatuksesta: Valittuja kirjoituksia ja puheita* [On education: Selected articles and speeches] (O. Kukkonen, Trans., pp. 145–154). Moskow, U.S.S.R.: Progress. (Original work published 1922)

Kubow, P. K., & Fossum, P. R. (2007). *Comparative education: Exploring issues in international context* (2nd ed.). Upper Saddle River, NJ: Pearson.

Kulkarni, G. R. (1940). A few practical problems in correlation: The experiment in the basic school at Rajpipla. In *One step forward: The report of the First Conference of Basic National Education, Poona, October 1939* (pp. 126–131). Segaon, India: Hindustani Talimi Sangh.

Kulkarni, G. R. (1949a). Our work in correlation. In *Two years of work: Report of the Second Basic Education Conference, Jamianagar, Delhi, April 1941* (3rd ed., pp. 174–180). Sevagram, India: Hindustani Talimi Sangh.

Kulkarni, G. R. (1949b). The Vijay Vidya-Mandir Avidha. In *Two years of work: Report of the Second Basic Education Conference, Jamianagar, Delhi, April 1941* (3rd ed., pp. 97–101). Sevagram, India: Hindustani Talimi Sangh.

Kumar, K. (2004). Educational quality and the new economic regime. In A. Vaugier-Chatterjee (Ed.), *Education and democracy in India* (pp. 113–127). New Delhi, India: Manohar.

Kumar, K. (2005). Political agenda of education: A study of colonialist and nationalist ideas (2nd ed.). New Delhi, India: Sage.

Kumar, R. (1991). Work experience/community service programme in Springdales Schools, New Delhi. In *Learning by doing: Report of the National Review Seminar on work experience, March 1990* (pp. 116–131). New Delhi, India: Department of Vocationalization of Education, National Council of Educational Research and Training.

Kuthiala, S. (2007, April 21). Building lives. *The Doon School Weekly*, 3.

Land, S. M., & Hannafin, M. J. (2000). Student-centered learning environments. In D. H. Jonassen & S. M. Land (Eds.), *Theoretical foundations of learning environments* (pp. 1–24). New York, NY: Routledge.

Land, S. M., Hannafin, M. J., & Oliver, K. (2012). Student-centered learning environments: Foundations assumptions and design. In D. Jonassen & S. Land (Eds.), *Theoretical foundations of learning environments* (2nd ed., pp. 3–25). New York, NY: Routledge.

Lauderdale, W. B. (1981). *Progressive education: Lessons from three schools*. Bloomington, IN: Phi Delta Kappa Educational Foundation.

Lauer, T. (2007). Mapping and sharing field trips on the Internet. In K. Carroll, *A guide to great field trips* (pp. 203–204). Chicago, IL: Zephyr Press.

Law of the Russian Federation of July 10, 1992, No. 3266–1, On Education. Moscow, Russia: Government of the Russian Federation.

Lenin, V. I. (1966a). On polytechnical education: Notes on theses by Nadezhda Konstantinovna. In V. I. Lenin, *Collected works: Vol. 36. 1900–1923* (A. Rothsein, Trans., Y. Sdobnikov, Ed., pp. 532–534). Moscow, U.S.S.R.: Progress. (Original work published 1929)

Lenin, V. I. (1966b). The tasks of the youth leagues: Speech delivered at the Third All-Russia Congress of the Russian Young Communist League. In V. I. Lenin, *Collected works: Vol. 31. April–December 1920* (J. Katzer, Ed., pp. 283–298). Moscow, U.S.S.R.: Progress. (Original work published 1920)

Lennert, J. W. (1981). A drainage model: A one-week project. *Science and Children, 18*(4), 12–14.

Leontovich, O. (2002). Russian Federation. In R. Marlow-Ferguson (Ed.), *World education encyclopedia: A survey of educational systems worldwide* (2nd ed., Vol. 2, pp. 1130–1151). Detroit, MI: Thomson Learning.

Lewin, K. M., Little, A. W., Xu, H., & Zheng, J. (1994). *Educational innovation in China: Tracing the impact of the 1985 reforms*. Essex, U.K.: Longman.

Li, J. (2017). Educational policy development in China for the 21st century: Rationality and challenges in a globalizing age. *Chinese Education & Society, 50*(3), 133–141.

Lian, F. (1958). Yi suo pu tong zhong xue de dao lu [The road of an ordinary middle school]. *Ren min jiao yu, 9*(8), 6–10.

Liao ning sheng ge ming wei yuan hui. (1968). Yi suo pin xia zhong nong zhang quan de min ban xiao xue [One local school managed by farmers]. *Hong qi, 11*(5), 46–51.

Lipchin, S. N. (1991). Uroki truda pod otkrytym nebom [Work lessons outdoors]. *Shkola i proizvodstvo, 22*(12), 62–63.

Liston, L. (1982). *Outdoor unified studies.* Escalante High School, Escalante, UT. ED No. 216828.

Littlejohn, G. (2009). Soy-powered learning. In T. Grant & G. Littlejohn (Eds.), *Teaching green: The high school years. Hands-on learning in grades 9–12* (pp. 216–217). Gabriola Island, Canada: New Society.

Liu, J. (1998). Liu jiping tong zhi zai quan guo jiao yu ting ju zhang hui yi shang de jiang hua [Comrade Liu Jiping's speech at the National Conference of the Bureau Directors of Education]. In D. He (Ed.), *Zhong hua ren min gong he guo zhong yao jiao yu wen xian: 1949–1975* [*The important educational documents of the People's Republic of China: Vol. 1. 1949–1975*] (pp. 1250–1255). Haikou, P.R.C.: Hainan Publishing.

Liu, J. (2006). *An introduction to Chinese philosophy: From ancient philosophy to Chinese Buddhism.* Malden, MA: Blackwell.

Liu, J., & Rong, G. (1982). Shang yang xiao xue kai zhan lao dong jiao yu huo quan mian feng shou [Shangyang Primary School achieved a lot through a work-based education system]. *Ren min jiao yu, 33*(3), 31–32.

Liu, K. (1956). Liao ning shi yan zhong xue deng san xiao kai she jin mu gong shi xi zuo ye he ji qi xue shi xi ke de qing kuang [Starting to work with metal, wood, and machinery in three schools like Liaoning Shiyan High School]. *Ren min jiao yu, 7*(10), 31–36.

Liu, S. (1998). Ban hao ban gong ban du xue xiao [Running schools well with part-time work and part-time study]. In D. He (Ed.), *Zhong hua ren min gong he guo zhong yao jiao yu wen xian: 1949–1975* [*The important educational documents of the People's Republic of China: Vol. 1. 1949–1975*] (pp. 1369–1371). Haikou, P.R.C.: Hainan Publishing. (Original work published 1993)

Liu, S., Cui, R., & Lu, G. (2013). The challenges of basic education curriculum change in rural primary schools in West China. In E. Kimonen & R. Nevalainen (Eds.), *Transforming teachers' work globally: In search of a better way for schools and their teachers* (pp. 175–198). Rotterdam, The Netherlands: Sense Publishing.

Liu, S., & Dou, K. (1988). Nong cun xiao xue zen yang wei ben di jing ji fa zhan fu wu [How a rural primary school serves a local economy]. *Ren min jiao yu, 39*(9), 15–16.

Liu, X., Gong, X., Wang, F.-Y., Sun, R., Gao, Y., Zhang, Y., Zhou, J., & Deng, X. (2017, June). *A new framework of science and technology innovation for K–12 in Qingdao, China.* Paper presented at the American Society for Engineering Education Conference, Columbus, OH.

Löfstedt, J.-I. (1980). *Chinese educational policy: Changes and contradictions 1949–79.* Stockholm, Sweden: Almqvist & Wiksell.

Long, D. H., & Long, R. A. (1999). *Education of teachers in Russia.* Westport, CT: Greenwood Press.

Lonzinger. (1921). Opyty stroitelstva novoy shkoly v Saratovskoy gub. obshchego i individualnogo kharaktera [General and individual experiences of creating a new school in the Saratovsky area]. *Vestnik narodnogo prosveshcheniya, 4*(1), 14–27.

Loop, C. A. (1936). Co-ordinating the new curriculum in Newport News High School. *Virginia Journal of Education, 29*(5), 208–210.

Losyuk, P. V. (1988). Shkolnyy trudovoy tsentr [School's work center]. *Shkola i proizvodstvo, 19*(6), 5.

Lu, D. (1998). Jiao yu bi xu yu sheng chan lao dong xiang jie he [Education must be combined with production and labor]. In D. He (Ed.), *Zhong hua ren min gong he guo zhong yao jiao yu wen xian: 1949–1975* [*The important educational documents of the People's Republic of China: Vol. 1. 1949–1975*] (pp. 852–857). Haikou, P.R.C.: Hainan Publishing. (Original work published 1958)

Makarenko, A. S. (1925). Perepiska A. S. Makarenko s A. M. Gorkim [Correspondence between A. S. Makarenko and A. M. Gorgy]. In A. S. Makarenko (1983), *Pedagogicheskie sochineniya v vosmi tomakh* [*Pedagogical essays in eight volumes*] (Vol. 1, pp. 217–219). Moskow, U.S.S.R.: Pedagogika.

Makarenko, A. S. (1933). Kommuna im. F. E. Dzerzhinskogo [The community named after F. E. Dzerzhynsky]. In A. S. Makarenko (1983), *Pedagogicheskie sochineniya v vosmi tomakh* [*Pedagogical essays in eight volumes*] (Vol. 1, p. 199). Moskow, U.S.S.R.: Pedagogika.

Makarenko, A. S. (1951). *Kasvatusopilliset katsomukseni* [*My pedagogical views*] (M. Lehmonen, Trans.). Helsinki, Finland: Kansankulttuuri.

Makarenko, A. (1965). *Problems of Soviet school education* (O. Shartse, Trans.). Moscow, U.S.S.R.: Progress. (Original work published 1949)

Malkovskaya, T. N., Avanesyan, I. D., & Butorina, T. S. (1983). *Vospitanie uchashchikhsya v protsesse trudovogo obucheniya* [*Educating students in connection with work education*]. Moskva, U.S.S.R.: Prosveshchenie.

Mallinson, V. (1957). *An introduction to the study of comparative education*. Melbourne, Australia: Heinemann.

Mallinson, V. (1975). *An introduction to the study of comparative education* (4th ed.). Oxford, U.K.: Heinemann.

Mallinson, V. (1981). *The Western European idea in education*. Oxford, U.K.: Pergamon Press.

Mand, C. L. (1967). *Outdoor education*. New York, NY: Pratt.

Mao, T. (1964). *Mao zhu xi yu lu* [*Quotations from Chairman Mao*]. Beijing, P.R.C.: Central Political Department of the Chinese People's Liberation Army.

Mao, T. (1965). The role of the Chinese Communist Party in the National War. In *Selected works of Mao Tse-tung* (Vol. 2, pp. 195–211). Peking, P.R.C.: Foreign Languages Press. (Original work published 1938)

Mao, T. (1966a). On contradiction. In T. Mao, *Four essays on philosophy* (pp. 23–78). Peking, P.R.C.: Foreign Languages Press. (Original work published 1937)

Mao, T. (1966b). On practice: On the relation between knowledge and practice, between knowing and doing. In T. Mao, *Four essays on philosophy* (pp. 1–22). Peking, P.R.C.: Foreign Languages Press. (Original work published 1937)

Mao, T. (1966c). On the correct handling of contradictions among the people. In T. Mao, *Four essays on philosophy* (pp. 79–133). Peking, P.R.C.: Foreign Languages Press. (Original work published 1957)

Mao, T. (1975). A talk to the editorial staff of Shansi-Suiyuan Daily. In *Selected works of Mao Tse-tung* (Vol. 4, pp. 241–245). Peking, P.R.C.: Foreign Languages Press. (Original work published 1948)

Mao, T. (1977). On the ten major relationships. In *Selected works of Mao Tse-tung* (Vol. 5, pp. 284–307). Oxford, U.K.: Pergamon Press. (Original work published 1956)

Mao, T. (1990). Remarks at the Spring Festival. In *Selected works of Mao Tse-tung* (Vol. 9, pp. 36–53). Secunderabad, India: Kranti. (Original work published 1964)

Mao, Z. (1998a). Gong zuo fang fa (cao an) (jie lu) [The work method (draft) (extract)]. In D. He (Ed.), *Zhong hua ren min gong he guo zhong yao jiao yu wen xian: 1949–1975 [The important educational documents of the People's Republic of China: Vol. 1. 1949–1975]* (pp. 796–797). Haikou, P.R.C.: Hainan Publishing. (Original work published 1991)

Mao, Z. (1998b). Zai chun jie zuo tan hui shang de tan hua [Talk at the seminar of the Chinese Spring Festival]. In D. He (Ed.), *Zhong hua ren min gong he guo zhong yao jiao yu wen xian: 1949–1975 [The important educational documents of the People's Republic of China: Vol. 1. 1949–1975]* (pp. 1249–1250). Haikou, P.R.C.: Hainan Publishing. (Original work published 1967)

Mao, Z. (1998c). Zai hang zhou hui yi shang de jiang hua [Speech at the Hangzhou meeting]. In D. He (Ed.), *Zhong hua ren min gong he guo zhong yao jiao yu wen xian: Vol. 1. 1949–1975 [The important educational documents of the People's Republic of China: Vol. 1. 1949–1975]* (p. 1383). Haikou, P.R.C.: Hainan Publishing. (Original work published 1967)

Marsh, C. J. (1997). *Planning, management and ideology: Key concepts for understanding curriculum 2* (revised and extended ed.). London, U.K.: Falmer Press.

Marx, K. (1968). Instruktionen für die Delegierten des Provisorischen Zentralrats zu den einzelnen Fragen [Instructions for the Delegates of the Provisional General Council concerning the specific questions]. In K. Marx & F. Engels, *Werke [Works]* (Vol. 16, pp. 190–199). Berlin, Germany: Dietz. (Original work published 1866)

Marx, K. (1974). *Pääoma: Kansantaloustieteen arvostelua. Vol. 1. Pääoman tuotanto-prosessi [Capital: A critique of political economy. Vol. 1. The process of production of capital]* (O. V. Louhivuori, Trans., T. Lehén & M. Ryömä, Eds.). Moskow, U.S.S.R.: Progress. (Original work published 1867)

Marx, K. (1978). Taloudellis-filosofiset käsikirjoitukset 1844 [Economic and philosophic manuscripts of 1844] (A. Tiusanen, Trans.). In K. Marx & F. Engels, *Valitut teokset* [*Selected works*] (Vol. 1, pp. 171–311). Moskow, U.S.S.R.: Progress. (Original work published in 1932)

Maslukova, L. V. (2000). A nature trail as environmental education. In M. Åhlberg (with A. Pölönen & P. Hynninen). (Eds.), *Case studies of environmental education and networking in Finland and Russia* (pp. 118–121). Joensuu, Finland: Savonlinna Department of Teacher Education, University of Joensuu, and Rantasalmi Institute of Environmental Education.

Mastrilli, T. (2005). Environmental education in Pennsylvania's elementary teacher education programs: A statewide report. *The Journal of Environmental Education, 36*(3), 22–30.

Matthews, M. (1982). *Education in the Soviet Union: Policies and institutions since Stalin.* London, U.K.: George Allen & Unwin.

Mayeno, A. S. (2000). *Environmental education needs and preferences of an inner city community of color* [Unpublished master's thesis]. San Francisco State University.

Mayhew, K. C., & Edwards, A. C. (1966). *The Dewey school: The Laboratory School of the University of Chicago 1896–1903.* New York, NY: Atherton Press. (Original work published 1936)

McCrea, E. J., & deBettencourt, K. (Eds.). (2000). *Environmental studies in the K–12 classroom: A teacher's view.* Washington, DC: North American Association for Environmental Education.

Mchitarjan, I. (2000). John Dewey and the development of education in Russia before 1930: Report on a forgotten reception. *Studies in Philosophy and Education, 19*(1–2), 109–131.

McKay, K. H., Adams, D. H., & Webb, R. C. (1991). "Kim: When we were in Foxfire...." In E. Wigginton and his students (Eds.), *Foxfire 25 years: A celebration of our first quarter century* (pp. 165–172). New York, NY: Doubleday.

Mead, G. H. (1934). *Mind, self & society: From the standpoint of a social behaviorist* (C. V. Morris, Ed.). Chicago, IL: University of Chicago Press.

Merritt, R. W. (1938). Community education in Ellerbe, North Carolina. *Progressive Education, 15*(2), 121–125.

Ministry of Education. (1950). *Syllabus for basic schools.* Delhi, India: Government of India.

Ministry of Education. (1956a). *Basic education in India: Report of the Assessment Committee on basic education.* Delhi, India: Government of India.

Ministry of Education. (1956b). *Experiments in primary and basic education.* Delhi, India: Government of India.

Ministry of Education. (1966). *Report of the Education Commission 1964–66: Education and national development* (5th ed.). Delhi, India: Government of India.

Ministry of Education and Scientific Research. (1956a). *The concept of basic education.* Delhi, India: Government of India.

Ministry of Education and Scientific Research. (1956b). *Handbook for teachers of basic schools.* Delhi, India: Government of India.

Ministry of Education and Social Welfare. (1977a). *Report of the Review Committee on the curriculum for the ten-year school: Including syllabus frames.* New Delhi, India: Government of India.

Ministry of Education and Social Welfare. (1977b). *Work-experience in schools: Third all India educational survey.* New Delhi, India: Government of India.

Ministry of Education of the C.P.G. (1998a). Jiao yu bu dang zu guan yu quan guo shi fan jiao yu hui yi de bao gao [The report by the Ministry of Education of the Central People's Government at the National Teacher Education Conference]. In D. He (Ed.), *Zhong hua ren min gong he guo zhong yao jiao yu wen xian: 1949–1975* [*The important educational documents of the People's Republic of China: Vol. 1. 1949–1975*] (pp. 1079–1081). Haikou, P.R.C.: Hainan Publishing.

Ministry of Education of the C.P.G. (1998b). Jiao yu bu guan yu shi xing quan ri zhi zhong xiao xue xin jiao xue ji hua (cao an) de tong zhi [Notification from the Ministry of Education of the Central People's Government on implementing the new teaching plan (draft) of the full-time primary and middle schools]. In D. He (Ed.), *Zhong hua ren min gong he guo zhong yao jiao yu wen xian: 1949–1975* [*The important educational documents of the People's Republic of China: Vol. 1. 1949–1975*] (pp. 1202–1205). Haikou, P.R.C.: Hainan Publishing.

Ministry of Education of the C.P.G. (1998c). Jiao yu bu guan yu shi xing quan ri zhi zhong xue zan xing gong zuo tiao li (shi xing cao an), quan ri zhi xiao xue zan xing gong zuo tiao li (shi xing cao an) de tong zhi [Notification from the Ministry of Education of the Central People's Government on the trial of provisional regulations of the work of full-time secondary and primary schools (trial draft)]. In D. He (Ed.), *Zhong hua ren min gong he guo zhong yao jiao yu wen xian: 1976–1990* [*The important educational documents of the People's Republic of China: Vol. 2. 1976–1990*] (pp. 1630–1639). Haikou, P.R.C.: Hainan Publishing.

Ministry of Education of the C.P.G. (1998d). Jia qiang si xiang jiao yu, lao dong jiao yu, ti chang qun zhong ban xue, qin jian ban xue [Strengthen ideological education, work education, and recommend masses run schools and, furthermore, do it economically]. In D. He (Ed.), *Zhong hua ren min gong he guo zhong yao jiao yu wen xian: 1949–1975* [*The important educational documents of the People's Republic of China: Vol. 1. 1949–1975*] (pp. 799–802). Haikou, P.R.C.: Hainan Publishing.

Ministry of Education of the C.P.G. (1998e). Zhong yang wen jiao xiao zu guan yu 1961 nian he jin hou yi ge shi qi wen hua jiao yu gong zuo an pai de bao gao [The report by the Ministry of Education of the Central People's Government on the cultural and educational work arrangement in 1961 and the future period]. In D. He (Ed.),

Zhong hua ren min gong he guo zhong yao jiao yu wen xian: 1949–1975 [*The important educational documents of the People's Republic of China: Vol. 1. 1949–1975*] (pp. 1027–1029). Haikou, P.R.C.: Hainan Publishing.

Ministry of Education of the P.R.C. (2003). Ji chu jiao yu ke cheng gai ge gang yao (shi xing) [Outline of the curriculum reform for basic education (trial)]. In D. He (Ed.), *Zhong hua ren min gong he guo zhong yao jiao yu wen xian: 1998–2002* [*The important educational documents of the People's Republic of China: Vol. 4. 1998–2002*] (pp. 907–909). Haikou, P.R.C.: Hainan Publishing.

Ministry of Education of the P.R.C. (2017). *Jiao yu bu guan yu yin fa "zhong xiao xue zong he shi jian huo dong ke cheng zhi dao gang yao" de tong zhi* [*Notice of the Ministry of Education of the P.R.C. on printing and distributing the outline of the curriculum for comprehensive practical activities in primary and secondary schools*]. http://www.moe.gov.cn/srcsite/A26/s8001/201710/t20171017_316616.html

Ministry of Higher Education of the C.P.G. (1998). Gao deng jiao yu bu guan yu zan ting yi jiu liu liu nian, yi jiu liu qi nian yan jiu sheng zhao sheng gong zuo de tong zhi [Notification from the Ministry of Higher Education of the Central People's Government on suspending the enrollment of post-graduate students in 1966 and 1967]. In D. He (Ed.), *Zhong hua ren min gong he guo zhong yao jiao yu wen xian: 1949–1975* [*The important educational documents of the People's Republic of China: Vol. 1. 1949–1975*] (p. 1403). Haikou, P.R.C.: Hainan Publishing.

Ministry of Human Resource Development. (2016). *National policy on education 2016: Report of the Committee for evolution of the new education policy*. New Delhi, India: Government of India.

Ministry of Information and Broadcasting. (1970). *India: A reference annual 1970*. New Delhi, India: Government of India.

Mitchinson, D. F. (1982, October). *Outdoor education residential programs: "Where we've been, where we are, where we're going."* Paper presented at the New York State Outdoor Education Association Conference, Buffalo, NY.

Moise, E. E. (1986). *Modern China: A history*. London, U.K.: Longman.

Montana State Department of Public Instruction. (1972). *Environmental education handbook*. Helena, MT: Author.

Naik, J. P. (1975). *Elementary education in India: A promise to keep*. Bombay, India: Allied.

Narayanan, M. (2001). Live skills: Learning by doing. In *Navchetna 2001* (p. 88). New Delhi, India: Mother's International School.

National and Community Service Act of 1990 (as amended through P.L. 106–170), 20 U.S.C. § 101, 111–112. (2009).

National Commission on Service-Learning. (2002). *Learning in deed: The power of service-learning for American schools*. Newton, MA: Education Development Center.

National Council of Educational Research and Training (NCERT). (1975). *The curriculum for the ten-year school: A framework*. New Delhi, India: Author.

National Defense Education Act of 1958, 20 U.S.C. § 101, 204, 303, 503, 701, 801, 901. (1958).

National Education Association. (1970). *Environmental education in the public schools: A pilot study.* Washington, DC: Author.

National Environmental Education Act, 20 U.S.C. § 5501–5504. (1990).

National Environmental Education and Training Foundation. (2002a). *Environmental education and educational achievement: Promising programs and resources.* Washington, DC: Author.

National Environmental Education and Training Foundation. (2002b). *Environmental learning in America: Working toward nationwide environmental literacy.* Washington, DC: Author.

NCERT. (1986). *National curriculum for primary and secondary education: A framework.* New Delhi, India: National Council of Educational Research and Training.

NCERT. (1988a). *Exemplar instructional material for work experience on scooter and motorcycle: Repair and maintenance. Classes IX–X.* New Delhi, India: National Council of Educational Research and Training.

NCERT. (1988b). *Guidelines and syllabi for upper primary stage: Classes VI–VIII.* New Delhi, India: National Council of Educational Research and Training.

NCERT. (1988c). *National curriculum for elementary and secondary education: A framework.* New Delhi, India: National Council of Educational Research and Training.

NCERT. (1989). *Exemplar instructional material for work experience on community work and social service: Classes IX–XII.* New Delhi, India: National Council of Educational Research and Training.

NCERT. (1992). *Fifth all India educational survey* (Vol. 2). New Delhi, India: National Council of Educational Research and Training.

NCERT. (1998). *Sixth all India educational survey: Agewise enrolment, repeaters, incentive schemes, etc. in schools* (Vol. 6). New Delhi, India: National Council of Educational Research and Training.

NCERT. (2000). *National curriculum framework for school education.* New Delhi, India: National Council of Educational Research and Training.

NCERT. (2001). *Guidelines and syllabi for secondary stage: Classes IX–X.* New Delhi, India: National Council of Educational Research and Training.

NCERT. (2005). *National curriculum framework 2005.* New Delhi, India: National Council of Educational Research and Training.

NCERT. (2006a). *National focus group on heritage grafts.* New Delhi, India: National Council of Educational Research and Training.

NCERT. (2006b). *Syllabus for classes at the elementary level* (Vol. 1). New Delhi, India: National Council of Educational Research and Training.

NCERT. (2008a). *Living craft traditions of India: Textbook in heritage crafts for class XI.* New Delhi, India: National Council of Educational Research and Training.

NCERT. (2008b). *National focus group on work and education*. New Delhi, India: National Council of Educational Research and Training.

NCERT. (2009). *National curriculum framework 2005: Abridged*. New Delhi, India: National Council of Educational Research and Training.

Nei meng gu wu yuan xian min zu gong she. (1973). Jian ku fen dou, qin jian ban xue [Work hard, build a school diligently and thriftily]. *Hong qi, 16*(6), 75–78.

Nesmith, S. M., Scott, L. M., LeCompte, K. N., & Johnsen, S. K. (2020). Connecting learning to the community: Pedagogical strategies for educators. In E. Kimonen & R. Nevalainen (Eds.), *Toward community-based learning: Experiences from the U.S.A., India, and China* (pp. 172–194). Leiden, The Netherlands: Brill Sense Publishing.

Neubauer, D. (2007). Globalization and education: Characteristics, dynamics, implications. In P. D. Hershock, M. Mason, & J. N. Hawkins (Eds.), *Changing education: Leadership, innovation and development in a globalizing Asia Pacific* (pp. 29–62). Hong Kong, P.R.C.: Comparative Education Research Centre, University of Hong Kong.

Nevalainen, R., Kimonen, E., & Alsbury, T. L. (2017). Educational change and school culture: Curriculum change in the Finnish school system. In E. Kimonen & R. Nevalainen (Eds.), *Reforming teaching and teacher education: Bright prospects for active schools* (pp. 195–224). Rotterdam, The Netherlands: Sense Publishers.

Nikandrov, N. D. (2014). Reforming education since the year 2000: The case of Russia. *International Dialogues on Education: Past and Present, 1*(1), pp. 29–41.

No Child Left Behind Act of 2001, 20 U.S.C. § 1001. (2002).

Nove, A. (1992). *An economic history of the USSR 1917–1991* (3rd ed.). London, U.K.: Benguin Books.

Odell, W. R. (1940). Two approaches to high school curriculum revision. *Curriculum Journal, 11*(3), 115–118.

Office of Education. (1966a). *PACE—Projects to advance creativity in education: Title III, Elementary and Secondary Education Act of 1965. A manual of guidelines for project applicants*. Washington, DC: U.S. Department of Health, Education, and Welfare.

Office of Education. (1966b). *Pacesetters in innovation: Descriptions of first projects approved. Title III, Elementary and Secondary Education Act of 1965. Supplementary centers and services program*. Washington, DC: U.S. Department of Health, Education, and Welfare.

Office of Education. (1966c). *PACE—Setting a new PACE through projects to advance creativity in education: Title III of the Elementary and Secondary Education Act of 1965. Supplementary centers and services*. Washington, DC: U.S. Department of Health, Education, and Welfare.

Office of Education. (1967). *Pacesetters in innovation: Vol. 1. Fiscal year 1966. Project resumes*. Washington, DC: Bureau of Elementary and Secondary Education, U.S. Department of Health, Education, and Welfare.

Office of Education. (1968). *Pacesetters in innovation: Vol. 2. Fiscal year 1967. Project resumes.* Washington, DC: Bureau of Elementary and Secondary Education, U.S. Department of Health, Education, and Welfare.

Office of Education. (1970). *Environmental education: Education that cannot wait.* Washington, DC: U.S. Department of Health, Education, and Welfare.

Okunkov, A. (1923). Shkola trudovogo promyshlennogo uchenichestva imeni Edissona [Edison School of Labor-Industrial Apprenticeship]. *Na putyakh k novoy shkole,* 2(1), 94–101.

Olkinuora, E. (1994). Oppimis-, tieto- ja opetuskäsitykset toimintaa koulussa ohjaavina taustatekijöinä [Concepts of learning, knowledge, and teaching as guiding factors in schoolwork]. In J. Tähtinen (Ed.), *Opettajaksi kasvaminen [Teacher professional growth]* (pp. 54–73). University of Turku, Faculty of Education, Publications B, No. 46.

Olsson, O. (1926). *Demokratiens skolväsen: Iakttagelser i amerikanska skolor [The school system of democracy: Observations in American schools].* Stockholm, Sweden: Norstedt & Söner.

Ong, E. K. (1970). Education in China since the Cultural Revolution. *Studies in Comparative Communism,* 3(3–4), 158–176.

Organisation for Economic Co-operation and Development. (2018). *The future of education and skills: Education 2030. The future we want.* Paris, France: Author.

Palese, A. (2009). *The Great Leap Forward (1958–1961): Historical events and causes of one of the biggest tragedies in People's Republic of China's history.* Lund, Sverige: Språk- och Litteraturcentrum, Lunds Universitet.

Pandit, J. (1949). Birla Basic School: Pilani. In *Two years of work: Report of the Second Basic Education Conference, Jamianagar, Delhi, April 1941* (3rd ed., pp. 121–122). Sevagram, India: Hindustani Talimi Sangh.

Pantsov, A. V. (with Levine, S. I.). (2012). *Mao: The real story.* New York, NY: Simon & Schuster.

Parikh, N. (1940). The basic syllabus in practice. In *One step forward: The report of the First Conference of Basic National Education, Poona, October 1939* (pp. 172–179). Segaon, India: Hindustani Talimi Sangh.

Parisio, R. (1986). Farm education at Stony Kill. *Outdoor Communicator,* 17(1), 30–34.

Parker, F. W. (1894). *Talks on pedagogics: An outline of the theory of concentration.* New York, NY: Kellogg.

Parkhurst, H. (1922). *Education on the Dalton Plan.* New York, NY: Dutton.

Parsons, T. (1934). Society. In R. A. Seligman & A. Johnson (Eds.), *Encyclopaedia of the social sciences* (Vol. 14, pp. 225–232). London, U.K.: Macmillan.

Parsons, T. (1966). *Societies: Evolutionary and comparative perspectives.* Englewood Cliffs, NJ: Prentice Hall.

Parsons, T. (1967). *Sociological theory and modern society.* New York, NY: Free Press.

Parsons, T. (1971). *The system of modern societies*. Englewood Cliffs, NJ: Prentice Hall.

Patel, S. P. (1988). *Curriculum guide in work experience for Navodaya Vidyalayas: Classes VI–VIII*. New Delhi, India: Department of Vocationalisation of Education, National Council of Educational Research and Training.

Pearson, L. (1990). *Children of glasnost: Growing up Soviet*. Seattle, WA: University of Washington Press.

Pearson, W. W. (1917). *Shantiniketan: The Bolpur School of Rabindranath Tagore*. London, U.K.: Macmillan.

Peirce, C. S. (1935a). The fixation of belief. In C. Hartshorne & P. Weiss (Eds.), *Collected papers of Charles Sanders Peirce: Vol. 5. Pragmatism and pragmaticism* (pp. 223–247). Cambridge, MA: Harvard University Press. (Original work published 1877)

Peirce, C. S. (1935b). Historical affinities and genesis. In C. Hartshorne & P. Weiss (Eds.), *Collected papers of Charles Sanders Peirce: Vol. 5. Pragmatism and pragmaticism* (pp. 6–9). Cambridge, MA: Harvard University Press. (Original work published 1906)

Peirce, C. S. (1935c). How to make our ideas clear. In C. Hartshorne & P. Weiss (Eds.), *Collected papers of Charles Sanders Peirce: Vol. 5. Pragmatism and pragmaticism* (pp. 248–271). Cambridge, MA: Harvard University Press. (Original work published 1878)

Peirce, C. S. (1935d). Pragmatism and abduction. In C. Hartshorne & P. Weiss (Eds.), *Collected papers of Charles Sanders Peirce: Vol. 5. Pragmatism and pragmaticism* (pp. 112–131). Cambridge, MA: Harvard University Press.

Peirce, C. S. (1935e). Questions concerning certain faculties claimed for man. In C. Hartshorne & P. Weiss (Eds.), *Collected papers of Charles Sanders Peirce: Vol. 5. Pragmatism and pragmaticism* (pp. 135–155). Cambridge, MA: Harvard University Press. (Original work published 1868)

Peirce, C. S. (1935f). Three types of reasoning. In C. Hartshorne & P. Weiss (Eds.), *Collected papers of Charles Sanders Peirce: Vol. 5. Pragmatism and pragmaticism* (pp. 94–111). Cambridge, MA: Harvard University Press.

Peirce, C. S. (1960). Phenomenology. In C. Hartshorne & P. Weiss (Eds.), *Collected papers of Charles Sanders Peirce: Vol. 1. Principles of philosophy* (pp. 139–308). Cambridge, MA: Harvard University Press. (Original work published 1931)

Peirce, C. S. (1966). The logic of drawing history from ancient documents. In A. W. Burks (Ed.), *Collected papers of Charles Sanders Peirce: Vol 7. Science and philosophy* (pp. 89–164). Cambridge, MA: Harvard University Press.

Pierce, P. R. (1941). The evolving pattern of a high school curriculum. *Curriculum Journal, 12*(2), 70–73.

Phillips, D. (2004). Toward a theory of policy attraction in education. In G. Steiner-Khamsi (Ed.), *The global politics of educational borrowing and lending* (pp. 54–67). New York, NY: Teachers College Press.

Pike, K. V. (1951). School camping has come to stay: Development of school camps and their special advantages in the educational program. *The Journal of the American Association for Health, Physical Education, and Recreation, 22*(6), 23–24.

Pinkevitch, A. P. (1929). *The new education in the Soviet Republic* (N. Perlmutter, Trans., G. S. Counts, Ed.). New York, NY: John Day.

Pipes, R. (1990). *The Russian revolution.* London, U.K.: Collins Harvill.

Pistrak, M. (1922). Shkola i fabrika: Chernovye itogi opyta 2 stupeni Shkolnoy Kommuny Narkomprosa [School and factory: Premilinary results concerning experiences of the school community of the Narcompros]. *Na putyakh k novoy shkole, 1*(2), 48–61.

Planning Commission. (1953). *First five year plan.* New Delhi, India: Government of India.

Planning Commission. (1956). *Second five year plan.* New Delhi, India: Government of India.

Planning Commission. (1961). *Third five year plan.* New Delhi, India: Government of India.

Polyzoi, E., & Nazarenko, T. (2004). A comparative analysis of four case studies of educational reform in Russia: Strategies of survival and change. *World Studies in Education, 5*(2), 65–80.

Prasad, C. S. (2008). *Economic survey of India: 1947–48 to 2008–09.* New Delhi, India: New Century.

Prasad, P. J. (1949). Basic syllabus at work: Two years of correlated teaching in the Basic School of Bihar. In *Two years of work: Report of the Second Basic Education Conference, Jamianagar, Delhi, April 1941* (3rd ed., pp. 133–149). Sevagram, India: Hindustani Talimi Sangh.

Prast, H. A., & Viegut, D. J. (2015). *Community-based learning: Awakening the mission of public schools.* Thousand Oaks, CA: Corwin Press.

Price, R. F. (2005). *Education in modern China.* London, U.K.: Routledge. (Original work published 1970)

Price, R. F. (1977). *Marx and education in Russia and China.* London, U.K.: Croom Helm.

Principles for future economic construction. (1991). In *Major documents of the People's Republic of China: December 1978–November 1989* (pp. 207–245). Beijing, P.R.C.: Foreign Languages Press. (Original work published 1981)

Provasoli, S. (2020, April). Sustainability passion projects. *Green Teacher, 35*(123), 14–18.

Putin, V. (with Gevorkyan, N., Timakova, N., & Kolesnikov, A.). (2000). *First person: An astonishingly frank self-portrait by Russia's president* (C. A. Fitzpatrick, Trans.). London, U.K.: Hutchinson.

Radchenko, A. (1922). Shkola s industrialnym uklonom v rayone 2-y opytnoy stantsii (Shaturskoy) [School with an industrial quality in the area of the Shatursky experimental station]. *Na putyakh k novoy shkole, 1*(2), 42–47.

Raju, P. T. (1992). *The philosophical traditions of India.* Delhi, India: Motilal Banarsidass.

Ranc, M.-H. (Executive Producer). (2019). *The Gulag—documentary examining Stalin's Gulag* (TV series). Arte France.

Rao, C. (2013). The reform and development of teacher education in China and Japan in an era of social change. In E. Kimonen & R. Nevalainen (Eds.), *Transforming teachers' work globally: In search of a better way for schools and their teachers* (pp. 261–301). Rotterdam, The Netherlands: Sense Publishing.

Rapacz, R. V. (1960). Polytechnical education and the new Soviet school reforms. In G. Z. F. Bereday & J. Pennar (Eds.), *The politics of Soviet education* (pp. 28–44). New York, NY: Frederick A. Praeger.

Ravitch, D. (1983). *The troubled crusade: American education, 1945–1980.* New York, NY: Basic Books.

Regents of the University of California. (1972). *OBIS—Outdoor biology instructional strategies: The lawn and the pond units.* Berkeley, CA: Author.

Ren min ri bao she lun 1967–1–22. (1998). Wu chan jie ji ge ming pai da lian he, duo zou zi ben zhu yi dao lu dang quan pai de quan [Uniting fully with proletarian revolutionaries, taking power from the power holders who use the capitalist road]. In D. He (Ed.), *Zhong hua ren min gong he guo zhong yao jiao yu wen xian: 1949–1975* [*The important educational documents of the People's Republic of China: Vol. 1. 1949–1975*] (pp. 1411–1412). Haikou, P.R.C.: Hainan Publishing.

Rheingold, A. (2007). Low-element challenge courses. In D. Prouty, J. Panicucci, & R. Collinson (Eds.), *Adventure education: Theory and applications* (pp. 141–159). Champaign, IL: Human Kinetics.

Riasanovsky, N. V., & Steinberg, M. D. (2005). *A history of Russia* (7th ed.). New York, NY: Oxford University Press.

Rigby, J. A. (1986). California treat: Three days in five ecosystems. *Science and Children,* 23(4), 20–23.

Riker, L. (2009). The living machine at Darrow School. In T. Grant & G. Littlejohn (Eds.), *Teaching green: The high school years. Hands-on learning in grades 9–12* (pp. 221–224). Gabriola Island, Canada: New Society.

Rizvi, F. (2007). Rethinking educational aims in an era of globalization. In P. D. Hershock, M. Mason, & J. N. Hawkins (Eds.), *Changing education: Leadership, innovation and development in a globalizing Asia Pacific* (pp. 63–91). Hong Kong, P.R.C.: Comparative Education Research Centre, University of Hong Kong.

Roberts, P. (2002). *Kids taking action: Community service learning projects, K–8.* Greenfield, MA: Northeast Foundation for Children.

Robertson, D. (1987). Down on the farm. *Camping Magazine,* 59(6), 24–27.

Rohnke, K. (1989). *Cowstails and cobras II: A guide to games, initiatives, ropes courses and adventure curriculum.* Dubuque, IA: Kendall & Hunt.

Roth, R. E. (1974). Environmental education in the United States: A status report 1974. *The Ohio Journal of Science,* 74(6), 390–395.

Roy, A. (1980). Schools and communities: An experience in rural India. *International Review of Education,* 26(3), 369–378.

Rugg, H. (1936). *American life and the school curriculum: Next steps toward schools of living*. Boston, MA: Ginn.

Ruhela, S. P. (2006). *Work experience education*. New Delhi, India: Diamond Books.

Rulison, L. L. (2007, September). Student "experts" in community character: An interdisciplinary unit for middle school grades. *Green Teacher, 22*(82), 13–17.

Ruskey, A., Wilke, R., & Beasley, T. (2001). A survey of the status of state-level environmental education in the United States—1998 update. *The Journal of Environmental Education, 32*(3), 4–14.

Rust, V. D., Soumaré, A., Pescador, O., & Shibuya, M. (1999). Research strategies in comparative education. *Comparative Education Review, 43*(1), 86–109.

Ryabtsev. (1929). Elektrotekhnicheskiy uklon v Shuyskoy shkole [Electric-technical approch at the Shuysky School]. *Trud v shkole i detskom dome, 1*(6), 32–35.

Sadler, M. E. (1900). How far can we learn anything of practical value from the study of foreign systems of education? Address at the Guildford Educational Conference on October 20, 1900. In Bereday, G. Z. F. (1964) Sir Michael Sadler's "Study of foreign systems of education." *Comparative Education Review, 7*(3), 307–314.

Sadovnik, A. R. (2011). Theory and research in the sociology of education. In A. R. Sadovnik (Ed.), *Sociology of education: A critical reader* (2nd ed., pp. 3–21). New York, NY: Routledge.

Sahlberg, P. (1997). *Opettajana koulun muutoksessa [As a teacher in school change]*. Porvoo, Finland: WSOY.

Salaamat-Ul-lah. (1949). Okhla Basic School. In *Two years of work: Report of the Second Basic Education Conference, Jamianagar, Delhi, April 1941* (3rd ed., pp. 106–109). Sevagram, India: Hindustani Talimi Sangh.

Salamatullah. (1970). *The school and the community*. New Delhi, India: Ministry of Education and Youth Services, Government of India.

Sardal, S. D. (1949). Basic schools of Tilak Maharashtra Vidyapith, Poona. In *Two years of work: Report of the Second Basic Education Conference, Jamianagar, Delhi, April 1941* (3rd ed., pp. 114–117). Sevagram, India: Hindustani Talimi Sangh.

Saunders, M. S. (1979). Locality and the curriculum: Towards a positive critique. *Comparative Education, 15*(2), 217–230.

Scales, P. C., & Roehlkepartain, E. C. (2004). *Community service and service-learning in U.S. public schools, 2004: Findings from a national survey*. St. Paul, MN: National Youth Leadership Council.

Schein, E. H. (1985). *Organizational culture and leadership*. San Francisco, CA: Jossey-Bass.

Schmierer, H. (1969). *Title III project in outdoor and conservation education: School districts, Town of North Hempstead. Project summary report (Pt. 2)*. North Hempstead, NY: Great Neck Public Schools.

Schneider, F. (1961). *Vergleichende Erziehungswissenschaft: Geschichte, Forschung, Lehre* [*Comparative education: History, research, instruction*]. Heidelberg, Germany: Quelle & Meyer.

Schoen, L. (2013). Supporting teachers' work: Insights from a study of differentially improving schools in the United States. In E. Kimonen & R. Nevalainen (Eds.), *Transforming teachers' work globally: In search of a better way for schools and their communities* (pp. 3–34). Rotterdam, The Netherlands: Sense Publishing.

Schramm, W. (1969). *Classroom out-of-doors: Education through school camping.* Kalamazoo, MI: Sequoia Press.

Schwartz, S. H. (1992). Universals in the content and structure of values: Theoretical advances and empirical tests in 20 countries. In M. P. Zanna (Ed.), *Advances in experimental social psychology* (Vol. 25, pp. 1–65). San Diego, CA: Academic Press.

Sehgal, G. C. S. (2001). *Work education.* New Delhi, India: APH.

Senge, P. M. (1990). *The fifth discipline: The art and practice of the learning organization.* London, U.K.: Century Business.

Serve America Act, 20 U.S.C. § 111, 1101. (2009).

Shang hai shi jiao yu yu sheng chan lao dong xiang jie he zhan lan hui. (1958). *Qin gong jian xue zai shi dong zhong xue* [*The work-study program of Shidong High School*]. Shanghai, P.R.C.: Shanghai Education Press.

Sharp, L. B. (1935). The public school camp. *The Camping Magazine, 7*(3), 25–29.

Sharp, L. B. (1941). Growth of the modern camping movement. *The Commonhealth, 28*(1), 4–6.

Sharp, L. B. (1947). Camping and outdoor education. *The Bulletin of the National Association of Secondary-School Principals, 31*(146), 32–38.

Sharp, L. B. (1952). What is outdoor education? *The School Executive, 71*(8), 19–22.

Sharp, L. B., & Osborne, E. G. (1940). Schools and camping: A review of recent developments. *Progressive Education, 17*(4), 236–241.

Shatsky, S. (1981a). First steps towards education through work. In S. Shatsky, *A teacher's experience: Collection* (C. Judelson, Trans., pp. 174–196). Moscow, U.S.S.R.: Progress.

Shatsky, S. (1981b). A teacher's path. In S. Shatsky, *A teacher's experience: Collection* (C. Judelson, Trans., pp. 23–40). Moscow, U.S.S.R.: Progress.

Shevchenko, N. A., Kucherkov, I. A., Shirev, D. A., & Miku, N. V. (2018). Public education in the Russian Empire at the end of the 19th century. *European Journal of Contemporary Education, 7*(1), 226–231.

Shmis, T., Ustinova, M., & Chugunov, D. (2020). *Learning environments and learning achievement in the Russian Federation: How school infrastructure and climate affect student success.* Washington, DC: World Bank Group.

Shulman, L. S. (2004). *The wisdom of practice: Essays on teaching, learning, and learning to teach* (S. M. Wilson, Ed.). San Francisco, CA: Jossey-Bass.

Sinclair, M. E. (with Lillis, K.). (1980). *School and community in the third world.* London, U.K.: Croom Helm.

Singh, M. (1998). *School enterprises: Combining vocational learning with production.* Berlin, Germany: UNEVOC.

Si ping shi yi ma lu xiao xue. (1959). Sheng chai you ji di, lao dong you ji hua [There are places for production, there are plans for work]. *Ji lin jiao yu, 4*(6), 19–21.

Skatkin, M. S., & Tsov'janov, G. S. (1994). Nadezhda Konstantinovna Krupskaya (1869–1939). *Prospects: Thinkers on Education, 3*(89–90), 49–60.

Smith, E. E. (2017). *The power of meaning: Finding fulfillment in a world obsessed with happiness.* Portland, OR: Broadway Books.

Smith, G. A., & Sobel, D. (2010). *Place- and community-based education in schools.* New York, NY: Routledge.

Smith, J. W. (1955). Adventure in outdoor education. *Journal of Health, Physical Education, Recreation, 26*(5), 8–9, 18.

Smith, J. W. (1958). Professional report from the First National Conference on outdoor education. *Journal of Health, Physical Education, Recreation, 29*(7), 8–9.

Smith, J. W. (1970). Where we have been, what we are, what we will become. *Journal of Outdoor Education, 5*(1), 3–7.

Smith, J. W., Carlson, R. E., Donaldson, G. W., & Masters, H. B. (1963). *Outdoor education.* Englewood Cliffs, NJ: Prentice Hall.

Smith, N. N., & Stahl, R. J. (1981). Overnight science. *Science and Children, 18*(6), 14–15.

Snyder, J., Bolin, F., & Zumwalt, K. (1992). Curriculum implementation. In P. W. Jackson (Ed.), *Handbook of research on curriculum* (pp. 402–435). New York, NY: Macmillan.

Solanki, A. B. (1958). *The technique of correlation in basic education.* Ahmedabad, India: Navajivan Trust.

Soloveychik, S. (1988). *V. A. Sukhomlinskiy o vospitanii [V. A. Sukhomlynsky on education].* Moskva, U.S.S.R.: Izdatelstvo politicheskoy literatury.

Spears, H. (1940). *The emerging high-school curriculum and its direction.* New York, NY: American Book Company.

Spencer, H. (1861). *Education: Intellectual, moral, and physical.* London, U.K.: Williams and Norgate.

Spranger, E. (1928). *Types of men: The psychology and ethics of personality* (P. J. W. Pigors, Trans.). Halle, Germany: Niemeyer; New York, NY: Hafner. (Original work published 1914)

Spring, K., Dietz, N., & Grimm, R., Jr. (2006). *Educating for active citizenship: Service-learning, school-based service and youth civic engagement.* Washington, DC: Corporation for National & Community Service.

Srivastava, J. M. (1991). The camp life in the implementation of S.U.P.W./W.E. programme. In *Learning by doing: Report of the National Review Seminar on work experience,*

March 1990 (pp. 100–102). New Delhi, India: Department of Vocationalization of Education, National Council of Educational Research and Training.

Stapp, W. B. (1969). The concept of environmental education. *The Journal of Environmental Education, 1*(1), 30–31.

State Council. (2003). Guo wu yuan guan yu ji chu jiao yu gai ge yu fa zhan de jue ding [The decision of the Central People's Government on basic education reform and development]. In D. He (Ed.), *Zhong hua ren min gong he guo zhong yao jiao yu wen xiun: 1998–2002* [*The important educational documents of the People's Republic of China: Vol. 4. 1998–2002*] (pp. 887–891). Haikou, P.R.C.: Hainan Publishing. (Original work published 2001)

State Council. (2017). *Guo wu yuan guan yu yin fa guo jia jiao yu shi ye fa zhan "shi san wu" gui hua de tong zhi* [*Notification of the Central People's Government on printing and distributing the 13th Five-Year Plan for the development of national education*]. Beijing, P.R.C. http://www.moe.gov.cn/jyb_xxgk/moe_1777/moe_1778/201701/t20170119_295319.html

State Education Commission of the P.R.C. (1995). *Education law of the People's Republic of China.* Beijing, P.R.C.: Author.

State Planning Commission of the U.S.S.R. (1933). *Summary of the fulfilment of the First Five-Year Plan for the development of the national economy of the U.S.S.R.* Report of the State Planning Commission of the Council of People's Commissars of the Union of Soviet Socialist Republics. Moscow, U.S.S.R.: Author.

Stein, D. (1998). *Situated learning in adult education.* ERIC. http://www.ericdigests.org/1998-3/adult-education.html

Steiner-Khamsi, G. (2016). New directions in policy borrowing research. *Asia Pacific Education Review, 17*(3), 381–390.

St. Clair, J. (1958). *The education curriculum philosophy of a select group of school camps* [Unpublished master's thesis]. State University of Iowa.

St. Preece, L. (1980). An outdoor education program. *Science and Children, 18*(1), 12–13.

Subbarao, C. S. (1958). *Basic education in practice.* Secunderabad, India: Ajanta.

Sukhomlinskiy, V. A. (1980). *Izbrannye pedagogicheskie sochineniya* [*Selected pedagogical essays in three volumes*] (Vol. 2). Moskva, U.S.S.R.: Pedagogika.

Sun, J. (1957). Lin xian yi zhong shi zen yang jin xing lao dong jiao yu de [How No. 1 High School in the County of Lin, Henan, started a work-based education program]. *Ren min jiao yu, 8*(10), 41–45.

Tagore, R. (1917). *Personality: Lectures delivered in America.* London, U.K.: Macmillan.

Tagore, R. (1961). *Towards universal man.* London, U.K.: Asia Publishing.

Tähtinen, U. (1964). *Non-violence as an ethical principle: With special reference to the views of Mahatma Gandhi.* Turku, Finland: University of Turku.

Tähtinen, U. (1970). *Mitä Gandhi todella sanoi* [*What Gandhi really said*]. Porvoo, Finland: Werner Söderström.

Tähtinen, U. (1979). *The core of Gandhi's philosophy*. New Delhi, India: Abhinav.

Tähtinen, U. (1982). *Non-violent theories of punishment: Indian and Western*. Helsinki, Finland: Academia Scientiarum Fennica.

Tähtinen, U. (1984). *Miksi elät? Intialaiset elämänarvot* [*Why do you live? Indian values of life*]. Helsinki, Finland: Gaudeamus.

Tähtinen, U. (1986). Mahatma Gandhin väkivallaton vastarinta [The nonviolent resistance of Mahatma Gandhi]. *Katsaus, 14*(4), 26–28.

Taloumis, T. (1980). Overnight camping with fourth-graders. *Science and Children, 18*(1), 16–18.

Tan, C. (2016). *Educational policy borrowing in China: Looking west or looking east?* London, U.K.: Routledge.

Tan, C., & Reyes, V. (2016). Neo-liberal education policy in China: Issues and challenges in curriculum reform. In S. Guo & Y. Guo (Eds.), *Spotlight on China: Changes in education under China's market economy* (pp. 19–33). Rotterdam, The Netherlands: Sense Publishing.

Taylor, C. (1971). Interpretation and the sciences of man. *The Review of Metaphysics, 25*(1), 3–51.

Taylor, N., Littledyke, M., Eames, C., & Coll, R. K. (2009). Environmental education in context: Observations, conclusions, and some recommendations. In N. Taylor, M. Littledyke, C. Eames, & R. K. Coll (Eds.), *Environmental education in context: An international perspective on the development of environmental education* (pp. 319–326). Rotterdam, The Netherlands: Sense Publishing.

Tchen, Y. (1977). Education and productive work in China. *Prospects: Quarterly Review of Education, 7*(3), 413–416.

Teng, H. (1978, May). Speech at the National Educational Work Conference. *Peking Review, 21*(18), 6–12.

Thomas, T. M. (1970). *Indian educational reforms in cultural perspective*. Delhi, India: Chand.

Thompson, A., Alibrandi, M., & Hagevik, R. (2000). Historical documentation of a culture. In R. Audet & G. Ludwig, *GIS in schools* (pp. 47–54). Redlands, CA: ESRI Press.

Tian jin shi si shi er zhong ge ming wei yuan hui. (1970). Wo men shi zen yang kai zhan "xue gong" huo dong de? [How do we carry out school activities?]. *Hong qi, 13*(8), 58–60.

Tillman, M. (1976). Non-formal education and rural development: A historical sketch and selected case studies. *New Frontiers in Education, 6*(1), 29–49.

Tolstoy, L. (1894). *The kingdom of God is within you: Or, Christianity not as a mystical doctrine but as a new life-conception* (A. Delano, Trans.). London, U.K.: Walter Scott.

Tolstoy, L. (1968). From count Leo Tolstoy. In S. Narayan (Ed.), *The selected works of Mahatma Gandhi: Vol. 5. Selected letters* (pp. 21–26). Ahmedabad, India: Navajivan Trust. (Original letter written in 1910)

Tynan, P. J. (2009). *Record book of socially useful productive work and community service: Fully covering the syllabus prescribed for ICSE examination.* New Delhi, India: Pitambar.

Uger, C. (1947). School camping. In E. G. Olsen (Ed.), *School and community: The philosophy, procedures, and problems of community study and service through schools and colleges* (pp. 225–247). New York, NY: Prentice Hall.

Ulich, R. (1961). *The education of nations: A comparison in historical perspective.* Cambridge, MA: Harvard University Press.

Urban, W. J., & Wagoner, J. L., Jr. (2009). *American education: A history* (4th ed.). New York, NY: Routledge.

Ushinsky, K. D. (1975). The psychological and educational significance of labour. In K. D. Ushinsky, *Selected works* (A. Bratov, Trans., A. I. Piskunov, Ed., pp. 208–239). Moscow, U.S.S.R.: Progress.

U.S.S.R. (1925). *Sosialististen Neuvostotasavaltojen Liiton perustuslaki* [*Constitution of the Union of Soviet Socialist Republics*]. Leningrad, U.S.S.R.: Kniga.

U.S.S.R. (1945). *Sosialististen Neuvostotasavaltojen Liiton perustuslaki* [*Constitution of the Union of Soviet Socialist Republics*]. Petroskoi, U.S.S.R.: Karjalaisen valtion kustannusliike.

U.S.S.R. (1961a). *Neuvostoliiton kommunistisen puolueen ohjelmasta: N. S. Hrushtshevin alustus NKP:n XXII edustajakokouksessa lokakuun 18 p:nä 1961* [*On the program of the C.P.S.U.: Introduction by N. S. Khrushchev at the 22nd Congress of the C.P.S.U. on October 18, 1961*]. Helsinki, Finland: Embassy of the U.S.S.R.

U.S.S.R. (1961b). *Programme of the Communist Party of the Soviet Union, adopted by the 22nd Congress of the C.P.S.U. October 31, 1961.* Moscow, U.S.S.R.: Foreign Languages Publishing.

U.S.S.R. (1963). *Narodnoye obrazovaniye v SSSR* [*Public education in the U.S.S.R.*]. Moscow, U.S.S.R.: Ministry of Education.

U.S.S.R. (1966). *23rd Congress of the Communist Party of the Soviet Union: Report on the directives for the five-year economic development plan of the USSR for 1966–1970.* Moscow, U.S.S.R.: Novosti Press.

U.S.S.R. (1971). *Report of the Central Committee of the Communist Party of the Soviet Union to the 24th Congress of the C.P.S.U., delivered by Leonid Brezhnev on March 30, 1971.* Moscow, U.S.S.R.: Novosti Press.

U.S.S.R. (1974). *Programma vosmiletnei shkoly na 1974/5 uchebny god: Nachalnye klassy i–iii* [*Program of an eight-year school for the 1974/5 academic year: Primary classes 1–3*]. Moscow, U.S.S.R.: Prosveshchenie.

U.S.S.R. (1977). *Sosialististen Neuvostotasavaltojen Liiton perustuslaki* [*Constitution of the Union of Soviet Socialist Republics, adopted on November 7, 1977 by the Supreme Soviet of the U.S.S.R.*]. Moscow, U.S.S.R.: Novosti Press.

U.S.S.R. (1986a). *Neuvostoliiton kommunistisen puolueen ohjelma* [*Program of the Communist Party of the Soviet Union, adopted by the 27th Congress of the C.P.S.U. in 1986*]. Moscow, U.S.S.R.: Novosti Press.

U.S.S.R. (1986b). *NKP XXVII: Neuvostoliiton taloudellisen ja sosiaalisen kehityksen perussuunnat vuosina 1986–1990 ja vuoteen 2000* [*N.K.P. XXVII: Report of the economic and social development of the U.S.S.R. during 1986–1990 and until 2000*]. Moscow, U.S.S.R.: Novosti Press.

U.S.S.R. (1987). Osnovnye napravleniya reformy obshcheobrazovatelnoy i professionalnoy shkoly, utverzhdeny postanovleniem Verkhovnogo Soveta CCCR 12 aprelya 1984 g [Guidelines to reform general and vocational schools, approved by the Supreme Soviet of the U.S.S.R. on April 12, 1984]. In N. E. Golubeva (Ed.), *Narodnoe obrazovanie v SSSR: Sbornik normativnykh aktov* [*Public education in the U.S.S.R.: Collection of statutes*] (pp. 9–25). Moskva, U.S.S.R.: Juridicheskaja literatura. (Original work published 1984)

U.S.S.R. (1988a). Perus-, keskiasteen ja korkeakoulujen uudistus ja puolueen tehtävät sen toteuttamiseksi: NKP:n keskuskomitean sihteerin Jegor Ligatshovin alustus [Reform of primary, secondary, and higher education, and the party's procedures for its implementation: Introduction by Yegor Ligachev, Secretary of the Central Committee of the C.P.S.U.]. In *Neuvostoliiton koulutusuudistus: NKP:n keskuskomitean täysistunto 17.–18.2.1988* [*Soviet education reform: The plenary session of the Central Commitee of the C.P.S.U. on February 17–18, 1988*] (pp. 45–94). Moscow, U.S.S.R.: Novosti Press.

U.S.S.R. (1988b). Uudistuksen ideologiaa vallankumoukselliselle perestroikalle: NKP:n keskuskomitean pääsihteeri Mihail Gorbatshovin puhe [On the ideology of reform for revolutionary perestroika: A speech by Mikhail Gorbachev, General Secretary of the Central Committee of the C.P.S.U.]. In *Neuvostoliiton koulutusuudistus: NKP:n keskuskomitean täysistunto 17.–18.2.1988* [*Soviet education reform: The plenary session of the Central Committee of the C.P.S.U. on February 17–18, 1988*] (pp. 3–42). Moscow, U.S.S.R.: Novosti Press.

U.S.S.R. (1990). *28th Congress of the Communist Party of the Soviet Union: Report and speeches, Policy statement of the Congress, and Resolutions*. Moscow, U.S.S.R.: Novosti.

Van Herpen, M. H. (2014). *Putin's wars: The rise of Russia's new imperialism*. Lanham, MD: Rowman and Littlefield.

Van Matre, S. (1972). *Acclimatization: A sensory and conceptual approach to ecological involvement*. Martinsville, IN: American Camping Association.

Van Matre, S. (1974). *Acclimatizing: A personal and reflective approach to a natural relationship*. Martinsville, IN: American Camping Association.

Van Matre, S. (1979). *Sunship Earth: An earth education pogram. Getting to know your place in space*. Martinsville, IN: American Camping Association.

Verhagen, F. C. (2009). The earth community school: A back-to-basics model of secondary education. In T. Grant & G. Littlejohn (Eds.), *Teaching green: The high school years. Hands-on learning in grades 9–12* (pp. 212–215). Gabriola Island, Canada: New Society.

Vinal, W. G. (1936). The school camp line-up for nature education. *The Clearing House*, 10(8), 462–466.

Vogel, E. F. (2011). *Deng Xiaoping and the transformation of China*. Cambridge, MA: Belknap of Harvard University Press.

Waks, L. J. (2007). The concept of fundamental educational change. *Educational Theory*, 57(3), 277–295.

Wang, D. (1958). Chang ge san zhong de xin qi xiang [New atmosphere in Changge School No. 3]. *Ren min jiao yu*, 9(4), 19, 34–37.

Wang, J., Chen, Y., & Wang, Z. (1991). Jiang su sheng tai xian liang xu xiang kai zhan zhong xue yu she hui shuang xiang fu wu [The Township of Liangxu in the County of Tai, Jiangsu, starts two-way service between a high school and society]. *Ren min jiao yu*, 43(Z1), 52–53.

Wang, R. S. (1975). Educational reforms and the cultural revolution: The Chinese evaluation process. *Asian Survey*, 15(9), 758–774.

Wang, S. (1988). Nan kai zhong xue de zheng ti gai ge [General reform in Nankai High School]. *Ren min jiao yu*, 39(11), 21–23.

Wang, Y., Wang, C., Bai, R., Sun, Z., Chen, W., Yu, S., Hu, S., Yu, X., & Fu, L. (1996). Qin gong jian xue [A work-study program]. In M. Xia (Ed.), *Ning bo shi jiao yu zhi [Educational memorandum of Ningbo, Zhejiang]* (pp. 290–295). Hangzhou, P.R.C.: Zhejiang Education Publishing.

Webb, L. D. (2006). *The history of American education: A great American experiment*. Upper Saddle River, NJ: Pearson.

Wegner, F. R., & Langworthy, H., Jr. (1936). Roslyn, N.Y., moves toward integration. *The Clearing House*, 11(2), 84–87.

Weil, T. T. (1950). The school camp: Our outdoor classroom. *The Journal of the American Association for Health, Physical Education, and Recreation*, 21(5), 284–285, 317–318.

Westbrook, M. A. (with Lurie, L. & Ivanov, M.). (1994). The independent schools of St. Petersburg: Diversification of schooling in postcommunist Russia. In A. Jones (Ed.), *Education and society in the new Russia* (pp. 103–117). Armonk, NY: M. E. Sharpe.

Whyte, M. K. (1974). Educational reform: China in the 1970s and Russia in the 1920s. *Comparative Education Review*, 8(1), 112–128.

Wilburn, D. (1983). Into the woods: A 6th-grade nature trail. *Childhood Education*, 59(3), 157–162.

Willis, K. (2005). *Theories and practices of development*. London, U.K.: Routledge.

Wilson, B. G. (1996). What is a constructivist learning environment? In B. G. Wilson (Ed.), *Constructivist learning environments: Case studies in instructional design* (pp. 3–8). Englewood Cliffs, NJ: Educational Technology.

Wood, J. K. (1986). Take a field trip close to home. *Science and Children, 24*(2), 26–27.

Wu yuan xian ge ming wei yuan hui. (1968). Yi suo li lun he shi ji yi zhi de xin xing xue xiao [One new-type school combining theory with practice]. *Hong qi, 11*(4), 24–31.

von Wright, G. H. (1971). *Explanation and understanding.* London, U.K.: Routledge & Kegan Paul.

Xi, J. (2017). *Secure a decisive victory in building a moderately prosperous society in all respects and strive for the great success of socialism with Chinese characteristics for a new era.* http://www.xinhuanet.com/english/download/Xi_Jinping's_report_at_ 19th_CPC_National_Congress.pdf

Xu, D. (1992). *A comparison of the educational ideas and practices of John Dewey and Mao Zedong in China: Is school society or society school?* San Francisco, CA: Mellen Research University Press.

Yadav, S. K. (2011). *National study on ten year school curriculum implementation.* New Delhi, India: Department of Teacher Education and Extension, National Council of Educational Research and Training.

Yahya, S., Ahmad, E. A., & Jalil, K. A. (2010). The definition and characteristics of ubiquitous learning: A discussion. *International Journal of Education and Development Using Information and Communication Technology, 6*(1), 117–127.

Yang, C., & Geng, D. (Eds.). (2009). *Service learning handbook.* New York, NY: Rural China Education Foundation.

Yao, X. (2013). The way of harmony in the *Four books. Journal of Chinese Philosophy, 40*(2), 252–268.

Zajda, J. I. (1980). *Education in the USSR.* Oxford, U.K.: Pergamon Press.

Zakir Husain Committee. (1938). *Basic national education: Report of the Zakir Husain Committee and the detailed syllabus with a foreword by Mahatma Gandhi* (3rd ed.). Segaon, India: Hindustani Talimi Sangh.

Zepper, J. T. (1960). *A study of N. K. Krupskaya's educational philosophy* [Unpublished doctoral dissertation]. University of Missouri.

Zhang, D. (2002). *Key concepts in Chinese philosophy* (E. Ryden, Ed. & Trans.). New Haven, CT: Yale University Press; Beijing, P.R.C.: Foreign Languages Press.

Zhang, K. (1980). Ban hao non zhong, wei nong ye xian dai hua fu wu [Start an agricultural high school to serve agricultural modernization]. *Ren min jiao yu, 31*(11), 34–36.

Zhao, Z. (1998a). Zheng fu gong zuo bao gao (jie lu) [The work report of the Central People's Government in 1983 (extract)]. In D. He (Ed.), *Zhong hua ren min gong he guo zhong yao jiao yu wen xian: 1976–1990* [The important educational documents of the People's Republic of China: Vol. 2. 1976–1990] (pp. 2098–2100). Haikou, P.R.C.: Hainan Publishing. (Original work published 1983)

Zhao, Z. (1998b). Zheng fu gong zuo bao gao (jie lu) [The work report of the Central People's Government in 1984 (extract)]. In D. He (Ed.), *Zhong hua ren min gong he guo zhong yao jiao yu wen xian: 1976–1990* [The important educational documents *of the People's Republic of China: Vol. 2. 1976–1990*] (pp. 2184–2185). Haikou, P.R.C.: Hainan Publishing. (Original work published 1984)

Zhao yuan he sui hua ge wei hui. (1971). Jian chi qin jian ban xue, wei wu chan jie ji zheng zhi fu wu [Continue a work-study program, serve proletarian politics]. *Hong qi, 14*(6), 47–51.

Zhou, E. (1998). Lun zhi shi fen zi wen ti [About the intelligentsia]. In D. He (Ed.), *Zhong hua ren min gong he guo zhong yao jiao yu wen xian: 1949–1975* [*The important educational documents of the People's Republic of China: Vol. 1. 1949–1975*] (pp. 1081–1085). Haikou, P.R.C.: Hainan Publishing. (Original work published 1984)

Zuo, Z. (1986). Wo men chang dao le jian chi lao dong ji shu jiao yu de tian tou [Benefits of continuous labor technique education]. *Ren min jiao yu, 37*(10), 28–29.

Index

Printed in the United States
by Baker & Taylor Publisher Services